W9-AXB-877

Paul R. Kroeger. 2018. *Analyzing meaning: An introduction to semantics and pragmatics* (Textbooks in Language Sciences 5). Berlin: Language Science Press.

DOI:10.5281/zenodo.1164112

Typesetting: Felix Kopecky, Paul Kroeger, Sebastian Nordhoff
Proofreading: Aleksandrs Berdicevskis, Andreas Hölzl, Anne Kilgus, Bev Erasmus, Carla Parra, Catherine Rudin, Christian Döhler, David Lukeš, David Nash, Eitan Grossman, Eugen Costetchi, Guohua Zhang, Ikmi Nur Oktavianti, Jean Nitzke, Jeroen van de Weijer, José Poblete Bravo, Joseph De Veaugh, Lachlan Mackenzie, Luigi Talamo, Martin Haspelmath, Mike Aubrey, Monika Czerepowicka, Myke Brinkerhoff, Parviz Parsafar, Prisca Jerono, Ritesh Kumar, Sandra Auderset, Torgrim Solstad, Vadim Kimmelman, Vasiliki Foufi
Fonts: Linux Libertine, Arimo, DejaVu Sans Mono, AR PL UMing
Typesetting software: XƎLaTeX

Language Science Press
Unter den Linden 6
10099 Berlin, Germany

Contents

Preface

This book provides an introduction to the study of meaning in human language, from a linguistic perspective. It covers a fairly broad range of topics, including lexical semantics, compositional semantics, and pragmatics. The approach is largely descriptive and non-formal, although some basic logical notation is introduced.

The book is written at level which should be appropriate for advanced undergraduate or beginning graduate students. It presupposes some previous coursework in linguistics, including at least a full semester of morpho-syntax and some familiarity with phonological concepts and terminology. It does not presuppose any previous background in formal logic or set theory.

Semantics and pragmatics are both enormous fields, and an introduction to either can easily fill an entire semester (and typically does); so it is no easy matter to give a reasonable introduction to both fields in a single course. However, I believe there are good reasons to teach them together.

In order to cover such a broad range of topics in relatively little space, I have not been able to provide as much depth as I would have liked in any of them. As the title indicates, this book is truly an INTRODUCTION: it attempts to provide students with a solid foundation which will prepare them to take more advanced and specialized courses in semantics and/or pragmatics. It is also intended as a reference for fieldworkers doing primary research on under-documented languages, to help them write grammatical descriptions that deal carefully and clearly with semantic issues. (This has been a weak point in many descriptive grammars.) At several points I have also pointed out the relevance of the material being discussed to practical applications such as translation and lexicography, but due to limitations of space this is not a major focus of attention.

The book is organized into six Units: (I) Foundational concepts; (II) Word meanings; (III) Implicature (including indirect speech acts); (IV) Compositional semantics; (V) Modals, conditionals, and causation; (VI) Tense & aspect. The sequence of chapters is important; in general, each chapter draws fairly heavily on preceding chapters. The book is intended to be teachable in a typical one-semester course module. However, if the instructor needs to reduce the amount of material to be covered, it would be possible to skip Chapters 6 (Lexical sense relations), 15 (Intensional contexts), 17 (Evidentiality), and/or 22 (Varieties of the perfect) without seriously affecting the students' comprehension of the other chapters. Alternatively, one might skip the entire last section, on tense & aspect.

Most of the chapters (after the first) include exercises which are labeled as being for "Discussion" or "Homework", depending on how I have used them in my own teaching. (Of course other instructors are free to use them in any way that seems best to them.) A few chapters have only "Discussion exercises", and two (Chapters 15 and 17) have no exercises at all in the current version of the book. Additional exercises for many of the topics covered here can be found in Saeed (2009) and Kearns (2000).

The book is available for collaborative reading on the PaperHive platform at https://paperhive.org/documents/remote?type=langsci&id=144. Suggestions which will help to improve any aspect of the book will be most welcome. *Soli Deo Gloria.*

References

Kearns, Kate. 2000. *Semantics* (Modern Linguistics series). New York: St. Martin's Press.

Saeed, John. 2009. *Semantics.* 3rd edn. Chichester, UK: Wiley-Blackwell.

Abbreviations

ACC	accusative
AUX	auxiliary
COMP	complementizer
COND	conditional
CONJECT	conjecture
CONT	continuous
CONTR	contrast
COP	copula
COS	Change of State
DAT	dative
DECL	declarative
DEIC	deictic
DEM	demonstrative
DEON	deontic
DET	determiner
DIM	diminutive
DIR	direct evidence
EMPH	emphatic
EPIS	epistemic
ERG	ergative
EXCL	exclusive
EXCLAM	exclamation
EXIS	existential
EXPER	experiential aspect
F	feminine
FRUS	frustrative
FUT	future
GEN	genitive
HON	honorific
IMP	imperative;
IMPF	imparfait (French)
INT	intimate speech
INTR	intransitive
INAN	inanimate
IND	indicative
IPFV	imperfective
LNK	linker
LOC	locative
M	masculine
NEC	necessity
NEG	negative
NOM	nominative
NPST	non-past
OBJ	object
PEJOR	pejorative
PFV	perfective
PL	plural
POL	polite
POSS	possessive
POTENT	potentive
PRED	predicative
PRF	perfect
PROB	probability
PROG	progressive
PRTCL	particle
PS	passé simple (French)
PST	past
PTCP	participle
Q	question
REL	relativizer
SBJV	subjunctive
SG	singular
STAT	stative
SUBJ	subject
TR	transitive

Unit I

Foundational concepts

1 The meaning of *meaning*

1.1 Semantics and pragmatics

The American author Mark Twain is said to have described a certain person as "a good man in the worst sense of the word." The humor of this remark lies partly in the unexpected use of the word *good*, with something close to the opposite of its normal meaning: Twain seems to be implying that this man is puritanical, self-righteous, judgmental, or perhaps hypocritical. Nevertheless, despite using the word in this unfamiliar way, Twain still manages to communicate at least the general nature of his intended message.

Twain's witticism is a slightly extreme example of something that speakers do on a regular basis: using old words with new meanings. It is interesting to compare this example with the following famous conversation from *Through the Looking Glass*, by Lewis Carroll:

(1) [Humpty Dumpty speaking] "There's glory for you!"
"I don't know what you mean by 'glory'," Alice said.
Humpty Dumpty smiled contemptuously. "Of course you don't – till I tell you. I meant 'there's a nice knock-down argument for you!' "
"But 'glory' doesn't mean 'a nice knock-down argument'," Alice objected.
"When I use a word," Humpty Dumpty said, in rather a scornful tone, "it means just what I choose it to mean – neither more nor less."
"The question is," said Alice, "whether you can make words mean so many different things."
"The question is," said Humpty Dumpty, "which is to be master – that's all."

Superficially, Humpty Dumpty's comment seems similar to Mark Twain's: both speakers use a particular word in a previously unknown way. The results, however, are strikingly different: Mark Twain successfully communicates (at least part of) his intended meaning, whereas Humpty Dumpty fails to communicate; throughout the ensuing conversation, Alice has to ask repeatedly what he means.

Humpty Dumpty's claim to be the "master" of his words – to be able to use words with whatever meaning he chooses to assign them – is funny because it is absurd. If people really talked that way, communication would be impossible. Perhaps the most important fact about word meanings is that they must be shared by the speech community: speakers of a given language must agree, at least most of the time, about what each word means.

Yet, while it is true that words must have agreed-upon meanings, Twain's remark illustrates how word meanings can be stretched or extended in various novel ways, without loss of comprehension on the part of the hearer. The contrast between Mark Twain's successful communication and Humpty Dumpty's failure to communicate suggests that the conventions for extending meanings must also be shared by the speech community. In other words, there seem to be rules even for bending the rules. In this book we will be interested both in the rules for "normal" communication, and in the rules for bending the rules.

The term SEMANTICS is often defined as the study of meaning. It might be more accurate to define it as the study of the relationship between linguistic form and meaning. This relationship is clearly rule-governed, just as other aspects of linguistic structure are. For example, no one believes that speakers memorize every possible sentence of a language; this cannot be the case, because new and unique sentences are produced every day, and are understood by people hearing them for the first time. Rather, language learners acquire a vocabulary (lexicon), together with a set of rules for combining vocabulary items into well-formed sentences (syntax). The same logic forces us to recognize that language learners must acquire not only the meanings of vocabulary items, but also a set of rules for interpreting the expressions that are formed when vocabulary items are combined. All of these components must be shared by the speech community in order for linguistic communication to be possible. When we study semantics, we are trying to understand this shared system of rules that allows hearers to correctly interpret what speakers intend to communicate.

The study of meaning in human language is often partitioned into two major divisions, and in this context the term SEMANTICS is used to refer to one of these divisions. In this narrower sense, semantics is concerned with the inherent meaning of words and sentences as linguistic expressions, in and of themselves, while PRAGMATICS is concerned with those aspects of meaning that depend on or derive from the way in which the words and sentences are used. In the above-mentioned quote attributed to Mark Twain, the basic or "default" meaning of *good* (the sense most likely to be listed in a dictionary) would be its semantic content. The negative meaning which Twain manages to convey is the result of pragmatic inferences triggered by the peculiar way in which he uses the word.

The distinction between semantics and pragmatics is useful and important, but as we will see in Chapter 9, the exact dividing line between the two is not easy to draw and continues to be a matter of considerable discussion and controversy. Because semantics and pragmatics interact in so many complex ways, there are good reasons to study them together, and both will be of interest to us in this book.

1.2 Three "levels" of meaning

In this book we will be interested in the meanings of three different types of linguistic units:

1. word meaning
2. sentence meaning
3. utterance meaning (also referred to as "speaker meaning")

The first two units (words and sentences) are hopefully already familiar to the reader. In order to understand the third level, "utterance meaning", we need to distinguish between sentences vs. utterances. A sentence is a linguistic expression, a well-formed string of words, while an utterance is a speech event by a particular speaker in a specific context. When a speaker uses a sentence in a specific context, he produces an utterance. As hinted in the preceding section, the term SENTENCE MEANING refers to the semantic content of the sentence: the meaning which derives from the words themselves, regardless of context.[1] The term UTTERANCE MEANING refers to the semantic content plus any pragmatic meaning created by the specific way in which the sentence gets used. Cruse (2000: 27) defines utterance meaning as "the totality of what the speaker intends to convey by making an utterance."

Kroeger (2005: 1) cites the following example of a simple question in Teochew (a Southern Min dialect of Chinese), whose interpretation depends heavily on context.

(2) a. Lɯ chyaʔ pa bɔy?
you eat full not.yet
'Have you already eaten?' (tones not indicated)

[1] As we will see, this is an oversimplification, because certain aspects of sentence meaning do depend on context; see Chapter 9, §3 for discussion.

The literal meaning (i.e., sentence meaning) of the question is, "Have you already eaten or not?", which sounds like a request for information. But its most common use is as a greeting. The normal way for one friend to greet another is to ask this question. (The expected reply is: "I have eaten," even if this is not in fact true.) In this context, the utterance meaning is roughly equivalent to that of the English expressions *hello* or *How do you do?* In other contexts, however, the question could be used as a real request for information. For example, if a doctor wants to administer a certain medicine which cannot be taken on an empty stomach, he might well ask the patient "Have you eaten yet?" In this situation the sentence meaning and the utterance meaning would be essentially the same.

1.3 Relation between form and meaning

For most words, the relation between the form (i.e., phonetic shape) of the word and its meaning is arbitrary. This is not always the case. ONOMATOPOETIC words are words whose forms are intended to be imitations of the sounds which they refer to, e.g. *ding-dong* for the sound of a bell, or *buzz* for the sound of a housefly. But even in these cases, the phonetic shape of the word (if it is truly a part of the vocabulary of the language) is partly conventional. The sound a dog makes is represented by the English word *bow-wow*, the Balinese word *kong-kong*, the Armenian word *haf-haf*, and the Korean words *mung-mung* or *wang-wang*.[2] This cross-linguistic variation is presumably not motivated by differences in the way dogs actually bark in different parts of the world. On the other hand, as these examples indicate, there is a strong tendency for the corresponding words in most languages to use labial, velar, or labio-velar consonants and low back vowels.[3] Clearly this is no accident, and reflects the non-arbitrary nature of the form-meaning relation in such words. The situation with "normal" words is quite different, e.g. the word for 'dog': Armenian *shun*, Balinese *cicin*, Korean *gae*, Tagalog *aso*, etc. No common phonological pattern is to be found here.

The relation between the form of a sentence (or other multi-word expression) and its meaning is generally not arbitrary, but COMPOSITIONAL. This term means that the meaning of the expression is predictable from the meanings of the words it contains and the way they are combined. To give a very simple example, suppose we know that the word *yellow* can be used to describe a certain class of

[2] http://www.psychologytoday.com/blog/canine-corner/201211/how-dogs-bark-in-different-languages (accessed 2018-01-22)

[3] Labial consonants such as /b, m/; velar consonants such as /g, ng/; or labio-velar consonants such as /w/. Low back vowels include /a, o/.

objects (those that are yellow in color) and that the word *submarine* can be used to refer to objects of another sort (those that belong to the class of submarines). This knowledge, together with a knowledge of English syntax, allows us to infer that when the Beatles sang about living in a *yellow submarine* they were referring to an object that belonged to both classes, i.e., something that was both yellow and a submarine.

This PRINCIPLE OF COMPOSITIONALITY is of fundamental importance to almost every topic in semantics, and we will return to it often. But once again, there are exceptions to the general rule. The most common class of exceptions are IDIOMS, such as *kick the bucket* for 'die' or *X's goose is cooked* for 'X is in serious trouble'. Idiomatic phrases are by definition non-compositional: the meaning of the phrase is not predictable from the meanings of the individual words. The meaning of the whole phrase must be learned as a unit.

The relation between utterance meaning and the form of the utterance is neither arbitrary nor, strictly speaking, compositional. Utterance meanings are derivable (or "calculable") from the sentence meaning and the context of the utterance by various pragmatic principles that we will discuss in later chapters. However, it is not always fully predictable; sometimes more than one interpretation may be possible for a given utterance in a particular situation.

1.4 What does *mean* mean?

When someone defines semantics as "the study of meaning", or pragmatics as "the study of meanings derived from usage", they are defining one English word in terms of other English words. This practice has been used for thousands of years, and works fairly well in daily life. But if our goal as linguists is to provide a rigorous or scientific account of the relationship between form and meaning, there are obvious dangers in using this strategy. To begin with, there is the danger of circularity: a definition can only be successful if the words used in the definition are themselves well-defined. In the cases under discussion, we would need to ask: What is the meaning of *meaning*? What does *mean* mean?

One way to escape from this circularity is to translate expressions in the OBJECT LANGUAGE into a well-defined METALANGUAGE. If we use English to describe the linguistic structure of Swahili, Swahili is the object language and English is the metalanguage. However, both Swahili and English are natural human languages which need to be analyzed, and both exhibit vagueness, ambiguities, and other features which make them less than ideal as a semantic metalanguage.

Many linguists adopt some variety of formal logic as a semantic metalanguage, and later chapters in this book provide a brief introduction to such an approach. Much of the time, however, we will be discussing the meaning of English expressions using English as the metalanguage. For this reason it becomes crucial to distinguish (object language) expressions we are trying to analyze from the (metalanguage) words we are using to describe our analysis. When we write "What is the meaning of *meaning*?" or "What does *mean* mean?", we use italics to identify object language expressions. These italicized words are said to be MENTIONED, i.e., referred to as objects of study, in contrast to the metalanguage words which are USED in their normal sense, and are written in plain font.

Let us return to the question raised above, "What do we mean by *meaning*?" This is a difficult problem in philosophy, which has been debated for centuries, and which we cannot hope to resolve here; but a few basic observations will be helpful. We can start by noting that our interests in this book, and the primary concerns of linguistic semantics, are for the most part limited to the kinds of meaning that people intend to communicate via language. We will not attempt to investigate the meanings of "body language", manner of dress, facial expressions, gestures, etc., although these can often convey a great deal of information. (In sign languages, of course, facial expressions and gestures do have linguistic meaning.) And we will not address the kinds of information that a hearer may acquire by listening to a speaker, which the speaker does not intend to communicate.

For example, if I know how your voice normally sounds, I may be able to deduce from hearing you speak that you have laryngitis, or that you are drunk. These are examples of what the philosopher Paul Grice called "natural meaning", rather than linguistic meaning. Just as smoke "means" fire, and a rainbow "means" rain, a rasping whisper "means" laryngitis. Levinson (1983: 15) uses the example of a detective questioning a suspect to illustrate another type of unintended communication. The suspect may say something which is inconsistent with the physical evidence, and this may allow the detective to deduce that the suspect is guilty, but his guilt is not part of what the suspect intends to communicate. Inferences of this type will not be a central focus of interest in this book.

An approach which has proven useful for the linguistic analysis of meaning is to focus on how speakers use language to talk about the world. This approach was hinted at in our discussion of the phrase *yellow submarine*. Knowing the meaning of words like *yellow* or *submarine* allows us to identify the class of objects in a particular situation, or universe of discourse, which those words can be used to refer to. Similarly, knowing the meaning of a sentence will allow us to determine whether that sentence is true in a particular situation or universe of discourse.

Technically, sentences like *It is raining* are neither true nor false. Only an utterance of a certain kind (namely, a statement) can have a truth value. When a speaker utters this sentence at a particular time and place, we can look out the window and determine whether or not the speaker is telling the truth. The statement is true if its meaning corresponds to the situation being described: is it raining at that time and place? This approach is sometimes referred to as the CORRESPONDENCE theory of truth.

We might say that the meaning of a (declarative) sentence is the knowledge or information which allows speakers and hearers to determine whether it is true in a particular context. If we know the meaning of a sentence, the principle of compositionality places an important constraint on the meanings of the words which the sentence contains: the meaning of individual words (and phrases) must be suitable to compositionally determine the correct meaning for the sentence as a whole. Certain types of words (e.g., *if, and,* or *but*) do not "refer" to things in the world; the meanings of such words can only be defined in terms of their contribution to sentence meanings.

1.5 Saying, meaning, and doing

The Teochew question in (2) illustrates how a single sentence can be used to express two or more different utterance meanings, depending on the context. In one context the sentence is used to greet someone, while in another context the same sentence is used to request information. So this example demonstrates that a single sentence can be used to perform two or more different SPEECH ACTS, i.e., things that people do by speaking.

In order to fully understand a given utterance, the addressee (= hearer) must try to answer three fundamental questions:

1. What did the speaker say? i.e., what is the semantic content of the sentence? (The philosopher Paul Grice used the term "What is said" as a way of referring to semantic content or sentence meaning.)

2. What did the speaker intend to communicate? (Grice used the term IMPLICATURE for intended but unspoken meaning, i.e., aspects of utterance meaning which are not part of the sentence meaning.)

3. What is the speaker trying to do? i.e., what speech act is being performed?

In this book we attempt to lay a foundation for investigating these three questions about meaning. We will return to the analysis of speech acts in Chapter 10; but for a brief example of why this is an important facet of the study of meaning, consider the word *please* in examples (3a–b).

(3) a. *Please* pass me the salt.
    b. Can you *please* pass me the salt?

What does *please* mean? It does not seem to have any real semantic content, i.e., does not contribute to the sentence meaning; but it makes an important contribution to the utterance meaning, in fact, two important contributions. First, it identifies the speech act which is performed by the utterances in which it occurs, indicating that they are REQUESTS. The word *please* does not occur naturally in other kinds of speech acts. Second, this word is a marker of politeness; so it indicates something about the manner in which the speech act is performed, including the kind of social relationship which the speaker wishes to maintain with the hearer. So we see that we cannot understand the meaning of *please* without referring to the speech act being performed.

The claim that the word *please* does not contribute to sentence meaning is supported by the observation that misusing the word does not affect the truth of a sentence. We said that it normally occurs only in requests. If we insert the word into other kinds of speech acts, e.g. *It seems to be raining, please*, the result is odd; but if the basic statement is true, adding *please* does not make it false. Rather, the use of *please* in this context is simply inappropriate (unless there is some contextual factor which makes it possible to interpret the sentence as a request).

The examples in (3) also illustrate an important aspect of how form and meaning are related with respect to speech acts. We will refer to the utterance in (3a) as a DIRECT request, because the grammatical form (imperative) matches the intended speech act (request); so the utterance meaning is essentially the same as the sentence meaning. We will refer to the utterance in (3b) as an INDIRECT request, because the grammatical form (interrogative) does not match the intended speech act (request); the utterance meaning must be understood by pragmatic inference.

1.6 "More lies ahead" (a roadmap)

As you have seen from the table of contents, the chapters of this book are organized into six units. In the first four units we introduce some of the basic tools, concepts, and terminology which are commonly used for analyzing and describing linguistic meaning. In the last two units we use these tools to explore the meanings of several specific classes of words and grammatical markers: modals, tense markers, *if*, *because*, etc.

The rest of this first unit is devoted to exploring two of the foundational concepts for understanding how we talk about the world: reference and truth. Chapter 2 deals with reference and the relationship between reference and meaning. Just as a proper name can be used to refer to a specific individual, other kinds of noun phrase can be used to refer to people, things, groups, etc. in the world. The actual reference of a word or phrase depends on the context in which it is used; the meaning of the word determines what things it can be used to refer to in any given context.

Chapter 3 deals with truth, and also with certain kinds of inference. We say that a statement is true if its meaning corresponds to the situation under discussion. Sometimes the meanings of two statements are related in such a way that the truth of one will give us reason to believe that the other is also true. For example, if I know that the statement in (4a) is true, then I can be quite certain that the statement in (4b) is also true, because of the way in which the meanings of the two sentences are related. A different kind of meaning relation gives us reason to believe that if a person says (4c), he must believe that the statement in (4a) is true. These two types of meaning-based inference, which we will call ENTAILMENT and PRESUPPOSITION respectively, are of fundamental importance to most of the topics discussed in this book.

(4) a. John killed the wasp.
    b. The wasp died.
    c. John is proud that he killed the wasp.

Chapter 4 introduces some basic logical notation that is widely used in semantics, and discusses certain patterns of inference based on truth values and logical structure.

Unit II focuses on word meanings, starting with the observation that a single word can have more than one meaning. One of the standard ways of demonstrating this fact is by observing the ambiguity of sentences like the famous headline in (5). Many of the issues we discuss in Unit II with respect to "content words" (nouns, verbs, adjectives, etc.), such as ambiguity, vagueness, idiomatic uses, co-occurrence restrictions, etc., will turn out to be relevant in our later discussions of various kinds of "function words" and grammatical morphemes as well.

(5) Headline: *Reagan wins on budget, but more lies ahead.*

Unit III deals with a pattern of pragmatic inference known as CONVERSATIONAL IMPLICATURE: meaning which is intended by the speaker to be understood by the hearer, but is not part of the literal sentence meaning. Many people consider the identification of this type of inference, by the philosopher Paul Grice in the 1960s, to be the "birth-date" of pragmatics as a distinct field of study. It is another foundational concept that we will refer to in many of the subsequent chapters. Chapter 10 discusses a class of conversational implicatures that has received a great deal of attention, namely indirect speech acts. As illustrated above in example (3b), an indirect speech act involves a sentence whose literal meaning seems to perform one kind of speech act (asking a question: *Can you pass me the salt?*) used in a way which implicates a different speech act (request: *Please pass me the salt*). Chapter 11 discusses various types of expressions (e.g. sentence adverbs like *frankly, fortunately*, etc., honorifics and politeness markers, and certain types of "discourse particles") whose meanings seem to contribute to the appropriateness of an utterance, rather than to the truth of a proposition. Some such meanings were referred to by Grice as a different kind of implicature.

Unit IV addresses the issue of compositionality: how the meanings of phrases and sentences can be predicted based on the meanings of the words they contain and the way those words are arranged (syntactic structure). It provides a brief introduction to some basic concepts in set theory, and shows how these concepts can be used to express the truth conditions of sentences. One topic of special interest is the interpretation of "quantified" noun phrases such as *every person, some animal*, or *no student*, using set theory to state the meanings of such phrases. In Unit V we will use this analysis of quantifiers to provide a way of understanding the meanings of modals (e.g. *may, must, should*) and *if* clauses.

Unit VI presents a framework for analyzing the meanings of tense and aspect markers. Tense and aspect both deal with time reference, but in different ways. As we will see, the use and interpretation of these markers often depends heavily on the type of situation being described.

Each of these topics individually has been the subject of countless books and papers, and we cannot hope to give a complete account of any of them. This book is intended as a broad introduction to the field as a whole, a stepping stone which will help prepare you to read more specialized books and papers in areas that interest you.

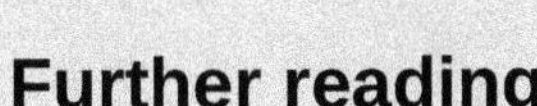

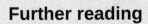

Further reading

For helpful discussions of the distinction between semantics vs. pragmatics, see Levinson (1983: ch. 1) and Birner (2012/2013: §1.2). Levinson (1983: ch. 1) also provides a helpful discussion of Grice's distinction between "natural meaning" vs. linguistic meaning.

2 Referring, denoting, and expressing

2.1 Talking about the world

In this chapter and the next we will think about how speakers use language to talk about the world. Referring to a particular individual, e.g. by using expressions such as *Abraham Lincoln* or *my father*, is one important way in which we talk about the world. Another important way is to describe situations in the world, i.e., to claim that a certain state of affairs exists. These claims are judged to be true if our description matches the actual state of the world, and false otherwise. For example, if I were to say *It is raining* at a time and place where no rain is falling, I would be making a false statement.

We will focus on truth in the next chapter, but in this chapter our primary focus is on issues relating to reference. We begin in §2.2 with a very brief description of two ways of studying linguistic meaning. One of these looks primarily at how a speaker's words are related to the thoughts or concepts he is trying to express. The other approach looks primarily at how a speaker's words are related to the situation in the world that he is trying to describe. This second approach will be assumed in most of this book.

In §2.3 we will think about what it means to "refer" to things in the world, and discuss various kinds of expressions that speakers can use to refer to things. In §2.4 we will see that we cannot account for meaning, or even reference, by looking only at reference. To preview that discussion, we might begin with the observation that people talk about the "meaning" of words in two different ways, as illustrated in (1). In (1a), the word *meant* is used to specify the reference of a phrase when it was used on a particular occasion, whereas in (1b-c), the word *means* is used to specify the kind of meaning that we might look up in a dictionary.

(1) a. When Jones said that he was meeting "a close friend" for dinner, he meant his lawyer.

b. *Salamat* means 'thank you' in Tagalog.

c. *Usufruct* means 'the right of one individual to use and enjoy the property of another.'[1]

[1]http://legal-dictionary.thefreedictionary.com/usufruct

We will introduce the term SENSE for the kind of meaning illustrated in (1b-c), the kind of meaning that we might look up in a dictionary. One crucial difference between sense and reference is that reference depends on the specific context in which a word or phrase is used, whereas sense does not depend on context in this way.

In §2.5 we discuss various types of AMBIGUITY, that is, ways in which a word, phrase or sentence can have more than one sense. The existence of ambiguity is an important fact about all human languages, and accounting for ambiguity is an important goal in semantic analysis.

In §2.6 we discuss a kind of meaning that does not seem to involve either reference to the world, or objective claims about the world. EXPRESSIVE meaning (e.g. the meanings of words like *ouch* and *oops*) reflects the speaker's feelings or attitudes at the time of speaking. We will list a number of ways in which expressive meaning is different from "normal" DESCRIPTIVE meaning.

2.2 Denotational semantics vs. cognitive semantics

Let us begin by discussing the relationships between a speaker's words, the situation in the world, and the thoughts or concepts associated with those words. These relationships are indicated in the figure in (2), which is a version of a diagram that is sometimes referred to as the Semiotic Triangle.

(2) (one version of) the Semiotic Triangle

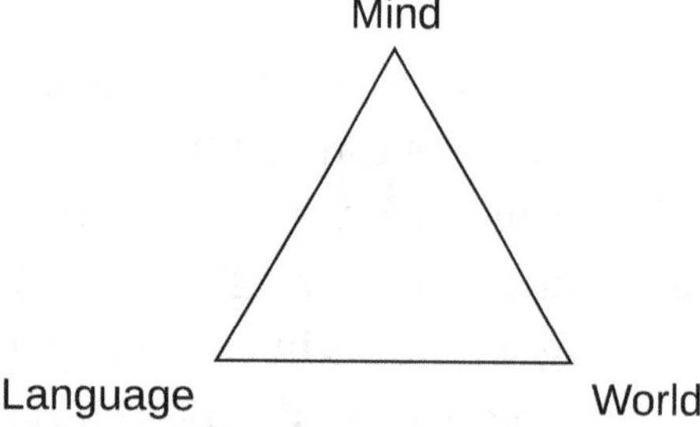

Semiotics is the study of the relationship between signs and their meanings. In this book we are interested in the relationship between forms and meanings in certain kinds of symbolic systems, namely human languages. The diagram is a way of illustrating how speakers use language to describe things, events, and situations in the world. As we will see when we begin to look at word meanings, what speakers actually describe is a particular CONSTRUAL of, or way of thinking about, the situation. Now the speaker's linguistic description rarely if ever includes everything that the speaker knows or believes about the situation, and what the speaker believes about the situation may not match the actual state of the world. Thus there is no one-to-one correspondence between the speaker's mental representation and either the actual situation in the world or the linguistic expressions used to describe that situation. However, there are strong links or associations connecting each of these domains with the others.

The basic approach we adopt in this book focuses on the link between linguistic expressions and the world. This approach is often referred to as DENOTATIONAL semantics. (We will discuss what DENOTATION means in §2.4 below.) An important alternative approach, COGNITIVE SEMANTICS, focuses on the link between linguistic expressions and mental representations. Of course, both approaches recognize that all three corners of the Semiotic Triangle are involved in any act of linguistic communication. One motivation for adopting a denotational approach comes from the fact that it is very hard to find direct evidence about what is really going on in a speaker's mind. A second motivation is the fact that this approach has proven to be quite successful at accounting for compositionality (how meanings of complex expressions, e.g. sentences, are related to the meanings of their parts).

The two foundational concepts for denotational semantics, i.e. for talking about how linguistic expressions are related to the world, are TRUTH and REFERENCE. As we mentioned in Chapter 1, we will say that a sentence is true if it corresponds to the actual situation in the world which it is intended to describe. It turns out that native speakers are fairly good at judging whether a given sentence would be true in a particular situation; such judgments provide an important source of evidence for all semantic analysis. Truth will be the focus of attention in Chapter 3. In the next several sections of this chapter we focus on issues relating to reference.

2.3 Types of referring expressions

Philosophers have found it hard to agree on a precise definition for *reference*, but intuitively we are talking about the speaker's use of words to "point to" something in the world; that is, to direct the hearer's attention to something, or to enable the hearer to identify something. Suppose we are told that Brazilians used to "refer to" Pelé as *o rei* 'the king'.[2] This means that speakers used the phrase *o rei* to direct their hearers' attention to a particular individual, namely the most famous soccer player of the 20th century. Similarly, we might read that

[2] Of course, Pelé rose to fame long after Brazil became a republic, so there was no king ruling the country at that time.

amyotrophic lateral sclerosis (ALS) is often "referred to" as Lou Gehrig's Disease, in honor of the famous American baseball player who died of this disease. This means that people use the phrase *Lou Gehrig's Disease* to direct their hearers' attention to that particular disease.

A REFERRING EXPRESSION is an expression (normally some kind of noun phrase) which a speaker uses to refer to something. The identity of the referent is determined in different ways for different kinds of referring expressions. A proper name like *King Henry VIII*, *Abraham Lincoln*, or *Mao Zedong*, always refers to the same individual. (In saying this, of course, we are ignoring various complicating factors, such as the fact that two people may have the same name. We will focus for the moment on the most common or basic way of using proper names, namely in contexts where they have a single unambiguous referent.) For this reason, they are sometimes referred to as RIGID DESIGNATORS. "Natural kind" terms, e.g. names of species (*camel, octopus, durian*) or substances (*gold, salt, methane*), are similar. When they are used to refer to the species as a whole, or the substance in general, rather than any specific instance, these terms are also rigid designators: their referent does not depend on the context in which they are used. Some examples of this usage are presented in (3).

(3) a. *The octopus* has eight tentacles and is quite intelligent.
  b. *Camels* can travel long distances without drinking.
  c. *Methane* is lighter than air and highly flammable.

For most other referring expressions, reference does depend on the context of use. DEICTIC elements (sometimes called INDEXICALS) are words which refer to something in the speech situation itself. For example, the pronoun *I* refers to the current speaker, while *you* refers to the current addressee. *Here* typically refers to the place of the speech event, while *now* typically refers to the time of the speech event.

Third person pronouns can be used with deictic reference, e.g. "Who is *he*?" (while pointing); but more often are used anaphorically. An ANAPHORIC element is one whose reference depends on the reference of another NP within the same discourse. (This other NP is called the ANTECEDENT.) The pronoun *he* in sentence (4) is used anaphorically, taking *George* as its antecedent.

(4) Susan refuses to marry George$_i$ because he$_i$ smokes.

Pronouns can be used with quantifier phrases, like the pronoun *his* in sentence (5a); but in this context, the pronoun does not actually refer to any specific individual. So in this context, the pronoun is not a referring expression.[3] For the same reason, quantifier phrases are not referring expressions, as illustrated in (5b). (The symbol "#" in (5b) indicates that the sentence is grammatical but unacceptable on semantic or pragmatic grounds.)

(5) a. [Every boy]$_i$ should respect his$_i$ mother.
  b. [Every American male]$_i$ loves football; #he$_i$ watched three games last weekend.

Some additional examples that illustrate why quantified noun phrases cannot be treated as referring expressions are presented in (6–8). As example (6a) illustrates, reflexive pronouns are normally interpreted as having the same reference as their antecedent; but this principle does not hold when the antecedent is a quantified noun phrase (6b).

(6) a. *John trusts himself* is equivalent to: *John trusts John.*
  b. *Everyone trusts himself* is not equivalent to: *Everyone trusts everyone.*

As we discuss in Chapter 3, a sentence of the form *X is Estonian and X is not Estonian* is a contradiction; it can never be true, whether X refers to an individual as in (7b) or a group of individuals as in (7c). However, when X is replaced by certain quantified noun phrases, e.g. those beginning with *some* or *many*, the sentence could be true. This shows that these quantified noun phrases cannot be interpreted as referring to either individuals or groups of individuals.[4]

(7) a. #X is Estonian and X is not Estonian.
  b. #John is Estonian and John is not Estonian.
  c. #My parents are Estonian and my parents are not Estonian.
  d. Some/many people are Estonian and some/many people are not Estonian.

As a final example, the contrast in (8) suggests that neither *every student* nor *all students* can be interpreted as referring to the set of all students, e.g. at a particular school. There is much more to be said about quantifiers. We will give a brief introduction to this topic in Chapter 3, and discuss them in more detail in Chapter 14.

[3] Pronouns used in this way are functioning as "bound variables", as described in Chapter 4.

[4] Peters & Westerståhl (2006: 49–52) present a mathematical proof showing that quantified noun phrases cannot be interpreted as referring to sets of individuals.

(8) a. The student body outnumbers the faculty.
b. #Every student outnumbers the faculty.
c. #All students outnumbers the faculty.

Common noun phrases may or may not refer to anything. Definite noun phrases (sometimes called DEFINITE DESCRIPTIONS) like those in (9) are normally used in contexts where the hearer is able to identify a unique referent. But definite descriptions can also be used generically, without referring to any specific individual, like the italicized phrases in (10).

(9) a. this book
b. the sixteenth President of the United States
c. my eldest brother

(10) Life's battles don't always go
To *the stronger or faster man*,
But sooner or later *the man who wins*
Is *the one who thinks he can.*[5]

INDEFINITE DESCRIPTIONS may be used to refer to a specific individual, like the object NP in (11a); or they may be non-specific, like the object NP in (11b). Specific indefinites are referring expressions, while non-specific indefinites are not.

(11) a. My sister has just married *a cowboy.*
b. My sister would never marry *a cowboy.*
c. My sister wants to marry *a cowboy.*

In some contexts, like (11c), an indefinite NP may be ambiguous between a specific vs. a non-specific interpretation. Under the specific interpretation, (11c) says that my sister wants to marry a particular individual, who happens to be a cowboy. Under the non-specific interpretation, (11c) says that my sister would like the man she marries to be a cowboy, but doesn't have any particular individual in mind yet. We will discuss this kind of ambiguity in more detail in Chapter 12.

[5]From the poem "Thinking" by Walter D. Wintle, first published 1905(?). This poem is widely copied and often mis-attributed. Authors wrongly credited with the poem include Napoleon Hill, C.W. Longenecker, and the great American football coach Vince Lombardi.

2.4 Sense vs. denotation

In §2.1 we noted that when people talk about what a word or phrase "means", they may have in mind either its dictionary definition or its referent in a particular context. The German logician Gottlob Frege (1848–1925) was one of the first people to demonstrate the importance of making this distinction. He used the German term *Sinn* (English SENSE) for those aspects of meaning which do not depend on the context of use, the kind of meaning we might look up in a dictionary.

Frege used the term *Bedeutung* (English DENOTATION)[6] for the other sort of meaning, which does depend on the context. The denotation of a referring expression, such as a proper name or definite NP, will normally be its referent. The denotation of a content word (e.g. an adjective, verb, or common noun) is the set of all the things in the current universe of discourse which the word could be used to describe. For example, the denotation of *yellow* is the set of all yellow things, the denotation of *tree* is the set of all trees, the denotation of the intransitive verb *snore* is the set of all creatures that snore, etc. Frege proposed that the denotation of a sentence is its truth value. We will discuss his reasons for making this proposal in Chapter 12; in this section we focus on the denotations of words and phrases.

We have said that denotations are context-dependent. This is not so easy to see in the case of proper names, because they always refer to the same individual. Other referring expressions, however, will refer to different individuals or entities in different contexts. For example, the definite NP *the Prime Minister* can normally be used to identify a specific individual. Which particular individual is referred to, however, depends on the time and place. The denotation of this phrase in Singapore in 1975 would have been Lee Kuan Yew; in England in 1975 it would have been Harold Wilson; and in England in 1989 it would have been Margaret Thatcher. Similarly, the denotation of phrases like *my favorite color* or *your father* will depend on the identity of the speaker and/or addressee.

The denotation of a content word depends on the situation or universe of discourse in which it is used. In our world, the denotation set of *talks* will include most people, certain mechanical devices (computers, GPS systems, etc.) and (perhaps) some parrots. In Wonderland, as described by Lewis Carroll, it will include playing cards, chess pieces, at least one white rabbit, at least one cat, a dodo bird, etc. In Narnia, as described by C.S. Lewis, it will include beavers, badgers, wolves, some trees, etc.

---

[6] The term *Bedeutung* is often translated into English as *reference*, but this can lead to confusion when dealing with non-referring expressions which nevertheless do have a denotation.

For each situation, the sense determines a denotation set, and knowing the sense of the word allows speakers to identify the members of this set. When Alice first hears the white rabbit talking, she may be surprised. However, her response would not be, "What is that rabbit doing?" or "Has the meaning of *talk* changed?" but rather "How can that rabbit be talking?" It is not the language that has changed, but the world. Sense is a fact about the language, denotation is a fact about the world or situation under discussion.

Two expressions that have different senses may still have the same denotation in a particular situation. For example, the phrases *the largest land mammal* and *the African bush elephant* refer to the same organism in our present world (early in the 21st century). But in a fictional universe of discourse (e.g., the movie *King Kong*), or in an earlier time period of our own world (e.g., 30 million BC, when the gigantic *Paraceratherium* —estimated weight about 20,000 kg— walked the earth), these two phrases could have different denotations. If two expressions can have different denotations in any context, they do not have the same sense.

Such examples demonstrate that two expressions which have different senses MAY have the same denotation in certain situations. However, two expressions that have the same sense (i.e., SYNONYMOUS expressions) must ALWAYS have the same denotation in any possible situation. For example, the phrases *my mother-in-law* and *the mother of my spouse* seem to be perfect synonyms (i.e., identical in sense). If this is true, then it will be impossible to find any situation where they would refer to different individuals when spoken by the same (monogamous) speaker under exactly the same conditions.

So, while we have said that we will adopt a primarily "denotational" approach to semantics, this does not mean that we are only interested in denotations, or that we believe that denotation is all there is to meaning. If meaning was just denotation, then phrases like those in (12), which have no referent in our world at the present time, would all either mean the same thing, or be meaningless. But clearly they are not meaningless, and they do not all mean the same thing; they simply fail to refer.

(12) a. the present King of France
  b. the largest prime number
  c. the diamond as big as the Ritz
  d. the unicorn in the garden

Frege's distinction allows us to see that non-referring expressions like those in (12) may not have a referent, but they do have a sense, and that sense is derived in a predictable way by the normal rules of the language.

2.5 Ambiguity

It is possible for a single word to have more than one sense. For example, the word *hand* can refer to the body part at the end of our arms; the pointer on the dial of a clock; a bunch of bananas; the group of cards held by a single player in a card game; or a hired worker. Words that have two or more senses are said to be AMBIGUOUS (more precisely, POLYSEMOUS; see Chapter 5).

A deictic expression such as *my father* will refer to different individuals when spoken by different speakers, but this does not make it ambiguous. As emphasized above, the fact that a word or phrase can have different denotations in different contexts does not mean that it has multiple senses, and it is important to distinguish these two cases. We will discuss the basis for making this distinction in Chapter 5.

If a phrase or sentence contains an ambiguous word, the phrase or sentence will normally be ambiguous as well, as illustrated in (13).

(13) LEXICAL AMBIGUITY

a. A boiled egg is hard to *beat.*
b. The farmer allows walkers to cross the field for free, but the bull *charges.*
c. I just turned 51, but I have a nice new *organ* which I enjoy tremendously.[7]

An ambiguous sentence is one that has more than one sense, or "reading". A sentence which has only a single sense may have different truth values in different contexts, but will always have one consistent truth value in any specific context. With an ambiguous sentence, however, there must be at least one conceivable context in which the two senses would have different truth values. For example, one reading of (13b) would be true at the same time that the other reading is false if there is a bull in the field which is aggressive but not financially sophisticated.

In addition to lexical ambiguity of the kind illustrated in (13), there are various other ways in which a sentence can be ambiguous. One of these is referred to as STRUCTURAL AMBIGUITY, illustrated in (14a–d). In such cases, the two senses (or readings) arise because the grammar of the language can assign two different structures to the same string of words, even though none of those words is itself ambiguous. The two different structures for (14d) are shown by the bracketing in (14e), which corresponds to the expected reading, and (14f) which corresponds to the Groucho Marx reading. Of course, some sentences involve both structural and lexical ambiguity, as is the case in (14c).

[7] From e-mail newsletter, 2011.

(14) STRUCTURAL AMBIGUITY[8]

a. Two cars were reported stolen by the Groveton police yesterday.
b. The license fee for altered dogs with a certificate will be $3 and for pets owned by senior citizens who have not been altered the fee will be $1.50.
c. For sale: mixing bowl set designed to please a cook with round bottom for efficient beating.
d. One morning I shot an elephant in my pajamas. How he got into my pajamas I'll never know.[9]
e. One morning I [shot an elephant] [in my pajamas].
f. One morning I shot [an elephant in my pajamas].

Structural ambiguity shows us something important about meaning, namely that meanings are not assigned to strings of phonological material but to syntactic objects.[10] In other words, syntactic structure makes a crucial contribution to the meaning of an expression. The two readings for (14d) involve the same string of words but not the same syntactic object.

A third type of ambiguity which we will mention here is REFERENTIAL AMBIGUITY. (We will discuss additional types of ambiguity in later chapters.) It is fairly common to hear people using pronouns in a way that permits more than one possible antecedent, e.g. *Adams wrote frequently to Jefferson while he was in Paris.* The pronoun *he* in this sentence has ambiguous reference; it could refer either to John Adams or to Thomas Jefferson. It is also possible for other types of NP to have ambiguous reference. For example, if I am teaching a class of 14 students, and I say to the Dean *My student has won a Rhodes scholarship*, there are multiple possible referents for the subject NP.

A famous example of referential ambiguity occurs in a prophecy from the oracle at Delphi, in ancient Greece. The Lydian king Croesus asked the oracle whether he should fight against the Persians. The oracle's reply was that if Croesus made war on the Persians, he would destroy a mighty empire. Croesus took this to be a positive answer and attacked the Persians, who were led by Cyrus the Great. The Lydians were defeated and Croesus was captured; the empire which Croesus destroyed turned out to be his own.

[8]These examples are taken from Pinker (1994: 102). The first three are said to be actual newspaper examples.
[9]Groucho Marx, in the movie *Animal Crackers*.
[10]Kennedy (2011: 514).

2.6 Expressive meaning: *Ouch* and *oops*

Words like *ouch* and *oops*, often referred to as EXPRESSIVES, present an interesting challenge to the "denotational" approach outlined above. They convey a certain kind of meaning, yet they neither refer to things in the world, nor help to determine the conditions under which a sentence would be true. In fact, it is hard to claim that they even form part of a sentence; they seem to stand on their own, as one-word utterances. The kind of meaning that such words convey is called EXPRESSIVE MEANING, which Lyons (1995: 44) defines as "the kind of meaning by virtue of which speakers express, rather than describe, their beliefs, attitudes and feelings." Expressive meaning is different from DESCRIPTIVE MEANING (also called PROPOSITIONAL MEANING or TRUTH- CONDITIONAL MEANING), the "normal" type of meaning which determines reference and truth values. If someone says *I just felt a sudden sharp pain*, he is describing what he feels; but when he says *Ouch!*, he is expressing that feeling.

Words like *ouch* and *oops* carry only expressive meaning, and seem to be unique in other ways as well. They may not necessarily be intended to communicate. If I hurt myself when I am working alone, I will very likely say *ouch* (or some other expressive with similar meaning) even though there is no one present to hear me. Such expressions seem almost like involuntary reactions, although the specific forms are learned as part of a particular language. But it is important to be aware of the distinction between expressive vs. descriptive meaning, because many "normal" words carry both types of meaning at once.

For example, the word *garrulous* means essentially the same thing as *talkative*, but carries additional information about the speaker's negative attitude towards this behavior.[11] There are many other pairs of words which seem to convey the same descriptive meaning but differ in terms of their expressive meaning: *father* vs. *dad*; *woman* vs. *broad*; *horse* vs. *nag*; *alcohol* vs. *booze*; etc. In each case either member of the pair could be used to refer to the same kinds of things in the world; the speaker's choice of which term to use indicates varying degrees of intimacy, respect, appreciation or approval, formality, etc.

The remainder of this section discusses some of the properties which distinguish expressive meaning from descriptive meaning.[12] These properties can be used as diagnostics when we are unsure which type of meaning we are dealing with.

[11] Barker (2002).

[12] Much of this discussion is based on Cruse (1986; 2000) and Potts (2007c).

2.6.1 Independence

Expressive meaning is independent of descriptive meaning in the sense that expressive meaning does not affect the denotation of a noun phrase or the truth value of a sentence. For example, the addressee might agree with the descriptive meaning of (15) without sharing the speaker's negative attitude indicated by the expressive term *jerk*. Similarly, the addressee in (16) might agree with the descriptive content of the sentence without sharing the speaker's negative attitude indicated by the pejorative suffix *-aco*.

(15) That *jerk* Peterson is the only real economist on this committee.

(16) Los vecinos tienen un pajarr-*aco* como mascota. [Spanish]
the neighbors have a bird-PEJOR as pet
Descriptive: The neighbors have a pet bird.
Expressive: The speaker has a negative attitude towards the bird.[13]

2.6.2 Nondisplaceability

Hockett (1958; 1960) used the term DISPLACEMENT to refer to the fact that speakers can use human languages to describe events and situations which are separated in space and time from the speech event itself. Hockett listed this ability as one of the distinctive properties of human language, one which distinguishes it, for example, from most types of animal communication.

Cruse (1986: 272) notes that this capacity for displacement holds only for descriptive meaning, and not for expressive meaning. A person can describe his own feelings in the past or future, e.g. *Last month I felt a sharp pain in my chest*, or *I will probably feel a lot of pain when the dentist drills my tooth tomorrow*; or the feelings of other people, e.g. *She was in a lot of pain.* But when a person says *Ouch!*, it must normally express pain that is felt by the speaker at the moment of speaking.

2.6.3 Immunity

Descriptive meaning can be negated (17a), questioned (17b), or challenged (17c). Expressive meaning is "immune" to all of these things, as illustrated in (18). As we will see in later chapters, negation, questioning, and challenging are three of the standard tests for identifying truth-conditional meaning. The fact that expressive

[13]Fortin (2011).

meaning cannot be negated, questioned, or challenged shows that it is not part of the truth-conditional meaning of the sentence.

(17) a. I am not feeling any pain.
   b. Are you feeling any pain?
   c. PATIENT: I just felt a sudden sharp pain.
   DENTIST: That's a lie – I gave you a double dose of Novocain.
   (Cruse 1986: 271)

(18) a. *Not ouch.
   b. *Ouch? (can only be interpreted as an elliptical form of the question: *Did you say "Ouch"?*)
   c. PATIENT: Ouch!
   DENTIST: #That's a lie.

2.6.4 Scalability and repeatability

Expressive meaning can be intensified through repetition (as seen in line g of Table 2.1 below), or by the use of intonational features such as pitch, length or loudness. Descriptive meaning is generally expressible in discrete units which correspond to the lexical semantic content of individual words. Repetition of descriptive meaning tends to produce redundancy, though we should note that a number of languages do use reduplication to encode plural number, repeated actions, etc.

2.6.5 Descriptive ineffability

"Effability" means 'expressibility'. The EFFABILITY HYPOTHESIS claims that "Each proposition can be expressed by some sentence in any natural language";[14] or in other words, "Whatever can be meant can be said."[15]

Potts (2007c) uses the phrase "descriptive ineffability" to indicate that expressive meaning often cannot be adequately stated in terms of descriptive meaning. A paraphrase based on descriptive meaning (e.g. *young dog* for *puppy*) is often interchangeable with the original expression, as illustrated in (19). Whenever (19a) is true, (19b) must be true as well, and vice versa. Moreover, this substitution is equally possible in questions, commands, negated sentences, etc. This is

[14]Katz (1978: 209).
[15]Searle (1969: 18); see also Katz (1972: 18–24); Carston (2002: 33).

not the case with expressives, even where a descriptive paraphrase is possible, as illustrated in (17–18) above.

(19) a. Yesterday my son brought home a puppy.
 b. Yesterday my son brought home a young dog.

For many expressives there is no descriptive paraphrase available, and speakers often find it difficult to explain the meaning of the expressive form in descriptive terms. For example, most dictionaries do not attempt to paraphrase the meaning of *oops*, but rather "define" it by describing the contexts in which it is normally used:

(20) a. "used typically to express mild apology, surprise, or dismay"[16]
 b. "an exclamation of surprise or of apology as when someone drops something or makes a mistake"[17]

This limited expressibility correlates with limited translatability. The descriptive meaning conveyed by a sentence in one language is generally expressible in other languages as well. (Whether this is always the case, as predicted by strong forms of the Effability Hypothesis, is a controversial issue.) However, it is often difficult to find an adequate translation equivalent for expressive meaning. One well known example is the ancient Aramaic term of contempt *raka*, which appears in the Greek text of Matthew 5:22 (and in many English translations), presumably because there was no adequate translation equivalent in Koine Greek. (Some of the English equivalents which have been suggested include: *good-for-nothing, rascal, empty head, stupid, ignorant.*) In 393 AD, St. Augustine offered the following explanation:

> Hence the view is more probable which I heard from a certain Hebrew whom I had asked about it; for he said that the word does not mean anything, but merely expresses the emotion of an angry mind. Grammarians call those particles of speech which express an affection of an agitated mind INTERJECTIONS; as when it is said by one who is grieved, 'Alas,' or by one who is angry, 'Hah.' And these words in all languages are proper names, and are not easily translated into another language; and this cause certainly compelled alike the Greek and the Latin translators to put the word itself, inasmuch as they could find no way of translating it."[18]

[16] http://www.merriam-webster.com

[17] *Collins English Dictionary – Complete and Unabridged,* ©HarperCollins Publishers 1991, 1994, 1998, 2000, 2003.

[18] *On the Sermon on the Mount,* Book I, ch. 9, §23; http://www.newadvent.org/fathers/16011.htm

Whether or not Augustine was correct in his view that *raka* was a pure expressive, he provides an excellent description of this class of words and the difficulty of translating them from one language to another. This quote also demonstrates that the challenges posed by expressives have been recognized for a very long time.

A similar translation problem helped to create an international incident in 1993 when the Malaysian Prime Minister, Dr. Mahathir Mohamad, declined an invitation to attend the first Asia-Pacific Economic Cooperation (APEC) summit. Australian Prime Minister Paul Keating, when asked for a comment, replied: "APEC is bigger than all of us; Australia, the US and Malaysia and Dr Mahathir and any other recalcitrants." Bilateral relations were severely strained, and both Malaysian government policies and Malaysian public opinion towards Australia were negatively affected for a long period of time. A significant factor in this reaction was the fact that the word *recalcitrant* was translated in the Malaysian press by the Malay idiom *keras kepala*, literally 'hard headed'. The two expressions have a similar range of descriptive meaning ('stubborn, obstinate, defiant of authority'), but the Malay idiom carries expressive meaning which makes the sense of insult and disrespect much stronger than in the English original. *Keras kepala* would be appropriate in scolding a child or subordinate, but not in referring to a head-of-government.

2.6.6 Case study: Expressive uses of diminutives

Diminutives are grammatical markers whose primary or literal meaning is to indicate small size; but diminutives often have secondary uses as well, and often these involve expressive content. Anna Wierzbicka (1985) describes one common use of diminutives in Polish as follows:

> In Polish, warm hospitality is expressed as much by the use of diminutives as it is by the 'hectoring' style of offers and suggestions. Characteristically, the food items offered to the guest are often referred to by the host by their diminutive names. Thus... one might say in Polish: *Wei jeszcze Sledzika! Koniecznie!* 'Take some more dear-little-herring (DIM). You must!' The diminutive praises the quality of the food and minimizes the quantity pushed onto the guest's plate. The speaker insinuates: "Don't resist! It is a small thing I'm asking you to do – and a good thing!". The target of the praise is in fact vague: the praise seems to embrace the food, the guest, and the action of the guest desired by the host. The diminutive and the imperative work hand in hand in the cordial, solicitous attempt to get the guest to eat more.

Markers of expressive meaning often have several possible meanings, which depend heavily on context, and this is true for the Spanish diminutive suffixes as illustrated in Table 2.1. Notice that the same diminutive suffix can have nearly opposite meanings (deprecation vs. appreciation; exactness vs. approximation; attenuation vs. intensification) in different contexts (and, in some cases, different dialects). These examples also illustrate the "scalability" of expressive meaning, the fact that it can be intensified through repetition, as in *chiqu-it-it-o*.

2.7 Conclusion

In this chapter we started with the observation that speakers use language to talk about the world, for example by referring to things or describing states of affairs. We introduced the distinction between sense and denotation, which is of fundamental importance in all that follows. Knowing the sense of a word is what makes it possible for speakers of a language to identify the denotation of that word in a particular context of use. In a similar way, as we discuss in Chapter 3, knowing the sense of a sentence is what makes it possible for speakers of a language to judge whether or not that sentence is true in a particular context of use. The issue of ambiguity (a single word, phrase, or sentence with more than one sense) is one that we will return to often in the chapters that follow. Finally, we demonstrated a number of ways in which this kind of descriptive meaning (talking about the world) is different from expressive meaning (expressing the speaker's emotions or attitudes). In the rest of this book, we will focus primarily on descriptive meaning rather than expressive meaning; but it is important to remember that both "dimensions" of meaning are involved in many (if not most) utterances.

Table 2.1: The expressive uses of Spanish diminutive suffixes. (Data from Fortin 2011.)

a.	Deprecation *mujer-zuela* woman-DIM	'disreputable woman' + disdain/mockery
b.	Appreciation *niñ-ito* boy-DIM	'boy' + endearment/affection
c.	Hypocorism (nick-name, pet name) *Carol-ita* Carol-DIM	'Carol' + endearment
d.	Exactness *igual-ito* the.same-DIM	'exactly the same'
e.	Approximation *floj-illo* lazy-DIM	'kind of lazy, lazy-ish'
f.	Attenuation *ahor-ita* now-DIM	'soon, in a little while' (Caribbean Spanish)
g.	Intensification *ahor-ita* now-DIM	'immediately, right now' (Latin American Spanish)
	chiqu-it-o small-DIM-MASC	'very small'
	chiqu-it-it-o small-DIM-DIM-MASC	'very, very small/teeny-weeny'
	chiqu-it-it-...-it-o small-DIM-DIM-...-DIM-MASC	'very, very, ..., very, small'

Further reading

Birner (2012/2013: Ch. 4) provides a helpful overview of reference and various related issues. Abbott (2010: Ch. 2) provides a good summary of early work by Frege and other philosophers on the distinction between sense and denotation; later chapters provide in-depth discussions of various types of referring expressions. For additional discussion of expressive meaning see Cruse (1986; 2000), Potts (2007a), and Kratzer (1999).

Discussion exercises

A: Sense vs. denotation. Which of the following pairs of expressions have the same sense? Which have the same denotation? Explain your answer.

a.	cordates (='animals with hearts')	renates (= 'animals with kidneys')
b.	animals with gills and scales	fish
c.	your first-born son	your oldest male offspring
d.	Ronald Reagan	the Governor of California
e.	my oldest sister	your Aunt Betty
f.	my pupils	the students that I teach
g.	the man who invented the phonograph	the man who invented the light-bulb

> Model answer for (a)
>
> In our world at the present time, all species that have hearts also have kidneys; so these two words have the same denotation in our world at the present time. They do not have the same sense, however, because we can imagine a world in which some species had hearts without kidneys, or kidneys without hearts; so the two words do not have the same denotation in all possible situations.

B: Referring expressions. Which of the following NPs are being used to *refer* to something?

a. I never promised you *a rose garden.*

b. St. Benedict, the father of Western monasticism, planted *a rose garden* at his early monastery in Subiaco near Rome.[a]

c. My sister wants to marry *a policeman.*

d. My sister married *a policeman.*

e. Leibniz searched for *the solution to the equation.*

f. Leibniz discovered *the solution to the equation.*

g. *No cat* likes being bathed.

h. *All musicians* are temperamental.

[a] http://www.scu.edu/stclaregarden/ethno/medievalgardens.cfm

Homework exercises

A: Idiomatic meaning. Try to find one phrasal idiom (an idiom consisting of two or more words) in a language other than English; give a word-for-word translation and explain its idiomatic meaning.

B: Expressive meaning. Try to find a word in a language other than English which has purely expressive meaning, like *oops* and *ouch*; and explain how it is used.

C: Referring expressions. For each of the following sentences, state whether or not the nominal expression in italics is being used to refer.

a. Abraham Lincoln was very close to *his step-mother.*

> Model answer
> The phrase *his step-mother* is used to refer to a specific person, namely Sarah Bush Lincoln, so it does refer

b. I'm so hungry I could eat *a horse.*

c. Senate Majority Leader Curt Bramble, R-Provo, was back in the hospital this weekend after getting kicked by *a horse.*[a]

d. Police searched the house for 6 hours but found *no drugs.*

e. Edward hopes that his on-line match-making service will help him find *the girl of his dreams.*

f. Susan married *the first man who proposed to her.*

g. *Every city* has pollution problems.

[a]Provo, UT *Daily Herald* Jan. 29, 2007.

3 Truth and inference

3.1 Truth as a guide to sentence meaning

Any speaker of English will "understand" the simple sentence in (1), i.e., will know what it "means". But what kind of knowledge does this involve? Can our hypothetical speaker tell us, for example, whether the sentence is true?

(1) *King Henry VIII snores.*

It turns out that a sentence by itself is neither true nor false: its truth value can only be determined relative to a specific situation (or state of affairs, or universe of discourse). In the real world at the time that I am writing this chapter (early in the 21st century), the sentence is clearly false, because Henry VIII died in 1547 AD. The sentence may well have been true in, say, 1525 AD; but most speakers of English probably do not know whether or not it was in fact true, because we do not have total knowledge of the state of the world at that time.

So knowing the meaning of a sentence does not necessarily mean that we know whether or not it is true in a particular situation; but it does mean that we know the kinds of situations in which the sentence would be true. Sentence (1) will be true in any universe of discourse in which the individual named *King Henry VIII* has the property of snoring. We will adopt the common view of sentence meanings expressed in (2):

(2) "To know the meaning of a [declarative] sentence is to know what the world would have to be like for the sentence to be true." (Dowty et al. 1981: 4)

The meaning of a simple declarative sentence is called a PROPOSITION. A proposition is a claim about the world which may (in general) be true in some situations and false in others. Some scholars hold that a sentence, as a grammatical entity, cannot have a truth value. Speakers speak truly when they use a sentence to perform a certain type of speech act, namely a statement (making a claim about the world), provided that the meaning (i.e., the sense) of the sentence corresponds to the situation about which the claim is being made. Under this view, when we speak of sentences as being true or false we are using a common but imprecise manner of speaking. It is the proposition expressed by the sentence, rather than the sentence itself, which can be true or false.

In §3.2 we will look at various types of propositions: some which must always be true, some which can never be true, and some (the "normal" case) which may be either true or false depending on the situation. In §3.3 we examine some important truth relations that can exist between pairs of propositions, of which perhaps the most important is the ENTAILMENT relation. Entailment is a type of inference. We say that proposition p "entails" proposition q if p being true makes it certain that q is true as well. Finally, in §3.4, we introduce another type of inference known as a PRESUPPOSITION. Presupposition is a complex and controversial topic, but one which will be important in later chapters.

3.2 Analytic sentences, synthetic sentences, and contradictions

We have said that knowing the meaning of a sentence allows us to determine the kinds of situations in which the proposition which it expresses would be true. In other words, the meaning of a sentence determines its TRUTH CONDITIONS. Some propositions have the interesting property of being true under all circumstances; there are no situations in which such a proposition would be false. We refer to sentences which express such propositions as ANALYTIC SENTENCES, or TAUTOLOGIES. Some examples are given in (3):

(3) a. *Today is the first day of the rest of your life.*[1]
    b. *Que será será.* 'What will be, will be.'
    c. Is this bill all that I want? Far from it. Is it all that it can be? Far from it. *But when history calls, history calls.*[2]

Because analytic sentences are always true, they are not very informative. The speaker who commits himself to the truth of such a sentence is making no claim at all about the state of the world, because the truth of the sentence depends only on the meaning of the words. But in that case, why would anyone bother to say such a thing? It is important to note that the use of tautologies is not restricted to

[1]Attributed to Charles Dederich (1913–1997), founder of the Synanon drug rehabilitation program and religious movement.

[2]Sen. Olympia Snowe explaining her vote in favor of the Baucus health care reform bill, Oct. 2009.

politicians and pop psychology gurus, who may have professional motivations to make risk-free statements which sound profound. In fact, all of us probably say such things more frequently than we realize. We say them because they do in fact have communicative value; but this value cannot come from the semantic (or truth conditional) content of the utterance. The communicative value of these utterances comes entirely from the pragmatic inferences which they trigger. We will talk in more detail in Chapter 8 about how these pragmatic inferences arise.

The opposite situation is also possible, i.e. propositions which are false in every imaginable situation. An example is given in (4). Propositions of this type are said to be CONTRADICTIONS. Once again, a speaker who utters a sentence of this type is not making a truth conditional claim about the state of the world, since there are no conditions under which the sentence can be true. The communicative value of the utterance must be derived by pragmatic inference.

(4) And a woman who held a babe against her bosom said, "Speak to us of children."And he said: "***Your children are not your children***. They are the sons and daughters of Life's longing for itself…"[3]

Propositions which are neither contradictions nor analytic are said to be SYNTHETIC. These propositions may be true in some situations and false in others, so determining their truth value requires not only understanding their meaning but also knowing something about the current state of the world or the situation under discussion. Most of the (declarative) sentences that speakers produce in everyday speech are of this type.

We would expect an adequate analysis of sentence meanings to provide an explanation for why certain sentences are analytic, and why certain others are contradictions. So one criterion for evaluating the relative merits of a possible semantic analysis is to ask how successful it is in this regard.

3.3 Meaning relations between propositions

Consider the pair of sentences in (5). The meanings of these two sentences are related in an important way. Specifically, in any situation for which (5a) is true, (5b) must be true as well; and in any situation for which (5b) is false, (5a) must also be false. Moreover, this relationship follows directly from the meanings of the two sentences, and does not depend on the situation or context in which they are used.

[3] From "On Children", in *The Prophet* (Kahlil Gibran, 1923).

(5) a. Edward VIII has abdicated the throne in order to marry Wallis Simpson.
b. Edward VIII is no longer the King.

This kind of relationship is known as ENTAILMENT; sentence (5a) ENTAILS sentence (5b), or more precisely, the proposition expressed by (5a) entails the proposition expressed by (5b). The defining properties of entailment are those mentioned in the previous paragraph. We can say that proposition *p* entails proposition *q* just in case the following three things are true:[4]

(a) whenever *p* is true, it is logically necessary that *q* must also be true;

(b) whenever *q* is false, it is logically necessary that *p* must also be false;

(c) these relations follow directly from the meanings of *p* and *q*, and do not depend on the context of the utterance.

This definition gives us some ways to test for entailments. Intuitively it seems clear that the proposition expressed by (6a) entails the proposition expressed by (6b). We can confirm this intuition by observing that asserting (6a) while denying (6b) leads to a contradiction (6c). Similarly, it would be highly unnatural to assert (6a) while expressing doubt about (6b), as illustrated in (6d). It would be unnaturally redundant to assert (6a) and then state (6b) as a separate assertion; this is illustrated in (6e).

(6) a. I broke your Ming dynasty jar.
b. Your Ming dynasty jar broke.
c. #I broke your Ming dynasty jar, but the jar didn't break.
d. #I broke your Ming dynasty jar, but I'm not sure whether the jar broke.
e. #I broke your Ming dynasty jar, and the jar broke.

Now consider the pair of sentences in (7). Intuitively it seems that (7a) entails (7b); whenever (7a) is true, (7b) must also be true, and whenever (7b) is false, (7a) must also be false. But notice that (7b) also entails (7a). The propositions expressed by these two sentences mutually entail each other, as demonstrated in (7c–d). Two sentences which mutually entail each other are said to be SYNONYMOUS, or PARAPHRASES of each other. This means that the propositions expressed

[4] Cruse (2000: 29).

by the two sentences have the same truth conditions, and therefore must have the same truth value (either both true or both false) in any imaginable situation.

(7) a. Hong Kong is warmer than Beijing (in December).
    b. Beijing is cooler than Hong Kong (in December).
    c. #Hong Kong is warmer than Beijing, but Beijing is not cooler than Hong Kong.
    d. #Beijing is cooler than Hong Kong, but Hong Kong is not warmer than Beijing.

A pair of propositions which cannot both be true are said to be INCONSISTENT or INCOMPATIBLE. Two distinct types of incompatibility have traditionally been recognized. Propositions which must have opposite truth values in every circumstance are said to be CONTRADICTORY. For example, any proposition *p* must have the opposite truth value from its negation (*not p*) in all circumstances. Thus the pair of sentences in (8) are contradictory; whenever the first is true, the second must be false, and vice versa.

(8) a. Ringo Starr is my grandfather.
    b. Ringo Starr is not my grandfather.

On the other hand, it is possible for two propositions to be inconsistent without being contradictory. This would mean that they cannot both be true, but they could both be false in a particular context. We refer to such pairs as CONTRARY propositions. An example is provided in (9a–b). These two sentences cannot both be true, so (9c) is a contradiction. However, they could both be false in a given situation, so (9d) is not a contradiction."

(9) a. Al is taller than Bill.
    b. Bill is taller than Al.
    c. #Al is taller than Bill and Bill is taller than Al.
    d. Al is no taller than Bill and Bill is no taller than Al.

Finally, two sentences are said to be INDEPENDENT when they are neither incompatible nor synonymous, and when neither of them entails the other. If two sentences are independent, there is no truth value dependency between the two propositions; knowing the truth value of one will not provide enough information to know the truth value of the other.

These meaning relations (incompatibility, synonymy, and entailment) provide additional benchmarks for evaluating a possible semantic analysis: how successful is it in predicting or explaining which pairs of sentences will be synonymous, which pairs will be incompatible, etc.?

3.4 Presupposition

In the previous section we discussed how the meaning of one sentence can entail the meaning of another sentence. Entailment is a very strong kind of inference. If we are sure that *p* is true, and we know that *p* entails *q*, then we can be equally sure that *q* is true. In this section we examine another kind of inference, that is, another type of meaning relation in which the utterance of one sentence seems to imply the truth of some other sentence. This type of inference, which is known as a PRESUPPOSITION, is extremely common in daily speech; it has been intensively studied but remains controversial and somewhat mysterious.

As a first approximation, let us define presupposition as information which is linguistically encoded as being part of the common ground at the time of utterance. The term COMMON GROUND refers to everything that both the speaker and hearer know or believe, and know that they have in common. This would include knowledge about the world, such as the fact that (in our world) there is only one sun and one moon; knowledge that is observable in the speech situation, such as what the speaker is wearing or carrying; or facts that have been mentioned earlier in that same conversation (or discourse).

Speakers can choose to indicate, by the use of certain words or grammatical constructions, that a certain piece of information is part of the common ground. Consider the following example:

(10) "Take some more tea," the March Hare said to Alice, very earnestly.
"I've had nothing yet," Alice replied in an offended tone, "so I can't take more."[5]

By using the word *more* (in the sense which seems most likely in this context, i.e. as a synonym for *additional*) the March Hare implies that Alice has already had some tea, and that this knowledge is part of their common ground at that point in the conversation. The word or grammatical construction which indicates the presence of a presupposition is called a TRIGGER; so in this case we can say that *more* "triggers" the presupposition that she has already had some tea. However, in this example the "presupposed" material is not in fact part of

[5] Lewis Carroll, *Alice's Adventures in Wonderland*, Chapter 7: "A Mad Tea-Party"

the common ground, because Alice has not yet had any tea. This is a case of PRESUPPOSITION FAILURE, which we might define as an inappropriate use of a presupposition trigger to signal a presupposition which is not in fact part of the common ground at the time of utterance. Notice that Alice is offended – not only by the impoliteness of her hosts in not offering her tea in the first place, but also by the inappropriate use of the word *more.*

3.4.1 How to identify a presupposition

There is an important difference between entailment and presupposition with regard to how the nature of the speech act being performed affects the inference. If p entails q, then any speaker who states that p is true (e.g. *I broke your jar*) is committed to believing that q (e.g. *your jar broke*) is also true. However, a speaker who asks whether p is true (*Did I break your jar?*) or denies that p is true (*I didn't break your jar*) makes no commitment concerning the truth value of q. In contrast, if p presupposes q, then the inference holds whether the speaker asserts, denies, or asks whether p is true. Notice that all of the three sentences in (11) imply that the vice president has falsified his dental records. (This presupposition is triggered by the word *regret.*)

(11) a. The vice president regrets that he falsified his dental records.
b. The vice president doesn't regret that he falsified his dental records.
c. Does the vice president regret that he falsified his dental records?

In most cases, if a positive declarative sentence like (12a) triggers a certain presupposition, that presupposition will also be triggered by a "family" of related sentences (sentences based on the same propositional content) which includes negative assertions, questions, *if*-clauses and certain modalities.[6] For example, (12a) presupposes that Susan has been dating an Albanian monk; this presupposition is triggered by the word *stop.* All of the other sentences in (12) trigger this same presupposition, as predicted.

(12) a. Susan has stopped dating that Albanian monk.
b. Susan has not stopped dating that Albanian monk.
c. Has Susan stopped dating that Albanian monk?
d. If Susan has stopped dating that Albanian monk, I might introduce her to my cousin.
e. Susan may have stopped dating that Albanian monk.

[6] Cherchia & McConnell-Ginet (1990).

In addition to the presupposition mentioned above, (12a) also entails that Susan is not currently dating the Albanian monk; but this entailment is not shared by any of the other sentences in (12). This contrast shows us that presuppositions are preserved under negation, questioning, etc. while entailments are not.[7]

The "family of sentences" test is one of the most commonly used methods for distinguishing entailments from presuppositions. To offer another example, the statement *The neighbor's dog killed my cat* presupposes that the speaker owned a cat, and entails that the cat is dead. If the statement is negated (*The neighbor's dog didn't kill my cat*) or questioned (*Did the neighbor's dog kill my cat?*), the presupposition still holds but entailment does not.

Von Fintel & Matthewson (2008) describe another test for identifying presuppositions. They point out that if a presupposition is triggered which is not in fact part of the common ground, the hearer can appropriately object by saying something like, "Wait a minute, I didn't know that!" This kind of challenge is not appropriate for information that is simply asserted, since speakers do not usually assert something which they believe that the hearer already knows:

> A presupposition which is not in the common ground at the time of utterance can be challenged by 'Hey, wait a minute!' (or other similar responses). In contrast, an assertion which is not in the common ground cannot be challenged in this way. This is shown in [13]... The 'Hey, wait a minute!' test is the best way we know of to test for presuppositions in a fieldwork context. (von Fintel & Matthewson 2008)

(13) A: The mathematician who proved Goldbach's Conjecture is a woman.
B_1: Hey, wait a minute. I had no idea that someone proved Goldbach's Conjecture.
B_2: #Hey, wait a minute. I had no idea that that was a woman.

A fairly large number of presupposition triggers have been identified in English; a partial listing is presented below. For many of these it seems that translation equivalents in a number of other languages may trigger similar presuppositions, but so far there has been relatively little detailed study of presuppositions in languages other than English.[8]

[7] A more technical way of expressing this is to say that presuppositions PROJECT through the operators illustrated in (12), while entailments do not.

[8] Exceptions to this generalization include Levinson & Annamalai (1992), Matthewson (2006), and Tonhauser et al. (2013).

a. Definite descriptions: the use of a definite singular noun phrase, such as Bertrand Russell's famous example *the King of France*, presupposes that there is a uniquely identifiable individual in the situation under discussion that fits that description. Similarly, the use of a possessive phrase (e.g. *my cat*) presupposes the existence of the possessee (in this case, the existence of a cat belonging to the speaker).

b. Factive predicates (e.g. *regret, aware, realize, know, be sorry that*) are predicates that presuppose the truth of their complement clauses, as illustrated in (11) above.[9]

c. Implicative predicates: *manage to* presupposes *try; forget to* presupposes *intend to*; etc.

d. Aspectual predicates: *stop* and *continue* both presuppose that the event under discussion has been going on for some time, as illustrated in (12) above; *resume* presupposes that the event was going on but then stopped for some period of time; *begin* presupposes that the event was not occurring before.

e. Temporal clauses (14a–b) and restrictive relative clauses (14c) presuppose the truth of their subordinate clauses, while counterfactuals (14d) presuppose that their antecedent (*if*) clauses are false (see Chapter 19). Comparisons like (14e) presuppose that the relevant statement holds true for the object of comparison.

(14) a. Before I moved to Texas, I had never attended a rodeo.
(presupposes that the speaker moved to Texas)
b. While his wife was in the hospital, John worked a full 40 hour week.
(presupposes that John's wife was in the hospital)
c. "I'm looking for the man who killed my father."[10]
(presupposes that some man killed the speaker's father)
d. If you had not written that letter, I would not have to fire you.
(presupposes that the hearer did write that letter)
e. Jimmy isn't as unpredictably gauche as Billy.[11]
(presupposes that Billy is unpredictably gauche)

[9]Kiparsky & Kiparsky (1970).
[10]Maddie Ross in the movie *True Grit*.
[11]Levinson (1983: 183).

The tests mentioned above seem to work for all of these types, but in other respects it seems that different kinds of presupposition have slightly different properties. This is one of the major challenges in analyzing presuppositions. We return in Chapter 8 to the issue of how to distinguish between different kinds of inference.

3.4.2 Accommodation: a repair strategy

Recall that we defined presuppositions as "information which is LINGUISTICALLY ENCODED as being part of the common ground at the time of utterance." We crucially did not require that implied information actually BE part of the common ground in order to count as a presupposition. We have already seen one outcome that may result from the use of presupposition triggers which do not accurately reflect the common ground at the time of utterance, namely presupposition failure (10 above). Another example of presupposition failure is provided in (15), taken from the 1939 movie *The Wizard of Oz*:

(15)
Glinda: Are you a good witch or a bad witch?
Dorothy: Who, me? I'm not a witch at all. I'm Dorothy Gale, from Kansas.
Glinda: Well, is that the witch?
Dorothy: Who, Toto? Toto's my dog.
Glinda: Well, I'm a little muddled. The Munchkins called me because a new witch has just dropped a house on the Wicked Witch of the East. And there's the house, and here you are and that's all that's left of the Wicked Witch of the East. What the Munchkins want to know is, are you a good witch or a bad witch?

Glinda's first question presupposes that one of the two specified alternatives (*good witch* vs. *bad witch*) is true of Dorothy, and both of these would entail that Dorothy is a witch. Dorothy rejects this presupposition quite vigorously. Glinda's second question (*Is that the witch?*), and in particular her use of the definite article, presupposes that there is a uniquely identifiable witch in the context of the conversation. The fact that these false inferences are triggered by questions is a strong hint that they are presuppositions rather than entailments.

Glinda's questions in this passage trigger presuppositions which Dorothy contests, because these inferences are not part of the common ground. However, presupposition failure is not the only possible outcome with such inferences.

Another possibility is that the hearer, confronted with a mismatch between a presupposition trigger and the current common ground, may choose to accept the presupposition as if it were part of the common ground; in effect, to add it to the common ground. This is most likely to happen if the presupposed information is uncontroversial and consistent with all information that is already part of the common ground; something that the hearer would immediately accept if the speaker asserted it. For example, suppose I notice that you have not slept well and you explain by saying *My cat got stuck on the roof last night*; and suppose that I did not previously know you had a cat. Technically the presupposition triggered by the possessive phrase *my cat* is not part of the common ground, but I am very unlikely to object or to consider your statement in any way inappropriate. Instead, I will add to my model of the common ground the fact that you own a cat. This process is called ACCOMMODATION.

It is not uncommon for speakers to encode new information as a presupposition, expecting it to be accommodated by the hearer. For this reason, definitions which state that presuppositions "must be mutually known or assumed by the speaker and addressee for the utterance to be considered appropriate in context" are misleading.[12] This fact has long been recognized in discussions of presupposition, as the following quotes illustrate:

> I am asked by someone who I have just met, "Are you going to lunch?" I reply, "No, I've got to pick up my sister." Here I seem to presuppose that I have a sister even though I do not assume that the speaker knows this. (Stalnaker 1974: 202).

> It is quite natural to say to somebody... "My aunt's cousin went to that concert," when one knows perfectly well that the person one is talking to is very likely not even to know that one had an aunt, let alone know that one's aunt had a cousin. So the supposition must be not that it is common knowledge but rather that it is non-controversial, in the sense that it is something that you would expect the hearer to take from you (if he does not already know). (Grice 1981: 190)

3.4.3 Pragmatic vs. semantic aspects of presupposition

Thus far we have treated presupposition primarily as a pragmatic issue. We defined it in terms of the common ground between a specific speaker and hearer at a particular moment, a pragmatic concept since it depends heavily on the context

[12] See for example http://en.wikipedia.org/wiki/Presupposition.

of the utterance and the identity of the speech act participants. Presupposition failure, where accommodation is not possible, causes the utterance to be pragmatically inappropriate or INFELICITOUS.[13] In contrast, we defined entailment in purely semantic terms: an entailment relation between two propositions must follow directly from the meanings of the propositions, and does not depend on the context of the utterance.

It turns out that presuppositions can have semantic effects as well. We have said that knowing the meaning (i.e. semantic content) of a sentence allows us to determine its truth value in any given situation. Now suppose a speaker utters (16a) in our modern world, where there is no King of France; or (16b) in a context where the individual John has no children; or (16c) in a context where John's wife had not been in the hospital. Under those circumstances, the sentences would clearly not be true; but would we want to say that they are false? If they were false, then their denials should be true; but the negative statements in (17), if read with normal intonation, would be just as "un-true" as their positive counterparts in the contexts we have just described.

(16) a. The present King of France is bald.[14]
  b. John's children are very well-behaved.
  c. While his wife was in the hospital, John worked a full 40 hour week.

(17) a. The present King of France is not bald.
  b. John's children are not very well-behaved.
  c. While his wife was in the hospital, John did not work a full 40 hour week.

We have already noted that the presupposition failure triggered by such statements makes them pragmatically inappropriate; but examples like (16–17) show that, at least in some cases, presupposition failure can also make it difficult to assign the sentence a truth value. Some of the earliest discussions of presuppositions defined them in purely semantic, truth-conditional terms:[15] "One sentence PRESUPPOSES another just in case the latter must be true in order that the former have a truth value at all."[16]

[13]We will give a more precise explanation of the term INFELICITOUS in Chapter 10, as part of our discussion of speech acts.

[14]Adapted from Russell (1905).

[15]e.g. Frege (1892); Strawson (1950; 1952).

[16]Stalnaker (1973: 447), summarizing the positions of Strawson and Frege. Stalnaker himself argued for a pragmatic analysis.

Under this definition, presupposition failure results in a truth-value "gap", or indeterminacy. But there are other cases where presupposition failure does not seem to have this effect. For example, if (18a) were spoken in a context where the vice president had not falsified his dental records, or (18b) in a context where Susan had never dated an Albanian monk, these sentences would be pragmatically inappropriate because of the presupposition failure. But it also seems reasonable to say they are false (the vice president can't regret something he never did; Susan can't stop doing something she never did), and that their negative counterparts in (19) have at least one reading (or sense) which is true.

(18) a. The vice president regrets that he falsified his dental records.
b. Susan has stopped dating that Albanian monk.

(19) a. The vice president doesn't regret that he falsified his dental records.
b. Susan has not stopped dating that Albanian monk.

However, there are various complications concerning the way negation gets interpreted in examples like (19). For example, intonation can affect the interpretation of the sentence. We will return to this issue in Chapter 8.

3.5 Conclusion

The principle that the meaning of a sentence determines its truth conditions (i.e., the kinds of situations in which the proposition it expresses would be true) is the foundation for most of what we talk about in this book, including word meanings. A proposition is judged to be true if it corresponds to the situation about which a claim is made.

A major goal of semantic analysis is to explain how a sentence gets its meaning, that is, why a given form has the particular meaning that it does. In this chapter we have mentioned a few benchmarks for success, things that we would expect an adequate analysis of sentence meanings to provide for us. These benchmarks include explaining why certain sentences are analytic (always true) or contradictions (never true); and predicting which pairs of sentences will be synonymous (always having the same truth value in every possible situation), incompatible (cannot both be true), etc.

In this chapter we have introduced two very important types of inference, entailment and presupposition, which we will refer to in many future chapters. Entailment is strictly a semantic relation, whereas presupposition has to do with pragmatic issues such as managing the common ground and appropriateness of use. However, we have suggested that presupposition failure can sometimes block the assignment of truth values as well.

Further reading

Good basic introductions to the study of logic are presented in Allwood et al. (1977: ch. 3) and Gamut (1991a: ch. 1). The literature dealing with presupposition is enormous. Helpful overviews of the subject are presented in Levinson (1983: ch. 4), Geurts & Beaver (2011), Zimmermann & Sternefeld (2013: ch. 9), and Birner (2012/2013: ch. 5). Potts (2015) also provides a good summary, including a comparison of presuppositions with conventional implicatures (which we will discuss in chapters 8 and 11). Von Fintel & Matthewson (2008: §4.1) discuss cross-linguistic issues.

Discussion exercises

A: Classifying propositions. State whether the propositions expressed by the following sentences are analytic, synthetic, or contradictions:

1. My sister is a happily married bachelor.
2. Even numbers are divisible by two.
3. All dogs are brown.
4. All dogs are animals.
5. The earth revolves around the sun.
6. The sun does not shine at night.
7. CO_2 becomes a solid when it boils.

B: Relationships between propositions. Identify the relationship between the following pairs of propositions (ENTAILMENT, PARAPHRASE, CONTRARY, CONTRADICTORY, INDEPENDENT):

(1) a. John killed the wasp.
b. The wasp died.

(2) a. John killed the wasp.
b. The wasp did not die.

(3) a. The wasp is alive.
b. The wasp is dead.

(4) a. The wasp is no longer alive.
b. The wasp is dead.

(5) a. Fido is a dog.
b. Fido is a cat.

(6) a. Fido is a dog.
b. Fido has four legs.

C: Presuppositions. Identify the presuppositions and presupposition triggers in the following examples:

1. John's children are very well-behaved.
2. Susan has become a vegan.
3. Bill forgot to call his uncle.
4. After he won the lottery, John had to get an unlisted phone number.
5. George is sorry that he broke your Ming dynasty jar.

D: Presuppositions vs. entailments. Show how you could use the negation and/or question tests to decide whether the (a) sentence ENTAILS or PRESUPPOSES the (b) sentence. Evaluate the two sentences if spoken by the same speaker at the same time and place.[a]

(1) a. Dave knows that Jim crashed the car.

b. Jim crashed the car.

> Model answer
>
> The statement *Dave knows that Jim crashed the car*, its negation *Dave doesn't know that Jim crashed the car*, and the corresponding question *Does Dave know that Jim crashed the car?* all lead the hearer to infer that Jim crashed the car. This suggests that the inference is a presupposition.

(2) a. Zaire is bigger than Alaska.
b. Alaska is smaller than Zaire.

(3) a. The minister blames her secretary for leaking the memo to the press.
b. The memo was leaked to the press.

(4) a. Everyone passed the examination.
b. No one failed the examination.

(5) a. Mr. Singleton has resumed his habit of drinking stout.
b. Mr. Singleton had a habit of drinking stout.

[a] Adapted from Saeed (2009: 114, ex. 4.8)

Homework exercises

A: Classifying propositions. Classify the following sentences as analytic, synthetic, or contradictions.

1. If it rains, we'll get wet.

> Model answer:
> Sentence 1. is synthetic, since we can imagine some contexts in which the sentence will be true, and other contexts in which it will be false (e.g., if I carry an umbrella).

2. If that snake is not dead then it is alive.
3. Shanghai is the capital of China.
4. My brother is an only child.
5. Abraham Lincoln was the 16th president of the United States.

B: Relationships between propositions. Identify the relationship between the following pairs of propositions (ENTAILMENT, PARAPHRASE, CONTRARY, CONTRADICTORY, INDEPENDENT):

(1) a. Michael is my advisor.
    b. I am Michael's advisee.

(2) a. Stewball was a race horse.
    b. Stewball was a mammal.

(3) a. Elvis died of cardiac arrhythmia.
    b. Elvis is alive.

C: Identifying entailments. For each pair of sentences, decide whether sentence (a) ENTAILS sentence (b). The two sentences should be evaluated as if spoken by the same speaker at the same time and place; so, for example, repeated names and definite NPs refer to the same individuals.

(1) a. Olivia passed her driving test.
    b. Olivia didn't fail her driving test.

> Model answer:
> If a is true, b must be true; if b is false, a must be false; this follows from the meanings of the sentences, and does not depend on context. So a entails b.

(2) a. Fido is a dog.
    b. Fido has four legs.

(3) a. That boy is my son.
    b. I am that boy's parent.

(4) a. Not all of our students will graduate.
    b. Some of our students will graduate.

D: Presuppositions vs. entailments. Show how you could use the negation test to decide whether the (a) sentence ENTAILS or PRESUPPOSES the (b) sentence. Again, evaluate the two sentences as being spoken by the same speaker at the same time and place.

(1) a. The boss realized that Jim was lying.
    b. Jim was lying.

> Model answer:
> Both *The boss realized that Jim was lying* and *The boss didn't realize that Jim was lying* lead the hearer to infer that Jim was lying. This suggests that the inference is a presupposition.

(2) a. Singapore is south of Kuala Lumpur.
    b. Kuala Lumpur is north of Singapore.

(3) a. I am sorry that Arthur was fired.
    b. Arthur was fired.

(4) a. Nobody is perfect.
    b. Everybody is imperfect.

(5) a. Leif Erikson returned to Greenland.
    b. Leif Erikson had previously visited Greenland.

4 The logic of truth

> *LOGIC, n. The art of thinking and reasoning in strict accordance with the limitations and incapacities of the human misunderstanding. The basic of logic is the syllogism, consisting of a major and a minor premise and a conclusion — thus:*
>
> | | |
> |---|---|
> | *Major Premise:* | *Sixty men can do a piece of work sixty times as quickly as one man.* |
> | *Minor Premise:* | *One man can dig a posthole in sixty seconds; therefore,* |
> | *Conclusion:* | *Sixty men can dig a posthole in one second.* |
>
> *This may be called the syllogism arithmetical, in which, by combining logic and mathematics, we obtain a double certainty and are twice blessed.*
>
> *[entry from The Devil's Dictionary by Ambrose Bierce 1911]*

4.1 What logic can do for you

In Chapter 1 we mentioned that semanticists often use formal logic as a metalanguage for representing the meanings of sentences and other expressions in human languages. For the most part, this book emphasizes prose description more than formalization; we will use the logical notation a fair bit in Unit IV but only sporadically in other sections of the book. Nevertheless, it will be helpful for you to become familiar with this notation, not only for the purposes of this book but also to help you read other books and articles about semantics.

In this chapter we will introduce some of the basic symbols and rules of inference for standard logic. Before we begin, it will probably be helpful to address a question which many readers may already be asking themselves, and which others are likely to ask before we get too far into the discussion: why are we doing this? How does translating English (or Samoan or Marathi) sentences into logical formulae help us to understand their meaning?

Representing the complexities of natural language using formal logic is no trivial task, but here are some of the reasons why many scholars have found the effort required in adopting this approach worthwhile. First, every human language is characterized by ambiguity, vagueness, figures of speech, etc. These features can actually be an advantage for communicative purposes, but they make it difficult to provide precise and unambiguous descriptions of word and sentence meanings in English (or Samoan or Marathi). Using formal logic as a metalanguage avoids most of these problems.

Second, we stated in Chapter 3 that one way of measuring the success or adequacy of a semantic analysis is to see whether it can explain or predict various meaning relations between sentences, such as entailment, paraphrase, or incompatibility. Logic is the science of inference. If the meanings of two sentences can be stated as logical formulae, logic provides very precise rules and methods for determining whether one follows as a logical consequence of the other (entailment), whether each follows as a logical consequence of the other (paraphrase), or whether the two are logically inconsistent, i.e. they cannot both be true (incompatibility).

Third, it is often useful to test a hypothesis about the meaning of a sentence by expressing it in logical form, and then using the rules of logical inference to see what the implications would be. For example, suppose our analysis predicts that a certain sentence should mean p, and suppose we can show that if a person believes p, he is logically committed to believing q. Now suppose that native speakers of the language feel that there would be no inconsistency in asserting the sentence in question but denying q. This mismatch between logical inference and speaker intuition may give us reason to think that p is not the correct meaning of the sentence after all. We will see examples of this kind of reasoning in future chapters.

Fourth, formal logic has proven to be a very powerful tool for modeling compositionality, i.e., for explaining how the meanings of sentences can be predicted from the meanings of the words they contain and the syntactic structure used to combine those words. As we noted in Chapter 1, this is one of the fundamental goals of semantic analysis. We will get a glimpse of how this can be done in Unit IV.

Finally, formal logic is a recursive system. This means that a relatively small number of symbols and rules can be used to form an unlimited number of different formulae. Any adequate metalanguage for describing the meanings of sentences in a human language must have this property, because (as we noted in Chapter 1) there is in principle no limit to the number of distinct meaningful sentences that can be produced in any human language.

To illustrate the recursive nature of the system, let us introduce the logical negation operator $\neg$ 'not'. The negation operator combines with a single proposition to form a new proposition. So, for example, if we let p represent the proposition 'It is raining,' then $\neg p$ (read 'not p') would represent the proposition 'It is not raining.' This proposition in turn can again combine with the negation operator to form a new proposition $\neg(\neg p)$ 'It is not the case that it is not raining.' There is in principle no limit to the number of formulae that can be produced in this way, though in practice sheer boredom would probably be a limiting factor.

We begin in §4.2 with a brief discussion of INFERENCE and some of the ways in which logic can help us distinguish valid from invalid patterns of inference. §4.3 deals with PROPOSITIONAL LOGIC, which specifies ways of combining simple propositions to form complex propositions. An important fact about this part of the logical system is that the inferences of propositional logic depend only on the truth values of the propositions involved, and not on their meanings. §4.4 deals with PREDICATE LOGIC, which provides a way to take into account the meanings of individual content words and to state inferences which arise due to the meanings of quantifier words such as *all, some, none*, etc.

4.2 Valid patterns of inference

If someone says to us, *Either Joe is crazy or he is lying, and he is not crazy*, and we believe the speaker to be truthful and well-informed, we will naturally conclude that Joe is lying. This is an example of INFERENCE: knowing that one fact or set of facts is true gives us an adequate basis for concluding that some other fact is also true.

Logic is the science of inference. One important goal of logic is to provide a systematic account for the kinds of reasoning or inference that we intuitively know to be correct, like the example mentioned in the previous paragraph. In thinking about such examples it is helpful to lay out each of the PREMISES (the facts which form the basis for the inference) and the CONCLUSION (the fact which is inferred) as shown in (1). For longer and more complex chains of inference, the same format can be used to lay out each step in the reasoning and thereby provide a PROOF that the conclusion is true.

(1) Premise 1: *Either Joe is crazy or he is lying.*
Premise 2: *Joe is not crazy.*
____
Conclusion: *Therefore, Joe is lying.*

As we will see, the kind of inference illustrated in (1) does not depend on the meanings of the "content words" (nouns, verbs, adjectives, etc.) but only on the meaning of the logical words, in this case *or* and *not.* Propositional logic, the topic of §4.3, deals with patterns of this type. Some other kinds of reasoning that we intuitively recognize as being correct are illustrated in (2):

(2) a. Premise 1: *All men are mortal.*
Premise 2: *Socrates is a man.*
______
Conclusion: *Therefore, Socrates is mortal.*

b. Premise 1: *Arthur is a lawyer.*
Premise 2: *Arthur is honest.*
______
Conclusion: *Therefore, some (= at least one) lawyer is honest.*

The kinds of inference illustrated in (2) are clearly valid, and have been studied and discussed for over 2000 years. But these patterns cannot be explained using propositional logic alone. Once again, these inferences do not depend on the meanings of the "content words" (*mortal, lawyer, honest,* etc.). In these examples the inferences follow from the meaning of the QUANTIFIERS *all* and *some.* Predicate logic, the topic of §4.4, provides a way of dealing with such cases.

Now consider the inference in (3):

(3) Premise: *John killed the wasp.*
______
Conclusion: *Therefore, the wasp died.*

This inference is not determined by the meanings of logical words or quantifiers, but only by the meanings of the verbs *kill* and *die.* Neither propositional logic nor predicate logic actually addresses this kind of inference. Logic deals with general patterns or forms of reasoning, rather that the meanings of individual words. However, predicate logic provides a notation for representing the meanings of the content words within each proposition, and thus gives us a way of expressing lexical entailments (e.g., *kill* entails *die*; see Chapter 6).

It is important to remember that a valid form of inference does not (by itself) guarantee a true conclusion. For example, the inferences in (4) both make use of a valid pattern discussed in §4.3.2, which is called MODUS TOLLENS 'method of rejecting/denying':

(4) a. Premise 1: *If dolphins are fish, they are cold-blooded.*
Premise 2: *Dolphins are not cold-blooded.*
______
Conclusion: *Dolphins are not fish.*

b. Premise 1: *If salmon are fish, they are cold-blooded.*
   Premise 2: *Salmon are not cold-blooded.*

   Conclusion: *Salmon are not fish.*

Even though both of these examples employ the same logic, the results are different: (4a) leads to a true conclusion while (4b) leads to a false conclusion. Obviously this difference is closely related to the premises which are used in each case: (4b) starts from a false premise, namely *Salmon are not cold-blooded.* Valid reasoning guarantees a true conclusion if the premises are true, but if one or more of the premises is false there is no guarantee.

Example (4b) shows that a false conclusion does not necessarily mean that the reasoning is invalid. Conversely, a true conclusion does not necessarily mean that the reasoning is valid. The examples in (5) both make use of an invalid form of reasoning called 'denying the antecedent.' This is in fact a common FALLACY, i.e., an invalid pattern of inference which people nevertheless often try to use to support an argument. Now, the conclusion in (5a) is true, but the truth of this statement (*Crocodiles are not warm-blooded*) does not show that the reasoning is valid. It is simply a coincidence that in our world, crocodiles happen to be cold-blooded. It is easy to imagine a slightly different sort of world which is much like our own except that crocodiles and other reptiles are warm-blooded. In that context, the same reasoning would lead to a false conclusion. This shows that the conclusion is not a necessary truth in all contexts for which the premises are true.

(5) a. Premise 1: *If crocodiles are mammals, they are warm-blooded.*
   Premise 1: *Crocodiles are not mammals.*

   Conclusion: *Crocodiles are not warm-blooded.*

b. Premise 1: *If bats are birds, then they have wings.*
   Premise 1: *Bats are not birds.*

   Conclusion: *Bats do not have wings.*

Another way of showing that this pattern of inference is invalid is to change the content words while preserving the same logical structure, as illustrated in (5b). In this example the conclusion is false even though both premises are true, showing that the logical structure of the inference is invalid.

We have said that one important goal of logic is to provide a systematic account for the kinds of reasoning or inference that we intuitively know to be correct. In addition, logic can help us move beyond our intuitions in at least two important ways. First, it provides a way of analyzing very complex arguments, for which our intuitions do not give reliable judgements. Second, our intuitive reasoning may sometimes be based on patterns of inference which are not in fact valid. Logic provides an objective method for distinguishing valid from invalid patterns of inference, and a way of proving which patterns belong to each of these types. We now procede to survey the basic notation and concepts used in the two primary branches of logic, beginning with propositional logic.

4.3 Propositional logic

4.3.1 Propositional operators

In §4.1 we introduced the logical negation operator "¬". (An alternate symbol for this is the tilde, "~"; so in logical notation, 'not p' can be written as either $\neg p$ or $\sim p$.) Logical negation is referred to as a "one-place" operator, because it combines with a single proposition to form a new proposition. The other basic operators of propositional logic are referred to as "two-place" operators, because they are used to combine two propositions to form a new complex proposition. The basic two-place operators include ∧ 'and', ∨ 'or', and the MATERIAL IMPLICATION operator → (generally read as 'if…then…'). If p and q are well-formed propositions, then the formulae $p \wedge q$ 'p and q', $p \vee q$ 'p or q', and $p \rightarrow q$ 'if p, (then) q' are also well-formed propositions. (The p and q in these formulae are VARIABLES which represent propositions.)

A word of caution is in order here. In reading logical formulae we use English words like *not, and, or,* and *if* to pronounce the logical operators, for convenience; but we cannot assume that the meanings of these English words are identical to the meanings of the corresponding operators. This turns out to be an interesting and somewhat controversial question, and we will return to it in chapters 9 and 19. For the purposes of this chapter, as a way to introduce the logical notation itself, we will use the English words as simple translation equivalents for the logical operators; but the reader should bear in mind that there is more to be said about this issue, and we will say some of it in later chapters.

These four operators determine the "syntax" of the complex propositions that they are used to create. They specify, for example, that $\neg p$ and $p \wedge q$ are valid formulae but $p\neg$ and $pq\wedge$ are not. These operators also determine certain aspects of the meaning of these complex propositions, specifically their truth values. For example, if we are told that proposition p is true in a given situation, we can be very sure that its negation ($\neg p$) is false in that situation. Conversely, if p is false in a given situation, we know that its negation ($\neg p$) must be true in that situation. We do not need to know what p actually means in order to make these predictions; all we need to know is its truth value.

The other operators also specify the truth values of the complex propositions that they form based only on the truth values of the individual propositions that they combine with. For this reason, the meanings of these operators (i.e., their contribution to the meaning of a proposition) can be fully specified in terms of truth values. When we have said that p and $\neg p$ must have opposite truth values in any possible situation, we have provided a definition of the negation operator; nothing needs to be known about the specific meaning of p. One common way of representing this kind of definition is through the use of a TRUTH TABLE, like that in (6). This table says that whenever p is true (T), *not p* must be false (F); and whenever p is false, *not p* must be true.

(6)

p	¬p
T	F
F	T

In the same way, the operator ∧ 'and' can be defined by the truth table in (7). This table says that $p \wedge q$ (which is also sometimes written $p\&q$) is true just in case both p and q are true, and false in all other situations.

(7)

p	q	p ∧ q
T	T	T
T	F	F
F	T	F
F	F	F

Again, the truth value of the complex proposition does not depend on the meaning of the simpler propositions it contains, but only on their truth values and the meaning of ∧. Nevertheless, we can assign arbitrary meanings to the variables in order to illustrate the function of the operator. Suppose for example that p represents the proposition 'It is raining,' and q represents the proposition 'The north wind is blowing.' The formula $p \wedge q$ would then represent the proposition 'It is raining and the north wind is blowing.' The truth table in (7) predicts that this proposition will only be true if, at the time of speaking, there is a north wind accompanied by rain; it will be false if the weather is different in either of these respects. This prediction seems to match our intuitions as speakers of English. We can see this by imagining someone saying to us, *It is raining and the north wind is blowing.* We would consider the speaker to have spoken truthfully just in case there was a north wind accompanied by rain, and falsely if the circumstances were otherwise.

The operator ∨ 'or' is defined by the truth table in (8). This table says that $p \vee q$ is true whenever either p is true or q is true; it is only false when both p and q are false. Notice that this *or* of standard logic is the INCLUSIVE *or*, corresponding to the English phrase *and/or*, because it includes the case where both p and q are true. Suppose, for example, that p represents the proposition 'It is raining,' and q represents the proposition 'It is snowing.' Imagine a meteorologist looking at a radar display and, based on what he sees there, saying: 'It is raining or it is snowing.' This statement would be true if it was raining at the time of speaking, or if it was snowing, or if both things were happening at the same time. (This last possibility is rare but not impossible.)

(8)

p	q	p ∨ q
T	T	T
T	F	T
F	T	T
F	F	F

In spoken English we often use the word *or* to mean 'either ... or ... but not both'. For example, this is normally the usage that we intend when we ask, "Would you like white wine or red?" Table (9) shows how we would define this EXCLUSIVE "sense" of *or*, abbreviated here as *XOR*. The table says that *p XOR q* will be true whenever either p or q is true, but not both; it is false whenever p and q have the same truth value. (We will return in Chapter 9 to the question of whether we should consider the English word *or* to have two distinct senses.)

(9)

p	q	p XOR q
T	T	F
T	F	T
F	T	T
F	F	F

The MATERIAL IMPLICATION operator (⟶) is defined by the truth table in (10). (The formula $p{\longrightarrow}q$ can be read as *if p (then) q*, *p only if q*, or *q if p*.) The truth table says that $p{\longrightarrow}q$ is defined to be false just in case p is true but q is false; it is true in all other situations.

(10)

p	q	p → q
T	T	T
T	F	F
F	T	T
F	F	T

In order to get an intuitive sense of what this definition means, suppose that a mother says to her children, *If it rains this afternoon, I will take you to a movie.* Under what circumstances would the mother be considered to have spoken falsely? In applying the truth table we let p represent *it rains this afternoon* and q represent *I will take you to a movie.* Now suppose that it does not rain. In that case p is false, and whether the family goes to a movie or not, no one would accuse the mother of lying or breaking her promise; and this is what the truth table predicts. If it does rain, then p is true; and if the mother takes her children to a movie, she has spoken the truth. Only if it rains but she does not take her children to a movie would her statement be considered false. Again, this is just what the truth table predicts. (It turns out that the material implication operator of standard logic does not always correspond to our intuitions about English *if*, and we will have much more to say about this in Chapter 19.)

For convenience we will introduce one additional operator here, which is referred to as the BICONDITIONAL operator (↔). The formula $p{\leftrightarrow}q$ (read as 'p if and only if q') is a short-hand or abbreviation for: $(p{\longrightarrow}q) \wedge (q{\longrightarrow}p)$. The biconditional operator is defined by the truth table in (11):

(11)

p	q	p↔q
T	T	T
T	F	F
F	T	F
F	F	T

This table says that $p{\leftrightarrow}q$ is true just in case p and q have the same truth value. Suppose the mother in our previous example had said *I will take you to a movie if and only if it rains this afternoon.* If it did not rain but she took her children to a movie anyway, the truth table says that she would have spoken falsely. This prediction seems linguistically correct, although her children would very likely have forgiven her in this case.

Having introduced the basic operators of propositional logic, let us see how they can be used to identify certain kinds of tautologies and contradictions, and to account for certain kinds of meaning relations between propositions (entailment, paraphrase, and incompatibility), namely those that are the result of logical structure alone.

4.3.2 Meaning relations and rules of inference

In addition to using truth tables to define logical operators, we can also use them to evaluate more complex logical formulae. To begin with a very simple example, the formula $p \vee (\neg p)$ represents the logical structure of sentences like *Either you will graduate or you will not graduate.* Sentences of this type are clearly tautologies, and we can show why using a truth table. We start by putting the basic proposition (p) at the top of the left column and the formula that we want to prove ($p \vee (\neg p)$) at the top of the last (right-most) right column, as shown in (12a). We can also fill in all the possible truth values for p in the left column.

(12) a.

p	p∨(¬p)
T	
F	

The proposition we are trying to prove ($p \vee (\neg p)$) is an *or* statement; that is, the highest operator is ∨. The two propositions conjoined by ∨ are p and $\neg p$. We already have a column for the truth values of p, so the next step is to create a column for the corresponding truth values of $\neg p$, as shown in (12b).

(12) b.

p	¬p	p∨(¬p)
T	F	
F	T	

The final step in the proof is to calculate the possible truth values of the proposition $p \vee (\neg p)$, using the truth table in (8) which defines the ∨ operator. The result is shown in (12c).

(12) c.

p	¬p	p∨(¬p)
T	F	T
F	T	T

Notice that both cells in the right-most column contain T. This means that the formula is always true, under any circumstances; in other words, it is a tautology. The truth of this tautology does not depend in any way on the meaning of *p*, but only on the definitions of the logical operators ∨ and ¬. Propositions which are necessarily true just because of their logical structure (regardless of the meanings of words they contain) are sometimes said to be "logically true".

Suppose we change the *or* in the previous example to *and*. This would produce the formula *p∧(¬p)*, which corresponds to the logical structure of sentences like *You will graduate and you will not graduate.* It is hard to imagine any context where such a sentence could be true, and using the truth table in (13) we can show why this is impossible. Sentences of this type are contradictions; they are never true, under any possible circumstance, as reflected in the fact that both cells in the right-most column contain F.

(13)

p	¬p	p∧(¬p)
T	F	F
F	T	F

Now let us consider a slightly more complex example: $((p \vee q) \wedge (\neg p)) \rightarrow q$. To construct a truth table which will allow us to evaluate this formula, we begin by putting the basic propositions *p* and *q* in the left-hand columns (1&2). We put the complete formula that we want to prove in the far right column (6). We introduce a new column for each constituent part of the complete formula and calculate truth values for each cell, building from left to right, as seen in (14). First, columns 1 & 2 are used to construct column 3, based on the truth table for ∨. Next, column 4 is calculated from column 1. Columns 3 & 4 are used to construct column 5, based on the truth table for ∧. Finally, columns 2 & 5 are used to construct column 6, based on the truth table for →.

(14)

1	2	3	4	5	6
p	q	p∨q	¬p	(p∨q)∧¬p	((p∨q)∧¬p) → q
T	T	T	F	F	T
T	F	T	F	F	T
F	T	T	T	T	T
F	F	F	T	F	T

Notice that every cell in the right-most column contains T. This means that the formula is always true, under any circumstances; in other words, it is a tautology. Furthermore, the truth of this tautology does not depend in any way on the meanings of *p* and *q*, but only on the definitions of the logical operators. This tautology predicts that whenever a proposition of the form *((p∨q) ∧ (¬p))* is true, the proposition *q* must also be true. For example, it explains why the sentence cited at the beginning of §4.2 (*Either Joe is crazy or he is lying, and he is not crazy*) must entail *Joe is lying*. A similar entailment relation will hold for any other pair of sentences that have the same logical structure.

As mentioned above, it is helpful to check the predictions of the logical formalism against our intuition as speakers by "translating" the formulae into English or some other human language (i.e., replacing the variables *p* and *q* with sentences that express propositions). We noted at the beginning of §4.2 that when we hear the sentence *Either Joe is crazy or he is lying, and he is not crazy*, we seem to reach the conclusion *Joe is lying* automatically and without effort. It takes a bit more effort to process a formula like *((p∨q) ∧ (¬p))*, but the table in (14) shows that the logical implication of this formula matches our intuition about the corresponding sentence.

Now consider the biconditional formula *(p∨q) ↔ ¬((¬p) ∧ (¬q))*. Using the procedure outlined above, we can construct the truth table in (15). First, columns 1 & 2 are used to construct column 3, based on the truth table for ∨. Next, columns 4 & 5 are used to construct column 6, based on the truth table for ∧. Column 7 is calculated from column 6, and finally columns 3 & 7 are used to construct column 8, based on the truth table for ↔.

(15)

p	q	p∨q	¬p	¬q	(¬p)∧(¬q)	¬((¬p)∧(¬q))	(p∨q) ↔ ¬((¬p) ∧ (¬q))
T	T	T	F	F	F	T	T
T	F	T	F	T	F	T	T
F	T	T	T	F	F	T	T
F	F	F	T	T	T	F	T

Once again we see that every cell in the right-most column contains T, which means that this formula must always be true, purely because of its logical form. The biconditional operator in this formula expresses mutual entailment, that is, a paraphrase relation. This formula explains why the sentence *Either he is crazy or he is lying* must always have the same truth value as *It is not the case that he is both not crazy and not lying*. The first sentence is a paraphrase of the second, simply because of the logical structures involved.

As we noted in an earlier chapter, tautologies are not very informative because they make no claim about the world. But for that very reason, these logical tautologies can be extremely useful because they define logically valid rules of inference. A few tautologies are so famous as rules of inference that they are given Latin names. One of these is called Modus Ponens 'method of positing/affirming', also called 'affirming the antecedent': $((p \rightarrow q) \wedge p) \rightarrow q$. The proof of this tautology is presented in (16).

(16)

p	q	p→q	(p→q) ∧ p	((p→q) ∧ p) → q
T	T	T	T	T
T	F	F	F	T
F	T	T	F	T
F	F	T	F	T

Modus Ponens defines one of the valid ways of deriving an inference from a conditional statement. It says that if we know that $p \rightarrow q$ is true, and in addition we know or assume that p is true, it is valid to infer that q is true. An illustration of this pattern of inference is presented as a syllogism in (17).

(17) Premise 1: *If John is Estonian, he will like this book.* (p→q)
Premise 2: *John is Estonian.* (p)

Conclusion: *He will like this book.* (q)

As we noted in §4.2, Modus Ponens guarantees a valid inference but does not guarantee a true conclusion. The conclusion will only be as reliable as the premises that we begin with. Suppose in this example it turns out that John is Estonian but hates the book. This does not disprove the rule of Modus Ponens; rather, it shows that the first premise is false, by providing a counter-example.

Another valid rule for deriving an inference from a conditional statement is MODUS TOLLENS 'method of rejecting/denying', also called 'denying the consequent': $((p \longrightarrow q) \land \neg q) \longrightarrow \neg p$. This rule was illustrated in example (4a) above, repeated here as (18). It says that if we know that $p \longrightarrow q$ is true, and in addition we know or assume that q is false, it is valid to infer that p is also false.

(18) Premise 1: *If dolphins are fish, they are cold-blooded.* $(p \longrightarrow q)$
Premise 2: *Dolphins are not cold-blooded.* $(\neg q)$
Conclusion: *Dolphins are not fish.* $(\neg p)$

The tautology which we proved in (14) is known as the DISJUNCTIVE SYLLOGISM: $((p \lor q) \land (\neg p)) \longrightarrow q$. Another example which illustrates this pattern of inference is provided in (19).

(19) Premise 1: *Dolphins are either fish or mammals.* $(p \lor q)$
Premise 2: *Dolphins are not fish.* $(\neg p)$
Conclusion: *Dolphins are mammals.* (q)

Finally, the tautology known as the HYPOTHETICAL SYLLOGISM is given in (20).

(20) $((p \longrightarrow q) \land (q \longrightarrow r)) \longrightarrow (p \longrightarrow r)$
Premise 1: *If Mickey is a rodent, he is a mammal.* $(p \longrightarrow q)$
Premise 2: *If Mickey is a mammal, he is warm-blooded.* $(q \longrightarrow r)$
Conclusion: *If Mickey is a rodent, he is warm-blooded.* $(p \longrightarrow r)$

The propositional logic outlined in this section is an important part of the logical metalanguage for semantic analysis, but it is not sufficient on its own because it is concerned only with truth values. We need a way to go beyond p and q, to represent the actual meanings of the basic propositions we are dealing with. PREDICATE LOGIC gives us a way to include information about word meanings in logical expressions.

4.4 Predicate logic

Consider the simple sentences in (21):

(21) a. John is hungry.
  b. Mary snores.
  c. John loves Mary.
  d. Mary slapped John.

Each of these sentences describes a property, event or relationship. The element of meaning which determines what kind of property, event or relationship is being described is called the PREDICATE. The words *hungry, snores, loves,* and *slapped* express the predicates in these examples. The individuals of whom the property or relationship is claimed to be true (*John* and *Mary* in these examples) are referred to as ARGUMENTS. As we can see from example (21), different predicates require different numbers of arguments: *hungry* and *snore* require just one, *love* and *slap* require two. When a predicate is asserted to be true of the right number of arguments, the result is a well-formed proposition, i.e., a claim about the world which can (in principle) be assigned a truth value, T or F.

In our logical notation we will write predicates in capital letters (to distinguish them from normal English words) and without inflectional morphology. We follow the common practice of using lower case initials to represent proper names. For predicates which require two arguments, the agent or experiencer is normally listed first. So the simple sentence *John is hungry* would be translated into the logical metalanguage as HUNGRY(j), while the sentence *John loves Mary* would be translated LOVE(j,m). Some additional examples are shown in (22).

(22)			
	a.	*Henry VIII snores.*	SNORE(h)
	b.	*Socrates is a man.*	MAN(s)
	c.	*Napoleon is near Paris.*	NEAR(n,p)
	d.	*Abraham Lincoln admired Queen Victoria.*	ADMIRE(a,v)
	e.	*Jocasta is Oedipus' mother.*	MOTHER_OF(j,o)
	f.	*Abraham Lincoln was tall and homely.*	TALL(a) ∧ HOMELY(a)
	g.	*Abraham Lincoln was a tall man.*	TALL(a) ∧ MAN(a)
	h.	*Joe is neither honest nor competent.*	¬ (HONEST(j) ∨ COMPETENT(j))

As these examples illustrate, semantic predicates can be expressed grammatically as verbs, adjectives, common nouns, or even prepositions. They can appear as part of the VP, or as modifiers within NP as in (22g).[1]

We have seen examples of one-place and two-place predicates; there are also predicates which take three arguments, e.g. *give, show, offer, send,* etc. Some predicates, including verbs like *say, think, believe, want,* etc., can take propositions as arguments:

(23) a. *Henry thinks that Anne is beautiful.* THINK(h, BEAUTIFUL(a))
b. *Susan wants to marry Ringo.* WANT(s, MARRY(s,r))

4.4.1 Quantifiers (an introduction)

All the predicates in examples (21–23) have proper names as arguments. Of course we need to be able to represent other kinds of arguments as well. We will discuss this issue in more detail in later chapters, but as a brief introduction let us consider the subject NPs in (24):

(24) a. *All students* are weary.
b. *Some men* snore.
c. *No crocodile* is warm-blooded.

The italicized phrases in (24) are examples of "quantified" NPs; they contain a special kind of determiner known as a QUANTIFIER. Sentence (24a) makes a universal generalization. It says that if you select anything within the universe of discourse that happens to be a student, that thing will also be weary. Notice that the phrase *all students* does not refer to any specific individual, or set of individuals; that is why we said in Chapter 2 that quantified NPs are generally not referring expressions. Rather, the phrase seems to express a kind of inference: if a given thing is a student, then it will also have the property expressed in the remainder of the sentence.

Sentence (24b) makes an existential claim. It says that there exists at least one thing within the universe of discourse that is both a man and snores. Actually, this sentence says that there must be at least two such things, but that is not part of the meaning of *some*; it follows from the fact that the noun *men* is plural. (We can show this by comparing (25a) with (25b).) *Some* simply means that there exists something within the universe of discourse that has both of the named

[1]VP = verb phrase, that is, the verb plus its non-subject arguments. NP = noun phrase.

properties (e.g., being a man and snoring). Sentence (24c) is a negative existential statement. It says that there does not exist anything within the universe of discourse that is both a crocodile and warm-blooded.

(25) a. *Some guy* in the back row was snoring. (at least one)
b. *Some guys* in the back row were snoring. (at least two)

Standard predicate logic makes use of two quantifier symbols: the Universal Quantifier ∀ and the Existential Quantifier ∃. As the mathematical examples in (26) illustrate, these quantifier symbols must introduce a VARIABLE, and this variable is said to be BOUND by the quantifier. The letters *x*, *y* or *z* are normally used as variables that represent individuals. (We can read "∀x" as 'for all individuals x', and "∃x" as 'there exists one or more individuals x'.)

(26) a. Universal Quantifier:
$\forall x[x+x = 2x]$
b. Existential Quantifier:
$\exists y[y+4 = y/3]$

Quantifier words must be interpreted relative to the current universe of discourse, that is, the set of individuals currently available for discussion. For example, in order to decide whether sentences like *All students are female* or *No student is wealthy* are true, we need to know what the currently relevant universe of discourse is. If we are discussing a secondary school for economically disadvantaged girls, both statements would be true. In other contexts, either or both of these statements might be false.

In the same way, variables bound by one of the logical quantifier symbols are assumed to be members of the currently relevant UNIVERSAL SET, i.e., the set of all elements currently available for consideration.[2] In mathematical contexts, the universal set is often a particular class of numbers, e.g. the integers or the real numbers. In order to evaluate a proposition involving quantifier symbols, like those in (26), the universal set must be specified or assumed from context.

Variables bound by a quantifier do not refer to a specific individual or entity, but rather allow for the arbitrary selection of any individual or entity within the universal set. Once a particular value is assigned to a given variable, the same assignment is understood to hold for all occurrences of that variable within the SCOPE of the quantifier (the material inside the square brackets). So for example, if we assume that the universal set in (26) is the set of all real numbers, (26a) can

[2]The concept of UNIVERSAL SET is discussed further in Chapter 13.

be interpreted as follows: "Choose any real number. If you add that number to itself, the sum will be equal to that number multiplied by two." The equation in (26b) can be interpreted as follows: "There exists some real number which, when added to four, will be equal to the quotient of that same number divided by three."

The value of an unbound (or "free") variable, that is, one which is not introduced by a quantifier or which occurs outside the scope of its quantifier, is not defined. The variables in (27) are not bound, and as a result the equations in which they occur are neither true nor false; they do not make any claim about the world, until some value is assigned to each variable. (In contrast, both of the equations in (26), where the variables are bound, can be shown to be true.) Of course, it is fairly easy to solve the equations in (27), that is, to find the values that must be assigned to each variable in order to make the equations true. But until some value is assigned, no truth value can be determined for the equations.

(27) a. $x-7 = 4x$
b. $y + 2z = 51$

The same applies to variables which occur within logical formulae. A proposition that contains unbound variables is called an OPEN PROPOSITION. Such a proposition cannot be assigned a truth value, unless some mechanism is provided for assigning values to the unbound variables.

The universal and existential quantifier symbols allow us to translate the sentences in (24) into logical notation, as shown in (28). (We will ignore for the moment the difference in interpretation between singular vs. plural nouns with *some.*)

(28) a. Universal Quantifier: *All students are weary.*
∀x[STUDENT(x) ⟶ WEARY(x)]
b. Existential Quantifier: *Some men snore.*
∃x[MAN(x) ∧ SNORE(x)]
c. Negative Existential: *No crocodile is warm-blooded.*
¬∃x[CROCODILE(x) ∧ WARM-BLOODED(x)]

Notice that *all* is translated differently from *some* or *no.* The universal quantifier is paired with material implication (⟶), while the existential quantifier introduces an *and* statement. We will discuss the reason for this difference in more detail in Unit IV, but the fundamental issue is that we want our logical translation to have the same interpretation as the English sentence it is meant to represent. We might interpret the formula in (28a) roughly as follows: "Choose something within the universe of discourse. We will temporarily call that thing 'x'. Is x a student? If so, then x will also be weary." This long-winded paraphrase seems to describe the same state of affairs as the original sentence *All students are weary*. However, if we replace ⟶ with ∧, we get the formula in (29), which means something very different.

(29) ∀x[STUDENT(x) ∧ WEARY(x)]
'Everything in the universe of discourse is a student and is weary.'

So far we have only considered quantifier phrases which occur as subject NPs, but of course they can occur in other syntactic positions as well. When we translate a sentence containing a quantified NP into logical notation, the quantifier always comes at the beginning of the proposition which it takes scope over, even when the quantified NP is functioning as direct object, oblique argument, etc. Some examples are presented in (30). Note that indefinite NPs are often translated as existential quantifiers, as illustrated in (30b–c).

(30) a. *John loves all girls.*
∀x[GIRL(x) ⟶ LOVE(j,x)]

b. *Susan has married a cowboy.*
∃x[COWBOY(x) ∧ MARRY(s,x)]

c. *Ringo lives in a yellow submarine.*
∃x[YELLOW(x) ∧ SUBMARINE(x) ∧ LIVE_IN(r,x)]

The patterns of inference observed in example (2) above illustrate two basic principles that govern the use of quantifiers. The first principle, which is called UNIVERSAL INSTANTIATION, states that anything which is true of all members of a particular class is true of any specific member of that class. This is the principle which licenses the inference shown in (2a), repeated here as (31a). The second principle, which is called EXISTENTIAL GENERALIZATION, licenses the inference shown in (2b), repeated here as (31b).

(31) a.

All men are mortal.	∀x[MAN(x) ⟶ MORTAL(x)]
Socrates is a man.	MAN(s)
Therefore, Socrates is mortal.	MORTAL(s)

b.

Arthur is a lawyer.	LAWYER(a)
Arthur is honest.	HONEST(a)
Therefore, some (= at least one) lawyer is honest.	∃x[LAWYER(x) ∧ HONEST(x)]

4.4.2 Scope ambiguities

When a quantifier combines with another quantifier, with negation, or with various other elements (to be discussed in Chapter 14), it can give rise to ambiguities of scope. In (32a) for example, one of the quantifiers must appear within the scope of the other, so there are two possible READINGS for the sentence.

(32) a. *Some man loves every woman.*
   i. $\exists x[\text{MAN}(x) \wedge (\forall y[\text{WOMAN}(y) \rightarrow \text{LOVE}(x,y)])]$
   ii. $\forall y[\text{WOMAN}(y) \rightarrow (\exists x[\text{MAN}(x) \wedge \text{LOVE}(x,y)])]$
 b. *All that glitters is not gold.*
   i. $\forall x[\text{GLITTER}(x) \rightarrow \neg\text{GOLD}(x)]$
   ii. $\neg\forall x[\text{GLITTER}(x) \rightarrow \text{GOLD}(x)]$

The quantifier that appears farthest to the left in the formula gets a WIDE SCOPE interpretation, meaning that it takes logical priority; the one which is embedded within the scope of the first quantifier gets a NARROW SCOPE interpretation. So the first reading for (32a) says that there exists some specific man who loves every woman. The second reading for (32a) says that for any woman you choose within the universe of discourse, there exists some man who loves her. Try to provide similar paraphrases for the two readings of (32b). Then try to verify that these sentences involve real ambiguities by finding contexts for each sentence where one reading would be true while the other is false.

4.5 Conclusion

In this chapter we mentioned some of the motivations for using formal logic as a semantic metalanguage. We discussed the notion of valid inference, and showed that valid patterns of reasoning guarantee a true conclusion only when the premises are true. We then showed how propositional logic accounts for certain kinds of inferences, namely those which are determined by the meanings of the logical operators 'and', 'or', 'not', and 'if'. In this way propositional logic helps to explain certain kinds of tautology and contradiction, as well as certain types of meaning relations between sentences (entailment, paraphrase, etc.), namely those which arise due to the logical structure of the sentences involved. Finally we gave a brief introduction to predicate logic, which allows us to represent the meanings of the propositions, and an even brief introduction to the use of quantifiers, which will be the topic of Chapter 14.

Our emphasis in this chapter was on translating sentences of English (or some other object language) into logical notation. In Unit IV we will discuss how we can give an interpretation for these propositions in terms of set theory, and how this helps us understand the compositional nature of sentence meanings.

Further reading

Good, brief introductions to propositional and predicate logic are provided in Allwood et al. (1977: chapters 4–5) and Kearns (2000: chapter 2). More detailed introductions are provided in J. N. Martin (1987) and Gamut (1991a).[a]

[a] L. T. F. Gamut is a collective pen-name for the Dutch logicians Johan van Benthem, Jeroen Groenendijk, Dick de Jongh, Martin Stokhof and Henk Verkuyl.

Discussion exercises

A. Create a truth table to prove each of the following tautologies:

a. Law of Double Negation: $\neg(\neg p) \leftrightarrow p$

b. Law of Contradiction: $\neg(p \wedge \neg p)$

c. Modus Tollens: $[(p \rightarrow q) \wedge \neg q] \rightarrow \neg p$

B. Construct syllogisms, using English sentences, to illustrate each of the following patterns of inference:

a. Modus Ponens: $[(p \rightarrow q) \wedge p] \rightarrow q$

b. Modus Tollens: $[(p \rightarrow q) \wedge \neg q] \rightarrow \neg p$

c. Hypothetical Syllogism: $[(p \rightarrow q) \wedge (q \rightarrow r)] \rightarrow (p \rightarrow r)$

d. Disjunctive Syllogism: $[(p \vee q) \wedge \neg p] \rightarrow q$

C. Translate the following sentences into logical notation:

a. All unicorns are herbivores.

b. No philosophers admire Nietzsche.

c. Some green apples are edible.

d. Bill feeds all stray cats.

Homework exercises

A. Using truth tables. Arthur has been selected to be a juror in a case which has generated a lot of local publicity. He is asked to promise not to read the newspaper or watch television until the trial is finished. There are two different ways in which he can make this commitment:

(1) a. I will not read the newspaper or watch television until the trial is finished.

b. I will not read the newspaper and I will not watch television until the trial is finished.

Construct truth tables for these two sentences to show why they are logically equivalent. You may omit the adverbial clause (*until the trial is finished*) from your table. (**Hint**: Let **p** stand for *I will read the newspaper* and **q** stand for *I will watch television.* Assume the following translation for sentence (a): $\neg(p \vee q)$. Construct a truth table for this proposition, and a second truth table for sentence (b). If the right-most column of the two tables is identical, that means that the two propositions must have the same truth value under any circumstances.)

(1′) a.

p	q	$p \vee q$	$\neg(p \vee q)$

b.

p	q			

B. Translate the following sentences into logical notation:

a. All famous linguists quote Chomsky.

b. David tutors some struggling students.

c. No president was Buddhist or Hindu.

d. Alice and Betty married Charlie and David, respectively.

Unit II

Word meanings

5 Word senses

5.1 Introduction

In Chapter 2 we introduced the important distinction between sense and denotation. We noted that a single word may have more than one sense, a situation referred to as LEXICAL AMBIGUITY. We also noted that two expressions which have different senses may have the same denotation in some particular context, but two expressions which have the same sense must have the same denotation in every imaginable context. So what if a single word can be used to refer to several different kinds of things? Does that mean it has several different senses? The answer is, sometimes yes and sometimes no. This chapter is designed to help you answer this kind of question for specific cases.

We begin in §5.2 with the observation that a speaker often has a variety of ways to refer to a particular thing. The various expressions which the speaker may use reflect different CONSTRUALS, or ways of thinking about the thing. In §5.3 we discuss several diagnostic tests that can be used to distinguish true lexical ambiguity from other similar patterns, such as vagueness and underspecification. We then distinguish two different types of lexical ambiguity, POLYSEMY vs. HOMONYMY, recognizing that making this distinction is not always easy; and we discuss the role of context in enabling hearers to choose the intended sense of ambiguous word forms.

In §5.4 we discuss some ways in which new senses of words can be created, including COERCION and figures of speech. In §5.5 we apply the principles developed in §5.3 to a certain pattern of variable denotation, illustrated by words like *book*, which can be used to name either a physical object or the text or discourse that it contains.

5.2 Word meanings as construals of external reality

Words give us a way to describe the world. However, our linguistic descriptions are never complete. In choosing a word to describe a particular thing or event, we choose to express certain bits of information and leave many others unexpressed.

For example, suppose that I am holding a rag in my right hand and moving it back and forth across the surface of a table. If you ask me what I am doing, I might reply with either (1a) or (1b).

(1) a. I am wiping the table.
  b. I am cleaning the table.
  c. I wiped/??cleaned the table but it is no cleaner than before.
  d. I cleaned/#wiped the table without touching it.

In this situation, both (1a) and (1b) would be true descriptions of the event, but they do not mean the same thing. By choosing the word *clean*, I would be specifying a certain change in the state of the table, but leaving the manner unspecified. By choosing the word *wipe*, I would be specifying a certain manner, but not asserting anything about a change of state. The different entailments associated with these two verbs can be demonstrated using examples like (1c–d).

To take a second example, suppose that you have a large quartz crystal on your desk, which you use as a paperweight. If I want to look more closely at this object, I could ask for it by saying: *May I look at your paperweight?*; or by saying: *May I look at that quartz crystal?* Clearly the words *paperweight* and *quartz crystal* do not mean the same thing; but in this context they can have the same referent. The lexical meaning of each word includes features which are true of this referent, but neither word encodes all of the properties of the referent. The choice of which word to use reflects the speaker's CONSTRUAL of (or way of thinking about) the object, and commits the speaker to certain beliefs but not others concerning the nature of the object.

In analyzing word meanings, we are trying to account for linguistically coded information, rather than all the encyclopedic knowledge (or knowledge about the world) which may be associated with a particular word. For example, the fact that a quartz crystal sinks in water is a fact about the world, but probably not a linguistic property of the word *quartz*. But we need to be aware that this distinction between linguistic knowledge vs. knowledge about the world is often difficult to make.

5.3 Lexical ambiguity

5.3.1 Ambiguity, vagueness, and indeterminacy

In Chapter 2 we discussed cases of lexical ambiguity like those in (2). These sentences are ambiguous because they contain a word-form which has more than one sense, and as a result can be used to refer to very different kinds of things. For example, we can use the word *case* to refer to a kind of container or to a legal proceeding; *lies* can be a noun referring to false statements or a verb specifying the posture or location of something. These words have a variety of referents because they have multiple senses, i.e., they are ambiguous. And as we noted in Chapter 2, the truth value of each of these sentences in a particular context will depend on which sense of the ambiguous word is chosen.

(2) a. The farmer allows walkers to cross the field for free, but the bull *charges.*
b. Headline: Drunk gets nine months in violin *case.*
c. Headline: Reagan wins on budget, but more *lies* ahead.

However, there are other kinds of variable reference as well, ways in which a word can be used to refer to different sorts of things even though it may have only a single sense. For example, I can use the word *cousin* to refer to a child of my parent's sibling, but the person referred to may be either male or female. Similarly, the word *kick* means to hit something with one's foot, but does not specify whether the left or right foot is used.[1] We will say that the word *cousin* is INDETERMINATE with respect to gender, and that the word *kick* is indeterminate with respect to which foot is used.[2] We will argue that such examples are not instances of lexical ambiguity: neither of these cases requires us to posit two distinct senses for a single word form. Our basis for making this claim will be discussed in §5.3.2 below.

Another kind of variable reference is observed with words like *tall* or *bald.* How tall does a person have to be to be called "tall"? How much hair can a person lose without being considered "bald"? Context is a factor; a young man who is considered tall among the members of his gymnastics club might not be considered tall if he tries out for a professional basketball team. But even if we restrict our discussion to professional basketball players, there is no specific height (e.g. two meters) above which a player is considered tall and below which he is not considered tall. We say that such words are VAGUE, meaning that the limits of their possible denotations cannot be precisely defined.[3]

[1]Lakoff (1970).

[2]We follow Kennedy (2011) in using the term INDETERMINACY; as he points out, some other authors have used the term GENERALITY instead. Gillon (1990) makes a distinction between the two terms, using GENERALITY for superordinate terms.

[3]A number of authors (Ruth M. Kempson 1977, Lakoff 1970, Tuggy 1993) have used the term VAGUENESS as a cover term which includes generality or indeterminacy as a sub-type.

Kennedy (2011) mentions three distinguishing characteristics of vagueness. First, context-dependent truth conditions: we have already seen that a single individual may be truly said to be tall in one context (a gymnastics club) but not tall in another (a professional basketball team). This is not the case with indeterminacy; if a certain person is my cousin in one context, he or she will normally be my cousin in other contexts as well.

Second, vague predicates have borderline cases. Most people would probably agree that a bottle of wine costing two dollars is cheap, while one that costs five hundred dollars is expensive. But what about a bottle that costs fifty dollars? Most people would probably agree that Einstein was a genius, and that certain other individuals are clearly not. But there are extremely bright people about whom we might disagree when asked whether the term *genius* can be applied to them; or we might simply say "I'm not sure". Such borderline cases do not typically arise with indeterminacy; we do not usually disagree about whether a certain person is or is not our cousin.

Gillon (1990) provides another example:

> Vagueness is well exemplified by such words as *city*. Though a definite answer does exist as to whether or not it applies to Montreal [1991 population: 1,016,376 within the city limits] or to Kingsville (Ontario) [1991 population: 5,716]; nonetheless, no definite answer exists as to whether or not it applies to Red Deer (Alberta) [1991 population: 58,145] or Moose Jaw (Saskatchewan) [1991 population: 33,593]. Nor is the lack of an answer here due to ignorance (at least if one is familiar with the geography of Western Canada): no amount of knowledge about Red Deer or Moose Jaw will settle whether or not *city* applies. Any case in which further knowledge will settle whether or not the expression applies is simply not a case evincing the expression's vagueness; rather it evinces the ignorance of its user... Vagueness is not alleviated by the growth of knowledge, ignorance is.

Third, vague predicates give rise to "little-by-little" paradoxes.[4] For example, Ringo Starr was clearly not bald in 1964; in fact, the Beatles' famous haircut was an important part of their image during that era. Now if in 1964 Ringo had allowed you to pluck out one of his hairs as a souvenir, he would still not have been bald. It seems reasonable to assume that a man who is not bald can always lose one hair without becoming bald. But if Ringo had given permission for every person in Europe to pluck out one of his hairs, he would have become bald

[4]The technical term is the *sorites* paradox, also known as the paradox of the heap, the fallacy of the beard, the continuum fallacy, etc.

long before every fan was satisfied. But it would be impossible to say which specific hair it was whose loss caused him to become bald, because *bald* is a vague predicate.

Another property which may distinguish vagueness from indeterminacy is the degree to which these properties are preserved in translation. Indeterminacy tends to be language-specific. There are many interesting and well-known cases where pairs of translation equivalents differ with respect to their degree of specificity. For example, Malay has no exact equivalent for the English words *brother* and *sister*. The language uses three terms for siblings: *abang* 'older brother', *kakak* 'older sister', and *adek* 'younger sibling'. The term *adek* is indeterminate with respect to gender, while the English words *brother* and *sister* are indeterminate with respect to relative age.

Mandarin has several different and more specific words which would all be translated by the English word *uncle*: 伯伯 (bóbo) 'father's elder brother'; 叔叔 (shūshu) 'father's younger brother'; 姑丈 (gūzhàng) 'father's sister's husband'; 舅舅 (jiùjiu) 'mother's brother'; 姨丈 (yízhàng) 'mother's sister's husband'.[5] Thus the English word *uncle* is indeterminate with respect to various factors that are lexically distinguished in Mandarin.

The English word *carry* is indeterminate with respect to manner, but many other languages use different words for specific ways of carrying. Tzeltal, a Mayan language spoken in the State of Chiapas (Mexico), is reported to have twenty-five words for 'carry':[6]

(3)
1. *cuch* 'carry on one's back'
2. *q'uech* 'carry on one's shoulder'
3. *pach* 'carry on one's head'
4. *cajnuc'tay* 'carry over one's shoulder'
5. *lats'* 'carry under one's arm'
6. *chup* 'carry in one's pocket'
7. *tom* 'carry in a bundle'
8. *pet* 'carry in one's arms'
9. *nol* 'carry in one's palm'
10. *jelup'in* 'carry across one's shoulder'
11. *nop'* 'carry in one's fist'
12. *lat'* 'carry on a plate'
13. *lip'* 'carry by the corner'

[5] http://www.omniglot.com/language/kinship/chinese.htm

[6] http://www-01.sil.org/mexico/museo/3di-Carry.htm

14. *chuy* 'carry in a bag'
15. *lup* 'carry in a spoon'
16. *cats'* 'carry between one's teeth'
17. *tuch* 'carry upright'
18. *toy* 'carry holding up high'
19. *lic* 'carry dangling from the hand'
20. *bal* 'carry rolled up (like a map)'
21. *ch'et* 'carry coiled up (like a rope)'
22. *chech* 'carry by both sides'
23. *lut'* 'carry with tongs'
24. *yom* 'carry several things together'
25. *pich'* 'carry by the neck'

In contrast, words which are vague in English tend to have translation equivalents in other languages which are also vague. This is because vagueness is associated with certain semantic classes of words, notably with scalar adjectives like *big, tall, expensive*, etc. Vagueness is a particularly interesting and challenging problem for semantic analysis, and we will discuss it again in later chapters.

5.3.2 Distinguishing ambiguity from vagueness and indeterminacy

The Spanish word *llave* can be used to refer to things which would be called *key, faucet* or *wrench/spanner* in English.[7] How do we figure out whether *llave* has multiple senses (i.e. is ambiguous), or whether it has a single sense that is vague or indeterminate? A number of linguistic tests have been proposed which can help us to make this decision.

The most common tests are based on the principle that distinct senses of an ambiguous word are ANTAGONISTIC.[8] This means that two senses of the word cannot both apply simultaneously. Sentences which seem to require two senses for a single use of a particular word, like those in (4), are called PUNS.

(4) a. The hunter went home with five bucks in his pocket.
b. The batteries were given out free of charge.
c. I didn't like my beard at first. Then it grew on me.
d. When she saw her first strands of gray hair, she thought she'd dye.
e. When the chair in the Philosophy Department became vacant, the Appointment Committee sat on it for six months.[9]

[7] Jonatan Cordova (p.c.) informs me that the word can also be used to mean 'lock' in wrestling.
[8] Cruse (1986: 61).
[9] Cruse (2000: 108).

Sentence (4d) illustrates a problem with English spelling, namely that words which are pronounced the same can be spelled differently (*dye* vs. *die*). Because linguistic analysis normally focuses on spoken rather than written language, we consider such word-forms to be ambiguous; we will discuss this issue further in the following section.

A clash or incompatibility of senses for a single word in sentences containing a co-ordinate structure, like those in (5), is often referred to using the Greek term ZEUGMA (pronounced [ˈzugmə]).

(5)
a. Mary and her visa expired on the same day.[10]
b. He carried a strobe light and the responsibility for the lives of his men.[11]
c. On his fishing trip, he caught three trout and a cold.[12]

The odd or humorous nature of sentences like those in (4) and (5) provides evidence that two distinct senses are involved; that is, evidence for a real lexical ambiguity. Another widely used test for antagonism between two senses is the IDENTITY TEST.[13] This test makes use of the fact that certain kinds of ellipsis require parallel interpretations for the deleted material and its antecedent. We will illustrate the test first with an instance of structural ambiguity:[14]

(6)
a. The fish is ready to eat.
b. The fish is ready to eat, and so is the chicken.
c. The fish is ready to eat, but the chicken is not.
d. #The potatoes are ready to eat, but the children are not.

Sentence (6a) is structurally ambiguous: the fish can be interpreted as either the agent or the patient of *eat*. Both of the clauses in example (6b) are ambiguous in the same way. This predicts that there should be four logically possible interpretations of this sentence; but in fact only two are acceptable to most English speakers. If the fish is interpreted as an agent, then the chicken must be interpreted as an agent; if the fish is interpreted as a patient, then the chicken must be interpreted as a patient. The parallelism constraint rules out readings where the fish is the eater while the chicken is eaten, or vice versa. The same holds true for

[10] Adapted from Cruse (1986: 61).
[11] Tim O'Brien, *The Things They Carried*, via grammar.about.com.
[12] http://dictionary.reference.com/browse/zeugma
[13] Lakoff (1970); Zwicky & Sadock (1975).
[14] Examples adapted from Kennedy (2011: 512).

example (6c). Sentence (6d) is odd because the nouns used strongly favor different interpretations for the two clauses: the potatoes must be the patient, while the children must be the agent, violating the parallelism constraint.

Example (7) illustrates the use of the identity test with an apparent case of lexical ambiguity: *duck* can refer to an action (lowering the head or upper body) or to a water fowl. (In fact, this is a fairly obvious case of lexical ambiguity since the two uses have different parts of speech, which is not normally possible with vagueness or indeterminacy. Our purpose here is to validate the test, showing that it gives the expected results in the clear cases, and thus provides a reasonable source of evidence for deciding the less obvious cases.)

Sentence (7a) is ambiguous, because the two senses of *duck* generate two different readings, and one of these readings could be true while the other was false in a particular situation. The same potential ambiguity applies to both of the clauses in (7b), so again we would predict that four interpretations should be logically possible; but in fact only two are acceptable. Sentence (7b) can mean either that John and Bill both saw her perform a certain action or that they both saw a water fowl belonging to her. The fact that the parallelism constraint blocks the "crossed" readings provides evidence that these two different interpretations of *duck* are truly distinct senses, i.e. that *duck* is in fact lexically ambiguous.

(7) a. John saw her duck.
    b. John saw her duck, and so did Bill.

Contrast this with the examples in (8). The word *cousin* in the first clause of (8a) refers to a male person, while the implicit reference to *cousin* in the second clause of (8a) refers to a female person. This difference of reference does not violate the parallelism constraint, because the two uses of *cousin* are not distinct senses, even though they would be translated by different words in a language like Italian. The identity test indicates that *cousin* is not lexically ambiguous, but merely unspecified for gender.

(8) a. John is my cousin, and so is Mary.
    b. John carried a briefcase, and Bill a backpack.
    c. That three-year old is quite tall, but then so is his father.

Similarly, the word *carry* in the first clause of (8b) probably describes a different action from the implicit reference to *carry* in the second clause. The sentence allows an interpretation under which John carried the briefcase by holding it at his side with one hand, while Bill carried the backpack on his back; in fact, this would be the most likely interpretation in most contexts. The fact that this interpretation is not blocked by the parallelism constraint indicates that *carry* is not lexically ambiguous, but merely unspecified (i.e., indeterminate) for manner. The two uses of *carry* would be translated by different words in a language like Tzeltal, but they are not distinct senses.

The actual height described by the word *tall* in the first clause of (8c) is presumably much less than the height described by the implicit reference to *tall* in the second clause. The fact that this interpretation is acceptable indicates that *tall* is not lexically ambiguous, but merely vague.

Example (9) shows how we might use the identity test to investigate the ambiguity of the Spanish word *llave* mentioned above. These sentences could appropriately be used if both Pedro and Juan bought, broke or found the same kind of thing, whether keys, faucets, or wrenches. But the sentences cannot naturally describe a situation where different objects are involved, e.g. if Pedro bought a key but Juan bought a wrench, etc.[15] This fact provides evidence that *llave* is truly ambiguous and not merely indeterminate or vague.

(9) a. Pedro compró/rompió una llave y también Juan.
Pedro bought/broke a key/etc. and also Juan
'Pedro bought/broke a key/faucet/wrench, and so did Juan.'

b. Pedro encontró una llave al igual que Juan.
Pedro found a key/etc. to.the same that Juan
'Pedro found a key/faucet/wrench, just like Juan did.'

Another test which is sometimes used is the SENSE RELATIONS TEST: distinct senses will have different sets of synonyms, antonyms, etc. (see discussion of sense relations in Chapter 6). For example, the word *light* has two distinct senses; one is the opposite of *heavy*, the other is the opposite of *dark*. However, Cruse (1986: 56–57) warns that this test is not always reliable, because contextual features may restrict the range of possible synonyms or antonyms for a particular use of a word which is merely vague or indeterminate.

Another kind of evidence for lexical ambiguity is provided by the TEST OF CONTRADICTION.[16] If a sentence of the form *X but not X* can be true (i.e., not a contradiction), then expression X must be ambiguous. For example, the fact that the statement in (10) is not felt to be a contradiction provides good evidence for the claim that the two uses of *child* represented here ('offspring' vs. 'preadolescent human') are truly distinct senses.

[15] Jonatan Cordova, Steve and Monica Parker (p.c.).

[16] Quine (1960); Zwicky & Sadock (1975); Kennedy (2011).

(10) (Aged mother discussing her grown sons and daughters)
They are not children any more, but they are still my children.

This is an excellent test in some ways, because the essential property of ambiguity is that the two senses must have different truth conditions, and this test involves asserting one reading while simultaneously denying the other. In many cases, however, it can be difficult to find contexts in which such sentences sound truly natural. A few attempts at creating such examples are presented in (11). The fact that such sentences are even possible provides strong evidence that the relevant words have two distinct senses.

(11) a. Criminal mastermind planning to stage a traffic accident in order to cheat the insurance company: *After the crash, you lie down behind the bus and tell the police you were thrown out of the bus through a window.*
Unwilling accomplice: *I'll lie there, but I won't lie.*

b. Foreman: *I told you to collect a sample of uranium ore from the pit and row it across the river to be tested.*
Miner: *I have the ore but I don't have the oar.*

c. Rancher (speaking on the telephone): *I've lost my expensive fountain pen; I think I may have dropped it while we were inspecting the sheep. Can you check the sheep pen to see if it is there?*
Hired hand: *I am looking at the pen, but I don't see a pen.*

An equivalent way of describing this test is to say that if there exists some state of affairs or context in which a sentence can be both truly affirmed and truly denied, then the sentence must be ambiguous.[17] An example showing how this test might be applied to two uses of the word *drink* (alcoholic beverage vs. any beverage) is quoted in (12):

(12) a. *Ferrell has a drink each night before going to bed.*

b. "Imagine… this state of affairs: Ferrell has a medical problem which requires that he consume no alcoholic beverages but that he have a glass of water each night before going to bed. One person knows only that he does not consume alcoholic beverages; another knows only that he has a glass of water each night at bedtime. The latter person

[17] Adapted from Gillon (1990: 407).

can truly affirm the sentence in (12a)... But the former person can truly deny it." (Gillon 1990: 407)

Gillon points out that this is a very useful test because "generality and indeterminacy do not permit a sentence to be both truly affirmed and truly denied" (1990: 410). Sentences like those in (13) can only be interpreted as contradictions; they require some kind of pragmatic inference in order to make sense.[18]

(13) a. # She is my cousin and she is not my cousin.
b. # I am carrying the bag and I am not carrying the bag.
c. # This creature is a vertebrate and it is not a vertebrate.

5.3.3 Polysemy vs. homonymy

Two types of lexical ambiguity are traditionally distinguished: POLYSEMY (one word with multiple senses) vs. HOMONYMY (different words that happen to sound the same). Both cases involve an ambiguous word form; the difference lies in how the information is organized in the speaker's mental lexicon.

Of course, it is not easy to determine how information is stored in the mental lexicon. This is not something that native speakers are consciously aware of, so asking them directly whether two senses are "the same word" or not is generally not a reliable procedure. The basic criterion for making this distinction is that in cases of polysemy, the two senses are felt to be "related" in some way; there is "an intelligible connection of some sort" between the two senses.[19] In cases of homonymy, the two senses are unrelated; that is, the semantic relationship between the two senses is similar to that between any two words selected at random.

It is difficult to draw a clear boundary between these two types of ambiguity, and some authors reject the distinction entirely. However, many ambiguous words clearly belong to one type or the other, and the distinction is a useful one. We will adopt a prototype approach, suggesting some properties that are prototypical of polysemy vs. homonymy while recognizing there will be cases which are very difficult to classify.

[18] The word *vertebrate* is more "general", in Gillon's terms, than words like *fish* or *dog*. We will discuss this kind of sense relation in the next chapter.

[19] Cruse (2000: 109).

Some general guidelines for distinguishing polysemy vs. homonymy:

a. Two senses of a polysemous word generally share at least one salient feature or component of meaning, whereas this is not in general true for homonyms.[20] For example, the sense of *foot* that denotes a unit of length ('12 inches') shares with the body-part sense the same approximate size. The sense of *foot* that means 'base' (as in *foot of a tree/mountain*) shares with the body-part sense the same position or location relative to the object of which it is a part. These common features suggest that *foot* is polysemous. In contrast, the two senses of *row* (pull the oars vs. things arranged in a line) seem to have nothing in common, suggesting that *row* is homonymous.

b. If one sense seems to be a figurative extension of the other (see discussion of figurative senses below), the word is probably polysemous. For example, the sense of *run* in *This road runs from Rangoon to Mandalay* is arguably based on a metonymy between the act of running and the path traversed by the runner, suggesting that this is a case of polysemy.

c. Beekman & Callow (1974) suggest that, for polysemous words, one sense can often be identified as the PRIMARY SENSE, with other senses being classified as secondary or figurative. The primary sense will typically be the one most likely to be chosen if you ask a native speaker to illustrate how the word X is used in a sentence, or if you ask a bilingual speaker what the word X means (i.e., ask for a translation equivalent). For homonymous words, neither sense is likely to be "primary" in this way.[21]

d. Etymology (historical source) is used as a criterion in most dictionaries, but it is not a reliable basis for synchronic linguistic analysis. (Speakers may or may not know where certain words come from historically, and their ideas about such questions are often mistaken.) However, there is often a correlation between etymology and the criteria listed above, because figurative extension is a common factor in semantic change over time, as discussed in §5.4. English spelling may give a clue about etymology, but again is not directly relevant to synchronic linguistic analysis, which normally focuses on spoken language.

[20] Beekman & Callow (1974) suggest that *all* the senses of a polysemous word will share at least one component of meaning, but this claim is certainly too strong.

[21] A similar point is made by Fillmore & Atkins (2000: 100).

Point (d) is a specific application of a more general principle in the study of lexical meaning: word meanings may change over time, and the historical meaning of a word may be quite different from its modern meaning. It is important to base our analysis of the current meanings of words on SYNCHRONIC (i.e., contemporaneous) evidence, unless we are specifically studying the DIACHRONIC (historical) developments. Lyons (1977: 244) expresses this principle as follows:

> A particular manifestation of the failure to respect the distinction of the diachronic and the synchronic in semantics ... is what might be called the ETYMOLOGICAL FALLACY: the common belief that the meaning of words can be determined by investigating their origins. The etymology of a lexeme is, in principle, synchronically irrelevant.

As an example, Lyons points out that it would be silly to claim that the "real" meaning of the word *curious* in Modern English is 'careful', even though that was the meaning of the Latin word from which it is derived.

A number of authors have distinguished between REGULAR or SYSTEMATIC polysemy vs. non-systematic polysemy. Systematic polysemy involves senses which are related in recurring or predictable ways. For example, many verbs naming a change of state (*break, melt, split,* etc.) have two senses, one transitive (V_{TR}) and the other intransitive (V_{INTR}), with V_{TR} meaning roughly 'cause to V_{INTR}'. Similarly, many nouns that refer to things used as instruments (*hammer, saw, paddle, whip, brush, comb, rake, shovel, plow, sandpaper, anchor, tape, chain, telephone,* etc.) can also be used as verbs meaning roughly 'to use the instrument to act on an appropriate object.' (A single sense can have only a single part of speech, so the verbal and nominal uses of such words must represent distinct senses.)

The kinds of regularities involved in systematic polysemy are similar to patterns which are associated with derivational morphology in some languages.[22] This means that the systematic relationships between senses can be stated in the form of rules. Some authors have suggested that only the base or core meaning needs to be included in the lexicon, because the secondary senses can be derived by rule.[23] But even in the case of systematic polysemy, secondary senses need to be listed because not every extended sense which the rules would license actually occurs in the language. For example, there are no verbal uses for some instrumental nouns, e.g. *scalpel, yardstick, hatchet, pliers, tweezers,* etc. For others, verbal uses are possible only for non-standard uses of the instrument or non-literal senses:

[22] See Apresjan (1974), Aronoff & Fudeman (2011: ch. 5).

[23] For example, Pustejovsky (1995).

(14) a. Australian Prime Minister Kevin Rudd has *axed* the carbon tax.
b. Alaska Airlines *axed* the flights as a precaution.
c. ?*John *axed* the tree.

Traditionally it has been assumed that all the senses of a polysemous word will be listed within a single lexical entry, while homonyms will occur in separate lexical entries. Most dictionaries adopt a format that reflects this organization of the lexicon. The format is illustrated in the partial dictionary listing for the word form *lean* presented in (15).[24] The verbal and adjectival uses of *lean* are treated as homonyms, each with its own lexical entry. Each of the homonyms is analyzed as being polysemous, with the various senses listed inside the appropriate entry.

(15) *lean*$_1$ (V): 1. to incline, deviate, or bend from a vertical position; 2. to cast one's weight to one side for support; 3. to rely on for support or inspiration; 4. to incline in opinion, taste, or desire (e.g., *leaning toward a career in chemistry*).

lean$_2$ (Adj): 1. lacking or deficient in flesh; 2. containing little or no fat (*lean meat*); 3. lacking richness, sufficiency, or productiveness (*lean profits, the lean years*); 4. deficient in an essential or important quality or ingredient, e.g. (a) of ore: containing little valuable mineral; (b) of fuel mixtures: low in combustible component.

This is not the only way in which a lexicon could be organized, but we will not explore the various alternatives here. The crucial point is that polysemous senses are "related" while homonymous senses are not.

5.3.4 One sense at a time

When a lexically ambiguous word is used, the context normally makes it clear which of the senses is intended. As Cruse (1986: 53) points out, a speaker generally intends the hearer to be able to identify the single intended sense based on context:

> [A] context normally also acts in such a way as to cause a single sense, from among those associated with any ambiguous word form, to become operative. When a sentence is uttered, it is rarely the utterer's intention that

[24]Adapted from the Merriam-Webster Online Dictionary (http://www.merriam-webster.com/dictionary/lean).

> it should be interpreted in two (or more) different ways simultaneously... This means that, for the vast majority of utterances, hearers are expected to identify specific intended senses for every ambiguous word form that they contain.

Cruse (1986: 54) cites the sentence in (16), which contains five lexically ambiguous words. (Note that the intended sense of *burn* in this sentence, 'a small stream', is characteristic of Scottish English.)

(16) Several rare ferns grow on the steep banks of the burn where it runs into the lake.

Cruse writes,

> In such cases, there will occur a kind of mutual negotiation between the various options [so as to determine which sense for each word produces a coherent meaning for the sentence as a whole]... It is highly unlikely that any reader of this sentence will interpret *rare* in the sense of 'undercooked' (as in *rare steak*), or *steep* in the sense of 'unjustifiably high' (as in *steep charges*)... or *run* in the sense of 'progress by advancing each foot alternately never having both feet on the ground simultaneously', etc.

A very interesting use of this principle occurs in the short story "Xingu", by Edith Wharton (1916). In the following passage, Mrs. Roby is describing something to the members of her ladies' club, which they believe (and which she allows them to believe) to be a deep, philosophical book. After the discussion is over, however, the other members discover that she was actually describing a river in Brazil. The words which are italicized below are ambiguous; all of them must be interpreted with one sense in a discussion of a philosophical work, but another sense in a discussion of a river.

(17) "Of course," Mrs. Roby admitted, "the difficulty is that one must give up so much time to it. It's very *long*."
"I can't imagine," said Miss Van Vluyck tartly, "grudging the time given to such a subject."
"And *deep* in places," Mrs. Roby pursued; (so then it was a book!) "And it isn't easy to *skip*."
"I never skip," said Mrs. Plinth dogmatically.
"Ah, it's dangerous to, in Xingu. Even at the start there are places where one can't. One must just *wade* through."

> "I should hardly call it wading ," said Mrs. Ballinger sarcastically.
> Mrs. Roby sent her a look of interest. "Ah – you always found it went *swimmingly*?"
> Mrs. Ballinger hesitated. "Of course there are difficult *passages*," she conceded modestly.
> "Yes; some are not at all *clear* – even," Mrs. Roby added, "if one is familiar with the *original*.[25]"
> "As I suppose you are?" Osric Dane interposed, suddenly fixing her with a look of challenge.
> Mrs. Roby met it by a deprecating smile. "Oh, it's really not difficult up to a certain point; though some of the *branches* are very little known, and it's almost impossible to get at the *source*."

Mrs. Roby's motives seem to be noble – she is rescuing the ladies of the club from further humiliation by an arrogant visiting celebrity, Mrs. Osric Dane (a popular author). But when the other members discover the deception, they are so provoked that they demand Mrs. Roby's resignation.

Cotterell & Turner (1989: 175) point out the implications of the "one sense at a time" principle for exegetical work:

> The context of the utterance usually singles out ... the *one* sense, which is intended, from amongst the various senses of which the word is potentially capable... When an interpreter tells us his author could be using such-and-such a word with sense *a*, or he could be using it with sense *b*, and then sits on the fence claiming perhaps the author means *both*, we should not too easily be discouraged from the suspicion that the interpreter is simply fudging the exegesis.

Sometimes, of course, the speaker does intend both senses to be available to the hearer; but this is normally intended as some kind of play on words, e.g. a pun. The humor in a pun (for those people who enjoy them) lies precisely in the fact that this is not the way language is normally used.

5.3.5 Disambiguation in context

Word meanings are clarified or restricted by their context of use in several different ways. If a word is indeterminate with respect to a certain feature, the feature can be specified by linguistic or pragmatic context. For example, the word *nurse*

[25] Apparently a play upon an archaic sense of *original* meaning 'source' or 'origin'.

is indeterminate with respect to gender; but if I say *The nurse who checked my blood pressure was pregnant*, the context makes it clear that the nurse I am referring to is female.

We noted in the preceding section that the context of use generally makes it clear which sense of a lexically ambiguous word is intended. This is not to say that misunderstandings never arise, but in a large majority of cases hearers filter out unintended senses automatically and unconsciously. It is important to recognize that knowledge about the world plays an important role in making this disambiguation possible. For example, a slogan on the package of Wasa crispbread proudly announces, *Baked since 1919.* There is a potential ambiguity in the aspect of the past participle here. It is our knowledge about the world (and specifically about how long breads and crackers can safely be left in the oven), rather than any feature of the linguistic context, which enables us to correctly select the habitual, rather than the durative, reading. The process is automatic; most people who see the slogan are probably not even aware of the ambiguity.

Because knowledge about the world plays such an important role, disambiguation will be more difficult with translated material, or in other situations where the content is culturally unfamiliar to the reader/hearer. But in most monocultural settings, Ravin & Leacock's (2000) assessment seems fair:

> Polysemy is rarely a problem for communication among people. We are so adept at using contextual cues that we select the appropriate senses of words effortlessly and unconsciously... Although rarely a problem in language use, except as a source of humour and puns, polysemy poses a problem for semantic theory and in semantic applications, such as translation or lexicography.

If lexical ambiguity is not (usually) a problem for human speakers, it is a significant problem for computers. Much of the recent work on polysemy has been carried out within the field of computational linguistics. Because computational work typically deals with written language, more attention has been paid to HOMOGRAPHS (words which are spelled the same) than to HOMOPHONES (words which are pronounced the same), in contrast to traditional linguistics which has been more concerned with spoken language. Because of English spelling inconsistencies, the two cases do not always coincide; Ravin & Leacock cite the example of *bass* [bæs] 'fish species' vs. *bass* [be^{j}s] 'voice or instrument with lowest range', homographs which are not homophones.

As Ravin & Leacock note, lexical ambiguity poses a problem for translation. The problem arises because distinct senses of a given word-form are unlikely to have the same translation equivalent in another language. Lexical ambiguity can cause problems for translation in at least two ways: either the wrong sense may be chosen for a word which is ambiguous in the source language, or the nearest translation equivalent for some word in the source language may be ambiguous in the target language. In the latter case, the translated version may be ambiguous in a way that the original version was not.

A striking example of the former type occurred in the English text of a bilingual menu in a Chinese restaurant, which offered 'deep-fried enema' rather than 'deep-fried sausage'. The Chinese name of the dish is *zhá guànchang* (炸灌腸). The last two characters in the name refer to a kind of sausage made of wheat flour stuffed into hog casings; but they also have another sense, namely 'enema'. The translator (whether human or machine) chose the wrong sense for this context.[26]

Much medieval and renaissance art, most famously the sculptural masterpiece by Michelangelo, depicts Moses with horns coming out of his forehead. This practice was based on the Latin Vulgate translation of a passage in Exodus which describes Moses' appearance when he came down from Mt. Sinai.[27] The Hebrew text uses the verb *qaran* to describe his face. This verb is derived from the noun *qeren* meaning 'horn', and in some contexts it can mean 'having horns';[28] but most translators, both ancient and modern, have agreed that in this context it has another sense, namely 'shining, radiant' or 'emitting rays'. St. Jerome, however, translated *qaran* with the Latin adjective *cornuta* 'horned'.[29]

As noted above, a translation equivalent which is ambiguous in the target language can create ambiguity in the translated version that is not present in the original. For example, the French word *apprivoiser* 'to tame' plays a major role in the book *Le Petit Prince* 'The Little Prince' by Antoine de Saint-Exupéry. In most (if not all) Portuguese versions this word is translated as *cativar*, which can mean 'tame' but can also mean 'catch', 'capture', 'enslave', 'captivate', 'enthrall', 'charm', etc. This means that the translation is potentially ambiguous in a way that the original is not. The first occurrence of the word is spoken by a fox, who

[26] http://languagelog.ldc.upenn.edu/nll/?p=2236

[27] Exodus 34:29–35.

[28] Psalm 69:31.

[29] There is some disagreement as to whether St. Jerome simply made a mistake, or whether he viewed the reference to horns as a live metaphor and chose to preserve the image in his translation. The latter view seems more likely since he was very familiar with the rendering of the Septuagint, which uses the word 'glorified'. The first artistic depiction of a horned Moses appeared roughly 700 years after Jerome's translation, which might be taken as an indication that the metaphorical sense was in fact understood by readers of the Vulgate at first, but was lost over time. (see Ruth Mellinkoff. 1970. *The Horned Moses in Medieval Art and Thought* (California Studies in the History of Art, 14). University of California Press.)

explains to the little prince what the word means; so in that context the intended sense is clear. However, the word occurs frequently in the book, and many of the later occurrences might be difficult for readers to disambiguate on the basis of the immediate context alone.

It is not surprising that homonymy should pose a problem for translation, because homonymy is an accidental similarity of form; there is no reason to expect the two senses to be associated with a single form in another language. If we do happen to find a pair of homonyms in some other language which are good translation equivalents for a pair of English homonyms, we regard it as a remarkable coincidence. But even with polysemy, where the senses are related in some way, we cannot in general expect that the different senses can be translated using the same word in the target language. Beekman & Callow (1974: 103) state:

> Whether multiple senses of a word arise from a shared [component] of meaning or from relations which associate the senses [i.e. figurative extensions—PK], the cluster of senses symbolized by a single word is always specific to the language under study.

Perhaps Beekman & Callow overstate the unlikelihood that a single word in the target language can carry some or all of the senses of a polysemous word in the source language. Since there is an intelligible relationship between polysemous senses, it is certainly possible for the same relationship to be found in more than one language; but often this turns out not to be the case, which is why polysemy can be a source of problems for translators.

5.4 Context-dependent extensions of meaning

Cruse (1986; 2000) distinguishes between ESTABLISHED VS. NON-ESTABLISHED senses. An established sense is one that is permanently stored in the speaker's mental lexicon, one which is always available; these are the senses that would normally be listed in a dictionary. A lexically ambiguous word is one that has two or more established senses.

We have seen how context determines a choice between existing (i.e., established) senses of lexically ambiguous words. But context can also force the hearer to "invent" a new, non-established sense for a word. When Mark Twain described a certain person as "a good man in the worst sense of the word," his hearers were forced to interpret the word *good* with something close to the opposite of its normal meaning (e.g., puritanical, self-righteous, or judgmental). Clearly this "sense" of the word *good* is not permanently stored in the hearer's mental lexicon, and we would not expect to see it listed in a dictionary entry for *good.* It exists only on the occasion of its use in this specific context.

A general term for the process by which context creates non-established senses is COERCION.[30] Coercion provides a mechanism for extending the range of meanings of a given word. It is motivated by the assumption that the speaker intends to communicate something intelligible, relevant to current purposes, etc. If none of the established senses of a word allow for a coherent or intelligible sentence meaning, the hearer tries to create an extended meaning for one or more words that makes sense in the current speech context.

Coerced meanings are not stored in the lexicon, but are calculated as needed from the established or default meaning of the word plus contextual factors; so there is generally some identifiable relationship between the basic and extended senses. Several common patterns of extended meaning were identified and named by ancient Greek philosophers; these are often referred to as TROPES, or "figures of speech".

5.4.1 Figurative senses

Some of the best-known figures of speech are listed in (18):

(18) **Some well-known tropes**

Metaphor: Traditionally defined as a figure of speech in which an implied comparison is made between two unlike things; but see comments below.

Hyperbole: A figure of speech in which exaggeration is used for emphasis or effect; an extravagant statement. (e.g., *I have eaten more salt than you have eaten rice.* – Chinese saying implying seniority in age and wisdom)

Euphemism: Substitution of an inoffensive term (such as *passed away*) for one considered offensively explicit (*died*).

Metonymy: A figure of speech in which one word or phrase is substituted for another with which it is closely associated (such as *crown* for *monarch*).

Synecdoche (/sɪˈnɛk də ki/): A figure of speech in which a part is used to represent the whole, the whole for a part, the specific for the

[30] This term was coined by Moens & Steedman (1988).

general, the general for the specific, or the material for the thing made from it. Considered by some to be a form of metonymy.

Litotes: A figure of speech consisting of an understatement in which an affirmative is expressed by negating its opposite (e.g. *not bad* to mean 'good').

Irony: A figure of speech in which the intended meaning of the expression is the opposite of its literal meaning.

The question of how metaphors work has generated an enormous body of literature, and remains a topic of controversy. For our present purposes, it is enough to recognize all of these figures of speech as patterns of reasoning that will allow a hearer to provide an extended sense when all available established senses fail to produce an acceptable interpretation of the speaker's utterance.

5.4.2 How figurative senses become established

As mentioned above, figurative senses are not stored in the speaker/hearer's mental lexicon; rather, they are calculated as needed, when required by the context of use. However, some figurative senses become popular, and after frequent repetition they lose the sense of freshness or novelty associated with their original use; we call such expressions "clichés". At this stage they are remembered, rather than calculated, but are perhaps not stored in the lexicon in the same way as "normal" lexical items; they are still felt to be figurative rather than established senses. Probable examples of this type include: *fishing for compliments, sowing seeds of doubt, at the end of the day, burning the candle at both ends, boots on the ground, lash out, …*

At some point, these frequently used figurative senses may become lexicalized, and begin to function as established senses. For example, the original sense of *grasp* is 'to hold in the hand'; but a new sense has developed from a metaphorical use of the word to mean 'understand'. Similar examples include *freeze* 'become ice' > 'remain motionless'; *broadcast* 'plant (seeds) by scattering widely' > 'transmit via radio or television'; and, more recently, the use of *hawk* and *dove* to refer to advocates of war and advocates of peace, respectively. Once this stage is reached, the hearer does not have to calculate the speaker's intended meaning based on specific contextual or cultural factors; the intended meaning is simply selected from among the established senses already available, as with normal cases of lexical ambiguity.

When established senses develop out of metaphors they are referred to as CONVENTIONAL METAPHORS, in contrast to "novel" or "creative" metaphors which are newly created. Conventional metaphors are sometimes referred to as "dead" or "frozen" metaphors, phrases which are themselves conventional metaphors expressing the intuition that the meaning of such expressions is static rather than dynamic.

Finally, in some cases the original "literal" sense of a word may fall out of use, leaving what was originally a figurative sense as the only sense of that word. This seems to be happening with the compound noun *night owl*, which originally referred to a type of bird. Many current dictionaries (including the massive *Random House Unabridged*) now list only the conventional metaphor sense, i.e., a person who habitually stays out late at night.

This discussion shows how figurative senses may lead to polysemy.[31] Earlier we noted that translation equivalents in different languages are unlikely to share the same range of polysemous senses. For example, the closest translation equivalent for *grasp* in Malay is *pĕgang*; but this verb never carries the sense of 'understand'. Novel (i.e., creative) metaphors can sometimes survive and be interpretable when translated into a different language, because the general patterns of meaning extension listed in (18), if they are not universal, are at least used across a wide range of languages. Conventional (i.e., "frozen") metaphors, however, are much less likely to work in translation, because the specific contextual features which motivated the creative use of the metaphor need no longer be present.

5.5 "Facets" of meaning

The sentences in (19–22) show examples of different uses which are possible for certain classes of words. These different uses are often cited as cases of systematic polysemy, i.e., distinct senses related by a productive rule of some kind.[32] However, Cruse (2000; 2004) argues that they are best analyzed as "facets" of a single sense, by which he means "fully discrete but non-antagonistic readings of a word".[33]

(19) *book* (Cruse 2004):

a. My chemistry book makes a great doorstop. [PHYSICAL OBJECT]

[31]Apresjan (1974: 16) makes the interesting observation that semantic extensions based on metonymy frequently lead to systematic polysemy, which he refers to as "regular polysemy". Polysemy based on metaphorical extension is typically non-systematic.

[32]See for example Pustejovsky (1995), Nunberg & Zaenen (1992).

[33]Cruse (2000: 116).

b. My chemistry book is well-organized but a bit dull. [INFORMATION CONTENT]

(20) *bank* (Cruse 2000: 116; similar examples include *school, university,* etc.):

a. The bank in the High Street was blown up last night. [PREMISES]

b. That used to be the friendliest bank in town. [PERSONNEL]

c. This bank was founded in 1575. [INSTITUTION]

(21) *Britain* (Cruse 2000: 117; Croft & Cruse 2004: 117):

a. Britain lies under one metre of snow. [LAND MASS]

b. Britain today is mourning the death of the Royal corgi. [POPULACE]

c. Britain has declared war on San Marino. [POLITICAL ENTITY]

(22) *chicken, duck,* etc. (Croft & Cruse 2004: 117):

a. My neighbor's chickens are noisy and smelly. [ANIMAL]

b. This chicken is tender and delicious. [MEAT]

Cruse describes facets as "distinguishable components of a global whole".[34] The word *book*, for example, names a complex concept which includes both the physical object (the tome) and the information which it contains (the text). In the most typical uses of the word, it is used to refer to both the object and its information content simultaneously. In contexts like those seen in (19), however, the word can be used to refer to just one facet or the other (text or tome).

Cruse's strongest argument against the systematic polysemy analysis is the fact that these facets are non-antagonistic; they do not give rise to zeugma effects, as illustrated in (23). In this they are unlike normal polysemous senses, which are antagonistic. Under the systematic polysemy analysis we might derive the senses illustrated in (19–22) by a kind of metonymy, similar to that illustrated in (24).[35] However, as the examples in (25) demonstrate, figurative senses are antagonistic with their literal counterparts. This suggests that facets are not figurative senses.

(23) a. This is a very interesting book, but it is awfully heavy to carry around.[36]

b. My religion forbids me to eat or wear rabbit.[37]

[34] Croft & Cruse (2004: 116).

[35] Nunberg (1979; 1995).

[36] Cruse (2004).

[37] Nunberg & Zaenen (1992).

(24) a. I'm parked out back.
  b. The ham sandwich at table seven left without paying.
  c. Yeats is widely read although he has been dead for over 50 years.
  d. Yeats is widely read, even though most of it is now out of print.

(25) a. # The ham sandwich at table seven was stale and left without paying.
  b. # The White House needs a coat of paint but refuses to ask Congress for the money.

We cannot pursue a detailed discussion of these issues here. It may be that some of the examples in question are best treated in one way, and some in the other. The different uses of animal names illustrated in (22), for example, creature vs. meat, seem like good candidates for systematic polysemy, because they differ in grammatical properties (mass vs. count nouns). But the non-antagonism of the other cases seems to be a problem for the systematic polysemy analysis.

5.6 Conclusion

In this chapter we described several ways of identifying lexical ambiguity, based on two basic facts. First, distinct senses of a single word are "antagonistic", and as a result only one sense is available at a time in normal usage. The incompatibility of distinct senses can be observed in puns, in zeugma effects, and in the identity requirements under ellipsis. Second, true ambiguity involves a difference in truth conditions; so sentences which contain an ambiguous word can sometimes be truly asserted under one sense of that word and denied under the other sense, in the same context. Neither of these facts applies to vagueness or indeterminacy.

Lexical ambiguity is actually quite common, but only rarely causes confusion between speaker and hearer. The hearer is normally able to identify the intended sense for an ambiguous word based on the context in which it is used. Where none of the established senses lead to a sensible interpretation in a given context, new senses can be triggered by coercion. In Chapter 8 we will discuss some of the pragmatic principles which guide the hearer in working out the intended sense.

Further reading

Kennedy (2011) provides an excellent overview of lexical ambiguity, indeterminacy, and vagueness. These issues are also addressed in Gillon (1990). Cruse (1986: ch. 3) and (2000, ch. 6) discusses many of the issues covered in this chapter, including tests for lexical ambiguity, "antagonistic" senses, polysemy vs. homonymy, and contextual modification of meaning. Aronoff & Fudeman (2011: ch. 5) introduce some ways of describing systematic polysemy in terms of zero-derivation.

Discussion exercises

A: State whether the italicized words illustrate ambiguity, vagueness, or indeterminacy:

1. She spends her afternoons *filing* correspondence and her fingernails.
2. He spends his afternoons *washing* clothes and dishes.
3. He was a *big* baby, even though both of his parents are *small.*
4. The weather wasn't very *bright,* but then neither was our tour guide.
5. Mr. Smith smokes *expensive* cigars but drives a *cheap* car.
6. That boy couldn't *carry* a tune in a bucket.

B: In each of the following examples, state which word is ambiguous as demonstrated by the antagonism or zeugma effect. Is it an instance of polysemy or homonymy?

1. "You are free to execute your laws, and your citizens, as you see fit."[a]
2. "... and covered themselves with dust and glory."[b]
3. Arthur declined my invitation, and Susan a Latin pronoun.
4. Susan can't bear children.

5. The batteries were given out free of charge.
6. My astrologer wants to marry a star.

C: Figurative senses. Identify the type of figure illustrated by the italicized words in the following passages:

1. Fear is the *lock* and laughter the *key* to your heart.[c]
2. The *White House* is concerned about terrorism.
3. She has six hungry *mouths* to feed.
4. That joke is *as old as the hills.*
5. It's *not the prettiest* quarter I've ever seen, Mr. Liddell.[d]
6. as *pleasant and relaxed* as a coiled rattlesnake[e]
7. Headline: Korean "*comfort women*" get controversial apology, compensation from Japanese government[f]

D: Semantic shift. Identify the figures of speech that provided the source for the following historical shifts in word meaning:

1. *bead* (< 'prayer')
2. *pastor*
3. *drumstick* (for 'turkey leg')
4. *glossa* (Greek) 'tongue; language'
5. *pioneer* (< Old French *peon(ier)* 'foot-soldier'; cognate: *pawn*)

---

[a] *Star Trek: The Next Generation*, via grammar.about.com
[b] Mark Twain, *The Adventures of Tom Sawyer*
[c] Crosby, Stills & Nash – "Suite: Judy Blue Eyes"
[d] Sam Mussabini in *Chariots of Fire.*
[e] Kurt Vonnegut in *Breakfast of Champions*
[f] news.com.au, December 30, 2015

Homework exercises

A: Lexical ambiguity. Do the uses of *strike* in the following two sentences represent distinct senses (lexical ambiguity), or just indeterminacy? Provide linguistic evidence to support your answer.

a. The California Gold Rush began when James Marshall *struck* gold at Sutter's Mill.

b. Balaam *struck* his donkey three times before it turned and spoke to him.

B: Dictionary entries. Without looking at any published dictionary, draft a dictionary entry for *mean*. Include the use of *mean* as a noun, as an adjective, and at least three senses of *mean* as a verb.

C: Polysemy etc.[a] How would you describe the relationship between the readings of the italicized words in the following pairs of examples? You may choose from among the following options: POLYSEMY, HOMONYMY, VAGUENESS, INDETERMINACY, FIGURATIVE USE. If none of these terms seem appropriate, describe the sense relation in prose.

(1) a. Mary ordered an *omelette*.
b. The *omelette* at table 6 wants his coffee now.

(2) a. They *led* the prisoner away.
b. They *led* him to believe that he would be freed.

(3) a. King George III was not very *intelligent* and could not read until he was eleven.
b. The squid is actually quite *intelligent*, for an invertebrate.

(4) a. My *cousin* married an actress.
b. My *cousin* married a policeman.

(5) a. Could you loan me your *pen*? Mine is out of ink.
b. The goats escaped from their *pen* and ate up my artichokes.

(6) a. Wittgenstein's Philosophical Investigations is too *deep* for me.
b. This river is too *deep* for my Land Rover to ford.

[a] Adapted from Cruse (2000).

6 Lexical sense relations

6.1 Meaning relations between words

A traditional way of investigating the meaning of a word is to study the relationships between its meaning and the meanings of other words: which words have the same meaning, opposite meanings, etc. Strictly speaking these relations hold between specific senses, rather than between words; that is why we refer to them as sense relations. For example, one sense of *mad* is a synonym of *angry*, while another sense is a synonym of *crazy*.

In §6.2 we discuss the most familiar classes of sense relations: synonymy, several types of antonymy, hyponymy, and meronymy. We will try to define each of these relations in terms of relations between sentence meanings, since it is easier for speakers to make reliable judgments about sentences than about words in isolation. Where possible we will mention some types of linguistic evidence that can be used as diagnostics to help identify each relation. In §6.3 we mention some of the standard ways of defining words in terms of their sense relations. This is the approach most commonly used in traditional dictionaries.

6.2 Identifying sense relations

Let's begin by thinking about what kinds of meaning relations are likely to be worth studying. If we are interested in the meaning of the word *big*, it seems natural to look at its meaning relations with words like *large*, *small*, *enormous*, etc. But comparing *big* with words like *multilingual* or *extradite* seems unlikely to be very enlightening. The range of useful comparisons seems to be limited by some concept of semantic similarity or comparability.

Syntactic relationships are also relevant. The kinds of meaning relations mentioned above (same meaning, opposite meaning, etc.) hold between words which are mutually substitutable, i.e., which can occur in the same syntactic environments, as illustrated in (1a). These relations are referred to as PARADIGMATIC sense relations. We might also want to investigate relations which hold between words which can occur in construction with each other, as illustrated in (1b). (In this example we see that *big* can modify some head nouns but not others.) These relations are referred to as SYNTAGMATIC relations.

(1) a. Look at that *big/large/small/enormous/?#discontinuous/*snore* mosquito!
    b. Look at that big *mosquito/elephant/?#surname/#color/*discontinuous/ *snore*!

We will consider some syntagmatic relations in Chapter 7, when we discuss selectional restrictions. In this chapter we will be primarily concerned with paradigmatic relations.

6.2.1 Synonyms

We often speak of synonyms as being words that "mean the same thing". As a more rigorous definition, we will say that two words are synonymous (for a specific sense of each word) if substituting one word for the other does not change the meaning of a sentence. For example, we can change sentence (2a) into sentence (2b) by replacing *frightened* with *scared.* The two sentences are semantically equivalent (each entails the other). This shows that *frightened* is a synonym of *scared.*

(2) a. John *frightened* the children.
    b. John *scared* the children.

"Perfect" synonymy is extremely rare, and some linguists would say that it never occurs. Even for senses that are truly equivalent in meaning, there are often collocational differences as illustrated in (3–4). Replacing *bucket* with *pail* in (3a) does not change meaning; but in (3b), the idiomatic meaning that is possible with *bucket* is not available with *pail.* Replacing *big* with *large* does not change meaning in most contexts, as illustrated in (4a); but when used as a modifier for certain kinship terms, the two words are no longer equivalent (*big* becomes a synonym of *elder*), as illustrated in (4b).

(3) a. John filled the *bucket*/*pail.*
    b. John kicked the *bucket*/??*pail.*

(4) a. Susan lives in a *big*/*large* house.
    b. Susan lives with her *big*/*large* sister.[1]

[1]Adapted from Saeed (2009: 66).

6.2.2 Antonyms

Antonyms are commonly defined as words with "opposite" meaning; but what do we mean by "opposite"? We clearly do not mean 'as different as possible'. As noted above, the meaning of *big* is totally different from the meanings of *multilingual* or *extradite*, but neither of these words is an antonym of *big*. When we say that *big* is the opposite of *small*, or that *dead* is the opposite of *alive*, we mean first that the two terms can have similar collocations. It is odd to call an inanimate object *dead*, in the primary, literal sense of the word, because it is not the kind of thing that could ever be *alive*. Second, we mean that the two terms express a value of the same property or attribute. *Big* and *small* both express degrees of size, while *dead* and *alive* both express degrees of vitality. So two words which are antonyms actually share most of their components of meaning, and differ only with respect to the value of one particular feature.

The term ANTONYM actually covers several different sense relations. Some pairs of antonyms express opposite ends of a particular scale, like *big* and *small*. We refer to such pairs as SCALAR or GRADABLE antonyms. Other pairs, like *dead* and *alive*, express discrete values rather than points on a scale, and name the only possible values for the relevant attribute. We refer to such pairs as SIMPLE or COMPLEMENTARY antonyms. Several other types of antonyms are commonly recognized as well. We begin with simple antonyms.

6.2.2.1 Complementary pairs (simple antonyms)

> "All men are created equal. Some, it appears, are created a little more equal than others." [Ambrose Bierce, In *The San Francisco Wasp* magazine, September 16, 1882]

Complementary pairs such as *open/shut*, *alive/dead*, *male/female*, *on/off*, etc. exhaust the range of possibilities, for things that they can collocate with. There is (normally) no middle ground; a person is either alive or dead, a switch is either on or off, etc. The defining property of simple antonyms is that replacing one member of the pair with the other, as in (5), produces sentences which are CONTRADICTORY. As discussed in Chapter 3, this means that the two sentences must have opposite truth values in every circumstance; one of them must be true and the other false in all possible situations where these words can be used appropriately.

(5) a. The switch is on.
  b. The switch is off.
  c. ??The switch is neither on nor off.

If two sentences are contradictory, then one or the other must always be true. This means that simple antonyms allow for no middle ground, as indicated in (5c). The negation of one entails the truth of the other, as illustrated in (6).

(6) a. ??The post office is not open today, but it is not closed either.
 b. ??Your headlights are not off, but they are not on either.

A significant challenge in identifying simple antonyms is the fact that they are easily coerced into acting like gradable antonyms.[2] For example, *equal* and *unequal* are simple antonyms; the humor in the quote by Ambrose Bierce at the beginning of this section arises from the way he uses *equal* as if it were gradable. In a similar vein, zombies are often described as being *undead*, implying that they are not dead but not really alive either. However, the gradable use of simple antonyms is typically possible only in certain figurative or semi-idiomatic expressions. The gradable uses in (7) seem natural, but those in (8) are not. The sentences in (9) illustrate further contrasts. For true gradable antonyms, like those discussed in the following section, all of these patterns would generally be fully acceptable, not odd or humorous.

(7) a. half-dead, half-closed, half-open
 b. more dead than alive
 c. deader than a door nail

(8) a. ?half-alive
 b. #a little too dead
 c. #not dead enough
 d. #How dead is that mosquito?
 e. #This mosquito is deader than that one.

(9) a. I feel fully/very/??slightly alive.
 b. This town/#mosquito seems very/slightly dead.

6.2.2.2 Gradable (scalar) antonyms

A defining property of gradable (or scalar) antonyms is that replacing one member of such a pair with the other produces sentences which are CONTRARY, as illustrated in (10a–b). As discussed in Chapter 3, contrary sentences are sentences which cannot both be true, though they may both be false (10c).

[2] Cann (2011: 463).

(10) a. My youngest son-in-law is extremely diligent.
b. My youngest son-in-law is extremely lazy.
c. My youngest son-in-law is neither extremely diligent nor extremely lazy.

Note, however, that not all pairs of words which satisfy this criterion would normally be called "antonyms". The two sentences in (11) cannot both be true (when referring to the same thing), which shows that *turnip* and *platypus* are INCOMPATIBLES; but they are not antonyms. So our definition of gradable antonyms needs to include the fact that, as mentioned above, they name opposite ends of a single scale and therefore belong to the same semantic domain.

(11) a. This thing is a turnip.
b. This thing is a platypus.

The following diagnostic properties can help us to identify scalar antonyms, and in particular to distinguish them from simple antonyms:[3]

a. Scalar antonyms typically have corresponding intermediate terms, e.g. *warm, tepid, cool* which name points somewhere between *hot* and *cold* on the temperature scale.

b. Scalar antonyms name values which are relative rather than absolute. For example, a small elephant will probably be much bigger than a big mosquito, and the temperature range we would call hot for a bath or a cup of coffee would be very cold for a blast furnace.

c. As discussed in Chapter 5, scalar antonyms are often vague.

d. Comparative forms of scalar antonyms are completely natural (*hotter, colder*, etc.), whereas they are normally much less natural with complementary antonyms, as illustrated in (8e) above.

e. The comparative forms of scalar antonyms form a converse pair (see below).[4] For example, *A is longer than B* ↔ *B is shorter than A*.

f. One member of a pair of scalar antonyms often has privileged status, or is felt to be more basic, as illustrated in (12).

[3] Adapted from Saeed (2009: 67); Cruse (1986: 204ff.).
[4] Cruse (1986: 232).

(12) a. How old/??young are you?
b. How tall/??short are you?
c. How deep/??shallow is the water?

6.2.2.3 Converse pairs

Converse pairs involve words that name an asymmetric relation between two entities, e.g. *parent-child, above-below, employer-employee.*[5] The relation must be asymmetric or there would be no pair; symmetric relations like *equal* or *resemble* are (in a sense) their own converses. The two members of a converse pair express the same basic relation, with the positions of the two arguments reversed. If we replace one member of a converse pair with the other, and also reverse the order of the arguments, as in (13–14), we produce sentences which are semantically equivalent (paraphrases).

(13) a. Michael is my advisor.
b. I am Michael's advisee.

(14) OWN(x,y) ↔ BELONG_TO(y,x)
ABOVE(x,y) ↔ BELOW(y,x)
PARENT_OF(x,y) ↔ CHILD_OF(y,x)

6.2.2.4 Reverse pairs

Two words (normally verbs) are called REVERSES if they "denote motion or change in opposite directions... [I]n addition... they should differ only in respect of directionality" (Cruse 1986: 226). Examples include *push/pull, come/go, fill/empty, heat/cool, strengthen/weaken*, etc. Cruse notes that some pairs of this type (but not all) allow an interesting use of *again*, as illustrated in (15). In these sentences, *again* does not mean that the action named by the second verb is repeated (REPETITIVE reading), but rather that the situation is restored to its original state (RESTITUTIVE reading).

(15) a. The nurse heated the instruments to sterilize them, and then cooled them *again*.
b. George filled the tank with water, and then emptied it *again*.

[5] Cruse (1986: 231) refers to such pairs as RELATIONAL OPPOSITES.

6.2.3 Hyponymy and taxonomy

When two words stand in a generic-specific relationship, we refer to the more specific term (e.g. *moose*) as the HYPONYM and to the more generic term (e.g. *mammal*) as the SUPERORDINATE or HYPERONYM. A generic-specific relationship can be defined by saying that a simple positive non-quantified statement involving the hyponym will entail the same statement involving the superordinate, as illustrated in (16). (In each example, the hyponym and superordinate term are set in boldface.) We need to specify that the statement is positive, because negation reverses the direction of the entailments (17).

(16) a. *Seabiscuit was a* ***stallion*** entails: *Seabiscuit was a* ***horse****.*
  b. *Fred* ***stole*** *my bicycle* entails: *Fred* ***took*** *my bicycle.*
  c. *John* ***assassinated*** *the Mayor* entails: *John* ***killed*** *the Mayor.*
  d. *Arthur looks like a* ***squirrel*** entails: *Arthur looks like a* ***rodent****.*
  e. *This pot is made of* ***copper*** entails: *This pot is made of* ***metal****.*

(17) a. *Seabiscuit was not a* ***horse*** entails: *Seabiscuit was not a* ***stallion****.*
  b. *John did not* ***kill*** *the Mayor* entails: *John did not* ***assassinate*** *the Mayor.*
  c. *This pot is not made of* ***metal*** entails: *This pot is not made of* ***copper****.*

TAXONOMY is a special type of hyponymy, a classifying relation. Cruse (1986: 137) suggests the following diagnostic: X is a TAXONYM of Y if it is natural to say *An X is a kind/type of Y*. Examples of taxonomy are presented in (18a–b), while the examples in (18c–d) show that other hyponyms are not fully natural in this pattern. (The word TAXONYMY is also used to refer to a generic-specific hierarchy, or system of classification.)

(18) a. *A beagle is a kind of dog.*
  b. *Gold is a type of metal.*
  c. ?*A stallion is a kind of horse.*
  d. ??*Sunday is a kind of day of the week.*

TAXONOMIC SISTERS are taxonyms which share the same superordinate term, such as *squirrel* and *mouse* which are both hyponyms of *rodent.*[6] Taxonomic

[6] More general labels for hyponyms of the same superordinate term, whether or not they are part of a taxonomy, include HYPONYMIC SISTERS and COHYPONYMS.

sisters must be incompatible, in the sense defined above; for example, a single animal cannot be both a squirrel and a mouse. But that property alone does not distinguish taxonomy from other types of hyponymy. Taxonomic sisters occur naturally in sentences like the following:

(19) a. *A beagle is a kind of dog, and so is a Great Dane.*
b. *Gold is a type of metal, and copper is another type of metal.*

Cruse notes that taxonomy often involves terms that name NATURAL KINDS (e.g., names of species, substances, etc.). Natural kind terms cannot easily be paraphrased by a superordinate term plus modifier, as many other words can (see §3 below):

(20) a. *"Stallion" means a male horse.*
b. *"Sunday" means the first day of the week.*
c. *??"Beagle" means a __ dog.*
d. *??"Gold" means a __ metal.*
e. *??"Dog" means a __ animal.*

We must remember that semantic analysis is concerned with properties of the object language, rather than scientific knowledge. The taxonomies revealed by linguistic evidence may not always match standard scientific classifications. For example, the authoritative *Kamus Dewan* (a Malay dictionary published by the national language bureau in Kuala Lumpur) gives the following definition for *labah-labah* 'spider':

(21) *labah-labah: sejenis* **serangga** *yang berkaki lapan*
'spider: a kind of **insect** that has eight legs'

This definition provides evidence that in Malay, *labah-labah* 'spider' is a taxonym of *serangga* 'insect', even though standard zoological classifications do not classify spiders as insects. (Thought question: does this mean that *serangga* is not an accurate translation equivalent for the English word *insect*?)

Similar examples can be found in many different languages. For example, in Tuvaluan (a Polynesian language), the words for 'turtle' and 'dolphin/whale' are taxonyms of *ika* 'fish'.[7] The fact that turtles, dolphins and whales are not zoologically classified as fish is irrelevant to our analysis of the lexical structure of Tuvaluan.

[7] Finegan (1999: 192).

6.2.4 Meronymy

A MERONYMY is a pair of words expressing a part-whole relationship. The word naming the part is called the meronym. For example, *hand, brain* and *eye* are all meronyms of *body*; *door, roof* and *kitchen* are all meronyms of *house*; etc.

Once again, it is important to remember that when we study patterns of meronymy, we are studying the structure of the lexicon, i.e., relations between words and not between the things named by the words. One linguistic test for identifying meronymy is the naturalness of sentences like the following: *The parts of an X include the Y, the Z, ...* (Cruse 1986: 161).

A meronym is a name for a part, and not merely a piece, of a larger whole. Human languages have many words that name parts of things, but few words that name pieces. Cruse (1986: 158–159) lists three differences between parts and pieces. First, a part has autonomous identity: many shops sell automobile parts which have never been structurally integrated into an actual car. A piece of a car, on the other hand, must have come from a complete car. (Few shops sell pieces of automobile.) Second, the boundaries of a part are motivated by some kind of natural boundary or discontinuity – potential for separation or motion relative to neighboring parts, joints (e.g. in the body), difference in material, narrowing of connection to the whole, etc. The boundaries of a piece are arbitrary. Third, a part typically has a definite function relative to the whole, whereas this is not true for pieces.

6.3 Defining words in terms of sense relations

Traditional ways of defining words depend heavily on the use of sense relations; hyponymy has played an especially important role. The classical form of a definition, going back at least to Aristotle (384–322 BC), is a kind of phrasal synonym; that is, a phrase which is mutually substitutable with the word being defined (same syntactic distribution) and equivalent or nearly equivalent in meaning.

The standard way of creating a definition is to start with the nearest superordinate term for the word being defined (traditionally called the *genus proximum*), and then add one or more modifiers (traditionally called the *differentia specifica*) which will unambiguously distinguish this word from its hyponymic sisters. So, for example, we might define *ewe* as 'an adult female sheep'; *sheep* is the superordinate term, while *adult* and *female* are modifiers which distinguish ewes from other kinds of sheep.

This structure can be further illustrated with the following well-known definition by Samuel Johnson (1709–1784), himself a famous lexicographer. It actually consists of two parallel definitions; the superordinate term in the first is *writer*, and in the second *drudge*. The remainder of each definition provides the modifiers which distinguish lexicographers from other kinds of writers or drudges.

(22) *Lexicographer*: A writer of dictionaries; a harmless drudge that busies himself in tracing the [origin], and detailing the signification of words.

Some additional examples are presented in (23). In each definition the superordinate term is bolded while the distinguishing modifiers are placed in square brackets.

(23) a. *fir* (N): a kind of **tree** [with evergreen needles].[8]
b. *rectangle* (N): a [right-angled] **quadrilateral**.[9]
c. *clean* (Adj): **free** [from dirt].[10]

However, as a number of authors have pointed out, many words cannot easily be defined in this way. In such cases, one common alternative is to define a word by using synonyms (24a–b) or antonyms (24c–d).

(24) a. *grumpy*: moodily cross; surly.[11]
b. *sad*: affected with or expressive of grief or unhappiness.[12]
c. *free*: not controlled by obligation or the will of another; not bound, fastened, or attached.[13]
d. *pure*: not mixed or adulterated with any other substance or material.[14]

Another common type of definition is the EXTENSIONAL definition. This definition spells out the denotation of the word rather than its sense as in a normal definition. This type is illustrated in (25).

(25) Definitions from Merriam-Webster on-line dictionary:

[8] Hartmann & James (1998: 62).
[9] Svensén (2009: 219).
[10] Svensén (2009: 219).
[11] http://www.merriam-webster.com/dictionary/
[12] http://www.merriam-webster.com/dictionary/
[13] http://www.thefreedictionary.com/free
[14] http://oxforddictionaries.com/us/definition/american_english/pure

a. *New England*: the NE United States comprising the states of Maine, New Hampshire, Vermont, Massachusetts, Rhode Island, & Connecticut

b. *cat*: any of a family (Felidae) of carnivorous, usually solitary and nocturnal, mammals (as the domestic cat, lion, tiger, leopard, jaguar, cougar, wildcat, lynx, and cheetah)

Some newer dictionaries, notably the COBUILD dictionary, make use of full sentence definitions rather than phrasal synonyms, as illustrated in (26).

(26) confidential: Information that is **confidential** is meant to be kept secret or private.[15]

6.4 Conclusion

In this chapter we have mentioned only the most commonly used sense relations (some authors have found it helpful to refer to dozens of others). We have illustrated various diagnostic tests for identifying sense relations, many of them involving entailment or other meaning relations between sentences. Studying these sense relations provides a useful tool for probing the meaning of a word, and for constructing dictionary definitions of words.

Further reading

Cruse (1986: chapters 4–12) offers a detailed discussion of each of the sense relations mentioned in this chapter. Cann (2011) provides a helpful overview of the subject.

[15] COBUILD dictionary, 3rd edition (2001); cited in Rundell (2006).

Discussion exercises

Identify the meaning relations for the following pairs of words, and provide linguistic evidence that supports your identification:

a.	*sharp*	*dull*		e.	*hyponym*	*hyperonym*
b.	*finite*	*infinite*		f.	*silver*	*metal*
c.	*two*	*too*		g.	*insert*	*extract*
d.	*arm*	*leg*				

Homework exercises

Antonyms.[a] Below is a list of incompatible pairs. (i) Classify each pair into one of the following types of relation: SIMPLE ANTONYMS, GRADABLE ANTONYMS, REVERSES, CONVERSES, or TAXONOMIC SISTERS. (ii) For each pair, provide at least one type of linguistic evidence (e.g. example sentences) that supports your decision, and where possible mention other types of evidence that would lend additional support.

a.	*legal*	*illegal*		e.	*lend to*	*borrow from*
b.	*fat*	*thin*		f.	*lucky*	*unlucky*
c.	*raise*	*lower*		g.	*married*	*unmarried*
d.	*wine*	*beer*				

[a] Adapted from Saeed (2009: 82), ex. 3.4.

7 Components of lexical meaning

7.1 Introduction

The traditional model of writing definitions for words, which we discussed in Chapter 6, seems to assume that word meanings can (in many cases) be broken down into smaller elements of meaning.[1] For example, we defined *ewe* as 'an adult female sheep', which seems to suggest that the meanings of the words *sheep*, *adult*, and *female* are included in the meaning of *ewe*.[2] In fact, if the phrase 'adult female sheep' is really a synonym for *ewe*, one might say that the meaning of *ewe* is simply the combination of the meanings of *sheep*, *adult*, and *female*. Another way to express this intuition is to say that the meanings of *sheep*, *adult*, and *female* are COMPONENTS of the meaning of *ewe*.

In this chapter we introduce some basic ideas about how to identify and represent a word's components of meaning. Most components of meaning can be viewed as entailments or presuppositions which the word contributes to the meaning of a sentence in which it occurs. We discuss lexical entailments in §7.2 and SELECTIONAL RESTRICTIONS in §7.3. Selectional restrictions are constraints on word combinations which rule out collocations such as *#Assassinate that cockroach!* or *#This cabbage is nervous*, and we will treat them as a type of presupposition.

In §7.4 we summarize one influential approach to word meanings, in which components of meaning were represented as binary distinctive features. We will briefly discuss the advantages and limitations of this approach, which is no longer widely used. In §7.5 we introduce some of the foundational work on the meanings of verbs.

---

[1]Engelberg (2011: 126).

[2]Svensén (2009: 218), in his *Handbook of Lexicography*, identifies such intensional definitions as "the classic type of definition". He explicitly defines intension (i.e. sense) in terms of components of meaning: "The term INTENSION denotes the content of the concept, which can be defined as the combination of the distinctive features comprised by the concept." Svensén seems to have in mind the representation of components of word meaning as binary distinctive features, the approach discussed in §7.4 below.

Our study of the components of word meanings will primarily be based on evidence from sentence meanings, for reasons discussed in earlier chapters. We focus here on descriptive meaning. Of course, words can also convey various kinds of expressive (or AFFECTIVE) meaning, signaling varying degrees of politeness, intimacy, formality, vulgarity, speaker's attitudes, etc., but we will not attempt to deal with these issues in the current chapter.

7.2 Lexical entailments

When people talk about the meaning of one word (e.g. *sheep*) being "part of", or "contained in", the meaning of some other word (e.g. *ewe*), they are generally describing a lexical entailment. Strictly speaking, of course, entailment is a meaning relation between propositions or sentences, not words. When we speak of "lexical entailments", we mean that the meaning relation between two words creates an entailment relation between sentences that contain those words. This is illustrated in (1–4). In each pair of sentences, the (a) sentence entails the (b) sentence because the meaning of the italicized word in the (b) sentence is part of, or is contained in, the meaning of the italicized word in the (a) sentence. We can say that *ewe* lexically entails *sheep*, *assassinate* lexically entails *kill*, etc.

(1) a. John *assassinated* the Mayor.
  b. John *killed* the Mayor.

(2) a. John is a *bachelor*.
  b. John is *unmarried*.

(3) a. John *stole* my bicycle.
  b. John *took* my bicycle.

(4) a. Fido is a *dog*.
  b. Fido is an *animal*.

These intuitive judgments about lexical entailments can be supported by additional linguistic evidence. Speakers of English feel sentences like (5), which explicitly describe the entailment relation, to be natural. Sentences like (6), however, which seem to cast doubt on the entailment relation, are unnatural or incoherent:[3]

[3]Examples from Cruse (1986: 14).

(5) a. It can't possibly be a dog and not an animal.
 b. It's a dog and therefore it's an animal.
 c. If it's not an animal, then it follows that it's not a dog.

(6) a. #It's not an animal, but it's just possible that it's a dog.
 b. #It's a dog, so it might be an animal.

Cruse (1986: 12) mentions several additional tests for entailments which can be applied here, including the following:

(7) Denying the entailed component leads to contradiction:

 a. #John killed the Mayor but the Mayor did not die.
 b. #It's a dog but it's not an animal.
 c. #John is a bachelor but he is happily married.
 d. #The child fell upwards.

(8) Asserting the entailed component leads to unnatural redundancy (or PLEONASM):

 a. #It's a dog and it's an animal.
 b. ??Kick it with one of your feet. (Cruse 1986: 12)
 c. ??He was murdered illegally. (Cruse 1986: 12)

7.3 Selectional restrictions

In addition to lexical entailments, another important aspect of word meanings has to do with constraints on specific word combinations. These constraints are referred to as SELECTIONAL RESTRICTIONS. The sentences in (9) all seem quite odd, not really acceptable except as a kind of joke, because they violate selectional restrictions.

(9) a. #This sausage doesn't appreciate Mozart.
 b. #John drank his sandwich and took a big bite out of his coffee.
 c. #Susan folded/perforated/caramelized her reputation.
 d. #Your exam results are sleeping.
 e. #The square root of oatmeal is Houston.
 f. *My Feet Are Smiling* (title of guitarist Leo Kottke's sixth album)

g. "They've a temper, some of them — particularly verbs: they're the proudest..." [Humpty Dumpty, in *Through the Looking Glass*]

As we noted in (7), denying an entailment leads to a contradiction. In contrast, violations of selectional restrictions like those in (9) lead to dissonance rather than contradiction.[4] Chomsky (1965: 95) proposed that selectional restrictions were triggered by syntactic properties of words, but McCawley, Lakoff and other authors have argued that they derive from word meanings. If they were purely syntactic, they should hold even in contexts like those in (10). The fact that these sentences are acceptable suggests that the constraints are semantic rather than syntactic in nature.

(10) a. He's become irrational – he thinks his exam results are sleeping.
b. You can't say that John drank his sandwich.

The lexical entailments of words which occur in questions or negated statements can often be denied without contradiction, as illustrated in (11). Selectional restrictions, in contrast, hold even in questions, negative statements, and other non-assertive environments (12). This suggests that they are a special type of presupposition, and we will assume that this is the case.[5]

(11) a. John didn't kill the Mayor; the Mayor is not even dead.
b. Is that a dog, or even an animal?
c. John is not a bachelor, he is happily married.
d. The snowflake did not fall, it floated upwards.

(12) a. #Did John drink his sandwich?
b. #John didn't drink his sandwich; maybe he doesn't like liverwurst.
c. #Are your exam results sleeping?
d. #My feet aren't smiling.

Selectional restrictions are part of the meanings of specific words; that is, they are linguistic in nature, rather than simply facts about the world. Cruse (1986: 21) points out that hearers typically express astonishment or disbelief on hearing a

[4] Such violations are sometimes called "category mistakes", or "sortal errors", especially in philosophical literature.

[5] The idea that selectional restrictions can be treated as lexical presuppositions was apparently first proposed by Fillmore, but was first published by McCawley (1968).

statement that is improbable, given what we know about the world (13–14). This is quite different from hearers' reactions to violations of selectional restrictions like those in (9). Those sentences are linguistically unacceptable, and hearers are more likely to respond, "You can't say that."

(13) A: Our kitten drank a bottle of claret.
B: No! Really? (Cruse 1986: 21)

(14) a. A: I know an old woman who swallowed a goat/cow/bulldozer.
B: That's impossible!
b. #I know an old woman who swallowed a participle/prime number.

It is fairly common for words with the same basic entailments to differ with respect to their selectional restrictions. German has two words corresponding to the English word *eat*: *essen* for people and *fressen* for animals. (One might use *fressen* to insult or tease someone – basically saying they eat like an animal.) In a Kimaragang[6] version of the Christmas story, the translator used the word *paalansayad* to render the phrase which is expressed in the King James Bible as *great with child.* This word correctly expresses the idea that Mary was in a very advanced stage of pregnancy when she arrived in Bethlehem; but another term had to be found when someone pointed out that *paalansayad* is normally used only for water buffalo and certain other kinds of livestock.

It is sometimes helpful to distinguish selectional restrictions (a type of presupposition triggered by specific words, as discussed above) from COLLOCATIONAL RESTRICTIONS.[7] Collocational restrictions are conventionalized patterns of combining two or more words. They reflect common ways of speaking, or "normal" usage, within the speech community. Some examples of collocational restrictions are presented in (15).

(15) a. John died/passed away/kicked the bucket.
b. My prize rose bush died/#passed away/#kicked the bucket.
c. When we're feeling under the weather, most of us welcome a big/#large hug.

[6] An Austronesian language of northern Borneo.

[7] We follow the terminology of Cruse (1986: 107, 279–280) here. Not everyone makes this distinction. In some work on translation principles, e.g. Beekman & Callow (1974), a violation of either type is referred to as a COLLOCATIONAL CLASH.

d. He is (stark) raving mad/#crazy.[8]

e. dirty/#unclean joke

f. unclean/#dirty spirit

Violations of a collocational restriction are felt to be odd or unnatural, but they can typically be repaired by replacing one of the words with a synonym, suggesting that collocational restrictions are not, strictly speaking, due to lexical meaning *per se*.

7.4 Componential analysis

Many different theories have been proposed for representing components of lexical meaning. All of them aim to develop a formal representation of meaning components which will allow us to account for semantic properties of words, such as their sense relations, and perhaps some syntactic properties as well.

One very influential approach during the middle of the 20th century was to treat word meanings as bundles of distinctive semantic features, in much the same way that phonemes are defined in terms of distinctive phonetic/phonological features.[9] This approach is sometimes referred to as COMPONENTIAL ANALYSIS of meaning. Some of the motivation for this approach can be seen in the following famous example from Hjelmslev (1953[1943]). The example makes it clear that the feature of gender is an aspect of meaning that distinguishes many pairs of lexical items within certain semantic domains. If we were to ignore this fact and just treat each word's meaning as an ATOM (i.e., an unanalyzable unit), we would be missing a significant generalization.

(16)

	horse	human	child	sheep
"he"	stallion	man	boy	ram
"she"	mare	woman	girl	ewe

Features like gender and adulthood are binary, and so lend themselves to representation in either tree or matrix format, as illustrated in (17). Notice that in addition to the values + and −, features may be unspecified (represented by ∅ in the matrix). For example, the word *foal* is unspecified for gender, and the word *horse* is unspecified for both age and gender.

[8] Jim Roberts, p.c.

[9] One early example of this approach is found in Nida (1951).

(17) Binary feature analysis for horse terms:

	[adult]	[male]
horse	∅	∅
stallion	+	+
mare	+	–
foal	–	∅
colt	–	+
filly	–	–

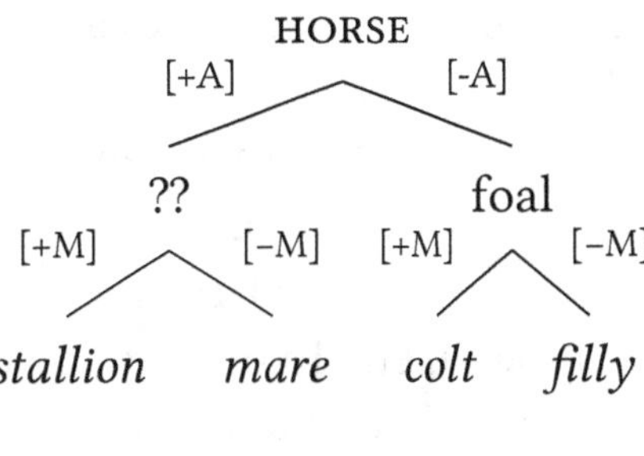

(18) Binary feature analysis for human terms:

	[adult]	[male]
man_1/human	∅	∅
man_2	+	+
woman	+	–
child	–	∅
boy	–	+
girl	–	–

Componential analysis provides neat explanations for some sense relations. Synonymous senses can be represented as pairs that share all the same components of meaning. Complementary pairs are perfectly modeled by binary features: the two elements differ only in the polarity for one feature, e.g. [+/– alive], [+/– awake], [+/– possible], [+/– legal], etc. The semantic components of a hyperonym (e.g. *child* [+human, –adult]) are a proper subset of the semantic components of its hyponyms (e.g. *boy* [+human, –adult, +male]); *girl* [+human, –adult, –male])). In other words, each hyponym contains all the semantic components of the hyperonym plus at least one more; and these "extra" components are the ones that distinguish the meanings of taxonomic sisters. Reverse pairs might be treated in a way somewhat similar to complementary pairs; they differ in precisely one component of meaning, typically a direction, with the dimension and manner of motion and the reference point held steady.

On the other hand, it is not so easy to define gradable antonyms, converse pairs, or meronyms in this way. Moreover, while many of the benefits of this kind of componential analysis are shared by other approaches, a number of problems have been pointed out which are specific to the binary feature approach.[10]

First, there are many lexical distinctions which do not seem to be easily expressible in terms of binary features, at least not in any plausible way. Species names, for example, are a well-known challenge to this approach. What features distinguish members of the cat family (*lion, tiger, leopard, jaguar, cougar, wildcat, lynx, cheetah*, etc.) from each other? Similar issues arise with color terms, types of metal, etc. In order to deal with such cases, it seems that the number of features would need to be almost as great as the number of lexical items.

Second, it is not clear how to use simple binary features to represent the meanings of two-place predicates, such as *recognize, offend, mother (of)*, etc. The word *recognize* entails a change of state in the first argument, while the word *offend* entails a change of state in the second argument. A simple feature matrix like those above cannot specify which argument a particular feature applies to.

Third, some word meanings cannot be adequately represented as an unordered bundle of features, whether binary or not. For example, many studies have been done concerning the semantic components of kinship terms in various languages. This is one domain in which the components need to be ordered or structured in some way; 'mother's brother's spouse' (one sense of *aunt* in English) would probably not, in most languages, be called by the same term as 'spouse's mother's brother' (no English term available). Verb meanings also seem to require structured components. For example, 'want to cause to die' (part of the meaning of *murderous*) is quite different from 'cause to want to die' (similar to one sense of *mortify*).

Fourth, we need to ask how many features would be needed to describe the entire lexicon of a single language? Binary feature analysis can be very efficient within certain restricted semantic domains, but when we try to compare a wider range of words, it is not clear that the inventory of features could be much smaller than the lexicon itself.

7.5 Verb meanings

Much of the recent research on lexical semantics has focused on verb meanings. One reason for this special interest in verbs is the fact that verb meanings have a direct influence on syntactic structure, and so syntactic evidence can be used to supplement traditional semantic methods.

[10] The following discussion is based on Engelberg (2011: 129–130); Lyons (1977: 317ff.).

A classic paper by Charles Fillmore (1970) distinguishes two classes of transitive verbs in English: "surface contact" verbs (e.g., *hit, slap, strike, bump, stroke*) vs. "change of state" verbs (e.g., *break, bend, fold, shatter, crack*). Fillmore shows that the members of each class share certain syntactic and semantic properties which distinguish them from members of the other class. He further argues that the correlation between these syntactic and semantic properties supports a view of lexical semantics under which the meaning of a verb is made up of two kinds of elements: (a) systematic components of meaning that are shared by an entire class; and (b) idiosyncratic components that are specific to the individual root. Only the former are assumed to have syntactic effects. This basic insight has been foundational for a large body of subsequent work in the area of verbal semantics.

Fillmore begins by using syntactic criteria to distinguish the two classes, which we will refer to for convenience as the *hit* class vs. the *break* class. Subsequent research has identified additional criteria for making this distinction. One of the best-known tests is the CAUSATIVE-INCHOATIVE alternation.[11] *Break* verbs generally exhibit systematic polysemy between a transitive and an intransitive sense. The intransitive sense has an INCHOATIVE (change of state) meaning while the transitive sense has a causative meaning (19). As illustrated in (20), *hit* verbs do not permit this alternation, and often lack intransitive senses altogether.

(19) a. John broke the window (with a rock).
     b. The window broke.

(20) a. John hit the tree (with a stick).
     b. * The tree hit.

Additional tests include "body-part possessor ascension" (21–22),[12] the CONATIVE alternation (23–24),[13] and the MIDDLE alternation (25).[14] Each of these tests demonstrates a difference between the two classes in terms of the potential syntactic functions (subject, direct object, oblique argument, or unexpressed) of the agent and patient.

(21) a. I {hit/slapped/struck} his leg.
     b. I {hit/slapped/struck} him on the leg.

[11]Fillmore (1970: 122–123).
[12]Fillmore (1970: 126).
[13]Guerssel et al. (1985); Levin (1993).
[14]Fillmore (1977); Hale & Keyser (1987); Levin (1993).

(22) a. I {broke/bent/shattered} his leg.
b. * I {broke/bent/shattered} him on the leg.

(23) a. Mary hit the piñata.
b. Mary hit at the piñata.
c. I slapped the mosquito.
d. I slapped at the mosquito.

(24) a. Mary broke the piñata.
b. * Mary broke at the piñata.
c. I cracked the mirror.
d. * I cracked at the mirror.

(25) a. This glass breaks easily.
b. * This fence hits easily.

These various syntactic tests (and others not mentioned here) show a high degree of CONVERGENCE; that is, the class of *break* verbs identified by any one test matches very closely the class of *break* verbs identified by the other tests. This convergence strongly supports the claim that the members of each class share certain properties in common. Fillmore (1970: 125) suggests that these shared properties are semantic components: "change of state" in the case of the *break* verbs and "surface contact" in the case of the *hit* verbs. Crucially, he provides independent semantic evidence for this claim, specifically evidence that *break* verbs do but *hit* verbs do not entail a change of state (26).[15] Sentence (26a) is linguistically acceptable, although surprising based on our knowledge of the world, while (26b) is a contradiction. Example (27) presents similar evidence for the entailment of "surface contact" in the case of the *hit* verbs.

(26) a. I *hit* the window with a hammer; it didn't faze the window, but the hammer shattered.
b. * I *broke* the window with a hammer; it didn't faze the window, but the hammer shattered.

(27) a. * I *hit* the window without touching it.
b. I *broke* the window without touching it.

[15] Fillmore (1970: 125).

Without this kind of direct semantic evidence, there is a great danger of falling into circular reasoning, e.g.: *break* verbs permit the causative-inchoative alternation because they contain the component "change of state", and we know they contain the component "change of state" because they permit the causative-inchoative alternation. As many linguists have learned to our sorrow, it is all too easy to fall into this kind of trap.

While *break* verbs (e.g., *break, bend, fold, shatter, crack*) all share the "change of state" component, they do not all mean the same thing. Each of these verbs has aspects of meaning which distinguish it from all the other members of the class, such as the specific nature of the change and selectional restrictions on the object/patient. Fillmore (1970: 131) suggests that only the shared component of meaning has syntactic consequences; the idiosyncratic aspects of meaning that distinguish one *break* verb from another do not affect the grammatical realization of arguments.

Levin (1993) builds on and extends Fillmore's study of verb classes in English. In her introduction she compares the *break* and *hit* verbs with two additional classes, *touch* verbs (*touch, pat, stroke, tickle,* etc.) and *cut* verbs (*cut, hack, saw, scratch, slash,* etc.). Using just three of the diagnostic tests discussed above, she shows that each of these classes has a distinctive pattern of syntactic behavior, as summarized in (28). The examples in (29–31) illustrate the behavior of *touch* verbs and *cut* verbs.[16]

(28) English transitive verb classes[17]

	touch verbs	*hit* verbs	*cut* verbs	*break* verbs
body-part possessor ascension	YES	YES	YES	NO
conative alternation	NO	YES	YES	NO
middle	NO	NO	YES	YES

(29) BODY-PART POSSESSOR ASCENSION:

a. I touched Bill's shoulder.

b. I touched Bill on the shoulder.

[16] Examples adapted from Levin (1993: 6–7).

[17] Levin (1993: 8)

c. I cut Bill's arm.
d. I cut Bill on the arm.

(30) CONATIVE ALTERNATION:

a. Terry touched the cat.
b. * Terry touched at the cat.
c. Margaret cut the rope.
d. Margaret cut at the rope.

(31) MIDDLE:

a. The bread cuts easily.
b. * Cats touch easily.

Levin proposes the following explanation for these observations. Body-part possessor ascension is possible only for verb classes which share the surface contact component of meaning. The conative alternation is possible only for verb classes whose meanings include both contact and motion. The middle construction is possible only for transitive verb classes whose meanings include a caused change of state. The four classes pattern differently with respect to these tests because each of the four has a distinctive set of meaning components, as summarized in (32).

(32) Shared components of meaning[18]

touch verbs	CONTACT
hit verbs	MOTION, CONTACT
cut verbs	MOTION, CONTACT, CHANGE
break verbs	CHANGE

These verb classes have been found to be grammatically relevant in other languages as well. Levin (2015) cites the following examples: DeLancey (1995; 2000) on Lhasa Tibetan; Guerssel et al. (1985) on Berber, Warlpiri, and Winnebago; Kroeger (2010) on Kimaragang Dusun; Vogel (2005) on Jarawara.

In the remainder of her book, Levin (1993) identifies 192 classes of English verbs, using 79 diagnostic patterns of DIATHESIS alternations (changes in the way that arguments are expressed syntactically). She shows that these verb classes are supported by a very impressive body of evidence. However, she states that establishing these classes is only a means to an end; the real goal is to understand meaning components:

[18]Adapted from Saeed (2009: 268).

> [T]here is a sense in which the notion of verb class is an artificial construct. Verb classes arise because a set of verbs with one or more shared meaning components show similar behavior... The important theoretical construct is the notion of meaning component, not the notion of verb class.[19]

Like Fillmore, Levin argues that not all meaning components are grammatically relevant, but only those which define class membership. The aspects of meaning that distinguish one verb from another within the same class (e.g. *punch* vs. *slap*) are idiosyncratic, and do not affect syntactic behavior. Evidence from diathesis alternations can help us determine the systematic, class-defining meaning components, but will not provide an analysis for the idiosyncratic aspects of the meaning of a particular verb.

As noted above, verb meanings cannot be represented as an unordered bundle of components, but must be structured in some way. One popular method, referred to as LEXICAL DECOMPOSITION, is illustrated in (33). This formula was proposed by Rappaport Hovav & Levin (1998: 109) as a partial representation of the systematic components of meaning for verbs like *break*. In this formula, *x* represents the agent and *y* the patient. The idiosyncratic aspects of meaning for a particular verb root would be associated with the STATE predicate (e.g. *broken*, *split*, etc.).

(33) [[x ACT] CAUSE [BECOME [y <STATE>]]]

7.6 Conclusion

The idea that verb meanings may consist of two distinct parts, a systematic, class-defining part vs. an idiosyncratic, verb-specific part, is similar to proposals that have been made for content words in general. Fillmore (1970: 131) notes that a very similar idea is found in the general theory of word meaning proposed by Katz & Fodor (1963). These authors suggest that word meanings are made up of systematic components of meaning, which they refer to as SEMANTIC MARKERS, plus an idiosyncratic residue which they refer to as the DISTINGUISHER.

This proposal is controversial, but there do seem to be some good reasons to distinguish systematic vs. idiosyncratic aspects of meaning. As we have seen, Fillmore and Levin demonstrate that certain rules of syntax are sensitive to some components of meaning but not others, and that the grammatically relevant components are shared by whole classes of verbs. Additional motivation for making

[19] Levin (1993: 9–10).

this distinction comes from the existence of systematic polysemy. It seems logical to expect that rules of systematic polysemy must be stated in terms of systematic aspects of meaning.

However, there is no general consensus as to what the systematic aspects of meaning are, or how they should be represented.[20] Some scholars even deny that components of meaning exist, arguing that word meanings are ATOMS, in the sense defined in §7.4.[21] Under this "atomic" view of word meanings, lexical entailments might be expressed in the form of MEANING POSTULATES like the following:

(34) $\forall x[\text{STALLION}(x) \rightarrow \text{MALE}(x)]$
$\forall x[\text{BACHELOR}(x) \rightarrow \neg\text{MARRIED}(x)]$

Many scholars do believe that word meanings are built up in some way from smaller elements of meaning. However, a great deal of work remains to be done in determining what those smaller elements are, and how they are combined.

Further reading

Engelberg (2011) provides a good overview of the various approaches to and controversies about lexical decomposition and componential analysis. Lyons (1977: 317ff.) discusses some of the problems with the binary feature approach to componential analysis. The first chapter of Levin (1993) gives a very good introduction to the Fillmore-type analysis of verb classes and what they can tell us about verb meanings, and Levin (2015) presents an updated cross-linguistic survey of the topic.

[20] For one influential proposal, see Pustejovsky (1995).

[21] E.g. Fodor (1975) and subsequent work.

Discussion exercises

A. Componential analysis of meaning. Construct a table of semantic components, represented as binary features, for each of the following sets of words:

1. *bachelor, spinster, widow, widower, husband, wife, boy, girl*
2. *walk, run, march, limp, stroll*
3. *cup, glass, mug, tumbler, chalice, goblet, stein*

B. Locative-alternation ("spray-load") verbs.[a] Based on the following examples, fill in the table below to show which verbs allow the goal or location argument to be expressed as direct object and which verbs allow the displaced theme argument to be expressed as direct object. Try to formulate an analysis in terms of meaning components to account for the patterns you find in the data.

(1) a. Jack sprayed paint on the wall.
    b. Jack sprayed the wall with paint.

(2) a. Bill loaded the cart with apples.
    b. Bill loaded the apples onto the cart.

(3) a. William filled his mug with guava juice.
    b. * William filled guava juice into his mug.

(4) a. *William poured his mug with guava juice.
    b. William poured guava juice into his mug.

(5) a. Ailbhe pushed the bicycle into the shed.
    b. #Ailbhe pushed the shed with the bicycle. [different meaning]

(6) a. Harvey pulled me onto the stage.
    b. #Harvey pulled the stage with me. [different meaning]

(7) a. Libby coated the chicken with oil.
    b. ?*Libby coated the oil onto the chicken.

(8) a. Mike covered the ceiling with paint.
b. * Mike covered the paint onto the ceiling.

Verb	Theme = object	Location = object
fill	no	yes
load		
spray		
cover		
coat		
pour		
push		
pull		

[a]Adapted from Saeed (2009), ch. 9.

Homework exercises

Causative/ inchoative alternation.[a] Rappaport Hovav & Levin (1998: 102–105) propose a semantic explanation for why some change of state verbs participate in the CAUSATIVE/ INCHOATIVE alternation (*John broke the window* vs. *the window broke*), while others do not. They suggest that verbs which name events that must involve an animate, intentional and volitional agent never appear in the intransitive form. This hypothesis predicts that only (but not necessarily all) verbs which allow an inanimate force as subject should participate in the alternation, as illustrated in (a–b). Your tasks: (i) construct examples like those in (a–b) to test this prediction for the following verbs, and explain what your examples show us about the hypothesis: *melt, write, shrink, destroy*; (ii) Use Levin & Rappaport Hovav's hypothesis to explain the contrasts in sentences (c–d).

a. A terrorist/*tornado assassinated the governor.
   *The governor assassinated.

b. The storm broke all the windows in my office.
   All the windows in my office broke.

c. The sky/*table cleared.

d. Paul's window/*contract/*promise broke.

[a] Adapted from Saeed (2009: 298), ex. 9.3.

Unit III

Implicature

8 Grice's theory of Implicature

8.1 Sometimes we mean more than we say

The story in (1) concerns a ship's captain and his first mate (second in command):

(1) **The Story of the Mate and the Captain** (Meibauer 2005, adapted from Posner 1980)

> A captain and his mate have a long-term quarrel. The mate drinks more rum than is good for him, and the captain is determined not to tolerate this behaviour any longer. When the mate is drunk again, the captain writes in the logbook: "Today, 11th October, the mate is drunk." When the mate reads this entry during his next watch, he gets angry. Then, after a short moment of reflection, he writes in the logbook: "Today, 14th October, the captain is not drunk."

The mate's log entry communicates something bad and false (namely that the captain is frequently or habitually drunk) by saying something good and true (the captain is not drunk today). It provides a striking example of how widely SENTENCE MEANING (the semantic content of the sentence) may differ from UTTERANCE MEANING. Recall that we defined utterance meaning as "the totality of what the speaker intends to convey by making an utterance;"[1] so utterance meaning includes the semantic content plus any pragmatic meaning created by the use of the sentence in a specific context.

In this chapter and the next we will explore the question of how this kind of context-dependent meaning arises. Our discussion in this chapter will focus primarily on the ground-breaking work on this topic by the philosopher H. Paul Grice. Grice referred to the kind of inference illustrated in (1) as a CONVERSATIONAL IMPLICATURE, and suggested that such inferences arise when there is a real or apparent violation of our shared default expectations about how conversations work.

In §8.2 we introduce the concept of conversational implicature, and in §8.3 we summarize the default expectations about conversation which Grice proposed

[1] Cruse (2000: 27).

as a way of explaining these implicatures. In §8.4 we distinguish two different types of conversational implicature, and mention briefly a different kind of inference which Grice referred to as CONVENTIONAL IMPLICATURE. In §8.5–§8.6 we discuss various diagnostic properties of conversational implicatures, and talk about how to distinguish conversational implicatures from entailments and presuppositions.

8.2 Conversational implicatures

Let us begin by considering the simple conversation in (2):

(2) **Arthur**: Can you tell me where the post office is?
Bill: I'm a stranger here myself.

As a reply to Arthur's request for directions, Bill's statement is clearly intended to mean 'No, I cannot.' But the sentence meaning, or semantic content, of Bill's statement does not contain or entail this intended meaning. The statement conveys the intended meaning only in response to that specific question. In a different kind of context, such as the one in (3), it could be intended to convey a very different meaning: willingness to engage in conversation on a wider range of topics, or at least sympathy for Arthur's situation.

(3) **Arthur**: I've just moved to this town, and so far I'm finding it pretty tedious; I haven't met a single person who is willing to talk about anything except next week's local elections.
Bill: I'm a stranger here myself.

When the same sentence is used in two different contexts, these are two distinct utterances which may have different utterance meanings. But since the sentence meaning is identical, the difference in utterance meaning must be due to pragmatic inferences induced by the different contexts. As mentioned above, Grice referred to the kind of pragmatic inference illustrated in these examples as CONVERSATIONAL IMPLICATURE. Examples (2–3) illustrate the following characteristics of conversational implicatures:

1. The implicature is different from the literal sentence meaning; in Grice's terms, what is implicated is different from "what is said".
2. Nevertheless, the speaker intends for the hearer to understand both the sentence meaning and the implicature; and for the hearer to be aware that the speaker intends this.

3. Conversational implicatures are context-dependent, as discussed above.

4. Conversational implicatures are often unmistakable, but they are not "inevitable", i.e. they are not logically necessary. In the context of (2), for example, Bill's statement is clearly intended as a negative reply; but it would not be logically inconsistent for Bill to continue as in (4). In Grice's terms we say that conversational implicatures are DEFEASIBLE, meaning that they can be cancelled or blocked when additional information is provided.

(4) **Arthur**: Can you tell me where the post office is?
Bill: I'm a stranger here myself; but it happens that I have just come from the post office, so I think I can help you.

Conversational implicatures are not something strange and exotic; they turn out to be extremely common in everyday language use. Once we become aware of them, we begin to find them everywhere. They are an indispensable part of the system we use to communicate with each other.

8.3 Grice's Maxims of Conversation

The connection between what is said and what is implicated, taking context into account, cannot be arbitrary. It must be rule-governed to a significant degree, otherwise the speaker could not expect the hearer to reliably understand the intended meaning.

Grice was not only the first scholar to describe the characteristic features of implicatures, but also the first to propose a systematic explanation for how they work. Grice's lecture series at Harvard University in 1967, where he laid out his analysis of implicatures, triggered an explosion of interest in and research about this topic. It is sometimes cited as the birth date of Pragmatics as a separate field of study. Of course a number of authors have proposed revisions and expansions to Grice's model, and we look briefly at some of these in the next chapter; but his model remains the starting point for much current work and is the model that we will focus on in this chapter.

Grice's fundamental insight was that conversation is a cooperative activity. In order to carry on an intelligible conversation, each party must assume that the other is trying to participate in a meaningful way. This is true even if the speakers involved are debating or quarreling; they are still trying to carry on a conversation. Grice proposed that there are certain default assumptions about how conversation works. He stated these in the form of a general COOPERATIVE PRINCIPLE (5) and several specific sub-principles which he labeled "maxims" (6):

(5) **The Cooperative Principle** (Grice 1975: 45)
Make your conversational contribution such as is required, at the stage at which it occurs, by the accepted purpose or direction of the talk exchange in which you are engaged.

(6) **The Maxims of Conversation** (Grice 1975: 45–46)
QUALITY: Try to make your contribution one that is true.
1. Do not say what you believe to be false.
2. Do not say that for which you lack adequate evidence.

QUANTITY:
1. Make your contribution as informative as is required (for the current purposes of the exchange).
2. Do not make your contribution more informative than is required.

RELATION (or RELEVANCE): Be relevant.

MANNER: Be perspicuous.
1. Avoid obscurity of expression.
2. Avoid ambiguity.
3. Be brief (avoid unnecessary prolixity).
4. Be orderly.

It is important to remember that Grice did not propose the Cooperative Principle as a code of conduct, which speakers have a moral obligation to obey. A speaker may communicate either by obeying the maxims or by breaking them, as long as the hearer is able to recognize which strategy is being employed. The Cooperative Principle is a kind of background assumption: what is necessary in order to make rational conversation possible is not for the speaker to follow the principle slavishly, but for speaker and hearer to share a common awareness that it exists.

We might draw an analogy with radio waves. Radio signals start with a "carrier wave" having a specific, constant frequency and amplitude. The informative part of the signal, e.g. the audio frequency wave that represents the music, news report, or football match being broadcast, is superimposed as variation in the frequency (for FM) or amplitude (for AM) of the carrier wave. The complex wave form which results is transmitted to receivers, where the intended signal is recovered by "subtracting" the carrier wave. In order for the correct signal to be recovered, the receiver must know the frequency and amplitude of the carrier wave.

Furthermore, the receiver must assume that variations from this base frequency and amplitude are intended to be meaningful, and are not merely interference due to lightning, sunspots, or the neighbors' electrical gadgets.

The analogue of the wave form for pragmatic inferences is the sentence meaning, i.e. the literal semantic content of the utterance. The Cooperative Principle and maxims specify the default frequency and amplitude of the carrier wave. When a speaker appears to violate one of the maxims, a pragmatic inference is created; but this is only possible if the hearer assumes that the speaker is actually being cooperative, and thus the apparent violations are intended to be meaningful.

For example, Bill's reply to Arthur's request for directions to the post office in (2) appears to violate the maxim of relevance. Arthur might interpret the reply as follows: "Bill's statement that he is a stranger here has nothing to do with the location of the post office. Bill seems to be violating the maxim of relevance, but I assume that he is trying to participate in a rational conversation; so he must actually be observing the conversational maxims, or at least the Cooperative Principle. I know that strangers in a town typically do not know where most things are located. I believe that Bill knows this as well, and would expect me to understand that his being a stranger makes it unlikely that he can provide the information I am requesting. If his reply is intended to mean 'No, I cannot,' then it is actually relevant and there is no violation. So in order to maintain the assumption that Bill is observing the Cooperative Principle, I must assume that this is what he intends to communicate."

Of course, the sentence meaning is not just a means to trigger implicatures; it is itself part of the meaning which is being communicated. Utterance meaning is composed of the sentence meaning plus any pragmatic inference created by the specific context of use. Grice's model is intended to explain the pragmatic part of the meaning. In example (2), the answer to Arthur's literal yes-no question is conveyed by pragmatic inference, while the sentence meaning explains the reason for this answer, and so is felt to be more polite than a blunt "No" would be.

Grice described several specific patterns of reasoning which commonly give rise to conversational implicatures. First, there are cases in which there is an apparent violation, but no maxim is actually violated. Our analysis of example (2) was of this type. Bill's statement *I am a stranger here myself* was an apparent violation of the maxim of relevance, but the implicature that it triggered actually was relevant; so there was no real violation. Two of Grice's classic examples of this type are shown in (7–8). In both cases the second speaker's reply is an apparent violation of the maxim of relevance, but it triggers an implicature that is relevant (*You can buy petrol there* in (7), *Maybe he has a girlfriend in New York* in (8)).[2]

(7) A: I am out of petrol [=gasoline].
B: There is a garage [=service station] around the corner.

(8) A: Smith doesn't seem to have a girlfriend these days.
B: He has been paying a lot of visits to New York lately.

Second, Grice noted cases in which an apparent violation of one maxim is the result of conflict with another maxim. He illustrates this type with the example in (9).

(9) A: Where does C live?
B: Somewhere in the South of France.

B's reply here seems to violate the maxim of quantity, specifically the first sub-maxim, since it is not as informative as would be appropriate in this context. A is expected to be able to infer that B cannot be more informative without violating the maxim of quality (second sub-maxim) by saying something for which he lacks adequate evidence. So the intended implicature is, "I do not know exactly where C lives."

Third, Grice described cases in which one of the maxims is "flouted", by which he meant a deliberate and obvious violation, intended to be recognized as such. Two of his examples of this type are presented in (10–11).

(10) A professor is writing a letter of reference for a student who is applying for a job as a philosophy teacher:
"Dear Sir, Mr. X's command of English is excellent, and his attendance at tutorials has been regular. Yours, etc."[3]

(11) Review of a vocal recital:
"Miss X produced a series of sounds that corresponded closely with the score of *Home sweet home*."[4]

The professor's letter in (10) flouts the maxims of quantity and relevance, since it contains none of the information that would be expected in an academic letter

[2]Examples (7–9) come from Grice (1975: 51).
[3]Grice (1975: 52).
[4]Grice (1975: 55).

of reference. The review in (11) flouts the maxim of manner, since there would have been a shorter and clearer way of describing the event, namely "Miss X sang *Home sweet home*."

As we noted in an earlier chapter, speakers sometimes utter sentences which are tautologies or contradictions. In such cases, the communicative value of the utterance comes primarily from the pragmatic inferences which are triggered; the semantic (i.e. truth conditional) content of the sentence contributes little or nothing. Grice observes that tautologies like those in (12) can be seen as flouting the maxim of quantity, since their semantic content is uninformative. Metaphors, irony, and other figures of speech like those in (13) can be seen as flouting the maxim of quality, since their literal semantic content is clearly untrue and intended to be recognized as such.

(12) a. War is war.
    b. Boys will be boys.

(13) a. You are the cream in my coffee.
    b. Queen Victoria was made of iron. (Levinson 1983: 110)
    c. A fine friend he turned out to be!

Von Fintel & Matthewson (2008) consider the question of whether Grice's Cooperative Principle and maxims hold for all languages. Of course, differences in culture, lexical distinctions, etc. will lead to differences in the specific implicatures which arise, since these are calculated in light of everything in the common ground between speaker and hearer.[5] They note a single proposed counter example to Grice's model, from Malagasy (Keenan 1974); but they endorse the response of Prince (1982), who points out that the speakers in Keenan's examples actually do obey Grice's principles, given their cultural values and assumptions. Their conclusion echoes that of Green (1990: 419):

> [I]t would astonish me to find a culture in which Grice's maxims were not routinely observed, and required for the interpretation of communicative intentions, and all other things being equal, routinely exploited to create implicature.

[5]See for example Matsumoto (1995).

8.4 Types of implicatures

8.4.1 Generalized Conversational Implicature

Grice distinguished two different types of conversational implicatures. He referred to examples like those we have considered up to this point as **PARTICULARIZED CONVERSATIONAL IMPLICATURES**, meaning that the intended inference depends on particular features of the specific context of the utterance. The second type he referred to as **GENERALIZED CONVERSATIONAL IMPLICATURES**. This type of inference does not depend on particular features of the context, but is instead typically associated with the kind of proposition being expressed. Some examples are shown in (14).

(14) a. She gave him the key and he opened the door.
IMPLICATURE: She gave him the key *and then* he opened the door.

b. The water is warm.
IMPLICATURE: The water is not hot.

c. It is possible that we are related.
IMPLICATURE: It is not necessarily true that we are related.

d. Some of the boys went to the rugby match.
IMPLICATURE: Not all of the boys went to the rugby match.

e. John has most of the documents.
IMPLICATURE: John does not have all of the documents.

f. That man is either Martha's brother or her boyfriend.
IMPLICATURE: The speaker does not know whether the man is Martha's brother or boyfriend.

Generalized conversational implicatures are motivated by the same set of maxims discussed above, but they typically do not involve a violation of the maxims. Rather, the implicature arises precisely because the hearer assumes that the speaker is obeying the maxims; if the implicated meaning were not true, then there would be a violation. In (14a) for example, assuming that the semantic content of English *and* is simply logical *and* ($\wedge$), the implicated sequential meaning ('and then') is motivated by the maxim of manner (sub-maxim: Be orderly). If the actual order of events was not the one indicated by the sequential order of the conjoined clauses, the speaker would have violated this maxim; therefore, unless there is evidence to the contrary, the hearer will assume that the sequential meaning is intended. (We will return in the next chapter to the question of whether this is an adequate analysis of the meaning of English *and*.)

A widely discussed type of generalized conversational implicature involves non-maximal degree modifiers, that is, words which refer to intermediate points on a scale. (Implicatures of this type are often referred to as SCALAR IMPLICATURES.) The word *warm* in (14b), for example, belongs to a set of words which identify various points on a scale of temperature: *frigid, cold, cool, lukewarm, warm, hot, burning/sizzling/scalding*, etc. The choice of the word *warm* implicates 'not hot' by the maxim of quantity. If the speaker knew that the water was hot but only said that it was warm, he would not have been as informative as would be appropriate in most contexts; a hearer stepping into a full bath tub, for example, would be justified in complaining if the water turned out to be painfully hot and not just warm. This inference does not depend on particular features of the context, but is normally triggered by any use of the word *warm* unless something in the context prevents it from arising. The same reasoning applies to *possible* in (14c), *some* in (14d), and *most* in (14e).

The maxim of quantity also motivates the implicature in (14f), since if the speaker knew which alternative was correct but only made an *or* statement, he would not have been as informative as would be appropriate in most contexts. Again, this inference would normally be triggered by any similar use of the word *or* unless something in the context prevents it from arising.

The indefinite article can trigger generalized conversational implicatures concerning the possessor of the indefinite NP, with different implicatures depending on whether the head noun is alienable as in (15a–b) or inalienable as in (15c–d).[6] How to account for this difference is somewhat puzzling.

(15) a. I walked into a house.
IMPLICATURE: The house was not my house.

b. Arthur is meeting a woman tonight.
IMPLICATURE: The woman is not Arthur's wife or close relative.

c. I broke a finger yesterday.
IMPLICATURE: The finger was my finger.

d. **Lady Glossop**: How would you ever support a wife, Mr. Wooster?
Bertie: Well, it depends on whose wife it was. I would've said a gentle pressure beneath the left elbow when crossing a busy street normally fills the bill.
[*Jeeves and Wooster*, Season 1, Episode 1; ITV1]

[6] Exx. (15a–b) are adapted from Grice (1975: 56).

8.4.2 Conventional Implicature

Grice identified another type of inference which he called CONVENTIONAL IMPLICATURES; but he said very little about them, and never developed a full-blown analysis. In contrast to conversational implicatures, which are context-sensitive and motivated by the conversational maxims, conventional implicatures are part of the conventional meaning of a word or construction. This means that they are not context-dependent or pragmatically explainable, and must be learned on a word-by-word basis. However, unlike the kinds of lexical entailments that we discussed in Chapter 6, conventional implicatures do not contribute to the truth conditions of a sentence, and for this reason have sometimes been regarded as involving pragmatic rather than semantic content.

Grice illustrated the concept of conventional implicature using the conjunction *therefore.* He suggested that this word does not affect the truth value of a sentence; the claim of a causal relationship is only conventionally implicated and not entailed:

> If I say (smugly), *He is an Englishman; he is, therefore, brave,* I have certainly committed myself, by virtue of the meaning of my words, to its being the case that his being brave is a consequence of (follows from) his being an Englishman. But while I have said that he is an Englishman, and said that he is brave, I do not want to say that I have said (in the favored sense [i.e. as part of the truth-conditional semantic content—PK]) that it follows from his being an Englishman that he is brave, though I have certainly indicated, and so implicated, that this is so. I do not want to say that my utterance of this sentence would be, strictly speaking, false should the consequence in question fail to hold. (Grice 1975: 44)

Frege had earlier expressed very similar views concerning words like *still* and *but,* though he never used the term "conventional implicature". He pointed out that the truth-conditional meaning of *but* is identical to that of *and.* The difference between the two is that *but* indicates a contrast or counter-expectation. But this is only conventionally implicated, in Grice's terms; if there is in fact no contrast between the two conjuncts, that does not make the sentence false.

> With the sentence *Alfred has still not come* one really says 'Alfred has not come' and, at the same time, hints that his arrival is expected, but it is only hinted. It cannot be said that, since Alfred's arrival is not expected, the sense of the sentence is therefore false... The word *but* differs from *and* in

> that with it one intimates that what follows is in contrast with what would be expected from what preceded it. Such suggestions in speech make no difference to the thought [i.e. the propositional content—PK]. [Frege 1918–1919/1956]

A few more examples of conventional implicatures (CI) are given in (16):

(16) a. I was in Paris last spring *too.*[7]
CI: some other specific/contextually salient person was in Paris last spring.

b. *Even* Bart passed the test.[8]
CI: Bart was among the least likely to pass the test.

Conventional implicatures turn out to have very similar properties to certain kinds of presuppositions, and there has been extensive debate over the question of whether it is possible or desirable to distinguish conventional implicatures from presuppositions. We will have more to say about conventional implicatures in Chapter 11.

8.5 Distinguishing features of conversational implicatures

Grice's analysis of conversational implicatures implies that they will have certain properties which allow us to distinguish them from other kinds of inference. We have already mentioned the most important of these, namely the fact that they are DEFEASIBLE. This term means that the inference can be cancelled by adding an additional premise. For example, conversational implicatures can be explicitly negated or denied without giving rise to anomaly or contradiction, as illustrated in (17). This makes them quite different from entailments, as seen in (18).

(17) a. Dear Sir, Mr. X's command of English is excellent, and his attendance at tutorials has been regular. *And, needless to say, he is highly competent in philosophy.* Yours, etc.

b. He has been paying a lot of visits to New York lately, *but I don't think he has a girlfriend there, either.*

c. John has most of the documents; *in fact, he has all of them.*

[7]Barbara Partee, 2009 lecture notes; http://people.umass.edu/partee/MGU_2009/materials/MGU098_2up.pdf

[8]Potts (2007b).

(18) John killed the wasp (#but the wasp did not die).

A closely related property is that conversational implicatures are SUSPENDABLE:[9] the speaker may explicitly choose not to commit to the truth or falsehood of the inference, without giving rise to anomaly or contradiction. This is illustrated in (19a). Again, the opposite is true for entailments, as seen in (19b).

(19) a. The water must be warm by now, *if not boiling.*
b. # The water must be warm by now, *if not cold.*

Conversational implicatures are CALCULABLE, that is, capable of being worked out on the basis of (i) the literal meaning of the utterance, (ii) the Cooperative Principle and its maxims, (iii) the context of the utterance, (iv) background knowledge, and (v) the assumption that (i)–(iv) are available to both participants of the exchange and that they are both aware of this. However, conversational implicatures are also INDETERMINATE: sometimes multiple interpretations are possible for a given utterance in a particular context.

Because conversational implicatures are not part of the conventional meaning of the linguistic expression, and because they are triggered by the semantic content of what is said rather than its linguistic form, replacing words with synonyms, or a sentence with its paraphrase as in (20), will generally not change the conversational implicatures that are generated, assuming the context is identical. Grice used the somewhat obscure term NONDETACHABLE to identify this property. He explicitly notes that implicatures involving the maxim of Manner are exceptions to this generalization, since in those cases it is precisely the speaker's choice of linguistic form which triggers the implicature.[10]

(20) A: Smith doesn't seem to have a girlfriend these days.
B1: He has been paying a lot of visits to New York lately.
B2: He travels to New York quite frequently, I have noticed.

Sadock (1978: 294) noted another useful diagnostic property, namely that conversational implicatures are REINFORCEABLE. He used this term to mean that the implicature can be overtly stated without creating a sense of anomalous redundancy (21a–b). This is another respect in which conversational implicatures differ from entailments (21c).

---

[9]Horn (1972); Sadock (1978).
[10]Grice (1975: 58).

(21) a. John is a capable fellow, *but I wouldn't call him a genius.*
b. Some of the boys went to the soccer match, *but not all.*
c. ?*Some of the boys went to the soccer match, *but not none.*

8.6 How to tell one kind of inference from another

The table in Table 8.1 summarizes some of the characteristic properties of entailments, conversational implicatures, and presuppositions.[11] In this section we will work through some examples showing how we can use these properties as diagnostic tools to help us determine which kind of inference we are dealing with in any particular example.

Two general comments need to be kept in mind. First, before we begin applying these tests, it is important to ask whether there is in fact a linguistic inference to be tested. The question is this: if a speaker whom we believe to be truthful and well-informed says *p*, would this utterance in and of itself give us reason to believe *q*? If so, we can apply the tests to determine the nature of the inference from *p* to *q*. But if not, applying the tests will only cause confusion. For example, if our truthful and well-informed speaker says *My bank manager has just been murdered*, it seems reasonable to assume that the bank will soon be hiring a new manager.[12] However, this expectation is based on our knowledge of how the world works, and not the meaning of the sentence itself; there is no linguistic inference involved. If the bank owners decided to leave the position unfilled, or even to close that branch office entirely, it would not render the speaker's statement false or misleading.

Second, any one test may give unreliable results in a particular example, because so many complex factors contribute to the meaning of an utterance. For this reason, it is important to use several tests whenever possible, and choose the analysis that best explains the full range of available data. Presuppositions are especially tricky, partly because they are not a uniform class; different sorts seem to behave differently in certain respects. Some specific issues regarding presuppositions are discussed below.

Let us begin with some simple examples. If our truthful and well-informed speaker makes the statement in (22), we would certainly infer that the wasp is dead. We can test to see whether this inference is cancellable/defeasible, as in (22a); the result is a contradiction. We can test to see whether the inference can

[11] Thanks to Seth Johnston for suggesting this type of summary table.

[12] This example comes from Saeed (2009: 54).

Table 8.1: Criteria for distinguishing Conversational Implicature from entailment and presupposition

		Entailment	Conversational Implicature	Presupposition
a.	Cancellable/ defeasible	NO	YES	sometimes[a]
b.	Suspendable	NO	YES	sometimes
c.	Reinforceable	NO	YES	NO
d.	Preserved under negation and questioning	NO	NO	YES

[a]Some presuppositions seem to be cancellable, but only if the clause containing the trigger is negated. Presuppositions triggered by positive statements are generally not cancellable.

be suspended, as in (22b); the result is quite unnatural. We can test to see whether the inference is reinforceable, as in (22c); the result is unnaturally redundant.

(22) STATED: *John killed the wasp.*
INFERRED: The wasp died.

a. # John killed the wasp, but the wasp did not die.
b. # John killed the wasp, but I'm not sure whether the wasp died.
c. ?# John killed the wasp, and the wasp died.
d. Did John kill the wasp?
e. John did not kill the wasp (and the wasp did not die).

In applying the final test, we are asking whether the same inference is created by a family of related sentences, which includes negation and questioning of the original statement. Clearly if someone asks the question in (22d), that would not give us any reason to believe that the wasp died. Similarly, the negative statement in (22e) gives us no reason to believe that the wasp died. We can demonstrate this by showing that it would not be a contradiction to assert, in the same sentence, that the wasp did not die; note the contrast with (22a), which is a contradiction. We have seen that all four tests in this example produce negative results. This pattern matches the profile of entailment; so we conclude that *John killed the wasp* entails *The wasp died.*

Now let us apply the tests to Grice's example (23); specifically we will be testing the inference that arises from B's reply, *There is a garage around the corner.* The sentences in (23a–c) show that this inference is defeasible (additional information can block the inference from arising), suspendable, and reinforceable. Neither the question in (23d) nor the negative statement in (23e) would give A any reason to believe that he could buy petrol around the corner. (The phrase *any more* could be added in (23e) to make the negative statement sound a bit more natural. In applying these tests, it is important to give the test every opportunity to succeed. Since naturalness is an important criterion for success, it is often helpful to adjust the test sentences as needed to make them more natural, provided the key elements of meaning are not lost or distorted.)

(23) A: *I am out of petrol.*
B: *There is a garage around the corner.*
INFERRED: You can buy petrol there.

a. There is a garage around the corner, but they aren't selling petrol today.
b. There is a garage around the corner, but I'm not sure whether they sell petrol.
c. There is a garage around the corner, and you can buy petrol there.
d. Is there a garage around the corner?
e. There is no garage around the corner (any more).

In this example the first three tests produce positive results, while the last one (the "family of sentences" test) is negative. This pattern matches the profile of conversational implicature; so we conclude that *There is a garage around the corner* (when spoken in the context of A's statement) conversationally implicates *You can buy petrol there.* Of course, we already knew this, based on our previous discussion. What we are doing here is illustrating and validating the tests by showing how they work with relatively simple cases where we think we know the answer. This gives us a basis for expecting that the tests will work for more complex cases as well.

Finally consider the inference shown in (24). The sentences in (24a–c) show that this inference is not defeasible (24a) or reinforceable (24c), but it is suspendable (24b). Both the question in (24d) and the negative statement in (24e) seem to imply that John used to chew betel nut. These results match the profile of a presupposition, as expected (*stopped chewing* presupposes *used to chew*).

(24) STATED: *John has stopped chewing betel nut.*
INFERRED: John used to chew betel nut.

a. # John has stopped chewing betel nut, and in fact he has never chewed it.
b. John has stopped chewing betel nut, if he (ever/really) did chew it.
c. ?# John has stopped chewing betel nut, and he used to chew it.
d. Has John stopped chewing betel nut?
e. John has not stopped chewing betel nut.

Recall that we mentioned in Chapter 3 another test which is useful for identifying presuppositions, the "Hey, wait a minute" test.[13] If a speaker's utterance presupposes something that is not in fact part of the common ground, it is quite appropriate for the hearer to object in the way shown in (25a). However, it is not appropriate for the hearer to object in this way just because the main point of the assertion is not in fact part of the common ground (25b). In fact, it would be unnatural for the speaker to assert something that is already part of the common ground.

(25) STATEMENT: *John has stopped chewing betel nut.*

a. RESPONSE 1: *Hey, wait a minute, I didn't know that John used to chew betel nut!*
b. RESPONSE 2: # *Hey, wait a minute, I didn't know that John has stopped chewing betel nut!*

We mentioned above that it is important to use several tests whenever possible, because any one test may run into unexpected complications in a particular context. For example, our discussion in §4.1 would lead us to believe that the word *most* should trigger the generalized conversational implicature *not all.* The examples in (26) are largely consistent with this prediction. They indicate that the inference is defeasible (26a), suspendable (26b), and reinforceable (26c). However, the "family of sentences" tests produce inconsistent results. The question in (26d) fails to trigger the inference, as expected, but the negative statement in (26e) seems to *entail* (not just implicate) that not all of the boys went to the soccer match.

(26) STATED: *Most of the boys went to the soccer match.*
INFERRED: Not all of the boys went to the soccer match.

[13] Von Fintel (2004).

a. Most of the boys went to the soccer match; in fact, I think all of them went.
b. Most of the boys went to the soccer match, if not all of them.
c. Most of the boys went to the soccer match, but not all of them.
d. Did most of the boys go to the soccer match?
e. Most of the boys didn't go to the soccer match.
f. If most of the boys went to the soccer match, dinner will probably be late this evening.

As mentioned in Chapter 4, combining clausal negation with quantified noun phrases often creates ambiguity; we see here that it can introduce other complexities as well. This is a situation where preservation under negation is not a reliable indicator. However, other members of the "family of sentences", including the question (26d) and conditional clause (26f), can be used, and show that the inference is not preserved. So the overall pattern of results confirms that this is a conversational implicature.

The table in Table 8.1 indicates that presuppositions are normally preserved under negation, and this is the first (and often the only) test that many people use for identifying presuppositions. But as we have seen, negating a sentence can introduce new complications. In discussing the presupposition in (24) we noted that the negative statement (24e), repeated here as (27a), seems to imply that John used to chew betel nut. This is true if the sentence is read with neutral intonation; but if it is read with what Jespersen (1933) calls "the peculiar intonation indicative of contradiction", indicated in (27b), it becomes possible to explicitly deny the presupposition without contradiction or anomaly. This is an instance of PRESUPPOSITION-CANCELLING NEGATION.

(27) a. John hasn't stopped chewing betel nut.
b. John hasn't STOPPED chewing betel nut, he never DID chew it.

Horn (1985; 1989) argues that cases of presupposition-cancelling negation like (27b) involve a special kind of negation which he refers to as METALINGUISTIC NEGATION. Metalinguistic negation is typically used to contradict something that the addressee has just said, implied, or implicitly accepted.[14] The negated clause is generally spoken with the special intonation pattern mentioned above, and is typically followed by a correction or "rectification" as in (27b).

[14] Karttunen & Peters (1979: 46–47).

Some additional examples of metalinguistic negation are presented in (28). These examples show clearly that metalinguistic negation is different from normal, logical negation which is used to deny the truth of a proposition. If the negation used in these examples was simply negating the propositional content, the sentences would be contradictions, because *horrible* entails *bad*, *all* entails *most*, etc. Horn claims that what is negated in such examples is not the propositional content but the conversational implicature: asserting *bad* implicates *not horrible*; asserting *most* implicates *not all*. Metalinguistic negation is used to reject the statements in the first clause as being inappropriate or "infelicitous", because they are not strong enough.

(28) a. That [1983] wasn't a BAD year, it was HORRIBLE.[15]
b. I'm not HUNGRY, I'm STARVING.
c. MOST of the boys didn't go to the soccer match, ALL of them went.

For our present purposes what we need to remember is that, in testing to see whether an inference is preserved under negation (one of the "family of sentences" tests), we must be careful to use normal, logical negation rather than metalinguistic negation.

8.7 Conclusion

Conversational implicatures are the paradigm example of a pragmatic inference: meaning derived not from the words themselves but from the way those words are used in a particular context. They are an indispensable part of our everyday communication. In order for a hearer to correctly interpret the part of the speaker's intended meaning which is not encoded by the words themselves, these implicatures must be derived in a systematic way, based on principles which are known to both speaker and hearer. Grice proposed a fairly simple account of these principles, starting with some basic assumptions about the nature of conversation as a cooperative activity. Some later modifications to Grice's theory will be mentioned in Chapter 9.

[15] A quote from the famous baseball player Reggie Jackson, cited in Horn (1989: 382).

Further reading

Levinson (1983: ch. 3) and Birner (2012/2013: ch. 2) present good introductions to Grice's treatment of conversational implicature. Grice's most famous papers (e.g. 1975; 1978; 1981) are also quite readable. (References to more recent work on conversational implicature will be provided in the next chapter.)

Discussion exercises

A. Identifying types of inference. For each of the examples in (1–4), determine whether the inference triggered by the statement is (A) a PARTICULARIZED CONVERSATIONAL IMPLICATURE, (B) a GENERALIZED CONVERSATIONAL IMPLICATURE, (C) a PRESUPPOSITION, (D) an ENTAILMENT, or (E) none of these.

(1) STATED: My mother is the mayor of Waxahachie.
INFERRED: The mayor of Waxahachie is a woman.

(2) STATED: That man is either Martha's brother or her boyfriend.
INFERRED: The speaker does not know whether the man is Martha's brother or boyfriend.

(3) STATED: My great-grandfather was arrested this morning for drag racing.
INFERRED: I have a great-grandfather.

(4) STATED: That's a great joke – Ham, Shem and Japheth couldn't stop laughing when they heard it from Noah.
INFERRED: The joke has lost some of its freshness.

For each of the sentences in (5), determine what inference is most likely to be triggered by the statement, and what kind of inference it is, using the same five options as above.

(5) a. I didn't realize that they are husband and wife.
b. Charles continues to wear a cabbage on his head.
c. It is possible that we are related.
d. Who stole my durian smoothie?
e. Q: Who is that guy over there?
A: That is the male offspring of my parents.[a]
f. Arthur is almost as unscrupulous as Susan.

(6) What kind of inference is involved in the following joke?
Q: How many months have 28 days?
A: All of them.

[a]Kearns (2000).

Homework exercises

A. Conversational implicature. For each pair of sentences, (i) identify the likely implicature carried by B's reply; (ii) state which maxim is most important in triggering the implicature, and (iii) explain how the implicature is derived.[a]

(1) A: Are you coming out for a pint tonight?
B: My in-laws are coming over for dinner.

Model answer:
The most likely implicature here is that B is unable to go out with A. It is triggered by the maxims of quantity and relevance: the literal meaning of B's reply does not provide the information requested (yes or no), and does not seem to be relevant. By assuming that B intends to communicate that he is obligated to eat with his in-laws, A can interpret B's statement as being both appropriately informative and relevant.

(2) A: Who is that couple?
B: That is my mother and her husband.

(3) A: Did you enjoy having your sister and her family come to visit?
B: The children were perfect angels. We didn't really want that antique table anyway, and I'm sure the cat likes to have its tail pulled.

(4) A: Jones has just taken a second mortgage on his house.
B: I think I saw him at the casino last weekend.

(5) A: Did you make us a reservation for dinner tonight?
B: I meant to.

B. Presupposition, Entailment, Implicature.[b] What is the relation (if any) between each statement and the bracketed statements which follow? Pick one of the following four answers: Presupposition; Entailment; Conversational Implicature; no inference.

(6) John is allegedly a good player.
[John is a good player.]

(7) Oscar and Jenny are middle-aged.
[Jenny is middle-aged.]

(8) Maria is an Italian radiologist.

a. [Some Italian is a radiologist.]
b. [Maria is Italian.]

(9) Not everyone will get the correct answer.
[Someone will get the correct answer.]

(10) Pete installed new cabinets after Hans painted the walls.
[Hans painted the walls.]

(11) Dempsey and Tunney fought in Philadelphia in September (1926).
[Dempsey and Tunney fought each other.]

(12) John believes that pigs do not have wings.
[Pigs do not have wings.]

(13) John realizes that pigs do not have wings.
[Pigs do not have wings.]

(14) Don is at home or at work.

a. [Don is at home.]
b. [I don't know whether Don is at home or at work.]

(15) My older brother called.
[I have an older brother.]

(16) Max has quit jogging, at least until his ankle heals.

a. [Max does not jog now.]
b. [Max used to jog.]

---

[a] adapted from Saeed (2009: 226, ex. 7.6).
[b] Adapted from MIT course notes.

9 Pragmatic inference after Grice

9.1 Introduction

Grice's work on implicatures triggered an explosion of interest in pragmatics. In the subsequent decades, a wide variety of applications, extensions, and modifications of Grice's theory have been proposed.

One focus of the theoretical discussion has been the apparent redundancy in the set of maxims and sub-maxims proposed by Grice. Many pragmaticists have argued that the same work can be done with fewer maxims.[1] In the extreme case, proponents of Relevance Theory have argued that only the Principle of Relevance is needed.

Rather than focusing on such theoretical issues directly, in this chapter we will discuss some of the analytical questions that have been of central importance in the development of pragmatics after Grice. In §9.2 we return to the question raised in Chapter 4 concerning the degree to which the English words *and*, *or*, and *if* have the same meanings as the corresponding logical operators. Grice himself suggested that some apparently distinct "senses" of these words could be analyzed as generalized conversational implicatures. §9.3 discusses a type of pragmatic "enrichment" that seems to be required in order to determine the truth-conditional meaning of a sentence. §9.4 discusses how the relatively clean and simple distinction between semantics vs. pragmatics which we have been assuming up to now is challenged by recent work on implicatures.

9.2 Meanings of English words vs. logical operators

As we hinted in Chapter 4, the logical operators $\wedge$ 'and', $\vee$ 'or', and $\rightarrow$ 'if... then' seem to have a different and often narrower range of meaning than the corresponding English words. A number of authors have claimed that the English words are ambiguous, with the logical operators corresponding to just one of the possible senses. Grice argued that each of the English words actually has only a single sense, which is more or less the same as the meaning of the corresponding

[1] See Birner (2012/2013: ch. 3) for a good summary of the competing positions on this issue.

logical operator, and that the different interpretations arise through pragmatic inferences. Before we examine these claims in more detail, we will first illustrate the variable interpretations of the English words, in order to show why such questions arise in the first place.

Let us begin with *and*.[2] The truth table in Chapter 4 makes it clear that logical $\wedge$ is commutative; that is, $p \wedge q$ is equivalent to $q \wedge p$. This is also true for some uses of English *and*, such as (1). In other cases, however, such as (2–4), reversing the order of the clauses produces a very different interpretation.

(1) a. The Chinese invented the folding umbrella and the Egyptians invented the sailboat.
b. The Egyptians invented the sailboat and the Chinese invented the folding umbrella.

(2) a. She gave him the key and he opened the door.
b. He opened the door and she gave him the key.

(3) a. The Lone Ranger jumped onto his horse and rode into the sunset.[3]
b. ?The Lone Ranger rode into the sunset and jumped onto his horse.

(4) a. The janitor left the door open and the prisoner escaped.
b. ?The prisoner escaped and the janitor left the door open.

It has often been noted that when *and* conjoins clauses which describe specific events, as (2–3), there is a very strong tendency to interpret it as meaning 'and then', i.e., to assume a sequential interpretation. When the second event seems to depend on or follow from the first, as in (4a), there is a tendency to assume a causal interpretation, 'and therefore'. The question to be addressed is, do such examples prove that English *and* is ambiguous, having two or three (or more) distinct senses?

We stated in Chapter 4 that the $\vee$ of standard logic is the "inclusive or", corresponding to the English *and/or*. We also noted that the English word *or* is often used in the "exclusive" sense (XOR), meaning 'either ... or ... but not both'. Actually either interpretation is possible, depending on the context, as illustrated in (5). (The reader should determine which of these examples contains an *or* that

[2]We focus here on the use of *and* to conjoin two clauses (or VPs), since this is closest to the function of logical $\wedge$. We will not be concerned with coordination of other categories in this chapter.

[3]Ruth. M. Kempson (1975: 56), cited in Gazdar (1979).

would most naturally be interpreted with the exclusive reading, and which with the inclusive reading.) Does this variable interpretation mean that English *or* is ambiguous?

(5) a. Every year the Foundation awards a scholarship to a student of Swedish or Norwegian ancestry.
b. You can take the bus or the train and still arrive by 5 o'clock.
c. If the site is in a particularly sensitive area, or there are safety considerations, we can refuse planning permission.[4]
d. Stop or I'll shoot![5]

Finally let us briefly consider the meaning of material implication (⟶) compared with English *if*. If these two meant the same thing, then according to the truth table for material implication in Chapter 4, all but one of the sentences in (6) should be true. (The reader can refer to the truth table to determine which of these sentences is predicted to be false.) However, most English speakers find all of these sentences very odd; many speakers are unwilling to call any of them true.

(6) a. If Socrates was a woman then $1 + 1 = 3$.[6]
b. If 2 is odd then 2 is even.[6]
c. If a triangle has three sides then the moon is made of green cheese.
d. If the Chinese invented gunpowder then Martin Luther was German.

Similarly, analyzing English *if* as material implication in (7) would predict some unlikely inferences, based on the rule of *modus tollens*.

(7) a. If you're hungry, there's some pizza in the fridge.
(predicted inference: #If there's no pizza in the fridge, then you're not hungry.)
b. If you really want to know, I think that dress is incredibly ugly.
(predicted inference: #If I don't think that dress is ugly, then you don't really want to know.)

Part of the oddness of the "true" sentences in (6) relates to the fact that material implication is defined strictly in terms of truth values; there does not have to

[4]Saeed (2009: 113).
[5]Saeed (2009: 113).
[6]http://en.wikipedia.org/wiki/Material_conditional

be any connection between the meanings of the two propositions. English *if*, on the other hand, is normally used only where the two propositions do have some sensible connection. Whether this preference can be explained purely in pragmatic terms is an interesting issue, as is the question of how many senses we need to recognize for English *if* and whether any of these senses are equivalent to $\rightarrow$. We will return to these questions in Chapter 19. In the present chapter we focus on the meanings of *and* and *or*.

9.2.1 On the ambiguity of *and*

In Chapter 8 we mentioned that the sequential ('and then') use of English *and* can be analyzed as a generalized conversational implicature motivated by the maxim of manner, under the assumption that its semantic content is simply logical *and* ($\wedge$). An alternative analysis, as mentioned above, involves the claim that English *and* is polysemous, with logical *and* ($\wedge$) and sequential 'and then' as two distinct senses. Clearly both uses of *and* are possible, given the appropriate context; example (8a) (like (1a) above) is an instance of the logical *and* use, while (8b) (like (1b-c) above) is most naturally interpreted as involving the sequential 'and then' use. The question is whether we are dealing with semantic ambiguity (two distinct senses) or pragmatic inference (one sense plus a potential conversational implicature). How can we decide between these two analyses?

(8) a. Hitler was Austrian and Stalin was Georgian.
 b. They got married and had a baby.

Horn (2004) mentions several arguments against the lexical ambiguity analysis for *and*:

i. The same two uses of *and* are found in most if not all languages. Under the semantic ambiguity analysis, the corresponding conjunction in (almost?) every language would just happen to be ambiguous in the same way as in English.

ii. No natural language contains a conjunction *shmand* that would be ambiguous between "and also" and "and earlier" readings so that *They had a baby shmand they got married* would be interpreted either atemporally (logical *and*) or as "They had a baby and, before that, they got married."

iii. Not only temporal but causal asymmetry ('and therefore', illustrated in (1d)) would need to be treated as a distinct sense. And a variety of other uses (involving "stronger" or more specific uses of the conjunction) arise in different contexts of utterance. How many senses are we prepared to recognize?

iv. The same "ambiguity" exhibited by *and* arises when two clauses describing related events are simply juxtaposed (*They had a baby. They got married.*). This suggests that the sequential interpretation is not in fact contributed by the conjunction *and*.

v. The sequential 'and then' interpretation is defeasible, as illustrated in (9). This strongly suggests that we are dealing with conversational implicature rather than semantic ambiguity.

(9) They got married and had a baby, but not necessarily in that order.

Taken together, these arguments seem quite persuasive. They demonstrate that English *and* is not polysemous; its semantic content is logical *and* (∧). The sequential 'and then' use can be analyzed as a generalized conversational implicature.

9.2.2 On the ambiguity of *or*

As noted in Chapter 4, similar questions arise with respect to the meaning(s) of *or*. The English word *or* can be used in either the inclusive sense (∨) or the exclusive sense (XOR). The inclusive reading is most likely in (10a–b), while the exclusive reading is most likely in (10c–d).

(10) a. Mary has a son or daughter.[7]
b. We would like to hire a sales manager who speaks Chinese or Korean.
c. I can't decide whether to order fried noodles or pizza.
d. Stop or I'll shoot![8]

Barbara Partee points out that examples like (11) are sometimes cited as sentences where only the exclusive reading of *or* is possible; but in fact, such examples do not distinguish the two senses. These are cases where our knowledge of the world makes it clear that both alternatives cannot possibly be true. She says that such cases involve "intrinsically mutually exclusive alternatives". Because we know that $p \wedge q$ cannot be true in such examples, $p \vee q$ and $pXORq$ are indistinguishable; if one is true, the other must be true as well.

[7]Barbara Partee, 2004 lecture notes. http://people.umass.edu/partee/RGGU_2004/RGGU047.pdf
[8]Saeed (2009: 113).

(11) a. Mary is in Prague or she is in Stuttgart.[9]
b. Christmas falls on a Friday or Saturday this year.

Grice (1978) argues that English *or*, like *and*, is not polysemous. Rather, its semantic content is inclusive *or* (∨), and the exclusive reading arises through a conversational implicature motivated by the maxim of quantity.

In fact, using *or* can trigger more than one implicature. If a speaker says *p or q* but actually knows that *p* is true, or that *q* is true, he is not being as informative as required or expected. So the statement *p or q* triggers the implicature that the speaker does not know *p* to be true or *q* to be true. By the same reasoning, it triggers the implicature that the speaker does not know either *p* or *q* individually to be false. Now if *p* and *q* are both true, and the speaker knows it, it would be more informative (and thus expected) for the speaker to say *p and q*. If he instead says *p or q*, he is violating the maxim of quantity. Thus the statement *p or q* also triggers the implicature that the speaker is not in a position to assert *p and q*.

So in contexts where the speaker might reasonably be expected to know if *p and q* were true, the statement *p or q* will trigger the implicature that *p and q* is not true, which produces the exclusive reading. When nothing can be assumed about the speaker's knowledge, it is harder to see how to derive the exclusive reading from Gricean principles; several different explanations have been proposed. But another reason for thinking that the exclusive reading arises through a conversational implicature is that it is defeasible, e.g. *I will order either fried noodles or pizza; in fact I might get both.*

Gazdar (1979: 81–82) presents another argument against analyzing English *or* as being polysemous. If *or* is ambiguous between an inclusive and an exclusive sense, then when sentences containing *or* are negated, the result should also be ambiguous, with senses corresponding to $\neg(p \vee q)$ vs. $\neg(pXORq)$. The crucial difference is that $\neg(pXORq)$ will be true and $\neg(p \vee q)$ false if $p \wedge q$ is true. (The reader should consult the truth tables in Chapter 4 to see why this is the case.) For example, if *or* were ambiguous, sentence (12a) should allow a reading which is true if Mary has both a son and a daughter, and (12b) should allow a reading under which I would allow my daughter to marry a man who both smokes and drinks. However, for most English speakers these readings of (12a–b) are not possible, at least when the sentences are read with normal intonation

(12) a. Mary doesn't have a son or daughter.[10]
b. The man who marries my daughter must not smoke or drink.

[9]Barbara Partee, 2004 lecture notes. http://people.umass.edu/partee/RGGU_2004/RGGU047.pdf
[10]Barbara Partee, 2004 lecture notes. http://people.umass.edu/partee/RGGU_2004/RGGU047.pdf

Grice (1978: 47), in the context of discussing the meaning of *or*, proposed a principle which he called **Modified Occam's Razor**: "Senses are not to be multiplied beyond necessity." This principle would lead us to favor an analysis of words like *and* and *or* as having only a single sense, with additional uses being derived by pragmatic inference, unless there is clear evidence in favor of polysemy.

9.3 Explicatures: bridging the gap between what is said vs. what is implicated

Grice's model seems to assume that the speaker meaning (total meaning that the speaker intends to communicate) is the sum of the sentence meaning ("what is said", i.e., the meaning linguistically encoded by the words themselves) plus implicatures. Moreover, implicatures were assumed not to affect the truth value of the proposition expressed by the sentence; truth values were assumed to depend only on sentence meaning.[11]

In many cases, however, the meaning linguistically encoded by the words themselves does not amount to a complete proposition, and so cannot be evaluated as being either true or false. Grice recognized that the proposition expressed by a sentence like (13a) is not complete, and its truth value cannot be determined, until the referents of pronouns and deictic elements are specified. Most authors also assume that any potential ambiguities in the linguistic form (like the syntactic and lexical ambiguities in 13b) must be resolved before the propositional content and truth conditions of the sentence can be determined.

(13) a. She visited me here yesterday.
b. Old men and women gathered at the bank.

Determining reference and disambiguation both depend on context, and so involve a limited kind of pragmatic reasoning. However, it turns out that there are many cases in which more significant pragmatic inferences are required in order to determine the propositional content of the sentence. Kent Bach (1994) identifies two sorts of cases where this is needed: "Filling in is needed if the sentence is semantically UNDER-DETERMINATE, and fleshing out will be needed if the speaker cannot plausibly be supposed to mean just what the sentence means."

The first type, which Bach refers to as SEMANTIC UNDER-DETERMINATION, involves sentences which fail to express a complete proposition (something capable

[11]Of course, the implicatures themselves also have propositional content, which may be true or false/misleading even if the literal sentence meaning is true.

of being true or false), even after the referents of pronouns and deictic elements have been determined and ambiguities resolved; some examples are presented in (14).[12]

(14) a. Steel isn't strong enough.
b. Strom is too old.
c. The princess is late.
d. Tipper is ready.

In these cases a process of COMPLETION (or "filling in" the missing information) is required to produce a complete proposition. This involves adding information to the propositional meaning which is unexpressed but implicit in the original sentence, as indicated in (15). The hearer must be able to provide this information from context and/or knowledge of the world. The truth values of these sentences can only be determined after the implicit constituent is added to the overtly expressed meaning.

(15) a. Steel isn't strong enough [to stop this kind of anti-tank missile].
b. Strom is too old [to be an effective senator].
c. The princess is late [for the party].
d. Tipper is ready [to dance].

The under-determination of the sentences in (14) is not due to syntactic deletion or ellipsis; they are semantically incomplete, but not syntactically incomplete. The examples in (16–17) show that the potential for occurring in such constructions may be lexically specific, and that close synonyms may differ in this respect.

(16) a. The king has arrived [at the palace].
b. * The king has reached.

(17) a. Al has finished [speaking].
b. * Al has completed.

The second type of sentence that Bach discusses involves those in which "there is already a complete proposition, something capable of being true or false (assuming linguistically unspecified references have been assigned and any ambiguities have been resolved), albeit not the one that is being communicated by the

[12] Examples (14–19) are adapted from K. Bach (1994).

speaker." For example, imagine that a mother says (18a) to her young son who is crying loudly because he cut his finger.

(18) a. You're not going to die.
 b. You're not going to die [from this cut].

Clearly she does not intend to promise immortality, although that is what the literal meaning of her words seems to say. In order to determine the intended propositional content of the sentence, the meaning has to be EXPANDED (or "fleshed out") as shown in (18b). Once again, the hearer must be able to provide this additional information from context and/or knowledge of the world. A more complex kind of pragmatic reasoning is required here than would be involved in assigning referents to deictic elements or resolving lexical ambiguities. Further examples are provided in (19), illustrating how identical sentence structures can be expanded differently on the basis of knowledge about the world.

(19) a. I have eaten breakfast [today].
 b. I have eaten caviar [before].
 c. I have nothing to wear [nothing appropriate for a specific event].
 d. I have nothing to repair [nothing at all].

Bach uses the term IMPLICITURE to refer to the kinds of inference illustrated in this section. The choice of this label is not ideal, because the words *impliciture* and *implicature* look so much alike. A very similar concept is discussed within Relevance Theory under the label EXPLICATURE,[13] expressing the idea that the overtly expressed content of the sentence needs to be explicated in order to arrive at the full sentence meaning intended by the speaker. In the discussion that follows we will adopt the term EXPLICATURE.[14]

K. Bach (1994: 11) describes the difference between "impliciture" (=explicature) and implicature as follows:

> Although both impliciture and implicature go beyond what is explicit in the utterance, they do so in different ways. An implicatum is completely separate from what is said and is inferred from it (more precisely, from the saying of it). What is said is one proposition and what is communicated in addition to that is a conceptually independent proposition, a proposition with perhaps no constituents in common with what is said...

[13] Sperber & Wilson (1986); Carston (1988).

[14] We are ignoring for now the relatively minor differences between Bach's notion of impliciture and the Relevance Theory notion of explicature; see K. Bach (2010) for discussion.

> In contrast, implicitures are built up from the explicit content of the utterance by conceptual strengthening ... which yields what would have been made fully explicit if the appropriate lexical material had been included in the utterance. Implicitures are, as the name suggests, implicit in what is said, whereas implicatures are implied by (the saying of) what is said.

In other words, implicatures are distinct from sentence meaning. They are communicated in addition to the sentence meaning and have independent truth values. A true statement could trigger a false implicature, or vice versa. Explicatures are quite different. The truth value of the sentence cannot be determined until the explicatures are added to the literal meanings of the words.

Since explicatures involve pragmatic reasoning, we must recognize the fact that pragmatic inferences can affect truth-conditional content. Further evidence that supports this same conclusion is discussed in the following section.

9.4 Implicatures and the semantics/pragmatics boundary

In Chapter 1 we defined the semantic content of an expression as the meaning that is associated with the words themselves, independent of context. We defined pragmatic meaning as the meaning which arises from the context of the utterance. We have implicitly assumed that the truth conditions of a sentence depend only on the "semantic content" or sentence meaning, and not on pragmatic meaning. Many authors have made the same assumption, using the term "truth conditional meaning" as a synonym for "sentence meaning". However, our discussion of explicatures has demonstrated that this view is too simplistic. Additional challenges to this simplistic view arise from research on implicatures.

As already discussed in Chapter 8, the conventional implicatures associated with words like *but* or *therefore* are part of the conventional meaning of these words, and not context-dependent; they would be part of the relevant dictionary definitions and must be learned on a word-by-word basis. Nevertheless, both Frege and Grice argued that these conventional implicatures do not contribute to the truth conditions of a sentence. So conventional meaning is not always truth-conditional. We will discuss this issue in more detail in Chapter 11.

The opposite situation has been argued to hold in the case of generalized conversational implicatures. In §9.2 above we presented compelling evidence which shows that the sequential 'and then' use of *and* is not due to lexical ambiguity (polysemy), but must be a pragmatic inference. It is often cited as a paradigm example of generalized conversational implicature. However, as noted by Levinson (1995; 2000) among others, this inference does affect the truth conditions of the sentence in examples like (20–21). Sentence (20a) could be judged to be true in the same context where (20b) is judged to be false. This difference can only be due to the sequential interpretation of *and*; if *and* means only $\wedge$, then the two sentences are logically equivalent. Similarly, if *and* means only $\wedge$, then (21) should be a contradiction; the fact that it is not can only be due to the sequential interpretation of *and*.

(20) a. If the old king has died of a heart attack and a republic has been declared, then Tom will be quite content.[15]

b. If a republic has been declared and the old king has died of a heart attack, then Tom will be quite content.[16]

(21) If he had three beers and drove home, he broke the law; but if he drove home and had three beers, he did not break the law.

Such examples have been extensively debated, and a variety of analyses have been proposed. For example, proponents of Relevance Theory argue that the sequential 'and then' use of *and* is an explicature: a pragmatic inference that contributes to truth conditions.[17] A similar analysis is proposed for most if not all of the inferences that Grice and the "neo-Griceans" have identified as generalized conversational implicatures: within Relevance Theory they are generally treated as explicatures.

This controversy is too complex to address in any detail here, but we might make one observation in passing. At the beginning of Chapter 8 we provided an example (the story of the captain and his mate) of how we can use a true statement to implicate something false. That example involved a particularized conversational implicature, but it is possible to do the same thing with generalized conversational implicatures as well. The following example involves a scalar implicature. It is taken from a news story about how Picasso's famous mural "Guernica" was returned to Spain after Franco's death. The phrase *Not all of them* in this context implicates *not none* (that is, 'I have some of them') by the maxim of Quantity, because *none* is a stronger (more informative) term than *not all*.

(22) To demonstrate that the Spanish Government had in fact paid Picasso to paint the mural in 1937 for the Paris International Exhibition, Mr.

[15] Cohen (1971: 58).

[16] Gazdar (1979: 69).

[17] Carston (1988; 2004).

> Fernandez Quintanilla had to secure documents in the archives of the late Luis Araquistain, Spain's Ambassador to France at the time. But Araquistain's son, poor and opportunistic, demanded $2 million for the archives, which Mr. Fernandez Quintanilla rejected as outrageous. He managed, however, to obtain from the son photocopies of the pertinent documents, which in 1979 he presented to Roland Dumas [Picasso's lawyer]...
> "This changes everything," a startled Mr. Dumas told the Spanish envoy when he showed him the photocopies of the Araquistain documents. "You of course have the originals?" the lawyer asked casually. "***Not all of them***," replied Mr. Fernandez Quintanilla, not lying but not telling the truth, either.
> [*The New York Times*, November 2, 1981; cited in Horn (1992)]

Mr. Fernandez Quintanilla was not lying, because the literal sentence meaning of his statement was true. But he was not exactly telling the truth either, because his statement triggered (and was clearly intended to trigger) an implicature that was false; in fact he had none of the originals.

Such examples show that generalized conversational implicatures can be used to communicate false information, even when the literal meaning of the sentence is true. It would be hard to account for this fact if these generalized conversational implicatures are considered to be explicatures, because explicatures do not have a truth value that is independent of the truth value of the literal sentence meaning. Rather, explicatures represent inferences that are needed in order to determine the truth value of the sentence.

9.4.1 Why numeral words are special

Scalar implicatures have received an enormous amount of attention in the recent pragmatics literature. Many early discussions of scalar implicatures relied heavily on examples involving cardinal numbers, which seem to form a natural scale (1, 2, 3, ...). However, various authors have pointed out that numbers behave differently from other scalar terms.

Horn (2004) uses examples (23–25) to bring out this difference. On the scale <*none, some, many, all*>, *all* is a stronger (more informative) term than *many*. Therefore, by the maxim of quantity, A's use of *many* in (23) entails '(at least) many' and implicates 'not all'.[18] B's reply states that the implicature does not

[18] *Many* is used here in its proportional sense; see Chapter 14 for discussion.

in fact hold in the current situation; but this does not render the propositional content of the sentence false. That is why it would be unnatural for B to begin the reply with *No*, as in B1. The acceptability of reply B2 follows from the fact that implicatures are defeasible.

(23) A: Did many of the guests leave?
B1: ?No, all of them.
B2: Yes, (in fact) all of them.

If numerals behaved in the same way as other scalars, we would expect A's use of *two* in (24) to entail 'at least two' and implicate 'not more than two'. However, if B actually does have more than two children, it seems to be more natural here for B to reply with *No* rather than *Yes*. This indicates that B is rejecting the literal propositional content of the question, not an implicature.

(24) A: Do you have two children?
B1: No, three.
B2: ?Yes, (in fact) three.

Such examples suggest that numerals like *two* allow two distinct readings: an 'at least 2' reading vs. an 'exactly 2' reading, and that neither of these is derived as an implicature from the other. A's question in (24) is most naturally interpreted as involving the 'exactly' reading. However, there are certain contexts (such as discussing a government subsidy that is available for families with two or more children) in which the 'at least' reading would be preferred, and in such contexts reply B2 would be more natural.

Example (25a) is acceptable under the 'exactly 3' reading of the numeral, under which *not three* is judged to be true whether the actual number is more than three or less than three. The fact that (25b) is unacceptable shows that the word *like* does not have an 'exactly (or merely) like' reading. Based on the scale <*hate, dislike, neutral, like, love/adore*>, using the word *like* entails 'at least like (=have positive feelings)' and implicates 'not more than like (not love/adore)'. Sentence (25b) attempts to negate the both the entailment and the implicature at the same time, and the result is unacceptable.[19]

(25) a. Neither of us has three kids – she has two and I have four.
b. # Neither of us liked the movie – she adored it and I hated it.

[19] Of course, as pointed out at the end of Chapter 8, given the right context and using a special marked intonation it is sometimes possible to negate the implicature alone, as in: "She didn't LÍKE the movie – she ADÓRED it."

Horn (1992) notes several other properties which set numerals apart from other scalar terms, and which demonstrate the two distinct readings for numerals:

1. Mathematical statements do not allow "at least" readings (26a). Also, round numbers are more likely to allow "at least" readings than very precise numbers (26b–c).

(26) a. * 2 + 2 = 3 (should be true under "at least 3" reading)
b. I have $200 in my bank account, if not more.
c. I have $201.37 in my bank account, #if not more.

2. Numerical scales are potentially reversible depending on the context (27–28); this kind of reversal is not possible with other scalar terms (29).

(27) a. That bowler is capable of breaking 100 (he might even score 150).
b. That golfer is capable of breaking 100 (he might even score 90).

(28) a. You can survive on 2000 calories per day (or more).
b. You can lose weight on 2000 calories per day (or less).

(29) a. He ate some of your mangoes, if not all/*none of them.
b. This classroom is always warm, if not hot/*cool.

3. The "at least" interpretation is only possible with the distributive reading of numerals, not the collective reading (30); this is not the case with other scalar quantifiers (31).

(30) a. Four salesmen have called me today, if not more.
b. Four students carried this sofa upstairs for me, #if not more.

(31) a. Most of the students have long hair, perhaps all of them.
b. Most of the students surrounded the stadium, perhaps all of them.

4. The "at least" interpretation is disfavored when a numeral is the focus of a question (32), but this is not the case with other scalar quantifiers (33):

(32) Q: Do you have two children?
A1: No, three.
A2: ?Yes, in fact three.

(33) Q: Are many of your friends linguists?
A1: ??No, all of them.
A2: Yes, in fact all of them.

It is important to bear in mind that sentences like (34) can have different truth values depending on which reading of the numeral is chosen:

(34) If Mrs. Smith has three children, there will be enough seatbelts for the whole family to ride together.

One possible analysis might be to treat the alternation between the 'at least *n*' vs. 'exactly *n*' readings as a kind of systematic polysemy. However, it seems that most pragmaticists prefer to treat numeral words as being underspecified or indeterminate between the two, with the intended reading in a given context being supplied by explicature.[20]

9.5 Conclusion

The large body of work exploring the implications of Grice's theory has forced us to recognize that Grice's relatively simple view of the boundary between semantics and pragmatics is not tenable. Early work in pragmatics often assumed that pragmatic inferences did not affect the truth-conditional content of an utterance, apart from the limited amount of contextual information needed for disambiguation of ambiguous forms, assignment of referents to pronouns, etc. Under this view, truth-conditional content is almost the same thing as conventional meaning.

In this chapter we have discussed various ways in which pragmatic inferences do contribute to truth-conditional content. We have seen that some (at least) generalized conversational implicatures affect truth-conditions, and we have seen that other types of pragmatic inferences, which we refer to as explicatures, are needed in order to determine the truth value of a sentence. In Chapter 11 we discuss the opposite kind of challenge, namely cases where conventional meaning (semantic content) does not contribute to the truth-conditional meaning of a sentence. But first, in Chapter 10, we discuss a special type of conversational implicature known as an INDIRECT SPEECH ACT.

[20] See for example Horn (1992) and Carston (1998).

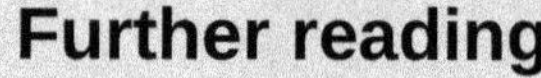

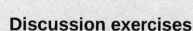

Further reading

Birner (2012/2013: ch. 3) presents a good overview of the issues discussed here, including a very helpful comparison of Relevance Theory with the "neo-Gricean" approaches of Levinson and Horn. Horn (2004) and Carston (2004) provide helpful surveys of recent work on implicature, Horn from a neo-Gricean perspective and Carston from a Relevance Theory perspective. K. Bach (2010) discusses the differences between his notion of "impliciture" and the Relevance Theory notion of explicature. Geurts (2011) provides a good introduction to, and a detailed analysis of, scalar and quantity implicatures.

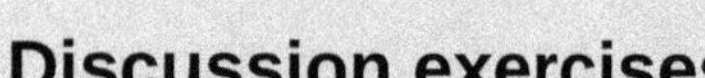

Discussion exercises

A. Explicature. Identify the explicatures which would be necessary in order to evaluate the truth value for each of the following examples:[a]

1. He arrived at the bank too early.
2. All students must pass phonetics.
3. No-one goes there anymore.
4. To buy a house in London you need money.
5. [Max: How was the party? Did it go well?]
   Amy: There wasn't enough drink and everyone left early.

B. Pragmatics in the lexicon. Horn (1972) observes that many languages have lexical items which express positive universal quantification (*all, every, everyone, everything, always, both,* etc.) and the corresponding negative concepts (*no, none, nothing, no one, never, neither,* etc.). In each case, the positive term can be paraphrased in terms of the corresponding negative, and vice versa. For example, *Everything is negotiable* can be paraphrased as *Nothing is non-negotiable.* However, most languages seem to lack negative counterparts to the existential quantifiers (*some, someone, sometimes,* etc.). In order to paraphrase an existential statement like *Something is negotiable,* we have to use a quantifying phrase, rather than a single word, as in *Not everything is non-negotiable.*

Try to formulate a pragmatic explanation for this lexical asymmetry, i.e., the fact that few if any languages have lexical items that mean *not everything, not everyone, not always, not both,* etc. (**Hint**: think about the kinds of implicatures that might be triggered by the various classes of quantifying words.)

[a]Examples (3-5) are taken from Carston & Hall (2012).

10 Indirect Speech Acts

10.1 Introduction

Deborah Tannen (1981) recounts the following experience as a visitor to Greece:

> While I was staying with a family on the island of Crete, no matter how early I awoke, my hostess managed to have a plate of scrambled eggs waiting on the table for me by the time I was up and dressed; and at dinner every evening, dessert included a pile of purple seeded grapes. Now I don't happen to like seeded grapes or eggs scrambled, but I had to eat them both because they had been set out—at great inconvenience to my hosts—especially for me. It turned out that I was getting eggs scrambled because I had asked, while watching my hostess in the kitchen, whether she ever prepared eggs by beating them, and I was getting grapes out of season because I had asked at dinner one evening how come I hadn't seen grapes since I had arrived in Greece. My hosts had taken these careless questions as hints—that is, indirect expressions of my desires. In fact, I had not intended to hint anything, but had merely been trying to be friendly, to make conversation.

Tannen's hosts believed that she was trying to communicate more than the literal meaning of her words, that is, that she was trying to implicate something without saying it directly. Moreover, the implicature which they (mistakenly) understood had the effect of doing more than the literal meaning of her words would do. Her utterances, taken literally, were simply questions, i.e., requests for information. Her hosts interpreted these utterances as implicated requests to provide her with scrambled eggs and grapes. In other words, Tannen's hosts interpreted these utterances as INDIRECT SPEECH ACTS.

A speech act is an action that speakers perform by speaking: offering thanks, greetings, invitations, making requests, giving orders, etc. A DIRECT SPEECH ACT is one that is accomplished by the literal meaning of the words that are spoken. An INDIRECT SPEECH ACT is one that is accomplished by implicature.

Tannen (1981) states that "misunderstandings like these are commonplace between members of what appear to (but may not necessarily) be the same culture.

However, such mix ups are especially characteristic of cross-cultural communication."[1] For this reason, indirect speech acts are a major focus of research in the areas of applied linguistics and second language acquisition. They also constitute a potential challenge for translation.

We begin this chapter in §10.2 with a summary of J.L. Austin's theory of speech acts, another foundational contribution to the field of pragmatics. Austin begins by identifying and analyzing a previously unrecognized class of utterances which he calls PERFORMATIVES. He then generalizes his account of performatives to apply to all speech acts.

In §10.3 we summarize Searle's theory of indirect speech acts. Searle builds on Austin's theory, with certain modifications, and goes on to propose answers to two fundamental questions: How do hearers recognize indirect speech acts (i.e., how do they know that the intended speech act is not the one expressed by the literal meaning of the words spoken), and having done so, how do they correctly identify the intended speech act? (Both of these issues tend to be difficult for even advanced language learners.) An important part of Searle's answer to these questions is the recognition that indirect speech acts are a special type of conversational implicature.

In §10.4 we touch briefly on some cross-linguistic issues, including the question of whether Searle's theory provides an adequate account for indirect speech acts in all languages.

10.2 Performatives

In Chapter 3 we cited the definition of sentence meaning repeated here in (1):

(1) "To know the meaning of a [declarative] sentence is to know what the world would have to be like for the sentence to be true."[2]

Perhaps you wondered, gentle reader, how we might define the meaning of a non-declarative sentence, such as a question or a command? It must be possible for someone to know the meaning of a question without knowing what the world would have to be like for the question to be true —a question is not the sort of thing which CAN be true, but clearly this does not mean that questions are meaningless.

The semantic analysis of questions and commands is an interesting and challenging area of research, but one that we will not attempt to address in the

[1] See also Tannen (1975; 1986).

[2] Dowty et al. (1981: 4).

present book. Even if we restrict our attention to declarative sentences, however, we find some for which the definition in (1) does not seem to be directly applicable. J.L. Austin, in a 1955 series of lectures at Harvard University (published as Austin 1962), called attention to a class of declarative sentences which cannot be assigned a truth value, because they do not make any claim about the state of the world. Some examples are presented in (2–3).[3]

Austin's examples:

(2) a. 'I do' (sc. take this woman to be my lawful wedded wife) – as uttered in the course of the marriage ceremony.
  b. 'I name this ship the Queen Elizabeth' – as uttered when smashing the bottle against the stem.
  c. 'I bet you sixpence it will rain tomorrow.'

(3) Further examples:
  a. I hereby sentence you to 10 years in prison.
  b. I now pronounce you man and wife.
  c. I declare this meeting adjourned.
  d. By virtue of the authority vested in me by the State of XX, and through the Board of Governors of the University of XX, I do hereby confer upon each of you the degree for which you have qualified, with all the rights, privileges and responsibilities appertaining.

Austin pointed out that when someone says *I now pronounce you man and wife* or *I hereby declare this meeting adjourned*, the speaker is not describing something, but doing something. The speaker is not making a claim about the world, but rather changing the world. For this reason, it doesn't make sense to ask whether these statements are true or false. It does, however, make sense to ask whether the person's action was successful or appropriate. Was the speaker licensed to perform a marriage ceremony at that time and place, or empowered to pass sentence in a court of law? Were all the necessary procedures followed completely and correctly? etc.

Austin called this special class of declarative sentences PERFORMATIVES. He argued that we need to recognize performatives as a new class of SPEECH ACTS (things that people can do by speaking), in addition to the commonly recognized speech acts such as statements, questions, and commands. Austin refers to the

[3] Much of the discussion in this section is based on Austin (1961), which is the transcript of an unscripted radio address he delivered on the BBC in 1956.

act which the speaker intends to perform by speaking as the ILLOCUTIONARY FORCE of the utterance.[4]

As noted above, it does not make sense to try to describe truth conditions for performatives. Instead, Austin says, we need to identify the conditions under which the performative speech act will be FELICITOUS, i.e. successful, valid, and appropriate. He identifies the following kinds of FELICITY CONDITIONS:

(4) Felicity Conditions (Austin 1962: 14–15):

(A.1) There must exist an accepted conventional procedure having a certain conventional effect, that procedure to include the uttering of certain words by certain persons in certain circumstances, and further,

(A.2) the particular persons and circumstances in a given case must be appropriate for the invocations of the particular procedure invoked.

(B.1) The procedure must be executed by all participants both correctly and

(B.2) completely.

(C.1) Where, as often, the procedure is designed for use by persons having certain thoughts or feelings, or for the inauguration of certain consequential conduct on the part of any participant, then a person participating in and so invoking the procedure must in fact have those thoughts or feelings, and the participants must intend so to conduct themselves, and further

(C.2) must actually so conduct themselves subsequently.[5]

Austin referred to violations of conditions A–B as MISFIRES; if these conditions are not fulfilled, then the intended acts are not successfully performed or are invalid. For example, if a person who is not licensed to perform a marriage ceremony says *I now pronounce you man and wife*, the couple being addressed does not become legally married as a result of this utterance. Violations of C Austin called ABUSES. If this condition is violated, the speech act is still performed and would be considered valid, but it is done insincerely or inappropriately. For example, if someone says *I promise to return this book by Sunday*, but has no intention

[4]Austin distinguished ILLOCUTIONARY ACT, the act which the speaker intends to perform "in speaking", from LOCUTIONARY ACT (the act of speaking) and PERLOCUTIONARY ACT (the actual result achieved "by speaking" the utterance).

[5]I have replaced Austin's "gamma" (Γ) with "C", for convenience.

of doing so, the utterance still counts as a promise; but it is an insincere promise, a promise which the speaker intends to break.

Performatives can be distinguished from normal declarative sentences by the following special features:

(5) Properties of explicit performatives:
- They always occur in indicative mood and simple present tense, with a non-habitual interpretation. As we will see in Chapter 20, the simple present form of an event-type verb in English typically requires a habitual interpretation; but this is not the case for the examples in (2–3).
- They frequently contain a PERFORMATIVE VERB, i.e. a verb which can be used either to describe or to perform the intended speech act (e.g. *sentence, declare, confer, invite, request, order, accuse,* etc.).
- Performative clauses normally occur in active voice with a first person subject, as in (2–3), but passive voice with second or third person subject is possible with certain verbs; see examples in (6).
- Performatives can optionally be modified by the performative adverb *hereby*; this adverb cannot be used with non-performative statements.

(6) a. Passengers are requested not to talk to the driver while the bus is moving.
b. You are hereby sentenced to 10 years in prison.
c. Permission is hereby granted to use this software for non-commercial purposes.
d. Richard Smith is hereby promoted to the rank of Lieutenant Colonel.

Austin refers to performative sentences which exhibit the features listed in (5) as EXPLICIT PERFORMATIVES. He notes that explicit performatives can often be paraphrased using sentences which lack some or all of these features. For example, the performative *I hereby order you to shut the door* is more commonly expressed using a simple imperative, *Shut the door!* Similarly, the performative *I hereby invite you to join me for dinner* would be more politely and naturally expressed using a question, *Would you like to join me for dinner?* Since the same speech act can be performed with either expression, it would seem odd to classify one as a performative but not the other. We will refer to utterances which function as paraphrases of explicit performatives but lack the features listed in (5) as IMPLICIT PERFORMATIVES.

Conversely, it turns out that most speech acts can be paraphrased using an explicit performative. For example, the question *Is it raining?* can be paraphrased as a performative: *I hereby ask you whether it is raining*. In the same way, simple statements can be paraphrased *I hereby inform you that...*, and commands can be paraphrased *I hereby order/command you to....* Once again, if the same speech act can be performed with either expression, it seems odd to classify one as a performative but not the other. These observations lead us to the conclusion that virtually all utterances should be analyzed as performatives, whether explicit or not.

But if all utterances are to be analyzed as performatives, then the label PERFORMATIVE doesn't seem to be very useful; what have we gained? In fact we have gained several important insights into the meaning of sentential utterances. First, in addition to their propositional content, all such utterances have an ILLOCUTIONARY FORCE, which is an important aspect of their meaning. In the case of explicit performatives, we can identify the illocutionary force by simply looking at the performative verb; but with implicit performatives, as discussed below, the illocutionary force depends partly on the context of the utterance.

Second, all utterances have Felicity Conditions. Certain speech acts (namely statements) also have truth conditions; but Felicity Conditions are something that needs to be analyzed for all speech acts, including statements. As discussed in the following section, in order to explain how indirect speech acts work, we need to identify the Felicity Conditions for the intended act.

The concept of Felicity Conditions is useful in other contexts as well. For example, it would be very odd for someone to say *The cat is on the mat, but I do not believe that it is.*[6] Austin suggests that this statement is not a logical contradiction but rather a violation of the Felicity Conditions for statements. One of the Felicity Conditions would be that a person should not make a statement which he knows or believes to be false (essentially equivalent to Grice's maxim of Quality). It is just as outrageous to make a statement and then explicitly deny that you believe it, as it is to make a promise and then explicitly deny that you intend to carry it out (*I promise that I shall be there, but I haven't the least intention of being there*). We might refer to such an utterance as a pragmatic contradiction.

A similar situation would arise if someone were to say *All of John's children are bald*, when in fact he knew perfectly well that John had no children. Austin says that the problem with this statement is the same as with a man who offers to sell a piece of land that does not belong to him. If a transaction were made under these circumstances, it would not be legally valid; the sale would be null

[6]This is an example of Moore's paradox.

and void. Austin says that the statement *All of John's children are bald* would similarly be "void for lack of reference" if John has no children. So Austin may have been the first to suggest that presupposition failure is a pragmatic issue (an infelicity), and not purely semantic.

10.3 Indirect speech acts

The Nigerian professor Ozidi Bariki describes a conversation in which he said to a friend:

> "I love your left hand." (The friend had a cup of tea in his hand). The friend, in reaction to my utterance, transferred the cup to his right hand. That prompted me to say: "I love your right hand". My friend smiled, recognized my desire for tea and told his sister, "My friend wants tea"... My friend's utterance addressed to his sister in reaction to mine was a representative, i.e. a simple statement: "my friend wants a tea". The girl rightly interpreted the context of the representative to mean a directive. In other words, her brother (my friend) was ordering her to prepare some tea. (Bariki 2008)

This brief dialogue contains two examples of indirect speech acts. In both cases, the utterance has the form of a simple statement, but is actually intended to perform a different kind of act: request in the first case and command in the second. The second statement, "My friend wants tea," was immediately and automatically interpreted correctly by the addressee. (In African culture, when an older brother makes such a statement to his younger sister, there is only one possible interpretation.) The first statement, however, failed to communicate. Only after the second attempt was the addressee able to work out the intended meaning, not automatically at all, but as if he was trying to solve a riddle.

Bariki uses this example to illustrate the role that context plays in enabling the hearer to identify the intended speech act. But it also shows us that context alone is not enough. In the context of the first utterance, there was a natural association between what was said (*your left hand*) and what was intended (a cup of tea); the addressee was holding a cup of tea in his left hand. In spite of this, the addressee was unable to figure out what the speaker meant. The contrast between this failed attempt at communication and the immediately understood statement *My friend wants tea*, suggests that there are certain principles and conventions which need to be followed in order to make the illocutionary force of an utterance clear to the hearer.

We might define an INDIRECT SPEECH ACT (following Searle 1975) as an utterance in which one illocutionary act (the PRIMARY ACT) is intentionally performed by means of the performance of another act (the LITERAL ACT). In other words, it is an utterance whose form does not reflect the intended illocutionary force. *My friend wants tea* is a simple declarative sentence, the form which is normally used for making statements. In the context above, however, it was correctly interpreted as a command. So the literal act was a statement, but the primary act was a command.

Most if not all languages have grammatical and/or phonological means of distinguishing at least three basic types of sentences: statements, questions, and commands. The default expectation is that declarative sentences will express statements, interrogative sentences will express questions, and imperative sentences will express commands. When these expectations are met, we have a DIRECT SPEECH ACT because the grammatical form matches the intended illocutionary force. Explicit performatives are also direct speech acts.

An indirect speech act will normally be expressed as a declarative, interrogative, or imperative sentence; so the literal act will normally be a statement, question, or command. One of the best-known types of indirect speech act is the Rhetorical Question, which involves an interrogative sentence but is not intended to be a genuine request for information.

Why is the statement *I love your left hand* not likely to work as an indirect request for tea? Searle (1969; 1975) proposes that in order for an indirect speech act to be successful, the literal act should normally be related to the Felicity Conditions of the intended or primary act in certain specific ways. Searle restated Austin's Felicity Conditions under four headings: PREPARATORY CONDITIONS (background circumstances and knowledge about the speaker, hearer, and/or situation which must be true in order for the speech act to be felicitous); SINCERITY CONDITIONS (necessary psychological states of speaker and/or hearer); PROPOSITIONAL CONTENT (the kind of situation or event described by the underlying proposition); ESSENTIAL CONDITION (the essence of the speech act; what the act "counts as"). These four categories are illustrated in Table 10.1 using the speech acts of promising and requesting.

Generally speaking, speakers perform an indirect speech act by stating or asking about one of the Felicity Conditions (apart from the essential condition). The examples in (7) show some sentences that could be used as indirect requests for tea. Sentences (7a–b) ask about the preparatory condition for a request, namely the hearer's ability to perform the action. Sentences (7c–d) state the sincerity condition for a request, namely that the speaker wants the hearer to perform the action. Sentences (7e–f) ask about the propositional content of the request, namely the future act by the hearer.

(7) a. Do you have any tea?
b. Could you possibly give me some tea?
c. I would like you to give me some tea.
d. I would really appreciate a cup of tea.
e. Will you give me some tea?
f. Are you going to give me some tea?

All of these sentences could be understood as requests for tea, if spoken in the right context, but they are clearly not all equivalent: (7b) is a more polite way of asking than (7a); (7d) is a polite request, whereas (7c) sounds more demanding; (7e) is a polite request, whereas (7f) sounds impatient and even rude.

Not every possible strategy is actually available for a given speech act. For example, asking about the sincerity condition for a request is generally quite unnatural: *#Do I want you to give me some tea?* This is because speakers do not normally ask other people about their own mental or emotional states. So that specific strategy cannot be used to form an indirect request.

Table 10.1: Felicity Conditions for promises and requests (Adapted from Searle 1969; 1975; S = speaker; H = hearer; A = action)

	promise	request
preparatory conditions	(i) S is able to perform A (ii) H wants S to perform A, and S believes that H wants S to perform A (iii) it is not obvious that S will perform A	H is able to perform A
sincerity condition	S intends to perform A	S wants H to perform A
propositional content	predicates a future act by S	predicates a future act by H
essential condition	counts as an under- taking by S to do A	counts as an attempt by S to get H to do A

We almost automatically interpret examples like (7b) and (7e) as requests. This tendency is so strong that it may be hard to recognize them as indirect speech acts. The crucial point is that their grammatical form is that of a question, not a request. However, some very close paraphrases of these sentences, such as those in (8), would probably not be understood as requests in most contexts.

(8) a. Do you currently have the ability to provide me with tea?
b. Do you anticipate giving me a cup of tea in the near future?

We can see the difference quite clearly if we try to add the word *please* to each sentence. As we noted in Chapter 1, *please* is a marker of politeness which is restricted to occurring only in requests; it does not occur naturally in other kinds of speech acts. It is possible, and in most cases fairly natural, to add *please* to any of the sentences in (7), even to those which do not sound very polite on their own. However, this is not possible for the sentences in (8). This difference provides good evidence for saying that the sentences in (8) are not naturally interpretable as indirect requests.

(9) a. Could you possibly give me some tea, please?
b. Will you give me some tea, please?
c. I would like you to give me some tea, please.
d. Are you going to give me some tea (?please)?
e. Do you currently have the ability to provide me with tea (#please)?
f. Do you anticipate giving me a cup of tea in the near future (#please)?

The contrast between the acceptability of (7b) and (7e) as requests vs. the unacceptability of their close paraphrases in (8) suggests that the form of the sentence, as well as its semantic content, helps to determine whether an indirect speech act will be successful or not. We will return to this issue below, but first we need to think about a more fundamental question: How does the hearer recognize an indirect speech act? In other words, how does he know that the primary (intended) illocutionary force of the utterance is not the same as the literal force suggested by the form of the sentence?

Searle suggests that the key to solving this problem comes from Grice's Cooperative Principle. If someone asks the person sitting next to him at a dinner *Can you pass me the salt?*, we might expect the addressee to be puzzled. Only under the most unusual circumstances would this question be relevant to the current topic of conversation. Only under the most unusual circumstances would the answer to this question be informative, since few people who can sit up at a dinner table are physically unable to lift a salt shaker. In most contexts, the addressee could only believe the speaker to be obeying the Co-operative Principle if the question is not meant as a simple request for information, i.e., if the intended illocutionary force is something other than a question.

Having recognized this question as an indirect speech act, how does the addressee figure out what the intended illocutionary force is? Searle's solution is essentially the Gricean method of calculating implicatures, enriched by an understanding of the Felicity Conditions for the intended speech act. Searle (1975) suggests that the addressee might reason as follows: "This question is not relevant to the current topic of conversation, and the speaker cannot be in doubt about my ability to pass the salt. I believe him to be cooperating in the conversation, so there must be another point to the question. I know that a preparatory condition for making a request is the belief that the addressee is able to perform the requested action. I know that people often use salt at dinner, sharing a common salt shaker which they pass back and forth as requested. Since he has mentioned a preparatory condition for requesting me to perform this action, I conclude that this request is what he means to communicate."

So it is important that we understand indirect speech acts as a kind of conversational implicature. However, they are different in certain respects from the implicatures that Grice discussed. For example, Grice stated that implicatures are "non-detachable", meaning that semantically equivalent sentences should trigger the same implicatures in the same context. However, as we noted above, this is not always true with indirect speech acts. In the current example, Searle points out that the question *Are you able to pass me the salt?*, although a close paraphrase of *Can you pass me the salt?*, is much less likely to be interpreted as a request (*#Are you able to please pass me the salt?*). How can we account for this?

Searle argues that, while the meaning of the indirect speech act is calculable or explainable in Gricean terms, the forms of indirect speech acts are partly conventionalized. Searle refers to these as "conventions of usage", in contrast to normal idioms like *kick the bucket* (for 'die') which we might call conventions of meaning or sense.

Conventionalized speech acts are different from normal idioms in several important ways. First, the meanings of normal idioms are not calculable or predictable from their literal meanings. The phrase *kick the bucket* contains no words which have any component of meaning relating to death.

Second, when an indirect speech act is performed, both the literal and primary acts are understood to be part of what is meant. In Searle's terms, the primary act is performed "by way of" performing the literal act. We can see this because, as illustrated in (10), the hearer could appropriately reply to the primary act alone (A1), the literal act alone (A2), or to both acts together (A3). Moreover, in reporting indirect speech acts, it is possible (and in fact quite common) to use matrix verbs which refer to the literal act rather than the primary act, as illustrated in (11–12).

(10) Q: Can you (please) tell me the time?
A1: It's almost 5:30.
A2: No, I'm sorry, I can't; my watch has stopped.
A3: Yes, it's 5:30.

(11) a. Will you (please) pass me the salt?
b. He asked me whether I would pass him the salt.

(12) a. I want you to leave now (please).
b. He told me that he wanted me to leave.

In this way indirect speech acts are quite similar to other conversational implicatures, in that both the sentence meaning and the pragmatic inference are part of what is communicated. They are very different from normal idioms, which allow either the idiomatic meaning (the normal interpretation), or the literal meaning (under unusual circumstances), but never both together. The two senses of a normal idiom are antagonistic, as we can see by the fact that some people use them to form (admittedly bad) puns:

(13) Old milkmaids never die – they just kick the bucket.[7]

Birner (2012/2013: 196) points out that under Searle's view, indirect speech acts are similar to generalized conversational implicatures. In both cases the implicature is part of the default interpretation of the utterance; it will arise unless it is blocked by specific features in the context, or is explicitly negated, etc. We have to work pretty hard to create a context in which the question *Can you pass the salt?* would not be interpreted as a request, but it can be done.[8]

Searle states that politeness is one of the primary reasons for using an indirect speech act. Notice that all of the sentences in (7), except perhaps (7f), sound more polite than the simple imperative: *Give me some tea!* He suggests that this motivation may help to explain why certain forms tend to be conventionalized for particular purposes.

[7] Richard Lederer (1988) *Get Thee to a Punnery*. Wyrick & Company.

[8] Searle (1975: 69) suggests that a doctor might ask such a question to check on the progress of a patient with an injured arm.

10.4 Indirect speech acts across languages

Searle states that his analysis of indirect speech acts as conventions of usage helps to explain why the intended illocutionary force is sometimes preserved in translation, and sometimes not. (This again is very different from the idiomatic meanings of normal idioms, which generally do not survive in translation.) He points out that literal translations of a question like *Can you help me?* would be understood as requests in French and German, but not in Czech. The reason that the intended force is sometimes preserved in translation is that indirect speech acts are calculable. They are motivated by Gricean principles which are widely believed to apply to all languages, subject to a certain amount of cultural variation. The reason that the intended force is not always preserved in translation is that indirect speech acts are partly conventionalized, and different languages may choose to conventionalize different specific forms.

It is often difficult for non-native speakers to recognize and correctly interpret indirect speech acts in a second language. Wierzbicka (1985: 175), for example, states: "Poles learning English must be taught the potential ambiguity of *would you–* sentences, or *why don't you–* sentences, just as they must be taught the polysemy of the word *bank*." This has been a major area of research in second language acquisition studies, and most scholars agree that this is a significant challenge even for advanced learners of another language.

There is less agreement concerning whether the same basic principles govern the formation of indirect speech acts in all languages. Numerous studies have pointed out cross-linguistic differences in the use of specific linguistic features, preferred or conventionalized patterns for specific speech acts, cultural variation in ways of showing politeness, contexts where direct vs. indirect speech acts are preferred, etc.

Wierzbicka (1985) argues that Searle's analysis of indirect speech acts is not universally applicable, but reflects an Anglo-centric bias. She points out for example that English seems to be unusual in its strong tendency to avoid the use of the imperative verb form. The strategy of expressing indirect commands via questions is so strongly preferred that it is no longer a marker of politeness; it is frequently used (at least in Australian English) in impolite speech laced with profanity, obscenity, or other expressives indicating anger, contempt, etc. Kalisz (1992) agrees with many of Wierzbicka's specific observations concerning differences between English and Polish, but argues that Searle's basic claims about the nature of indirect speech acts are not disproven by these differences.

It is certainly true that there is a wide range of variation across languages in terms of what counts as an apology, promise, etc., and in the specific features that distinguish appropriate from inappropriate ways for performing a particular speech act. For example, Olshtain & Cohen (1989) recount the following incidents to illustrate differences in acceptable apologies between English and Israeli Hebrew:

> One morning, Mrs G., a native speaker of English now living in Israel, was doing her daily shopping at the local supermarket. As she was pushing her shopping cart she unintentionally bumped into Mr Y., a native Israeli. Her natural reaction was to say "I'm sorry" (in Hebrew). Mr Y. turned to her and said, "Lady, you could at least apologize". On another occasion the very same Mr Y. arrived late for a meeting conducted by Mr W. (a native speaker of English) in English. As he walked into the room he said "The bus was late", and sat down. Mr W. obviously annoyed, muttered to himself "These Israelis, why don't they ever apologize!" [Olshtain & Cohen 1989: 53]

In a similar vein, Egner (2002) shows that in many African cultures, a promise only counts as a binding commitment when it is repeated. Clearly there are many significant differences across languages in the conventional features of speech acts; but this does not necessarily mean that the underlying system which makes it possible to recognize and interpret indirect speech acts is fundamentally different.

Searle's key insights are that indirect speech acts are a type of conversational implicature, and that the felicity conditions for the intended act play a crucial role in the interpretation of these implicatures. Given our current state of knowledge, it seems likely that these basic principles do in fact hold across languages. But like most cross-linguistic generalizations in semantics and pragmatics, this hypothesis needs to be tested across a wider range of languages.

10.5 Conclusion

A speech act is an action that speakers perform by speaking. Languages typically have grammatical ways of distinguishing sentence types (moods) corresponding to at least three basic speech acts: statements, commands, and questions. When the speaker's intended speech act (or ILLOCUTIONARY FORCE) corresponds to the sentence type that is chosen, a direct speech act is performed. In addition, the declarative sentence type is generally used for a special class of direct speech acts which we call EXPLICIT PERFORMATIVES. When the speaker's intended speech act does not correspond to the sentence type that is chosen, an indirect speech act is performed. Indirect speech acts are conversational implicatures, and their interpretation can be explained in Gricean terms; but in addition, they are often partly conventionalized.

All speech acts are subject to felicity conditions, that is, conditions that must be fulfilled in order for the speech act to be FELICITOUS (i.e., valid and appropriate). Successful indirect speech acts typically involve literal sentence meanings which state or query the felicity conditions for the primary (i.e., intended) speech act.

Further reading

Birner (2012/2013: ch.6) presents a useful overview of the issues addressed in this chapter. Austin (1961), based on a radio address he delivered on the BBC, provides a readable, non-technical introduction to his theory of performatives. Searle (1975) provides a concise summary of his theory of indirect speech acts. Brown & Levinson (1978) is the foundational study of sociolinguistic and pragmatic aspects of politeness across languages. The volumes edited by Blum-Kulka et al. (1989) and Gass & Neu (2006) contain studies on indirect speech acts in cross-cultural and second language communication.

Discussion exercises

A. Identifying indirect speech acts. Identify both the literal and primary act in each of the following indirect speech acts (square brackets are used to provide [context]):

1. [S1: My motorcycle is out of the shop; let's go for another ride.]
   S2: *Do you think I'm crazy?*

2. [senior citizen dialing the police:]
   I'm alone in the house and someone is trying to break down my door.

3. [S1: I'm really sorry for bumping into your car.]
   S2: *Don't give it another thought.*

B. Indirect speech act strategies. Assume that the felicity conditions for offers are essentially the same as for promises. (The main difference is that an offer does not count as a commitment on the part of the speaker unless and until the addressee accepts it.) Try to make up one example of a sentence that would work as an indirect offer for each of the following strategies:

1. by querying the preparatory conditions of the direct offer;
2. by stating the preparatory conditions of the direct offer;
3. by stating the propositional content of the direct offer;
4. by stating the sincerity condition of the direct offer.

Homework exercises

A. Performatives.[a] State whether the following utterances would be naturally interpreted as explicit performatives, and explain the evidence which supports your conclusion.

1. I acknowledge you as my legal heir.

> Model answer
> *I hereby acknowledge you as my legal heir* is quite natural. The verb is simple present tense, referring to a single event with no habitual meaning. It is active indicative with first person singular subject. Therefore this utterance is an explicit performative.

2. Smith acknowledges you as his legal heir.
3. I request the court to reconsider my petition.
4. I'm promising Mabel to take her to a movie next week.
5. I promised Mabel to take her to a movie next week.
6. I expect that you will arrive on time from now on.
7. You are advised that anything you say may be used as evidence against you.

B. Indirect speech acts (1). For each of the following indirect speech acts, identify both the literal and primary act.

1. [young woman to man who has just proposed to her]
   I hope that we can always remain friends.

   > Model answer
   >
   > literal act = statement; primary act = refusal.

2. [housewife to next-door neighbor]
   Can you spare a cup of sugar?
3. [flight attendant to passenger who is standing in the aisle]
   The captain has turned on the "fasten seatbelt" sign.
4. [host to friend who has just arrived for a visit]
   How would you like a cup of coffee?
5. [office manager to colleague who has invited him to go out for lunch]
   Look at that pile of papers in my inbox!
6. [addressing neighbor who has a broken arm]
   I will mow your lawn for you this month.

C. Indirect speech acts (2). Based on felicity conditions for requests, and using your own examples, try to form one indirect request for each of the following strategies.

1. by querying the preparatory condition of the direct request

   > Model answer
   >
   > preparatory condition = Hearer is able to perform action.
   >
   > Possible ISAs using this strategy:
   >
   > Can you give me a ride to church tomorrow?
   >
   > Would you be able to give me a ride to church tomorrow?

2. by stating the preparatory condition of the direct request;
3. by querying the propositional content of the direct request;
4. by stating the sincerity condition of the direct request.

---

[a]Sections A-C are modeled after Saeed (2009: 251–253).

11 Conventional implicature and use-conditional meaning

11.1 Introduction

In Chapter 8 we mentioned the somewhat mysterious concept of CONVENTIONAL IMPLICATURE. This term was coined by Grice, but he commented only briefly on what he meant by it. The most widely cited example of an expression that carries a conventional implicature is the word *but*. Grice used the example in (1a), based on a cliché of the Victorian era:

(1) a. She is poor but she is honest.
  b. She is poor and she is honest. [Grice 1961: 127]

Grice argued that a speaker who says (1a) only ASSERTS (1b). The word *but* provides an additional element of meaning, indicating that the speaker believes there to be a contrast between poverty and honesty. This extra element of meaning (implied contrast or counter-expectation) is the conventional implicature. It is said to be conventional because it is an inherent part of the meaning of *but*, and is not derived from the context of use. Grice called it an "implicature" because he, like Frege before him, felt that if this additional element of meaning is false but (1b) is true, we would not say that the person who says (1a) is making a false statement. In other words, the conventional implicature does not contribute to the truth conditions of the statement.[1]

Nevertheless, someone might object to (1a) as in (2), claiming that the word *but* has been misused. The core of this objection would not be the truth of the statement in (1a) but the appropriateness of the conjunction that was chosen.

(2) What do you mean "but"? There is no conflict between poverty and honesty!

Recent work by Christopher Potts and others has tried to clarify the nature of conventional implicature, and has greatly extended the range of expressions

[1]Recall similar comments by Frege regarding *but*, which were quoted in Chapter 8.

which are included under this label. In this chapter we will look at some of these expression types.

A core property of conventional implicatures is that they do not change the conditions under which the sentence will be true, but rather the conditions under which the sentence can be appropriately used. For this reason, some authors have made a distinction between TRUTH-CONDITIONAL MEANING VS. USE-CONDITIONAL MEANING.[2] The truth-conditional meaning that is asserted in (1a) would be equivalent to the meaning of (1b), while the implied contrast between *poor* vs. *honest* comes from the use-conditional meaning of *but*. The term "use-conditional meaning" seems to cover essentially the same range of phenomena as "conventional implicature", and we will treat these terms as synonyms.[3]

We begin in §11.2 with a discussion of the definition and diagnostic properties of conventional implicatures, as described by Potts. We illustrate this discussion using certain types of adverbs in English which seem to contribute use-conditional meaning rather than truth-conditional meaning. In the rest of the chapter we look at some use-conditional expressions in other languages: honorifics in Japanese (§11.3), politeness markers in Korean (§11.4), honorific pronouns and other polite register lexical choices (§11.5), and discourse particles in German (§11.6).

11.2 Distinguishing truth-conditional vs. use-conditional meaning

11.2.1 Diagnostic properties of conventional implicatures

A passage from Grice's comments on conventional implicatures was quoted in Chapter 8, which included the following discussion of the meaning of *therefore*:

> If I say (smugly), *He is an Englishman; he is, therefore, brave,* I have certainly committed myself, by virtue of the meaning of my words, to its being the case that his being brave is a consequence of (follows from) his being an Englishman... I do not want to say that my utterance of this sentence would be, strictly speaking, false should the consequence in question fail to hold. (Grice 1975: 44)

Based on Grice's comments, Potts formulates a definition of conventional implicatures that includes the following points: (i) conventional implicatures are

[2] Gutzmann (2015), Recanati (2004).

[3] In this we follow the usage of Gutzmann (2015).

(normally) beliefs of the speaker ("I have certainly committed MYSELF"), and so in a sense "speaker-oriented"; (ii) they are part of the intrinsic, conventional meaning of a given expression or construction ("by virtue of the meaning of my words"), and so are not cancellable; (iii) they do not contribute to the truth-conditional content which is the main point of the assertion.[4]

Potts uses the term AT-ISSUE CONTENT to refer to the main point of an utterance: the core information that is asserted in a statement or queried in a question. So in Grice's example, the at-issue content of the assertion is *He is English and brave*. The conventional implicature contributed by *therefore* is that a causal relationship exists between two situations (in this case, between being an Englishman and being brave).

The definition outlined above leads us to expect that conventional implicatures will have certain properties that allow us to distinguish them from other kinds of meaning. Potts suggests that conventional implicatures are:[5]

CONVENTIONAL, i.e., semantic in nature rather than pragmatic (as we defined those terms in Chapter 9). They must be learned as part of the meaning of a given word or construction, and cannot be calculated from context.

SECONDARY: not part of the at-issue content, but rather used to provide supporting content, contextual information, editorial comments, evaluation, etc.

INDEPENDENT: separate from and logically independent of the at-issue content.

"SCOPELESS": since conventional implicatures are not part of the at-issue content, they are typically not altered by negation, interrogative mood, etc. Often they take scope over the whole sentence even when embedded in subordinate clauses.

NOT PRESUPPOSED:[6] not assumed to be shared by the addressee, in contrast to presuppositions. So, for example, while the addressee might challenge a conventional implicature, as illustrated in (2) above, the "Hey, wait a minute" response seems less natural (3d).

Many of these properties are similar to the properties of expressive meaning that we listed in Chapter 2. This is no accident, since expressives provide a clear example of use-conditional meaning. The expressive term *jerk* in example (3a) reflects a negative attitude toward Peterson, and this negative attitude is a belief of the speaker. The negative attitude is not calculated from the context, but comes directly from the conventional meaning of the word *jerk*. It is not part of the at-issue content of the sentence, so a hearer who does not share this negative

[4]Potts (2005; 2012); see also Horn (1997: 39).

[5]Potts (2015); a similar list is presented for expressives in Potts (2007c).

[6]Potts uses the term "Backgrounded" for this concept.

attitude would not judge (3a) to be a false statement. The negative attitude is still expressed if the sentence is negated or questioned (3b–c).

(3) a. That jerk Peterson is the only economist on this committee.
    b. That jerk Peterson isn't the only economist on this committee.
    c. Is that jerk Peterson the only economist on this committee?
    d. #Hey, wait a minute! I didn't know that Peterson was a jerk!

Potts lists a wide variety of other expression types that illustrate these properties, including non-restrictive relative clauses and other kinds of parenthetical comments. In the remainder of this section we will focus on certain types of adverbs which seem to express use-conditional meanings.

11.2.2 Speaker-oriented adverbs

In this section we will discuss two classes of English adverbs. EVALUATIVE ADVERBS (e.g. *(un)fortunately, oddly, sadly, surprisingly, inexplicably*) provide information about the speaker's attitude toward the proposition being expressed. SPEECH ACT ADVERBIALS (e.g. *frankly, honestly, seriously, confidentially*) provide information about the manner in which the speaker is making the current statement. We will use the term SPEAKER-ORIENTED ADVERBS as a generic term that includes both of these classes.[7]

There are several reasons for thinking that speaker-oriented adverbs do not contribute to the truth-conditional content of the sentence. The adverbs in (4), for example, seem to contradict the asserted proposition: one cannot tell a lie *frankly*; the faculty are unlikely to make their demand *confidentially*; and the mayor, it seems, was not curious enough. Yet these sentences are not contradictions, precisely because these adverbs are not understood as contributing to the at-issue propositional content of the sentence. Rather, they provide information about the manner in which the speech act is being performed (4a–b) or the speaker's attitude toward the proposition expressed (4c).

(4) a. *Frankly*, your cousin is a habitual liar.
    b. *Confidentially*, the faculty are planning to demand that the provost resign.
    c. *Curiously* the mayor never asked where all the money came from.

[7]The label EVALUATIVE ADVERBS comes from Ernst (2009). Ernst uses the term SPEAKER-ORIENTED ADVERBS as to include not only evaluative adverbs and speech act adverbials, but also modal adverbs like *probably*. Potts (2005) uses the term SPEAKER-ORIENTED ADVERBS to refer to the class that I call EVALUATIVE ADVERBS.

Because they do not contribute to the proposition that is being asserted, it would be inappropriate to challenge the truth of a statement based on the content expressed by these adverbs (5–6). The hearer may express disagreement with the adverbial content by saying something like: *I agree that p, but I do not consider that curious/fortunate/etc.* But this would not be grounds for calling the original statement false.

(5) A: *Curiously/fortunately* the mayor never asked where all the money came from.
B: That's not true; he asked me just last week.
B': #That's not true; he never asked, but there is nothing curious/ fortunate about that.

(6) A: *Frankly/confidentially,* Jones is not the best-qualified candidate for this job.
B: That's not true; he is the only candidate who holds a relevant degree.
B': #That's not true; he is not qualified, but you are not speaking frankly/ confidentially.

Further evidence for the claim that these speaker-oriented adverbs are not part of the propositional content being asserted comes from their behavior under negation and questioning. When a sentence containing an evaluative or speech act adverbial is negated or questioned, the adverb itself cannot be interpreted as part of what is being negated or questioned. For example, (7a) cannot mean 'It is not fortunate that the best team won' but only 'It is fortunate that the best team did not win.' Example (7b) cannot mean 'Was it unfortunate that he lost the vision in that eye?' but only 'Did he lose the vision in that eye? If so, it was unfortunate.' Speech act adverbials in questions like (7c) are not part of what is being questioned, but generally describe the manner in which the speaker wants the addressee to answer the question. As such examples show, evaluative and speech act adverbials are not interpreted as being under the scope of sentence negation or interrogative mood.

(7) a. ... the best team *fortunately* didn't win on this occasion.[8]
b. Was it ok or did he *unfortunately* lose the vision in that eye?[9]

[8] http://sportwitness.ning.com/forum/topics/nextgen

[9] https://www.inspire.com/groups/preemie/discussion/rop-after-2-ops-scarring-is-pulling-the-retina-away/

c. Is he, *frankly*, combative enough? (referring to a potential presidential candidate)[10]

These claims about speaker-oriented adverbs apply only to their use as sentence adverbs, where the speaker uses them to describe his own manner of speaking or attitude toward the current speech act. Sentence adverbs occur most freely in sentence initial position, as in (8a) and (9a); but other positions are also possible (normally with the adverb set off from the rest of the sentence by pauses) as illustrated in (8b–d) and (9b–d).

(8)
   a. *Curiously*, the mayor never asked where all the money came from.
   b. The mayor, *curiously*, never asked where all the money came from.
   c. The mayor never asked, *curiously*, where all the money came from.
   d. The mayor never asked where all the money came from, *curiously*.

(9)
   a. *Frankly/confidentially*, Jones is not the best-qualified candidate for this job.
   b. Jones, *confidentially*, is not the best-qualified candidate for this job.
   c. Jones is not, *frankly*, the best-qualified candidate for this job.
   d. Jones is not the best-qualified candidate for this job, *frankly*.

A number of speech act adverbials also have a second use as manner adverbs, typically occurring within the VP as in (10A). In this use they describe the manner of the agent of a reported speech act. When these forms are used as manner adverbs, they do contribute to the "at issue" content of the sentence. We can see that this is so because the truth of an assertion can be challenged if such an adverb is misused, as in (10B).

(10) A: Jones told the committee *frankly/confidentially* about his criminal record.
   B: That's not true; he told them, but he did not speak frankly/confidentially.

Moreover, these manner adverbs are part of the propositional content which can be negated (11b) and questioned (12b). This contrasts with the behavior of the same forms used as sentence adverbs, which are not interpreted as being included under negation (11a) or questioning (12a).

[10] www.wbur.org/2011/12/21/romney-nh-6

(11) a. Jones did not, *confidentially*, inform the committee about his criminal record.
  b. Jones did not inform the committee *confidentially* about his criminal record; he told them in a public hearing.

(12) a. *Confidentially*, did Jones tell the committee about this?
  b. Did Jones tell you this *confidentially*, or can we inform the other members of the committee?

A number of the evaluative adverbs are morphologically related to an adjective that takes a propositional argument. In simple sentences, the adverbial and adjectival forms of a given root can be used to paraphrase each other, as seen in (13–15).

(13) a. *Fortunately*, Jones doesn't realize how valuable this parchment is.
  b. It is *fortunate* that Jones doesn't realize how valuable this parchment is.

(14) a. *Curiously* the mayor never asked where all the money came from.
  b. It is *curious* that the mayor never asked where all the money came from.

(15) a. *Oddly*, Jones never got that parchment appraised before he put it up for auction.
  b. It is *odd* that Jones never got that parchment appraised before he put it up for auction.

However, evaluative adjectives, in contrast to the corresponding evaluative adverbs, do contribute to the at-issue content of the utterance. They can provide grounds for challenging the truth of a statement, as in (16), and they are part of the propositional content which can be negated (17) or questioned (18).

(16) A: It is *curious/fortunate* that the mayor never asked where all the money came from.
B: That's not true; the fact that he never asked is {not curious at all/most unfortunate}.

(17) It is not *odd* that Jones asked for an appraisal before he bought that parchment; it seems natural under the circumstances.

(18) A: Was it *odd* that Jones did not ask for an appraisal?
B. No, I think it was fairly natural under the circumstances.

To summarize, we have argued that evaluative adverbs and speech act adverbials in English contribute use-conditional rather than truth-conditional meaning to the utterances in which they occur. We argued this on the grounds that they are independent of and secondary to the "at issue" propositional content of the utterance, they cannot be negated or questioned, and they do not affect the truth value of a statement. But clearly the meaning that these adverbs contribute is conventional: it has to be learned, rather than being calculated from the context of use. Moreover, they are not presupposed, that is, they are not treated as if they were already part of the common ground.

11.3 Japanese honorifics

Honorifics are grammatical markers that speakers use to show respect or deference to someone whom they consider to be higher in social status than themselves. Japanese has two major types of honorifics. One type is used to show respect toward someone referred to in the sentence, with different forms used for subjects vs. non-subjects. We will refer to this type as ARGUMENT HONORIFICS . The other type is used to show respect to the addressee, and so are considered to be a mark of polite speech. This type is often referred to as "performative honorifics", because they indicate something about the context of the current speech event, specifically the relationship between speaker and addressee. We will instead refer to this second type as ADDRESSEE HONORIFICS.[11]

The use of an argument honorific to indicate the speaker's respect for a person referred to in the sentence is illustrated in (19a), which shows respect for the referent of the subject NP (Prof. Sasaki). The use of an addressee honorific to indicate the speaker's respect for the addressee is illustrated in (19b).

(19) a. Sasaki sensei=wa watasi=ni koo **o**-hanasi.**ni.nat**-ta.
Sasaki teacher=TOP 1sg=DAT this.way speak.HON-PAST
'Prof. Sasaki told me this way.' [Harada 1976: 501]

[11]The term *argument honorifics* is adapted from Potts (2005), who referred to this type as "argument-oriented honorifics". Harada (1976), one of the first detailed discussions of these issues in English, refers to this type as "propositional honorifics". Harada was the original source of the term "performative honorifics" for those which show respect to the addressee, a terminology which is now widely adopted.

b. Watasi=wa sono hito=ni koo hanasi-**masi**-ta.
1SG=TOP that man=DAT this.way speak-HON-PAST
'I told him (=that man) this way.' (polite speech) [Harada 1976: 502]

Argument honorifics are only allowed in sentences that refer to someone socially superior to the speaker; sentence (20a) is unacceptable, because no such person is referred to. But addressee honorifics are not subject to this constraint (20b).

(20) a. *Ame=ga **o**-huri.**ni.nat**-ta.
rain=NOM fall.HON-PAST
(intended: 'It rained.') [Harada 1976: 502]

b. Ame=ga huri-**masi**-ta.
rain=NOM fall-HON-PAST
'It rained.' (polite speech) [Harada 1976: 502]

In the remainder of this section we will focus primarily on addressee honorifics. Potts (2005) analyzes addressee honorifics as conventional implicature triggers, specifically as a kind of expressive. This means that addressee honorifics do not contribute to the truth-conditional at-issue content of the sentence. The truth conditions of (20b) would not be changed if the honorific marker were deleted. Misuse of the honorific (e.g. for referring to someone socially inferior), or dropping the honorific when it is expected, would not make the statement false, only rude and/or inappropriate.[12]

As we would predict under Pott's proposal, the honorific meaning cannot be part of the propositional content that is negated or questioned. (21a–b) are felt to be just as polite as (20b); the element of respect is neither negated in (21a) nor questioned in (21b).

(21) a. Ame=ga huri-**mas-en** desi-ta.
rain=NOM fall-HON-NEG COP-PAST
'It didn't rain.' (polite speech)

b. Ame=wa huri-**masi**-ta-ka?
rain=TOP fall-HON-PAST-Q
'Did it rain?' (polite speech)

[12]Thanks to Eric Shin Doi for very helpful discussion of these issues, and for providing the examples in (21).

We have seen that addressee honorifics express beliefs or attitudes of the speaker. They are independent of and secondary to the at-issue propositional content of the utterance. They cannot be negated or questioned, and do not affect the truth value of a statement. Thus they clearly fit Potts' definition of conventional implicatures.

11.4 Korean speech style markers

Korean also has the same two types of honorifics as Japanese, argument honorifics vs. addressee honorifics.[13] As part of the addressee honorific system, Korean distinguishes grammatically six levels of politeness, often referred to as SPEECH STYLES: formal, semiformal, polite, familiar, intimate, and plain.[14] A seventh level, "super-polite", was used for addressing kings and queens; it is now considered archaic, and is used mostly in prayers. The choice of speech style marking depends on "(i) the *relationship* between speaker and addressee (e.g., intimacy, politeness), and (ii) the *formality* of the situation".[15] The uses of these styles, as described by Pak (2008: 120), are summarized in Table 11.1.

Speech style is marked grammatically by a verbal suffix referred to as the "sentence ender". Since Korean is an SOV language, the main clause verb typically occurs at the end of the sentence and hosts the sentence ender. The sentence ender is actually a portmanteau suffix which encodes three distinct grammatical features: (a) speech style (i.e. politeness); (b) "special mood" (not discussed here); and (c) sentence type (i.e. speech act; this corresponds to the major mood category in other languages).[16] Korean has an unusually rich inventory of speech act markers. The exact number is a topic of controversy; Sohn (1999) lists four major sentence types (declarative, interrogative, imperative, and "propositive" or hortative); plus several minor types including admonitive (warning), promissive, exclamatory, and apperceptive (new or currently perceived information?). Combinations of four of the speech styles with two sentence types (declarative and imperative) are illustrated in Table 11.2; the sentence enders are italicized.[17]

Like Japanese honorifics, the Korean speech style markers contribute information about the current speech act, specifically the relationship between speaker and hearer, rather than contributing to the at-issue propositional content of the

[13]Kim & Sells (2007)

[14]S. E. Martin (1992), Pak (2008), Sohn (1999)

[15]Pak et al. (2013)

[16]Sohn (1999), Pak (2008).

[17]These examples are taken from Pak et al. (2013).

Table 11.1: Use of Korean speech styles following Pak (2008: 120)

Speech styles	Contexts of use
Formal	used for speaking to someone to whom deference is due (e.g., ones superior or employer, a professor, a high official, etc.); or on formal occasions such as oral news reports and public lectures
Semiformal	could be used by a husband speaking to his wife, or by a younger superior speaking to an older subordinate; gradually disappearing from daily usage
Polite	used by adults for speaking to adults who are not close friends or family members; to address a socially equal or superior person; or by children speaking to adults in a polite way
Familiar	mostly used by male adults, for speaking to male adult friends, an adolescent, or a son-in-law
Intimate ("half-talk")	used for talking to family members or close friends
Plain	used by adults for speaking to children or younger siblings, and by children among themselves; also used in written texts and newspapers

utterance. Use of the wrong speech style marker in a particular situation would not cause a statement to be considered false, but would be felt to be inappropriate. A speaker who committed such an error would probably be corrected quickly and emphatically. Moreover, the information contributed by the speech style markers cannot be negated or questioned. The negative statement in (22b) and the question in (22c) are felt to be just as polite as the corresponding positive statement in (22a), and would be appropriate in the same range of situations.[18]

[18]Thanks to Shin-Ja Hwang for very helpful discussion of these issues.

Table 11.2: Declaratives and imperatives in Korean

	Declarative	Imperative
Formal	Chayk=ul ilk-ess-*supnita*. book=ACC read-PAST-DECL.FORM 'I read the book.'	Chayk=ul ilk-*usipsio*. book=ACC read-IMP.FORM 'Please read the book!'
Polite	Chayk=ul ilk-ess-*eyo*. book=ACC read-PAST-DECL.POL 'I read the book.'	Chayk=ul ilk-*useyyo*. book=ACC read-IMP.POL 'Please read the book.'
Intimate	Chayk=ul ilk-ess-*e*. book=ACC read-PAST-DECL.INT 'I read the book.'	Chayk=ul ilk-*e*. book=ACC read-IMP.INT 'Read the book!'
Plain	Chayk=ul ilk-ess-*ta*. book=ACC read-PAST-DECL 'I read the book.'	Chayk=ul ilk-*ela*. book=ACC read-IMP 'Read the book'

(22) a. Pi=ka w-ayo.
rain=NOM come-DECL.POL
'It is raining.' (polite)

b. Pi=ka an-w-ayo.
rain=NOM NEG-come-DECL.POL
'It is not raining.' (polite)

c. Pi=ka w-ayo?
rain=NOM come-DECL.POL
'Is it raining?' (polite) [Sohn 1999: 269–270]

11.5 Other ways of marking politeness

Honorific markers and speech style markers like those discussed in the previous two sections have no descriptive content, but only a use-conditional, utterance modifying function. However, there are words in many languages which express both normal descriptive content plus a use-conditional function as a marker of politeness.

One of the most common ways across languages of showing respect or politeness to the addressee is by distinguishing polite vs. familiar forms of the second person pronoun, e.g. *vous* vs. *tu* in French, *Sie* vs. *du* in German, etc. Malay has a very complex system of first and second person pronouns. The neutral first person singular form is *saya*; *aku* is considered more intimate, for use with friends and family members. *Beta* is the first person singular form used by royalty, and *patik* is the first person singular form used by commoners when addressing royalty. There is no native Malay second person singular pronoun which is truly neutral; *kamu*, *awak*, and *engkau* are all felt to be informal or intimate to varying degrees. The term *anda* was invented as part of the standardization of Malaysian as a national language to fill this gap, but is rarely used in conversational speech. Second person pronouns tend to be avoided when addressing royalty or other highly respected people, by using titles, kin terms, etc. instead.

Lexical substitution as a means of honorification is not limited to pronouns. Balinese and Javanese are famous for their speech levels, or registers. In these languages, two or more forms are available for thousands of lexical items, e.g. Balinese *makita* (high) vs. *edot* (low) 'want'; *sanganan* (high) vs. *jaja* (low) 'cake'.[19] The choice of which form to use is determined by the relative social status, caste, etc. of the speaker and addressee. Korean and Japanese also have suppletive forms for some words, e.g. Korean *pap* (plain) vs. *cinci* (polite) 'cooked rice, meal'. The primary meaning contributed by words of this sort is to the truth-conditional content of the sentence; their use-conditional politeness function is in a sense secondary.

11.6 Discourse particles in German

German and Dutch are well-known for their large inventories of discourse particles. These particles have been intensively studied, but their meanings are difficult to define or paraphrase. Those that occur in the "middlefield" (i.e., between the V2/Aux position and the position of clause-final verbs) have traditionally been referred to as *Modalpartikeln* 'modal particles' in German, although they do not express modality in the standard sense of that term.[20] Some examples and a description from Zimmermann (2011: 2013) are presented in (23).

(23) a. Max ist *ja* auf See.
     b. Max ist *doch* auf See.

[19] Arka (2005).
[20] Palmer (1986: 45–46).

c. Max ist *wohl* auf See.
'Max is PRTCL at sea.'

> The sentences in (23a–c) do not differ in propositional content: they all have the same truth-conditions... A difference in the choice of the particle (*ja, doch, wohl*) leads to a difference in felicity conditions, however, such that each sentence will be appropriate in a different context. As a first approximation, (23a) indicates that the speaker takes the hearer to be aware of the fact that Max is at sea. In contrast, (23b) signals that the speaker takes the hearer not to be aware of this fact at the time of utterance. (23c), finally, indicates a degree of speaker uncertainty concerning the truth of the proposition expressed. In each case, the discourse particle does not contribute to the descriptive, or propositional, content of the utterance, but to its expressive content.

Most of the German modal particles are homophonous with a stressed variant belonging to one of the standard parts of speech. For example, stressed *ja* means 'yes' and stressed *wohl* means 'probably'. However, when used as particles these words are unstressed and take on a variety of meanings, many of which are difficult to paraphrase or translate. Some of the variant meanings of *ja* and *doch* are illustrated in (24–25).

(24) a. Die Malerei war *ja* schon immer sein Hobby.
'<*As you know*>, painting has always been his hobby.'

b. Dein Mantel ist *ja* ganz schmutzig.
'<*Hey*> your coat is all dirty.' (not previously known to hearer)

c. Fritz hat *ja* noch gar nicht bezahlt.
'<*Hey*> Fred has not paid yet.' (newly discovered by speaker) [21]

(25) a. A: Maria kommt mit. 'Maria is coming with me.'
B: Sie ist *doch* verreist. 'She has left, <*hasn't she*>?'

b. Das ist *doch* der Hans! Was macht der hier?
'That's Hans over there <*surprise*>! What is he doing here?'

c. Ich war *doch* letztes Jahr schon dort.
'<*Did you forget?*> I was here last year.'[22]

[21]Examples from König 1991; König et al. 1990; Waltereit 2001.

[22]Examples from Karagjosova (2000); Grosz (2010); http://en.wikipedia.org/wiki/German_modal_particle.

In the passage quoted above, Zimmermann (2011) states that these particles contribute to the expressive content of the utterance rather than its descriptive, or at-issue, content; they affect the felicity conditions of the utterance, but not its truth-conditions. So, for example, all of the sentences in (23) would be true if Max is in fact at sea at the time of speaking. Using the wrong particle would make the utterance infelicitous, but not false. Other authors have reached similar conclusions. Waltereit (2001) states:

> [Modal particles] modify the preparatory conditions, as they evoke a speech situation in which the desired preparatory conditions are fulfilled... Preparatory conditions describe the way the speech act fits into the social relation of speaker and addressee, and they describe how their respective interests are concerned by the act.[23]

Karagjosova (2000) states that "[modal particles] indicate if and how incoming information in dialogue is processed by the interlocutors in terms of its consistency with the information or beliefs the interlocutors already have." For example, modal particles may indicate whether a proposition has succeeded in becoming GROUNDED, i.e., part of the shared assumptions (COMMON GROUND) of the speaker and hearer. She continues:

> [T]he meaning of [modal particles] seems not to be part of the proposition indeed and thus not part of the truth conditions of the sentence they occur in. ... [W]e conclude that *doch* does not contribute to the sentence meaning but to the utterance meaning and represents thus semantically an utterance modifier rather than a sentence modifier.

The hypothesis that German modal particles function as utterance modifiers, and do not contribute to truth-conditional content, is supported by the fact that they cannot be negated, as seen in (26). Moreover, they cannot be questioned and cannot function as the answer to a question.[24]

(26) Hein ist *ja* nicht zuhause.
 '*As you know*, Hein is not at home.' [Gutzmann 2015, sec. 7.2.2.2]
 (cannot mean: 'You do not know that Hein is not at home.')

---

[23] cf. Searle (1969).

[24] This point is mentioned in most descriptions of the German modal particles, including Bross (2012) and Gutzmann (2015).

11.7 Conclusion

In this chapter we have looked at several types of expressions in various languages that seem to contribute "use-conditional" rather than truth-conditional meanings. The characteristic properties of such expressions are those identified by Potts in his work on conventional implicatures. They tend to be speaker-oriented; independent of and secondary to the at-issue, truth-conditional content of the utterance; excluded from negation and questioning; and not assumed to be part of common ground.

We noted that speech act adverbials in English (e.g. *frankly, confidentially*) can function either as sentence adverbs with use-conditional meanings, or as manner adverbs with truth-conditional meanings. In future chapters we will see that similar ambiguities arise with certain conjunctions, notably *because* (Chapter 18) and *if* (Chapter 19). We will argue that, at least for *because*, such ambiguities need not be treated as polysemy (distinct senses), but can be seen as a kind of pragmatic ambiguity: a single sense that can function on two levels, modifying the sentence meaning or the utterance meaning. In the first case, it contributes truth-conditional meaning, while in the second case it contributes use-conditional meaning.

Further reading

Potts (2007a,b) and (2012) provide concise introductions to his analysis of conventional implicatures. Potts (2007c) focuses more specifically on expressives. Scheffler (2013) applies this analysis to sentence adverbs in English and German. Gutzmann (2015) presents an introduction to the idea of use-conditional meaning in chapter 2, and an analysis of the German "modal particles" in chapter 7.

Discussion exercises

A. Use the kinds of evidence discussed in this chapter to determine whether the italicized expressions in the following examples contribute truth-conditional or use-conditional meaning:

1. Sir Richard Whittington, *a medieval cloth merchant*, served four terms as Lord Mayor of London.
2. Wilma *probably* loves sauerkraut.
3. Fred loves sauerkraut *too*.
4. Mrs. Natasha Griggs, *who served six years as MP for Darwin*, is a cancer survivor.
5. Baxter *reportedly* supported Suharto.

Unit IV

Compositional semantics

12 How meanings are composed

12.1 Introduction

One of the central goals of semantics is to explain how meanings of sentences are related to the meanings of their parts. In Chapter 3 we discussed the simple sentence in (1), and how the meaning of the sentence determines the conditions under which it would be true.

(1) *King Henry VIII snores.*

Let us now consider the question of how the meaning of this sentence is composed from the meanings of its parts. What are the parts, and what kinds of meanings do they express? Any syntactic description of the sentence will recognize two immediate constituents: the subject NP *King Henry VIII* and the intransitive verb (or VP) *snores*. These two phrases express different kinds of meaning. The subject NP is a referring expression, specifically a proper name, which refers to an individual in the world. The intransitive VP expresses a property which may be true of some individuals but not of others in a given situation. The result of combining them, i.e. the meaning of the sentence as a whole, is a PROPOSITION (or claim about the world) which may be true in some situations and false in others. Sentence (1) expresses an assertion that the individual named by the subject NP (King Henry VIII) has the property named by the VP (he snores). This pattern for combining NP meanings with VP meanings is seen in many, perhaps most, simple declarative sentences.

The same basic principle holds not just for sentences but for any expression (apart from idioms) consisting of more than one word: the meaning of the whole is composed, or built up, in a predictable way from the meanings of the parts. This is what makes it possible for us to understand newly-created sentences. One way of expressing this principle is the following:

(2) PRINCIPLE OF COMPOSITIONALITY:
the meaning of a complex expression is determined by the meanings of its constituent expressions and the way in which they are combined.

Many semanticists adopt as a working hypothesis a stronger version of this principle, which says (roughly speaking) that there must be a one-to-one correspondence between the syntactic rules that build constituents and the semantic rules that provide interpretations for those constituents. Adopting this stronger version of the principle places significant constraints on the way these rules get written.[1] In Chapter 13 we will see a few very simple examples of how syntactic and semantic rules can be correlated.

In this chapter we lay a foundation for discussing compositionality in the more general sense expressed in (2). We are trying to understand what is involved in the claim that the meanings of phrases and sentences are predictable based on the meanings of their constituents and the manner in which those constituents get combined.

We begin in §12.2 by describing two very simple examples of compositional meaning: first, the combination of a subject NP with a VP to form a simple clause (*Henry snores*); and second, the combination of a modifying adjective with a common noun (*yellow submarine*). In Chapter 13 we will formulate rules to account for these patterns, among others.

In §12.3 we provide some historical context for the study of compositionality by sketching out some ideas from the German logician Gottlob Frege (1848–1925). We will summarize Frege's arguments for the claim that denotations, as well as senses, must be compositional. But Frege also pointed out that there are some contexts where the denotation of a complex expression is not fully predictable from the denotations of its constituents. We discuss one such context in §12.4, namely complement clauses of verbs like *think*, *believe*, *want*, etc. In §12.5 we discuss a particular type of ambiguity which can arise in such contexts.

12.2 Two simple examples

Let us return now to the question of how the meaning of the simple sentence in (1) is composed from the meanings of its parts. As we noted, the sentence contains two immediate constituents: the subject NP *King Henry VIII* and the intransitive verb (or VP) *snores*. The NP *King Henry VIII* is a proper name, a "rigid designator", and so always refers to the same individual; its denotation does not depend on the situation. The intransitive VP *snores* expresses a property which may be true of a particular individual at one time or in one situation, but not in other times or situations; so its denotation does depend on the situation in

[1] Partee (1995: 322).

which it is used. We will refer to the set of all things which snore in the current universe of discourse as the DENOTATION SET of the predicate *snores.* The result of combining the subject NP with the intransitive VP is a sentence whose meaning is a proposition, and this proposition will be true if and only if the individual named *King Henry VIII* is a member of the denotation set of *snores*; i.e., if the king has the property of snoring in the time and situation being described.

This same basic rule of interpretation works for a great many simple declarative sentences: the proposition expressed by the sentence as a whole will be true if and only if the referent of the subject NP is a member of the denotation set of the VP. Of course there are many other cases for which this simple rule is not adequate; but in the present book we will touch on these only briefly.

The Principle of Compositionality also applies to complex expressions which are smaller than a sentence, including noun phrases. Even though these phrasal expressions do not have truth values, they do have denotations which are determined compositionally. In Chapter 1 we briefly discussed the compositionality of the phrase *yellow submarine.* Suppose we refer to the denotation set of the word *yellow* (i.e., the set of all yellow things in our universe of discourse) as Y, and the denotation set of the word *submarine* (i.e., the set of all submarines in our universe of discourse) as S. The meaning of the phrase *yellow submarine* is predictable from the meaning of its individual words and the way they are combined. Knowing the rules of English allows speakers to predict that the denotation set of the phrase will be the set of all things which belong both to Y and to S; in other words, the set of all things in our universe of discourse which are both yellow and submarines.

As these simple examples illustrate, our analysis of denotations and truth values will be stated in terms of set membership and relations between sets. For this reason we will introduce some basic terms and concepts from set theory at the beginning of Chapter 13. These elements of set theory will also be crucial for analyzing the meanings of quantifiers (words and phrases such as *everyone, some people, most countries,* etc.). Quantifiers (the focus of Chapter 14) are an interesting and important topic of study in their own right, but they are also important because certain other kinds of expressions can actually be analyzed as quantifiers (see Chapter 16, for example).

But before we proceed with a more detailed discussion of these issues, it will be helpful to review some of Frege's insights.

12.3 Frege on compositionality and substitutivity

Many of the foundational concepts in truth-conditional semantics come from the work of Gottlob Frege, whose distinction between Sense and Denotation we discussed in Chapter 2. The Principle of Compositionality in (2) is often referred to as "Frege's principle". Frege himself never expressed the principle in these words, and there is some disagreement as to whether he actually believed it.[2] But there are passages in several of his works that seem to imply or assume that sentence meanings are compositional in this sense, including the following:

> It is astonishing what language accomplishes. With a few syllables it expresses a countless number of thoughts [=propositions], and even for a thought grasped for the first time by a human it provides a clothing in which it can be recognized by another to whom it is entirely new. This would not be possible if we could not distinguish parts in the thought that correspond to parts of the sentence, so that the construction of the sentence can be taken to mirror the construction of the thought... The question now arises how the construction of the thought proceeds, and by what means the parts are put together so that the whole is something more than the isolated parts.[3]

In this passage Frege argues for the compositionality of "thoughts", i.e. propositions; but the same kind of reasoning requires that the meaning of smaller expressions (e.g. noun phrases) be compositional as well. And in many cases, not only senses but also denotations are compositional. One way of seeing this involves substituting one expression for another which is co-referential, i.e., has the same denotation in that particular context.

In our world, the expressions *Abraham Lincoln* and *the 16th president of the United States* refer to the same individual. For this reason, if we replace one of these expressions with the other as illustrated in (3–4), the denotation of the larger phrase is not affected.

(3) a. the wife of Abraham Lincoln
    b. the wife of the 16th president of the United States

[2] Specifically, there is debate as to whether Frege believed that compositionality holds for senses, as well as denotations (Gamut 1991b: 12). Pelletier (2001), for example, argues that he did not. A number of modern scholars have argued against the Principle of Compositionality; see Goldberg (2015) for a summary.

[3] Frege (1923–1926), "Logische Untersuchungen. Dritter Teil: Gedankengefüge", quoted in Heim & Kratzer (1998: 2).

(4) a. the man who killed Abraham Lincoln
b. the man who killed the 16th president of the United States

Both of the NPs in (3) refer to Mary Todd Lincoln; both of the NPs in (4) refer to John Wilkes Booth. This is what we expect if the denotation of the larger phrase is compositional, i.e., predictable from the denotations of its constituent parts: replacing one of those parts with another part having the same denotation does not affect the denotation of the whole. (This principle is referred to as the principle of SUBSTITUTIVITY.)

A second way of observing the compositionality of denotations arises when non-referring expressions occur as constituents of a larger expression. In a world where there is no such person as Superman, i.e., a world in which this name lacks a denotation, phrases which contain the name *Superman* (like those in (5)) will also lack a denotation, i.e. will fail to refer.

(5) a. the mother of Superman
b. the man who Superman rescued

These observations support the claim that the denotation of a complex expression is (often) predictable from the denotations of its constituent parts. Since sentences are formed from constituent parts (words and phrases) which have denotations, this suggests that the denotations of sentences might also be compositional. In his classic paper *Über Sinn und Bedeutung* 'On sense and denotation', Frege (1892) argued that this is true; but he recognized that it may seem odd (at least at first) to suggest that sentences have denotations as well as senses. Sentences are not "referring expressions" in the normal sense of that term, so what could their denotation be?

Frege considered the possibility that the denotation of a sentence is the proposition that it expresses. But this hypothesis leads to unexpected results when we substitute one co-referential expression for another. Samuel Clemens was an American author who wrote under the pen name Mark Twain; so these two names both refer to the same individual. Since the two names have the same denotation, we expect that replacing one name with the other, as illustrated in (6), will not affect the denotation of the sentence as a whole.

(6) a. *The Prince and the Pauper* was written by Mark Twain.
b. *The Prince and the Pauper* was written by Samuel Clemens.

Of course, the resulting sentences must have the same truth value; it happens that both are true. However, a person who speaks English but does not know very much about American literature could, without inconsistency, believe (6a) without believing (6b). For Frege, if a rational speaker can simultaneously believe one sentence to be true while believing another to be false, the two sentences cannot express the same proposition.

Examples like (7) lead to the same conclusion. Abraham Lincoln was the 16th president of the United States, so replacing the phrase *Abraham Lincoln* with the phrase *the 16th president of the United States* should not change the denotation of the sentence as a whole. But the facts of history could have been different: Abraham Lincoln might have died in infancy, or lost the election in 1860, etc. Under those conditions, sentence (7b) might well be true while sentence (7a) is false. This again is evidence that the two sentences do not express the same proposition, since a single proposition cannot be simultaneously true and false in any single situation.

(7) a. Abraham Lincoln ended slavery in America.
    b. The 16th president of the United States ended slavery in America.

Frege concludes that the denotation of a (declarative) sentence is not the proposition which it expresses, but rather its truth value. Frege identifies the proposition expressed by a sentence as its sense.

There are clear parallels between the truth value of a sentence and the denotation of a noun phrase. First, neither can be determined in isolation, but only in relation to a specific situation or universe of discourse. Second, both may have different values in different situations. Third, both are preserved under substitution of co-referring expressions. This was illustrated for noun phrases in (3–4), and for sentences in (6–7). Finally, we noted that NPs which contain non-referring expressions as constituents, like those in (5), will also fail to refer, i.e., will lack a denotation. In the same way, Frege argued that sentences which contain non-referring expressions will lack a truth value. He states that sentences like those in (8) are neither true nor false; they cannot be evaluated, because their subject NPs fail to refer. These parallels provide strong motivation for considering the denotation of a sentence to be its truth value.

(8) a. Superman rescued the Governor's daughter.
    b. The largest even number is divisible by 7.

However, certain types of sentences, such as those in (9), contain a non-referring expression but nevertheless do seem to have a truth value. Even in a world where there is no Santa Claus and no fountain of youth, it would be possible to determine whether these sentences are true or false. Sentences of this type are said to be REFERENTIALLY OPAQUE, meaning that their denotation is not predictable from the denotations of their constituent parts. In these specific examples, the opacity is due to special properties of verbs like *believe* and *hope*. (We will discuss other types of opacity in Chapter 15.)

(9) a. The Governor still believes in Santa Claus.
 b. Ponce de León hoped to find the fountain of youth.

12.4 Propositional attitudes

Believe and *hope* belong to a broad class of verbs which are often referred to as PROPOSITIONAL ATTITUDE VERBS, because they take a propositional argument (expressed as a complement clause) and denote the mental state or attitude of an experiencer toward this proposition. Other verbs in this class include *think, expect, want, know,* etc. As we have just mentioned, the complement clauses of these verbs are referentially opaque. Some further examples of sentences involving such verbs are presented in (10).

(10) a. John believes [that the airplane was invented by an Irishman].
 b. Henry wants [to marry a Catholic].
 c. Mary knows [that Abraham Lincoln ended slavery in America].

Frege pointed out that when we substitute one co-referential expression for another in the complement clause of a propositional attitude verb, the truth value of the sentence as a whole can be affected. For example, since *Mark Twain* and *Samuel Clemens* refer to the same individual, the principle of substitutivity predicts that the positive statement in (11a) and its corresponding negative statement in (11b) should have opposite truth values. However, it is clearly possible for both sentences to be true at the same time (and for the same person named *Mary*). By the same token, the principle of substitutivity predicts that (11c) and (11d) should have the same truth value. However, it is hard to imagine a person of normal intelligence of whom (11d) could be true.

(11) a. Mary knows [that *The Prince and the Pauper* was written by Mark Twain].
 b. Mary does not know [that *The Prince and the Pauper* was written by Samuel Clemens].
 c. Mary does not know [that Samuel Clemens is Mark Twain].
 d. ?#Mary does not know [that Samuel Clemens is Samuel Clemens].

As mentioned above, this property of propositional attitude verbs is called REFERENTIAL OPACITY; the complements of propositional attitude verbs are an example of an OPAQUE CONTEXT, that is, a context where denotation does not appear to be compositional, because the principle of substitutivity fails. Frege used the following pair of examples to further illustrate referential opacity. Both of the complement clauses in (12) are true statements, but only the first is something that Copernicus actually believed (he believed that the planetary orbits were circles). Since the denotation of a declarative clause is its truth value, and since the two complement clauses have the same truth value if considered on their own, the principle of substitutivity would predict that sentences (12a) and (12b) as a whole should have the same denotation, i.e., the same truth value. But in fact (12a) is true while (12b) is false.

(12) a. Copernicus believed [that the earth revolves around the sun].
  b. Copernicus believed [that the planetary orbits are ellipses].

Propositional attitude verbs pose a significant problem for the principle of Compositionality. Frege's solution was to propose that the denotation of a clause or NP "shifts" in opaque contexts, so that in these contexts they refer to their customary sense, rather than to their normal denotation. For example, the denotation of the complement clauses in (12), because they occur in an opaque context, is not their truth value but the proposition they express (their customary sense). This shift explains why NPs or clauses with different senses are not freely substitutable in these contexts, even though they may seem to have the same denotation.

Frege's proposal is analogous in some ways to the referential "shift" which occurs in contexts where a word or phrase is MENTIONED, as in (13b), rather than USED, as in (13a). In such contexts, the quoted word or phrase refers only to itself. Substitutivity fails when referring expressions are mentioned, as illustrated in (13c–d). Even though both names refer to the same individual when used in the normal way, these two sentences are not equivalent: (13c) is true, but (13d) is false.

(13) a. Maria is a pretty girl.
  b. *Maria* is a pretty name.
  c. Samuel Clemens adopted the pen name *Mark Twain.*
  d. Mark Twain adopted the pen name *Samuel Clemens.*

We can now understand why sentences like those in (14), which contain a non-referring expression, nevertheless can have a truth value. *Hope* and *want* are propositional attitude verbs. Thus the denotation of their complement clauses is not their truth value but the propositions they express. The denotation (i.e., truth value) of the sentence as a whole can be derived compositionally, because all the constituents have well-defined denotations.

(14) a. Ponce de León hoped to find the fountain of youth.
 b. James Thurber wanted to see a unicorn.

12.5 *De dicto* vs. *de re* ambiguity

Another interesting property of opaque contexts, including the complements of propositional attitude verbs, is that definite NPs occurring in such contexts can sometimes receive two different interpretations. They can either be used to refer to a specific individual, as in (15a), or they can be used to identify a type of individual, or property of individuals, as in (15b).

(15) a. I hope to meet with *the Prime Minister* next year, (after he retires from office).
 b. I hope to meet with *the Prime Minister* next year; (we'll have to wait for the October election before we know who that will be).

The former reading, which refers to a specific individual, is known as the *de re* ('about the thing') interpretation. The latter reading, in which the NP identifies a property of individuals, is known as the *de dicto* ('about the word' or 'about what is said') interpretation. The same kind of ambiguity is illustrated in (16).

(16) a. I wanted *my husband* to be a Catholic, (but he said he was too old to convert).
 b. I wanted *my husband* to be a Catholic, (but I ended up marrying a Sikh).

Under the *de re* interpretation, the definite NP denotes a particular individual: the person who is serving as Prime Minister at the time of speaking in (15a), and the individual who is married to the speaker at the time of speaking in (16a). Under the *de dicto* interpretation, the semantic contribution of the definite NP is not what it refers to but its sense: a property (e.g. the property of being Prime Minister, or the property of being married to the speaker) rather than a specific individual. This "shift" from denotation to sense in opaque contexts is similar to the facts about complement clauses discussed in the previous section. A similar type of ambiguity is observed with indefinite NPs, as illustrated in (17).

(17) a. The opposition party wants to nominate *a retired movie* star for President.
b. The Dean believes that I am collaborating with *a famous linguist.*

With indefinites, the two readings are often referred to as SPECIFIC VS. NON-SPECIFIC; but we can apply the terms *de dicto* vs. *de re* to these cases as well.[4] Under the specific (*de re*) reading, the phrase *a retired movie star* in (17a) refers to a particular individual, e.g. Ronald Reagan or Joseph Estrada (former president of the Philippines); so under this reading sentence (17a) means that the opposition party has a specific candidate in mind, who happens to be a retired actor (whether the party leaders realize this or not). Under the non-specific (*de dicto*) reading, the phrase refers to a property or type, rather than a specific individual. Under this reading sentence (17a) means that the opposition party does not have a specific candidate in mind, but knows what kind of person they want; and being a retired actor is one of the qualifications they are looking for.

These *de dicto–de re* ambiguities involve true semantic ambiguity, as seen by the fact that the two readings have different truth conditions. For example, suppose I am collaborating with Noam Chomsky on a book of political essays. The Dean knows about this collaboration, but knows Chomsky only through his political writings, and does not realize that he is also a famous linguist. In this situation, sentence (17b) will be true under the *de re* reading but false under the *de dicto* reading.

As we will see in our discussion of quantifiers (Chapter 14), *de dicto–de re* ambiguities can often be explained or analyzed as instances of SCOPE AMBIGUITY. However, the specific vs. non-specific ambiguity of indefinite NPs is found even in contexts where no scope effects are involved.[5]

12.6 Conclusion

The passage from Frege quoted at the beginning of §12.3 describes the astonishing power of human language: "[E]ven for a thought grasped for the first time by a human it provides a clothing in which it can be recognized by another to whom it is entirely new." It is this productivity, the ability to communicate novel ideas, that we seek to understand when we try to account for the compositionality of sentence meanings.

[4]We follow von Heusinger (2011) in using the terms this way.
[5]Fodor & Sag (1982).

In the next two chapters we offer a very brief introduction to a widely-used method for modeling how meanings of complex expressions are composed from the meanings of their constituent parts. Building on Frege's intuition (discussed in §12.3 above) that the denotation of a sentence is its truth value, we describe a method for composing denotations of words and phrases to derive the truth conditions of the proposition expressed by a sentence. Then in Chapter 15 we discuss additional contexts where, as with the propositional attitude verbs discussed in §12.4 above, a purely denotational treatment is inadequate.

Further reading

Abbott (2010: §2.1.) provides a good summary of Frege's famous paper on sense and denotation. Goldberg (2015) and Pagin & Westerståhl (2010) discuss some of the challenges to the Principle of Compositionality. Zalta (2011) provides an overview of Frege's life and work.

Discussion exercises

A. Discuss the validity of the following inference (assuming that (a) and (b) are true):

a. Oedipus wants to marry Jocasta.

b. Jocasta is Oedipus' mother.

---

c. Therefore, Oedipus wants to marry his mother.

13 Modeling compositionality

13.1 Introduction

We have said that one of the most important goals of semantic theory is to understand the compositional nature of meaning, i.e., the knowledge which allows speakers to correctly predict how word meanings will combine in complex expressions. One way of exploring this topic is to construct formal rule systems which model the abilities of speakers in this respect.

Just as syntacticians try to construct rule systems which replicate the judgments of native speakers about the grammaticality of sentences, semanticists try to construct rule systems which replicate the ability of speakers to identify the denotation of an expression in a particular context of use, and in particular, to determine the truth values of sentences in a given context. A crucial step in this kind of analysis is to describe the situation under discussion in very explicit terms, so that predictions about denotations can be easily checked. The explicit description of a situation is called a MODEL, so this general approach to semantics is often referred to as MODEL THEORY.[1]

This chapter provides a very brief introduction to the Model Theory approach to the study of compositionality. This approach, which has proven to be remarkably productive, involves stating rules of semantic interpretation for the constituents that are formed by productive syntactic processes. We mentioned two such processes in Chapter 12: the combination of subject NP with VP, and the combination of modifying adjective with head noun. In this chapter we will provide a bit more detail about how we might formulate the rules of semantic interpretation for these and other constituents.

Our goal in this chapter is not to provide detailed explanation of the Model Theory approach, but merely to give a glimpse of how it works and some sense of what the goals are. This will provide helpful context for our discussion in future chapters of topics such as quantifiers, modality, tense, etc.

[1] A MODEL can also be defined an interpretation under which a given sentence or set of sentences is true (Hodges 2013). But by spelling out the denotations of the basic expressions used in the sentence(s) under discussion, the model also specifies the relevant facts about a particular situation.

§13.2 provides a brief description of the rationale behind this approach. In §13.3 we introduce some basic terms and concepts for describing sets and relations between sets, because our rules of interpretation will be stated in terms of set relations. §13.4 introduces the formal notation that is used for specifying a MODEL, in the sense defined above, and §13.5 gives some examples of how rules of semantic interpretation might be stated for several types of syntactic constituents. The overarching goal of all these steps is to account for the ability of native speakers to determine whether the proposition expressed by a given sentence is true or false in some particular context. This, you will recall, has been our benchmark for the analysis of sentence meanings.

13.2 Why a model might be useful

Language is a very complex system. In earlier chapters we have studied a variety of factors that affect how hearers will interpret the meanings of sentences: lexical ambiguity, vagueness, figurative and other coerced senses, implicatures and other pragmatic inferences, knowledge about the world, etc. In order to make progress in understanding how compositionality works, the Model Theory approach attempts to isolate the rules for combining word meanings from these other complicating factors. This same basic strategy is adopted in many other fields of research as well. For example, if medical researchers are investigating genetic factors which may contribute to heart disease or diabetes, they will do everything possible to control for other contributing factors such as diet, age, exercise, lifestyle, environmental factors, etc. The specification of a test situation in terms of an explicit model, as illustrated below, within which the rule system can be tested, is a way of controlling for lexical ambiguity, vagueness, incomplete knowledge about the world, etc.

A model must specify two things: first, the set of all individual entities in the situation; and second, the denotations of the basic vocabulary items of the language, at least those that occur in the expressions being analyzed. This would include words which function as predicates (verbs, adjectives, and common nouns), and proper names, but not non-denoting words like *not, and, if,* etc. Our semantic analysis can then be stated in terms of rules of interpretation, which will specify the denotation of complex expressions formed by combining these vocabulary items according to the syntactic rules of the language.

As a preliminary example, imagine a very simple situation which contains just three individuals: King Henry VIII, Anne Boleyn, and Thomas More. Our model of this situation would include the listing of these individuals, plus the denotation sets for the content words available for use. Let us begin with a limited vocabulary consisting of just three proper names (*Henry*, *Anne*, and *Thomas*) plus three predicate words: *snore*, *man*, and *woman*. The denotation set for *man* would include Henry VIII and Thomas More. The denotation set for *woman* would include just Anne Boleyn. Let's assume that King Henry VIII is the only person in this situation who snores; then he would be the only member of the denotation set for *snore*. The denotation of the proper name *Thomas* would be the individual Thomas More, etc.

In Chapter 12 we stated a rule of interpretation for simple sentences: the proposition expressed by a (declarative) sentence will be true if and only if the referent of the subject NP is a member of the denotation set of the VP. We can use this rule to evaluate sentence (1a) relative to the situation described by the model we have just constructed. The rule says that the sentence will be true if and only if the individual named *Henry* (i.e., King Henry VIII) is a member of the denotation set of *snore*. Since this is true in our model, the sentence is true relative to this model. The same rule of interpretation allows us to determine that sentence (1b) is false relative to this model. In Chapter 14 we will discuss additional rules that will allow us to evaluate (1c), which is false relative to this model, and (1d), which is true relative to this model.

(1) a. Henry snores.
  b. Anne snores.
  c. All men snore.
  d. No women snore.

Notice that this approach seeks to provide an account for compositional meaning, but not for the meanings (i.e., senses) of individual content words. In other words, Model Theory does not try to represent the process by which speakers of English determine that King Henry VIII would be referred to as a *man* and Anne Boleyn would be referred to as a *woman*, etc. We simply start with a model which specifies the denotation sets for content words. In adopting this approach, we are not denying the important role that word senses play in our use of language, or treating word meanings as a trivial issue that can be taken for granted. In fact, accounting for word meanings is a very complex and difficult undertaking, as our earlier discussions of the issue have demonstrated. Rather, the Model Theory approach assumes that it is possible to make progress in understanding compositionality without solving all of the difficult questions surrounding word meanings; and this strategy has proven to be extremely successful and productive.

As we have already hinted, the rules of interpretation which we formulate will be stated in terms of set membership and relations between sets. For that reason, before we proceed with our discussion of compositionality, we need to introduce some of the basic terminology and notation used for speaking about sets.

13.3 Basic concepts in set theory

A SET (in the mathematical sense) is a clearly-defined collection of things. We use braces, or "curly brackets", to represent sets. So, for example, the denotation set of the word *man* in the simple model described above could be written as shown in (2a). This is a set which contains two elements, or MEMBERS, both of which are men. If we focus on denotation sets of content words, the members of a set will normally all be the same kind of thing, as in (2a). For sets in general, however, this does not have to be the case. The set defined in (2b) contains four members which are very different from each other; but this is still a well-defined set.

(2) a. {King Henry VIII, Thomas More}
    b. {Orwell's novel *1984*, Noam Chomsky, $\sqrt{2}$, Sally McConnell-Ginet's breakfast muffin on 4-Sept-1988}[2]

The identity of a set is defined by its membership. If two sets have the same members, they are in fact the same set. When we list the members of a set, the order in which the members are listed is irrelevant; so all of the orderings shown in (3) describe the same set:

(3) {a,b,c} = {b,a,c} = {c,a,b} = {a,b,c,b,a}, etc.

We use the Greek letter epsilon to indicate that a certain element belongs to a given set. The formula "$x \in B$" can be read as: "x is a member (or element) of set B". This would be true, for example, if B = {x,y,z}; but false if B = {w,y,z}. The formula "$x \notin B$" means that x is not a member of set B.

It is possible for a set to have an infinite number of members. Examples of such sets include the set of all integers; the set of all rational numbers (i.e., quotients of integers); the set of all finite strings of letters of the Roman alphabet; the set of all finite strings of words found in the Oxford English Dictionary; and the set of all real numbers. (The membership of this last set turns out to be a higher order of infinity than that of the other sets just mentioned; but that topic will not concern us here.)

[2] This example is taken from Cherchia & McConnell-Ginet (1990: 431).

It is possible for a set to have no members. In fact, there is exactly one set of this kind, and it is called the EMPTY SET (often symbolized as "∅"). The fact that there can be only one empty set follows from the principle that a set is defined by its membership. (If there were two sets, A and B, both of which had no members, then they would contain exactly the same members; and so by the principle stated above, they would be the same set.)

A set is distinct from any of its members. A set containing just one element is a different thing from the element itself. For example, the set consisting of a single individual, e.g. {Paul Kroeger}, is not the same thing as the individual himself. {Paul Kroeger} is an abstract concept, but Paul Kroeger is (at the time of writing) a living, breathing human being. To take another example, the empty set is not the same as nothing; it is a set that contains nothing. And the set containing the empty set is not itself empty; it has exactly one member, namely the empty set:

(4) $\{\emptyset\} \neq \emptyset$

The CARDINALITY of a set is the number of members or elements which belong to that set. For example, the cardinality of the set {a,b,c} is 3, because it has three members. We use the symbol |B| to refer to the cardinality of set B; so $|\{a,b,c\}| = 3$. Some further examples are given below:

(5) $|\{a,b,c,d,f\}| = 5$
$|\emptyset| = 0$
$|\{\emptyset\}| = 1$

In order for a given collection of things to be a well-defined set, it must be possible to determine precisely what is and is not a member of the set. For example, the phrase *the set of all sets that do not contain themselves* does not identify a well-defined set. This is because its membership cannot be precisely determined. In fact, the proposed definition of the set gives rise to a paradox. Suppose that such a set exists. Does this set contain itself? If so, then it is not a "set that does not contain itself" and so should not be a member of the set. But if it is not a member of the set, then it does not contain itself, and so it must belong to the set.[3]

The membership of a set can be specified either by listing its members, as in (2–3), or by stating a rule of membership (e.g., *the set of all female British monarchs,*

[3]This puzzle is a version of "Russell's paradox", which Bertrand Russell discovered in 1901 and described in a letter to Frege on June 16, 1902. Apparently it had also been noticed by Ernst Zermelo a few years earlier. It posed a major challenge to Frege's work on the foundations of mathematics.

the set of all months whose name includes the letter "r", the set of all integers, etc.). A general notation for defining the membership of a set is illustrated in (6), which is one way of describing the set of all even numbers (we will call this set E): 'the set of all numbers which are divisible by 2'. In this notation, the variable is assumed to be an element of the currently relevant UNIVERSAL SET, or universe of discourse.[4] The colon in this notation stands for 'such that'. (Some authors use a vertical bar | instead of the colon.) If we assume that the currently relevant universal set is the set of all real numbers, then the set description in (6) can be read as: 'the set of all real numbers x such that x/2 is an integer.'

(6) E = {x: $\frac{x}{2}$ is an integer}

13.3.1 Relations and functions

Up to this point all of our examples have involved sets of individuals: numbers, letters, people, etc. But we can also define sets of couples (or triples, quadruples, etc.) of individuals. For example, the set of all married couples who crossed the Atlantic ocean on the *Mayflower* in the autumn of 1620 is a well defined set. This set contained 18 members, and each member of the set was a pair of people: {Isaac & Mary Allerton, William & Dorothy Bradford, William & Mary Brewster, Myles & Rose Standish, Edward & Elizabeth Winslow, ...}. Since the set is defined as a set of pairs, William Bradford (the first governor of the Plymouth Bay colony) was not himself a member of this set; but he was a member of a pair that did belong to the set.

In this example, the members of each pair can be distinguished by the title "Mr." vs. "Mrs.", no matter which one is mentioned first; but this is not always the case. As we will see, it is often useful to define sets of pairs of things in which the members of each pair are distinguished by specifying the order in which they occur. We refer to such pairs as ORDERED PAIRS, using the notation ⟨x,y⟩ to represent the pair which consists of x followed by y. Unlike sets, two ordered pairs may have the same members but still be distinct, if those members occur in different orders. So ⟨x,y⟩ and ⟨y,x⟩ are two distinct ordered pairs, but {x,y} and {y,x} are two different ways of representing the same set.

A set of ordered pairs is called a RELATION. The DOMAIN of the relation is the set of all the first elements of each pair and its RANGE is the set of all the second elements. So, referring to the two sets defined in (7), the domain of A is the set {a,c,f}, while the range of A is the set {3,4,6,7}. The domain of B is the set {2,3,4,5,6,7}, while the range of B is the set {2,3,4,7}.

[4]See Chapter 4.

(7) A = {⟨a,3⟩, ⟨f,4⟩, ⟨c,6⟩, ⟨a,7⟩}
B = {⟨2,3⟩, ⟨3,2⟩, ⟨4,7⟩, ⟨5,2⟩, ⟨6,7⟩, ⟨7,4⟩}

A set of ordered pairs defines a MAPPING, or correspondence, from the domain onto the range. The mappings defined by sets A and B are shown in (8):

(8) a. Set A

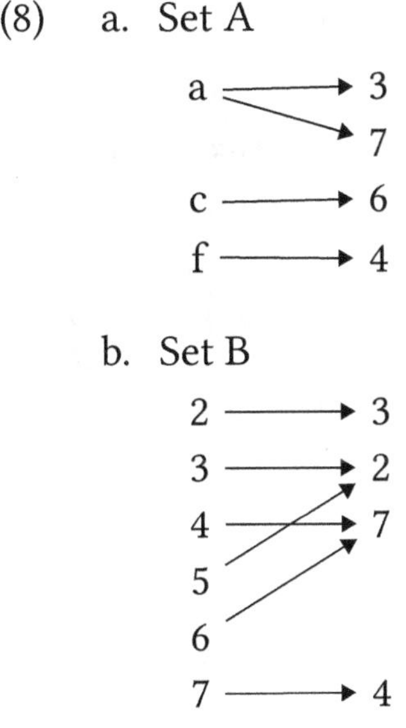

A FUNCTION is a relation (= a set of ordered pairs) in which each element of the domain is mapped to a single, unique value in the range. The relation which corresponds to set A above is not a function, because A contains two distinct ordered pairs which have the same first element (⟨a,3⟩ and ⟨a,7⟩). The relation which corresponds to set B is a function, even though B contains distinct ordered pairs which have the same second element (⟨3,2⟩ and ⟨5,2⟩; ⟨4,7⟩ and ⟨6,7⟩). What matters is that each member of the domain occurs in just one ordered pair.

The function B is defined in (7) by listing all the ordered pairs which belong to it. Another way of defining this same function is shown in (9). The first member of each ordered pair is called an ARGUMENT of the function, while the second member of each ordered pair is called a VALUE. The information in (9) is equivalent to that in (8b), showing how the function maps each argument onto a unique value. The format in (9) is more convenient for stating the value which corresponds to a single argument, when we do not need to list the entire set.

(9) B(2) = 3
B(3) = 2
B(4) = 7
B(5) = 2

B(6) = 7
B(7) = 4

The membership of any set S can be expressed as a function which maps the elements of S onto the set {1,0}. In this context, 1 represents "True" and 0 represents "False". Functions of this kind are called the CHARACTERISTIC FUNCTIONS (or, sometimes, "membership functions"). For example, the characteristic function of set C (members of the Beatles, as specified in 10a), is the function f_1 as defined in (11a). The characteristic function of set D (numbers between 10 and 20, as specified in 10b) is the function f_2 as defined in (11b). (The abbreviation "iff" stands for "if and only if".)

(10) a. C = {John, Paul, George, Ringo}
b. D = {x: 10 < x < 20}

(11) a. f_1(John) = 1
f_1(Paul) = 1
f_1(George) = 1
f_1(Ringo) = 1
in all other cases, $f_1(x) = 0$
b. $f_2(x) = 1$ iff $10 < x < 20$
in all other cases, $f_2(x) = 0$

13.3.2 Operations and relations on sets

When we use set concepts and terminology as a tool for interpreting sentences, we will often want to say something about the relationship between two sets, or to combine two or more sets in certain ways to define a new set. In order for this to be possible, we must assume that the elements of each of the sets under discussion are drawn from the same universal set. This universal set is referred to as U.

A very important relation which may hold between two sets is the SUBSET relation, also referred to as SET INCLUSION. We say that set A is a SUBSET of set B (written "A⊆B") if A is included in B; that is, if all the elements which are members of A are also members of B. We can illustrate this situation using the sets defined in (12). The universal set U is assumed to be the set of all integers between 1 and 10. By comparing the elements in set A with those in set B, we see that all the elements which are members of A are also members of B; so in this context, "A⊆B" is a true proposition. However, "B⊆A" would be false in this context, because there are some members of B which are not members of A, namely 2, 5, and 7.

(12) U = {1,2,3,4,5,6,7,8,9,10}
A = {3,4,6}
B = {2,3,4,5,6,7}

Figure 13.1 illustrates the subset relation in the form of a diagram, where each oval represents one of the sets.[5] Additional examples in standard set notation are provided in (13).

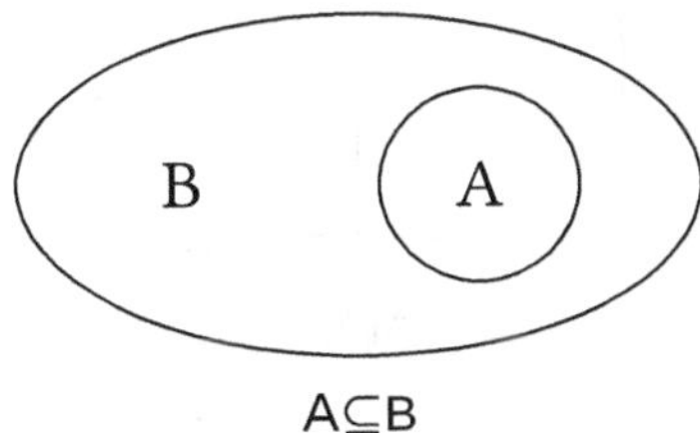

Figure 13.1: Set inclusion (the subset **relation)**

(13) a. $\{a,b,c\} \subseteq \{a,b,c,d,f\}$
b. $\{a,b,c\} \not\subseteq \{c,d,f\}$
c. $\{a,b,c\} \subseteq \{a,b,c\}$
d. $\forall S$ (where S is a set), $\varnothing \subseteq S$

Every set is a subset of itself, because all the elements which are members of set A are by definition members of set A. For this reason, the proposition "$A \subseteq A$" will be true whenever A is a well-defined set, as illustrated in (13c). If we want to specify that set A is a subset of set B, but that the two sets are not equal, we can write "$A \subset B$". This symbol means that set A is a PROPER SUBSET of set B. The proposition "$A \subset A$" will be false for any set A.

Since the elements of every set must be members of the current universal set U, "$A \subseteq U$" must always be true. If "$U \subseteq A$" is true, than it must be the case that A=U.

The INTERSECTION of two sets, written "$A \cap B$", is defined as the set consisting of all elements which are both members of A and members of B. We can illustrate this situation using the sets defined in (14). By comparing the elements in set A with those in set B, we see that the two sets share only the following elements in common: 3, 4, and 6; so $A \cap B = \{3,4,6\}$.

[5] This way of representing sets is called a Venn diagram.

(14) U = {1,2,3,4,5,6,7,8,9,10}
A = {2,3,4,6}
B = {3,4,5,6,7,8}

Figure 13.2 illustrates set intersection in the form of a diagram: the ovals represent two sets, labeled A and B, while the shaded portion which is included in both ovals represents the intersection of the two sets (A∩B). Another example in standard set notation is provided in (15).

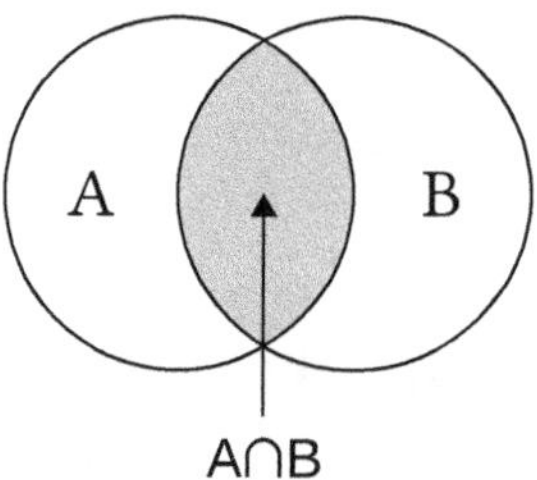

Figure 13.2: : Set intersection

(15) {a,b,c} ∩ {c,d,f} = {c}

The UNION of two sets, written "A∪B", is the set consisting of all elements which are either members of A or members of B. Returning to the sets defined in (14), the union of the two sets is formed by combining all the elements from both, which yields the following result: A∪B = {2,3,4,5,6,7,8}. Figure 13.3 illustrates this in the form of a diagram, and another example in standard set notation is provided in (16).

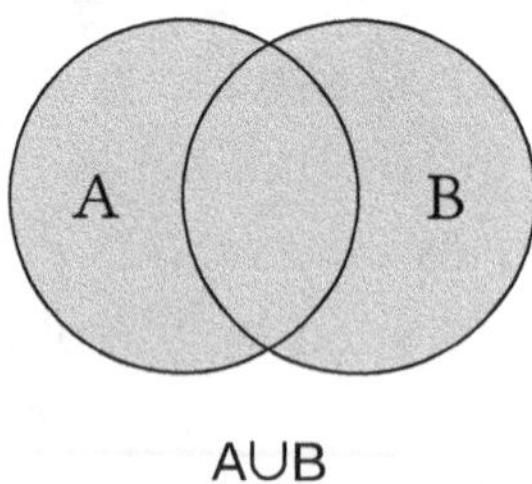

Figure 13.3: Set union

(16) {a,b,c} ∪ {c,d,f} = {a,b,c,d,f}

The COMPLEMENT of set A, written as $\overline{A}$ or A', is defined as the set which contains all the elements of U that are not elements of A. Some simple examples are shown in (17). Here, the only elements of U which are not in A are 1 and 5, so $\overline{A}$ = {1,5}. Similarly, the elements of U which are not in B are 1, 2, 5, and 6; so $\overline{B}$ = {1,2,5,6}.

(17) U = {1,2,3,4,5,6}
A = {2,3,4,6}
$\overline{A}$ = {1,5}
B = {3,4}
$\overline{B}$ = {1,2,5,6}

This basic notion of complement set involves complements relative to the universal set U. It is often useful to refer to the complement of one set relative to some other set. The complement of A relative to B, written "B–A", is the set consisting of all elements which are members of B but not members of A.[6] Another way of expressing this definition is the following: B–A = B∩$\overline{A}$. Figure 13.4 illustrates this in the form of a diagram, and several examples in standard set notation are provided in (18).

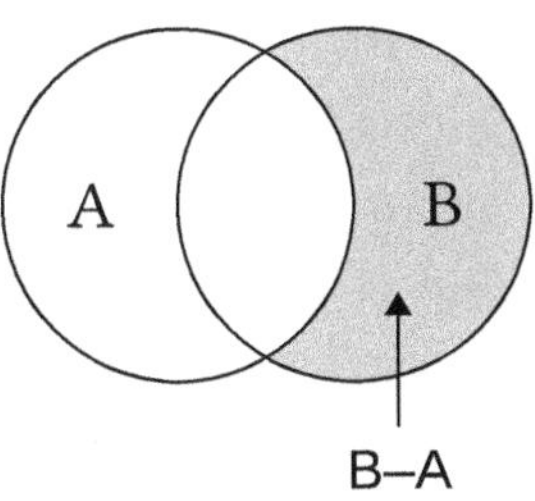

Figure 13.4: Set complementation

(18) {a,b,c} – {b,c} = {a}
{a,b,c,d,f} – {a,b,c,j,k,p} = {d,f}
A – ∅ = A
∅ – A = ∅
U – A = $\overline{A}$

To summarize, we have defined three basic operations on sets (INTERSECTION, UNION, and COMPLEMENT or "difference"), and one relation between sets, namely

[6]This operation is sometimes referred to as "set subtraction."

INCLUSION (the SUBSET relation). The three operations provide ways of combining two existing sets to define a new set. It is important to note that "A∩B", "A∪B", and "B–A" are names of sets; but "A⊆B" is a proposition, a claim about the membership of the two sets, which could be true or false.

More precise definitions of set intersection, union, complementation, and inclusion (the subset relation) are provided in (19). These definitions will help us to understand, for example, why the interpretation of an "and" statement frequently involves the intersection of two sets while the interpretation of an "or" statement frequently involves the union of two sets.

(19) $\forall x\ [x \in (A \cap B) \leftrightarrow ((x \in A) \wedge (x \in B))]$ [INTERSECTION]
$\forall x\ [x \in (A \cup B) \leftrightarrow ((x \in A) \vee (x \in B))]$ [UNION]
$\forall x\ [x \in (A - B) \leftrightarrow ((x \in A) \wedge (x \notin B))]$ [COMPLEMENT]
$(A \subseteq B) \leftrightarrow \forall x\ [(x \in A) \rightarrow (x \in B)]$ [SUBSET]

13.4 Truth relative to a model

We have noted several times that denotations, including the denotations of referring expressions and truth values of sentences, can only be evaluated relative to a particular situation of use. In order to develop and test a set of interpretive rules, which can correctly predict the denotation of a particular expression in any given situation, it is important to provide very explicit descriptions for the test situations. As stated above, this kind of description of a situation is called a MODEL, and must include two types of information: (i) the DOMAIN, i.e., the set of all individual entities in the situation; and (ii) the denotation sets for the basic vocabulary items in the expressions being analyzed.

As a first illustration of how the system works, let us return to our simple situation containing just three individuals: King Henry VIII, Anne Boleyn, and Thomas More. Our model of this situation, which we might call Model 1, would provide the information listed in (20). We often use the name "U" as a convenient way to refer to the domain (the "universal set" of individuals). The notation ⟦x⟧ represents the denotation (or "semantic value") of x within the current model. This notation can be used either for object language expressions or for logical formulae; so, for example, ⟦SNORE⟧ names the same set as ⟦*snores*⟧. By convention we use small letters for logical "constants", e.g. proper names, and capital letters for predicates.

(20) Model 1

i. the set of individuals U = { King Henry VIII, Anne Boleyn, Thomas More }

ii. denotations:
$[\![MAN]\!]$ = {King Henry VIII, Thomas More}
$[\![WOMAN]\!]$ = {Anne Boleyn}
$[\![SNORE]\!]$ = {King Henry VIII}
$[\![a]\!]$ = Anne Boleyn
$[\![h]\!]$ = King Henry VIII
$[\![t]\!]$ = Thomas More

The denotation sets encode information about the current state of the world. For example, this model indicates that King Henry VIII is the only person in the current situation who snores. We can use the defined vocabulary items to build simple declarative sentences about the individuals in this situation, and then try to provide interpretations for each sentence in terms of set membership, as illustrated in Table 13.1. These interpretations express the truth conditions for each sentence. We can use them to evaluate the truth of each sentence relative to Model 1. For example, the sentence in Table 13.1a, *Thomas More is a man*, will be true in any situation where the individual Thomas More is a member of the denotation set of the word *man*. Since this is the case in Model 1, the sentence is true relative to this model.

Table 13.1: Sentence interpretation examples

English sentence	logical form	interpretation	truth value
a. *Thomas More is a man.*	MAN(t)	Thomas More $\in [\![MAN]\!]$	T
b. *Anne Boleyn is a man or a woman.*	MAN(a) $\vee$ WOMAN(a)	Anne Boleyn $\in$ ($[\![MAN]\!] \cup [\![WOMAN]\!]$)	T
c. *Henry VIII is a man who snores.*	MAN(h) $\wedge$ SNORE(h)	Henry VIII $\in$ ($[\![MAN]\!] \cap [\![SNORE]\!]$)	T
d. *All men snore.*	$\forall$x[MAN(x) $\rightarrow$ SNORE(x)]	$[\![MAN]\!] \subseteq [\![SNORE]\!]$	F
e. *No women snore.*	$\neg\exists$x[WOMAN(x) $\wedge$ SNORE(x)]	$[\![WOMAN]\!] \cap [\![SNORE]\!] = \emptyset$	T

The interpretations in Table 13.1b–e can be derived from the corresponding logical forms, based on the definitions of intersection, union, and subset provided in (19). For example, the *or* statement in Table 19b constitutes a claim that a certain individual (Anne Boleyn) is a member of the union of two sets, because the definition of A∪B involves an *or* statement. Once the truth conditions are stated in terms of set relations, we can determine the truth values for each sentence by inspecting the membership of the denotation sets specified in the model. The statement in (Table 13.1b) is true relative to Model 1 because the individual Anne Boleyn is a member of the set ⟦WOMAN⟧ , and thus a member of ⟦MAN⟧∪⟦WOMAN⟧ .

13.5 Rules of interpretation

Stating the truth conditions for individual sentences like those in Table 13.1 is a useful first step, but does not yet replicate what speakers can do in their productive use of the language. Ultimately our goal is to provide general rules of interpretation which will predict the correct truth conditions for sentences based on their syntactic structure. As a further step toward this goal, let us return to the sentence in (21a), which we have already discussed several times.

(21) a. King Henry VIII snores.
  b. Anne Boleyn snores.

We have already stated an informal rule of interpretation for simple sentences: the proposition expressed by a (declarative) sentence will be true if and only if the referent of the subject NP is a member of the denotation set of the VP. We can now restate this rule in a slightly more formal manner. We will assume that the basic syntactic structure of the clause is [NP VP]. The semantic rule we wish to state operates in parallel with the syntactic rule which licenses this structure, as suggested in (22). (Recall that the semantic value, i.e. the denotation, of a sentence is its truth value.)

(22) **syntax**: S ⟶ NP_{subj} VP
semantics: The semantic value of a sentence is 'true' if the semantic value of the subject is a member of the set which is the semantic value of the VP, and 'false' otherwise;
$[\![S]\!]$ = 'true' iff $[\![NP_{subj}]\!] \in [\![VP]\!]$

Applying this rule to the sentence in (21a), we get the formula in (23). This formula says that the sentence will be true just in case King Henry VIII is a member of the denotation set of *snores*. Since this is true in our model, the sentence is true relative to this model. The same rule of interpretation allows us to determine that sentence (21b) is false relative to this model.

(23) $[\![$*King Henry VIII snores*$]\!]$ = 'true' iff $[\![$*King Henry VIII*$]\!] \in [\![$*snores*$]\!]$

The statement in (23) can be expressed in logical notation as in (24a). This formula is a specific instance of the general rule for evaluating the truth of propositions involving a one-place predicate. This general rule, shown in (24b), states that the proposition $P(\alpha)$ is true if and only if the entity denoted by α is an element of the denotation set of *P*.

(24) a. $[\![$SNORE(h)$]\!]$ = 'true' iff $[\![$h$]\!] \in [\![$SNORE$]\!]$
b. if α refers to an entity and P is a one-place predicate,
then $[\![$P(α)$]\!]$ = 'true' iff $[\![\alpha]\!] \in [\![$P$]\!]$

Let us now add a few more vocabulary items to our simple model, calling the new version Model 1′. This revised model presumably reflects the early period of the marriage, ca. 1532–1533 AD, when Henry and Anne were happy and in love. Note also that Thomas More had fallen out of favor with the king around this time.

(25) Model 1′
i. the set of individuals U = {King Henry VIII, Anne Boleyn, Thomas More}
ii. denotations:

$[\![$MAN$]\!]$ = {King Henry VIII, Thomas More}

$[\![$WOMAN$]\!]$ = {Anne Boleyn}

$[\![$SNORE$]\!]$ = {King Henry VIII}

$[\![$HAPPY$]\!]$ = {King Henry VIII, Anne Boleyn}

$[\![$LOVE$]\!]$ = { ⟨King Henry VIII, Anne Boleyn⟩, ⟨Anne Boleyn, King Henry VIII⟩ }

$[\![$ANGRY_AT$]\!]$ = { ⟨King Henry VIII, Thomas More⟩ }

$[\![$a$]\!]$ = Anne Boleyn

$[\![$h$]\!]$ = King Henry VIII

$[\![$t$]\!]$ = Thomas More

Model 1′ includes some two-place (i.e, transitive) predicates, and should allow us to evaluate simple transitive sentences like those in (26). The denotation set of a transitive predicate like LOVE or ANGRY_AT is not a set of individuals, but a set of ordered pairs. Sentence (26a) expresses the proposition stated by the logical formula in (27a). The truth conditions for this proposition are stated in terms of set membership in (27b): the proposition will be true if and only if the ordered pair ⟨King Henry VIII, Anne Boleyn⟩ is a member of the denotation set of LOVE. Since this is true in Model 1′, sentence (26a) is true with respect to this model. The formula in (27b) is an instance of the general pattern stated in (27c).

(26) a. King Henry VIII loves Anne Boleyn.
b. King Henry VIII is angry at Thomas More.

(27) a. LOVE(h,a)
b. $[\![\text{LOVE(h,a)}]\!]$ = 'true' iff $\langle [\![\text{h}]\!], [\![\text{a}]\!] \rangle \in [\![\text{LOVE}]\!]$
c. if α, β refer to entities and P is a two-place predicate, then $[\![\text{P}(\alpha,\beta)]\!]$ = 'true' iff $\langle [\![\alpha]\!], [\![\beta]\!] \rangle \in [\![\text{P}]\!]$

So far we have been dealing with the meanings of complete sentences all at once. This is possible only for the very simple kinds of sentences discussed thus far, but more importantly, it misses the point of the exercise. If we hope to account for the compositional nature of sentence meaning, modeling speakers' and hearers' ability to interpret novel sentences, we need to pay attention to syntactic structure. The sentences in (26) share the same basic syntactic structure as those in (21), namely [NP VP]. This suggests that the rule of interpretation stated in (22) should apply to the sentences in (26) as well.

The main syntactic difference between the sentences in (26) and those in (21) is the structure of VP: transitive in (26), intransitive in (21). In order to apply rule (22) to the sentences in (26), we need another rule which will provide the semantic value of a transitive VP. Intuitively, rule (22) says that the proposition expressed by a (declarative) sentence will be true if and only if the referent of the subject NP is a member of the denotation set of the VP. So we need to say that sentence (26a) will be true if and only if King Henry VIII belongs to a certain set. What is the relevant set? It would be the set of all individuals that love Anne Boleyn. This set will be the denotation set of the VP *loves Anne Boleyn.* The standard notation for defining such a set is shown in (28a), which says that the denotation set of this VP will be the set of all individuals x such that the ordered pair ⟨x, Anne Boleyn⟩ is an element of the denotation set of the transitive verb *love.*

(28) a. $[\![\textit{loves Anne Boleyn}]\!] = \{\text{x: } \langle \text{x, Anne Boleyn} \rangle \in [\![\text{LOVE}]\!]\}$

b. **syntax**: VP $\longrightarrow$ V_{trans} NP_{obj}
semantics: The semantic value of a VP containing a transitive verb meaning P together with an object NP meaning α is the set of all individuals x for which P(x,α) is true;
$[\![VP]\!] = \{x: \langle x, [\![NP_{obj}]\!]\rangle \in [\![V_{trans}]\!]\}$

The general rule for deriving denotation sets of transitive VPs is stated in (28b). The denotation sets formed by this rule are sets of individuals, so it makes sense to ask whether the referent of a subject NP is a member of one of these denotation sets. In other words, the denotation sets formed by rule (28b) are the right kind of sets to function as VP denotations in rule (22). So this approach allows us to model the stepwise derivation of sentence denotations. The rule of interpretation stated in (22) applies to both transitive and intransitive sentences. In the case of transitive sentences, rule (28b) "feeds", or provides the input to, rule (22).

Rule (22) can also be applied to intransitive sentences with non-verbal predicates like those in (29), provided we can determine the denotation set of the VP.

(29) a. King Henry VIII is happy.
b. King Henry VIII is a man.
c. King Henry VIII is a happy man.

We can assume that the semantic contribution of the copular verb *is* is essentially nil (apart from tense, which we are ignoring for the moment). That means that the denotation set of the VP *is happy* will be identical to $[\![HAPPY]\!]$, which is a set of individuals. For now we will also assume that the semantic contribution of the indefinite article in a predicate NP is nil.[7] So the denotation set of the VP *is a man* will be identical to $[\![MAN]\!]$, which is also a set of individuals. In general, the denotation sets of common nouns and many adjectives are of the same type as the denotation sets of intransitive verbs; this is observable in the denotations assigned in (25). So no extra work is needed to interpret sentences (29a–b), using rule (22).

Sentence (29c) is more complex, because the predicate NP contains a modifying adjective as well as the head noun. As with transitive verbs, we can determine the denotation set of the VP (in this case, *is a happy man*) by asking what set the sentence asserts that Henry VIII belongs to? Here the relevant set is the set of happy men, i.e., the set of all individuals who are both happy and men.

[7]This assumption applies only to predicate NPs, and not to indefinite NPs in argument positions.

The combination of word meanings in *happy man* follows the same pattern we have already discussed in connection with the phrase *yellow submarine.* The proposition asserted in (29c) might be represented by the formula in (30a). The truth conditions for this proposition are stated in terms of set membership in (30b). (Recall the definition of intersection given in (19).) The general rule for interpreting modifying adjectives is stated in (30c); we use the category label N′ for the constituent formed by A+N. Ignoring once again any possible semantic contribution of the copula and the indefinite article, the denotation set of the VP *is a happy man* is simply ⟦HAPPY⟧∩⟦MAN⟧. This is a set of individuals, and so rule (22) will apply correctly to sentence (29c) as well.

(30) a. HAPPY(h) ∧ MAN(h)

b. ⟦HAPPY(h) ∧ MAN(h)⟧ = 'true' iff ⟦h⟧∈(⟦HAPPY⟧∩⟦MAN⟧)

c. **syntax**: N′ → A N
semantics: The semantic value of an N′ constituent containing a modifying adjective and a head noun is the intersection of the semantic values of the adjective and noun;
⟦A N⟧ = ⟦A⟧∩⟦N⟧

13.6 Conclusion

In this chapter we have worked through a compositional analysis for the meanings of simple sentences like those in (4), (26), and (29). We have developed a rule of semantic interpretation for simple clauses of the form [NP VP] (see rule 22), a similar rule for transitive VPs (rule 28b), and a rule for adjective modifiers (30c). We have shown how these rules can be applied in a stepwise fashion to derive the truth-conditions of a simple sentence from the denotations of the words that it contains and the manner in which those words are combined syntactically.

In discussing the meanings of quantifiers, conditionals, tense markers etc. in later chapters we will focus more on understanding the phenomena than on formalizing the rule system, but we will still draw heavily on the concepts introduced in this chapter. Moreover, an important assumption in everything that follows is that our description of the meanings of these elements must be compatible with the kind of compositional analysis illustrated in this chapter.

Further reading

Good brief introductions to set theory are provided in Allwood et al. (1977: ch. 2), J. N. Martin (1987: ch. 2), Coppock (2016: ch. 2); and McCawley (1981a: ch. 5). Readable introductory textbooks include Halmos (1960) and Enderton (1977). Formal introductions to truth-conditional semantics are provided in Dowty et al. (1981) and Heim & Kratzer (1998). An informal discussion of this approach is presented in E. Bach (1989). A brief introduction to Model Theory is provided by Hodges (2013). Standard textbooks for this topic include Chang & Keisler (1990) and Hodges (1997).

Discussion exercises

A. Set theory Fill in the following tables:

	Set A	Set B	A∩B
a.	the set of all mammals	the set of all animals that lay eggs	the set of all MONOTREMES[a]
b.	{p,q,s,t}	{q,t,w,x}	
c.	the set of all odd numbers	the set of all even numbers	
d.	the set containing all members of the Beatles	the set of all people with 2-syllable first names	
e.	the set of all Hollywood stars	the set of all governors of California (past and present)	

	Set A	Set B	A∪B
a.	the set of all the books of the Old Testament	the set of all the books of the New Testament	the set of the canonical books of the Bible
b.	{p,q,s,t}	{q,t,w,x}	
c.	the set of all odd numbers	the set of all even numbers	
d.	the set of all members of the British House of Lords	the set of all members of the British House of Commons	
e.	the set of all female British monarchs	the set of all female French monarchs[b]	

	Set A	Set B	A–B
a.	nations that have won at least one FIFA World Cup title	nations that have won a FIFA World Cup title playing in their own homeland	{Brazil, Spain} (as of Dec. 2016)
b.	{p,q,s,t}	{q,t,w,x}	
c.	the set of all integers	the set of all even numbers	
d.	the set of all cordates	the set of all renates	
e.	the set of all French monarchs	the set of all female French monarchs	

	Set A	Set B	A⊆B?
a.	the set of all MONOTREMES	the set of all mammals	
b.	{p,q,s,t}	{q,t,w,x}	
c.	the set of all odd numbers	the set of all integers	
d.	the set of all cordates	the set of all renates	
e.	the set of all Indo-European languages	the set of all SVO languages	

B. Model theory

(1) Sketch a picture of the situation defined by the following model:

a. the set of individuals U = {Able, Baker, Charlie, Doug, Echo, Fred, Geronimo}

b. denotation assignments:
⟦FISH⟧ = {Able, Baker, Charlie, Doug}

⟦SUBMARINE⟧ = {Echo}
⟦SEAHORSE⟧ = {Fred, Geronimo}
⟦RED⟧ = {Able, Baker, Fred}
⟦GREEN⟧ = {Charlie, Geronimo}
⟦BLUE⟧ = {Doug, Echo}
⟦SWIM⟧ = {Able, Baker, Charlie, Doug, Fred, Geronimo}
⟦OCTOPUS⟧ = ∅
⟦FOLLOW⟧ = {⟨Able, Echo⟩, ⟨Doug, Able⟩, ⟨Doug, Echo⟩, ⟨Charlie, Fred⟩}
⟦a⟧ = Able
⟦b⟧ = Baker
⟦c⟧ = Charlie
⟦d⟧ = Doug
⟦e⟧ = Echo
⟦f⟧ = Fred
⟦g⟧ = Geronimo

(2) Complete the following table by providing logical formulae and set-theoretic interpretations for sentences (e–i), and evaluate the truth value of each sentence relative to the model provided above.

English sentence	logical form	set interpretation	
a. *Geronimo is a seahorse.*	SEAHORSE(g)	Geronimo $\in$⟦SEAHORSE⟧	T
b. *Doug is a blue fish.*	BLUE(d) $\wedge$ FISH(d)	Doug $\in$ (⟦BLUE⟧$\cap$⟦FISH⟧)	T
c. *Charlie is red or green.*	RED(c) $\vee$ GREEN(c)	Charlie $\in$ (⟦RED⟧$\cup$⟦GREEN⟧)	T
d. *All fish are red.*	$\forall$x[FISH(x) $\longrightarrow$ RED(x)]	⟦FISH⟧$\subseteq$⟦RED⟧	F
e. *Echo swims.*			
f. *All fish swim.*			
g. *No submarine is red.*			
h. *Some seahorse is green.*			
i. *Two fish are red.*			

(3) Draw annotated tree diagrams for the following sentences showing how their truth conditions would be derived compositionally from our rules of interpretation:

a. Henry snores.
b. Henry loves Jane.
c. Henry is a happy man.

[a]Platypus plus four species of echidna
[b]Note: there were no female French monarchs.

Homework exercises

A: Assume that the following individuals are included in our universe of discourse:

$[\![b]\!]$ = Mrs. Bennet
$[\![c]\!]$ = Mr. Collins
$[\![d]\!]$ = Mr. Darcy
$[\![e]\!]$ = Elizabeth (Bennet)
$[\![l]\!]$ = Lydia (Bennet)
$[\![w]\!]$ = Mr. Wickham

For each of the following logical formulae, provide an English translation and an interpretation stated in terms of set notation. Then create a model under which sentences (2–3) will be false, and the rest (including 1) will be true.[a]

1. LOVE(d,e)

   Model answer
   English translation: 'Mr. Darcy loves/loved Elizabeth.'
   truth conditions: ⟨Darcy, Elizabeth⟩ $\in [\![\text{LOVE}]\!]$

2. REJECT(e,c)
3. ∀x [(MAN(x) ∧ WEALTHY(x)) ⟶ ADMIRE(b,x)]
4. ∃x [MAN(x) ∧ WEALTHY(x) ∧ ADMIRE(b,x)]
5. ¬∃x [WOMAN(x) ∧ LOVE(x,c)]
6. DECEIVE(w,l) ∧ RESCUE(d,l)
7. ∀x [WOMAN(x) ⟶ CHARM(w,x)] ∧∀y [MAN(y) ⟶ ANGER(w,y)]

[a] Patterned loosely after Saeed (2009: 350).

14 Quantifiers

14.1 Introduction

As we noted in Chapter 13, sentences like those in (1a–c) seem to require some modifications to the simple rules of interpretation we have developed thus far:

(1) a. All men snore.
  b. No women snore.
  c. Some man snores.

Most of the sentences that we discussed in that chapter had proper names for arguments. We analyzed those sentences as asserting that a specific individual (the referent of the subject NP) is a member of a particular set (the denotation set of the VP). The sentences in (1a–c) present a new challenge because the subject NPs are quantified noun phrases, and do not refer to specific individuals.

Quantifier words like *all*, *some*, and *no* have been intensively studied by semanticists, and the present chapter summarizes some of this research. In §14.2 we present evidence for the somewhat surprising claim that quantifier words express a relationship between two sets. This insight, which we will argue follows from the general principle of compositionality, provides the critical foundation for all that follows. In §14.3 we show why the standard predicate logic notation that we introduced in Chapter 4 cannot express the meanings of certain kinds of quantifiers. We then introduce a different format, called the RESTRICTED QUANTIFIER notation, which overcomes this problem. In §14.4 we discuss two classes of quantifier words, CARDINAL QUANTIFIERS vs. PROPORTIONAL QUANTIFIERS, which differ in both semantic properties and syntactic distribution. §14.5 discusses an important property of quantifiers which was mentioned briefly in Chapter 4, namely their potential for ambiguous scope relations with other quantifiers (or various other types of expressions) occurring within the same sentence.

14.2 Quantifiers as relations between sets

Let us begin by asking what claim sentence (1a) makes about the world. Under what circumstances will it be true? Intuitively, it will be true in any situation in which all of the individuals that are men have the property of snoring; that is, when every member of the denotation set ⟦MAN⟧ is also a member of the denotation set ⟦SNORE⟧. But this is equivalent to saying that ⟦MAN⟧ is a subset of ⟦SNORE⟧, as indicated in (19) of Chapter 13 (page 240).

Now let us think about how this meaning is composed. We have said that the sentence *All men snore* expresses an assertion that the set of all men is a subset of the set of entities that snore. This interpretation is expressed in the formula in (2). Clearly the semantic contribution of *men* is ⟦MAN⟧, and the semantic contribution of *snore* is ⟦SNORE⟧. That means that the semantic contribution of *all* can only be the subset relation itself.

(2) ⟦*All men snore*⟧ = true ↔ ⟦MAN⟧ ⊆ ⟦SNORE⟧

Now it may seem odd to suggest that *all* really means 'subset', but that is what the principle of compositionality seems to lead us to. The subset relation is a relation between two sets. More abstractly, we can think of the determiner *all* as naming a relation between two sets, in this case the set of all men and the set of all individuals that snore.

Now let us consider sentence (1b), *No women snore.* Under what circumstances will this sentence be true? Intuitively, it will be true in any situation in which no individual who is a woman has the property of snoring; that is, when no individual is a member both of the denotation set ⟦WOMAN⟧ and of the denotation set ⟦SNORE⟧. But this is equivalent to saying that the intersection of ⟦WOMAN⟧ with ⟦SNORE⟧ is empty, as indicated in (19) of Chapter 13 (page 240). This interpretation is expressed in the formula in (3). By the same reasoning that we used above, the principle of compositionality leads us to the conclusion that the determiner *no* means 'empty intersection'. Once again, this is a relation between two sets.

(3) ⟦*No woman snores*⟧ = true ↔ (⟦WOMAN⟧ ∩ ⟦SNORE⟧ = ∅)

Sentence (1c), *Some man snores*, will be true in any situation in which at least one individual who is a man has the property of snoring. This is equivalent to saying that the intersection of ⟦MAN⟧ with ⟦SNORE⟧ is non-empty, as indicated in (4). The principle of compositionality leads us to the conclusion that the determiner *some* means 'non-empty intersection'.

(4) $[\![\textit{Some man snores}]\!] = \text{true} \leftrightarrow ([\![\text{MAN}]\!] \cap [\![\text{SNORE}]\!] \neq \varnothing)$

The key insight which has helped semanticists understand the meaning contributions of quantifier words like *all, some,* and *no,* is that these words name relations between two sets. The table in (5) lists these and several other quantifying determiners, showing their interpretations stated as a relation between two sets. In these examples the two sets are $[\![\text{STUDENT}]\!]$ (the set of all students), which for convenience we will refer to as S, and $[\![\text{BRILLIANT}]\!]$ (the set of all brilliant individuals) which for convenience we will refer to as B.

(5) a. All students are brilliant. $S \subseteq B$
b. No students are brilliant. $S \cap B = \varnothing$
c. Some students are brilliant. $|S \cap B| \geq 2$
d. A/Some student is brilliant. $S \cap B \neq \varnothing$; or: $|S \cap B| \geq 1$
e. Four students are brilliant. $|S \cap B| = 4$[1]
f. Most students are brilliant. $|S \cap B| > |S - B|$; or: $|S \cap B| > ½|S|$
g. Few students are brilliant. $|S \cap B| <$ some contextually defined number
h. Both students are brilliant. $S \subseteq B \wedge |S| = 2$

Notice that we have distinguished plural vs. singular uses of *some* by stating that plural *some* (ex. 5c) indicates an intersection with cardinality of two or more. The interpretation suggested in (h) indicates that the meaning of *both* includes the subset relation and the assertion that the cardinality of the first set equals two. This amounts to saying that *both* means 'all two of them'. Strictly speaking, it might be more accurate to treat the information about cardinality as a presupposition, because that part of the meaning is preserved in questions (*Are both students brilliant?*), conditionals (*If both students are brilliant, then* ...), etc. However, we will not pursue that issue here.

All of the examples in (5) involve relations between two sets. We might refer to quantifiers of this type as two-place quantifiers. Three-place quantifiers are also possible, i.e., quantifiers that express relations among three sets. Some examples are provided in (6).

(6) a. *Half as many* guests attended *as* were invited.
$|\,[\![\text{GUEST}]\!] \cap [\![\text{ATTEND}]\!]\,| = ½|\,[\![\text{GUEST}]\!] \cap [\![\text{INVITE}]\!]\,|$

[1]Recall from Chapter 9 that numerals seem to allow two different interpretations. In light of that discussion, this sentence could mean either $|S \cap B| = 4$ or $|S \cap B| \geq 4$ depending on context. For the purposes of this chapter we will ignore the 'at least' reading.

b. In every Australian election from 1967 to 1998, *more* men *than* women voted for the Labor party.
$| [\![\text{MAN}]\!] \cap \{x: \langle x,l \rangle \in [\![\text{VOTE\_FOR}]\!] \}| > | [\![\text{WOMAN}]\!] \cap \{x: \langle x,l \rangle \in [\![\text{VOTE\_FOR}]\!] \}|$

The kinds of meanings expressed by quantifying determiners can also be expressed by adverbs. D. Lewis (1975) refers to adverbs like *always, sometimes, never*, etc. as "unselective quantifiers", because they can quantify over various kinds of things. The examples in (7) show these adverbs quantifying over times: *always* means 'at all times', *never* means 'at no time', etc. The examples in (8) show these same adverbs quantifying over individual entities. If *usually* in (8b) were interpreted as quantifying over times, it would imply that the color of a dog's eyes might change from one moment to the next. If *sometimes* in (8c) were interpreted as quantifying over times, it would imply that the sulfur content of a lump of coal might change from one moment to the next.

(7) Quantifying over times:

a. In his campaigns Napoleon *always* relied upon surprise and speed.[2]
b. Churchill *usually* took a nap after lunch.
c. De Gaulle *sometimes* scolded his aide-de-camp (= Chief of Staff).
d. George Washington *never* told a lie.

(8) Quantifying over individual entities:

a. A triangle *always* has three sides. (= '*All* triangles have three sides.')
b. Dogs *usually* have brown eyes. (= '*Most* dogs have brown eyes.')
c. Bituminous coal *sometimes* contains more than one percent sulfur by weight. (= '*Some* bituminous coal contains more than one percent sulfur by weight.')
d. A rectangle *never* has five corners. (= '*No* rectangles have five corners.')

In a number of languages, including English, quantifying determiners like *all* can optionally occur in adverbial positions, as illustrated in (9). This alternation is often referred to as QUANTIFIER FLOAT:

[2] http://www.usafa.edu/df/dfh/docs/Harmon28.pdf

(9) a. *All* the children will go to the party.
 b. The children will *all* go to the party.

Not all languages make use of quantifying determiners; adverbial quantifiers seem to be more common cross-linguistically. Other strategies for expressing quantifier meanings are attested as well: quantificational verb roots, verbal affixes, particles, etc. For some languages it has been claimed that the syntactic means available for expressing quantification limits the range of quantifier meanings which can be expressed.[3] Most of the examples in our discussion below involve English quantifying determiners, and these have been the focus of a vast amount of study. However, we should not forget that other quantification strategies are also common.

14.3 Quantifiers in logical form

Our analysis of *all* as denoting a subset relation, *no* as meaning 'empty intersection', and *some* as meaning 'non-empty intersection', is reflected in the logical forms we proposed in Chapter 4 for sentences involving these words. These logical forms are repeated here in (10).

(10) a. All men snore. $\forall x[\text{MAN}(x) \longrightarrow \text{SNORE}(x)]$
 b. No women snore. $\neg\exists x[\text{WOMAN}(x) \wedge \text{SNORE}(x)]$
 c. Some man snores. $\exists x[\text{MAN}(x) \wedge \text{SNORE}(x)]$

Now we are in a position to understand why these forms work as translations of the English quantifier words. The use of material implication (⟶) in (10a) follows from the definition of the subset relation which we presented in Chapter 13, repeated here in (11a). The use of logical ∧ 'and' in (10b–c) follows from the definition of set intersection presented in Chapter 13, repeated here in (11b).

(11) a. $(A \subseteq B) \leftrightarrow \forall x[(x{\in}A) \longrightarrow (x{\in}B)]$ [SUBSET]
 $([\![\text{MAN}]\!] \subseteq [\![\text{SNORE}]\!]) \leftrightarrow \forall x[(x{\in}[\![\text{MAN}]\!]) \longrightarrow (x{\in}[\![\text{SNORE}]\!])]$
 b. $\forall x[x \in (A{\cap}B) \leftrightarrow ((x{\in}A) \wedge (x{\in}B))]$ [INTERSECTION]
 $([\![\text{MAN}]\!] \cap [\![\text{SNORE}]\!] \neq \emptyset) \leftrightarrow \exists x[(x{\in}[\![\text{MAN}]\!]) \wedge (x{\in}[\![\text{SNORE}]\!])]$

Many other quantifier meanings can also be expressed using the basic predicate logic notation. For example, the NP *four men* could be translated as shown in (12):

[3] Baker (1995); Bittner (1995); Koenig & Michelson (2010).

(12) *Four men snore.*
$\exists w \exists x \exists y \exists z[w \neq x \neq y \neq z \wedge \text{MAN}(w) \wedge \text{MAN}(x) \wedge \text{MAN}(y) \wedge \text{MAN}(z) \wedge \text{SNORE}(w) \wedge \text{SNORE}(x) \wedge \text{SNORE}(y) \wedge \text{SNORE}(z)]$

As we can see even in this simple example, the standard predicate logic notation is a somewhat clumsy tool for this task. Moreover, it turns out that there are some quantifier meanings which cannot be expressed at all using the predicate logic we have introduced thus far. For example, the interpretation for *most* suggested in (5f) is that the cardinality of the intersection of the two sets is greater than half of the cardinality of the first set. The basic problem here is that the logical predicates we have been using thus far represent properties of individual entities. This type of logic is called FIRST-ORDER LOGIC. However, the cardinality of a set is not a property of any individual, but rather a property of the set as a whole. What we would need in order to express quantifier meanings like *most* is some version of SECOND-ORDER LOGIC, which deals with properties of sets of individuals.

For example, we could define the denotation set of a NP like *most men* to be the set of all properties which are true of most men. The sentence *Most men snore* would be true just in case the property of snoring is a member of ⟦*most men*⟧.[4] However, the mathematical formalism of this approach is more complex than we can handle in the present book. Rather than trying to work out all the technical details, we will proceed from here on with a more descriptive approach.

One convenient way of expressing propositions which contain quantifier meanings like *most* is called the RESTRICTED QUANTIFIER notation. This notation consists of three parts: the quantifier operator, the restriction, and the nuclear scope. In example (13a), the operator is *most*; the restriction is the open proposition "STUDENT(x)"; and the nuclear scope is the open proposition "BRILLIANT(x)". This same format can be used for other quantifiers as well, as illustrated in (13b–c).

(13) a. *Most students are brilliant.* [*most* x: STUDENT(x)] BRILLIANT(x)
(OPERATOR = "*most*"; RESTRICTION = "STUDENT(x)";
SCOPE = "BRILLIANT(x)")
b. *No women snore.* [*no* x: WOMAN(x)] SNORE(x)
c. *All brave men are lonely.* [*all* x: MAN(x) ∧ BRAVE(x)] LONELY(x)

[4] This analysis, under which quantified NPs denote sets of sets, is called the Generalized Quantifier approach. The meanings of the quantified NPs themselves are referred to as Generalized Quantifiers, which leads to a certain amount of ambiguity in the use of the word *quantifier*. Sometimes it is used to refer to the whole NP, and sometimes just to the quantifying determiner.

In contrast to the standard logical notation, using this restricted quantifier notation allows us to adopt a uniform procedure for interpreting sentences which contain quantifying determiners:

- the quantifying determiner itself specifies the operator;
- the remainder of the NP which contains the quantifying determiner specifies the material in the restriction;
- the rest of the sentence specifies the material in the nuclear scope.

For example, the quantifying determiner in (13c) is *all*; this determines the operator. The remainder of the NP which contains the quantifying determiner is *brave men*; this specifies the material in the restriction (MAN(x) ∧ BRAVE(x)). The rest of the sentence (*are lonely*) specifies the material in the nuclear scope (LONELY(x)). Some additional examples are provided in (14).

(14) a. *Most men who snore are libertarians.*
[*most* x: MAN(x) ∧ SNORE(x)] LIBERTARIAN(x)
b. *Few strict Baptists drink or smoke.*
[*few* x: BAPTIST(x) ∧ STRICT(x)] DRINK(x) ∨ SMOKE(x)

Of course, translations in this format do not tell us what the quantifying determiners actually mean; the meaning of each quantifier needs to be defined separately, as illustrated in (15):

(15) a. [*all* x: P(x)] Q(x) $\leftrightarrow$ $[\![P]\!] \subseteq [\![Q]\!]$
b. [*no* x: P(x)] Q(x) $\leftrightarrow$ $[\![P]\!] \cap [\![Q]\!] = \varnothing$
c. [*four* x: P(x)] Q(x) $\leftrightarrow$ $|\ [\![P]\!] \cap [\![Q]\!]\ | = 4$
d. [*most* x: P(x)] Q(x) $\leftrightarrow$ $|\ [\![P]\!] \cap [\![Q]\!]\ | > ½\ |\ [\![P]\!]\ |$

As these definitions show, a quantifying determiner names a relation between two sets: one defined by the predicate(s) in the restriction (represented by P in the formulae in 15), and the other defined by the predicate(s) in the scope (represented by Q). Interpretations for the examples in (13) are shown in (16). Use these examples to study how the content of the restriction and scope of the logical form in restricted quantifier notation get inserted into the set theoretic interpretation.

(16) a. *Most students are brilliant.*
[*most* x: STUDENT(x)] BRILLIANT(x)
| ⟦STUDENT⟧ ∩ ⟦BRILLIANT⟧ | > ½ | ⟦STUDENT⟧ |

b. *No women snore.*
[*no* x: WOMAN(x)] SNORE(x)
⟦WOMAN⟧ ∩ ⟦SNORE⟧ = ∅

c. *All brave men are lonely.*
[*all* x: MAN(x) ∧ BRAVE(x)] LONELY(x)
(⟦MAN⟧ ∩ ⟦BRAVE⟧) ⊆ ⟦LONELY⟧

This same procedure applies whether the quantified NP is a subject, object, or oblique argument. Some examples of quantified object NPs are given in (17).

(17) a. *John loves all pretty girls.*
[*all* x: GIRL(x) ∧ PRETTY(x)] LOVE(j,x)
(⟦GIRL⟧ ∩ ⟦PRETTY⟧) ⊆ {x: <j,x> ∈ ⟦LOVE⟧ }

b. *Susan has married a cowboy who teases her.*
[*an* x: COWBOY(x) ∧ TEASE(x,s)] MARRY(s,x)
(⟦COWBOY⟧ ∩ {x: <x,s> ∈ ⟦TEASE⟧) ∩ {y: <s,y> ∈ ⟦MARRY⟧ } ≠ ∅

At least for the moment, we will provisionally treat the articles *the* and *a(n)* as quantifying determiners. We will discuss the definite article below in §14.4. For now we will treat the indefinite article as an existential quantifier, as illustrated in (17b). (Note that this applies to indefinite articles occurring in argument NPs, not predicate NPs. We suggested in Chapter 13 that indefinite articles occurring in predicate NPs typically do not contribute any independent meaning.)

Compound words such as *someone, everyone, no one, something, nothing, anything, everywhere,* etc. include a quantifier root plus another root that restricts the quantification to a general class (people, things, places, etc.). It is often helpful to include this "classifier" meaning as a predicate within the restriction of the quantifier, as illustrated in (18).

(18) a. *Everyone loves Snoopy.* [*all* x: PERSON(x)] LOVE(x,s)
b. *Columbus discovered something.* [*some* x: THING(x)] DISCOVER(c,x)
c. *Nowhere on Earth is safe.* [*no* x: PLACE(x) ∧ ON(x,e)] SAFE(x)

14.4 Two types of quantifiers

Quantifier determiners like *all*, *every*, and *most*, are referred to as PROPORTIONAL QUANTIFIERS because they express the idea that a certain proportion of one class is included in some other class. Certain complex determiners like *four out of (every) five* are also proportional quantifiers. Quantifier determiners like *no*, *some*, *four*, and *several*, in contrast, are referred to as CARDINAL QUANTIFIERS because they provide information about the cardinality of the intersection of two sets.[5] *Several* is vague; for most speakers it probably indicates a set containing more than two members, but not too much more (less than ten? less than seven?). Nevertheless, it clearly expresses cardinality rather than proportion.

The determiners *many* and *few* are ambiguous between a cardinal sense and a proportional sense. Sentence (19a) can be interpreted in a way which is not a contradiction, even though the student body at Cal Tech is a tiny fraction of the total population of America. However, this interpretation must involve the proportional senses of *many* and *few*; the cardinal senses would give rise to a contradiction. Sentence (19b) can only be interpreted as involving the cardinal senses of *many* and *few*, since the sentence does not invoke any specific set of problems or solutions from which a certain proportion could be specified.

(19) a. Few people in America have an IQ over 145, but many students at Cal Tech are in that range.
  b. Today we are facing many problems, but we have few solutions.

Both the cardinal and proportional senses of *many* and *few* are vague, and this can make it tricky to distinguish the two senses in some contexts. Cardinal *many* probably means more than several, but how much more? Generally speaking, proportional *many* should probably be more than half, and proportional *few* should probably be less than half; but how much more, or how much less? And in certain contexts, even this tendency need not hold. In a country where 80% of the citizens normally come out to vote, we might say *Few people bothered to vote this year* if the turnout dropped below 60%. In a city where less than 20% of the citizens normally bother to vote in local elections, we might say *Many people came to vote this year* if the turnout reached 40%. So, like other vague expressions, the meanings of *many* and *few* are partly dependent on context.

[5] Proportional quantifiers are sometimes referred to as STRONG QUANTIFIERS, and cardinal quantifiers are sometimes referred to as WEAK QUANTIFIERS.

Relationships expressed by cardinal quantifiers are generally symmetric, as illustrated in the examples in (20–23):[6]

(20) a. No honest men are lawyers. (a entails b)
b. No lawyers are honest men.

(21) a. Three senators are Vietnam War veterans. (a entails b)
b. Three Vietnam War veterans are senators.

(22) a. Some drug dealers are federal employees. (a entails b)
b. Some federal employees are drug dealers.

(23) a. Several Indo-European languages are verb-initial. (a entails b)
b. Several verb-initial languages are Indo-European.

Relationships expressed by proportional quantifiers, in contrast, are not symmetric, as illustrated in the examples in (24–26):

(24) a. All brave men are lonely. (a does not entail b)
b. All lonely men are brave.

(25) a. Most Popes are Italian. (a does not entail b)
b. Most Italians are Popes.

(26) a. Few people are Zoroastrians. (a does not entail b, in proportional sense of *few*)
b. Few Zoroastrians are people.

There are several distributional differences which distinguish these two classes of determiners. The best known of these has to do with existential constructions. Only cardinal quantifiers can occur as the "pivot" in the existential *there* construction; proportional quantifiers are ungrammatical in this environment.[7] (It is important to distinguish the existential *there* from several other constructions involving *there*. Sentences like (27b–c) might be grammatical with the locative *there*, or with the list *there* as in *There's John, there's Bill, there's all our cousins...*; but these other uses are irrelevant to the present discussion.)

[6]This symmetry follows from the fact that cardinal quantifiers generally have meanings of the form $|A \cap B| = n$; and the intersection function is commutative ($A \cap B = B \cap A$).
[7]Milsark (1977).

(27) a. There are several/some/no/many/six unicorns in the garden.
b. * There are all/most unicorns in the garden.
c. * There is every unicorn in the garden.

This contrast may be related to the fact that proportional quantifiers seem to presuppose the existence of a contextually relevant and identifiable set.[8] In order for sentence (28a) to be a sensible statement, a special context is required which specifies the relevant set of people. For example, we might be discussing a town where most people are Baptist. Similarly, if sentence (28b) is intended to be a sensible statement, a special context is required to specify the relevant set of students. For example, we might be discussing graduation requirements for a particular linguistics program. This "discourse familiarity" of the restriction set is required by proportional quantifiers, but not by cardinal quantifiers. The sentences in (29) do not require any specific context in order to be acceptable. (Of course context could be relevant in determining what the vague quantifier *many* means.)

(28) a. Most people attend the Baptist church.
b. All students are required to pass phonetics.

(29) a. Many people attend the Baptist church.
b. Six hundred students got grants from the National Science Foundation this year.
c. No aircraft are allowed to fly over the White House.

Discourse familiarity is of course one type of definiteness. We suggested above that the indefinite article *a(n)* could be analyzed as an existential quantifier, roughly synonymous with singular *some*. Under this analysis, *a(n)* would be a cardinal quantifier, because it specifies a non-empty intersection. Similarly, one way of analyzing the definite article *the* is to treat it as a special universal quantifier, meaning something like 'all of them' with plural nouns and 'all one of them' with singular nouns. Since *all* is a proportional quantifier, this analysis predicts that *the* should also function as a proportional quantifier. The use of *the* seems to trigger a presupposition that the individual or group named by the NP in which it occurs is uniquely identifiable in the context of the utterance.

[8] Barwise & Cooper (1981) suggest that asserting existence is a tautology for most proportional quantifier phrases, vacuously true if the reference set is empty and necessarily true if it is not empty. It is a contradiction for proportional quantifiers like *neither*.

This presupposition might be seen as following from the general requirement of discourse familiarity for the restriction set of a proportional quantifier.[9]

This analysis of the articles gets some support from the observation that *a(n)* can, but *the* cannot, occur with existential *there.* This is exactly what we would expect if *a(n)* is a cardinal quantifier while *the* is a proportional quantifier.

(30) There is a/*the unicorn in the garden. (under existential reading)

14.5 Scope ambiguities

As noted in Chapter 4, when a quantifier combines with another quantifier, negation, or certain other kinds of elements, it can give rise to ambiguities of scope. For example, the sentence *I did not find many valuable books* allows for two readings, as shown in (31). The first reading could be paraphrased as 'there were many valuable books which I did not find'. The second reading could be paraphrased as 'there were not many valuable books which I found.' The difference in the two readings depends on the scope of negation: it takes scope over the quantified NP in reading (b), but not in reading (a).

(31) *I did not find many valuable books.*

   a. [*many* x: BOOK(x) ∧ VALUABLE(x)] ¬FIND(speaker,x)

   b. ¬[*many* x: BOOK(x) ∧ VALUABLE(x)] FIND(speaker,x)

This is a real semantic ambiguity because the two readings have different truth conditions. For example, suppose that a library contains 10,000 books, of which 600 are considered valuable. One day the library catches fire. The next day the librarian goes in to search for the surviving books, and finds 300 which are considered valuable. In this context, 300 books could plausibly be described as "many", in which case the first reading would be true while the second reading would be false.

In Chapter 4 we noted that the proverb *All that glitters is not gold* actually has two possible readings. Once again the ambiguity arises from the interaction between the quantifier and clausal negation: either may occur within the scope of the other, as shown in (32). However, many English speakers are not aware of any ambiguity in this proverb. The mock syllogism in (33) has been proposed as an example of fallacious reasoning. In fact, the reasoning is sound under one possible reading of the proverb (the (a) reading), but not under the intended reading of the proverb (the (b) reading).

[9] Kearns (2000).

(32) *All that glitters is not gold.*

a. [*all* x: GLITTER(x)] ¬GOLD(x)

b. ¬[*all* x: GLITTER(x)] GOLD(x)

(33) All that glitters is not gold.
This rock glitters.
Therefore, this rock is not gold.[10]

Part of the reason that speakers do not feel the proverb to be ambiguous is that only one reading is consistent with what we know about the world. However, it also seems to be the case that the (b) reading is generally preferred in sentences of this type. On the other hand, naturally occurring examples of the (a) reading can be found as well, such as those listed in (34). (In each case the context makes it clear that the intended reading gives widest scope to the quantifier; so (34c) for example is intended to mean that no person is perfect.)

(34) a. All social features are not working.

b. All external storage devices are not being detected as drives.

c. Every person is not perfect.

Example (35) illustrates how ambiguity can (and frequently does) arise from the interaction between the two quantifiers: either may occur within the scope of the other. The (a) reading says that there are many individual linguists who have read every paper by Chomsky. The (b) reading says that for any given paper by Chomsky there are many individual linguists who have read it. It would be possible for the (b) reading to be true while the (a) reading is false under the same circumstances.

(35) *Many linguists have read every paper by Chomsky.*

a. [*many* x: LINGUIST(x)] ([*every* y: PAPER(y) ∧ BY(y,c)] READ(x,y))

b. [*every* y: PAPER(y) ∧ BY(y,c)] ([*many* x: LINGUIST(x)] READ(x,y))

A similar example is presented in (36). The (a) reading says that every student in some contextually-determined set, e.g. all those enrolled in a certain course, knows two languages; but each student could know a different pair of languages. The (b) reading says that there is some specific pair of languages, e.g. Urdu and Swahili, which every student in the relevant set knows. (Another example of this type was mentioned in Chapter 4, ex. 28a.)

[10] http://www.fallacyfiles.org/scopefal.html

(36) *Every student knows two languages.*

a. [*every* x: STUDENT(x)] ([*two* y: LANGUAGE(y)] KNOW(x, y))
b. [*two* y: LANGUAGE(y)] ([*every* x: STUDENT(x)] KNOW(x, y))

Scope ambiguities can also arise when a quantifier combines with a modal auxiliary, as illustrated in (37–40). (The symbol $\Diamond$ stands for 'possibly true' and the symbol $\Box$ stands for 'necessarily true'.) As we will see in Chapter 16, many modals appear to be lexically ambiguous, but that is not the source of the ambiguity in these examples. As with negation, the modal operator can either be interpreted within the scope of the quantifier (the (a) readings), or it can take scope over the quantifier (the (b) readings). Try to paraphrase the two readings for each of these sentences.

(37) *Every student might fail the course.*[11]

(38) $\forall x[\text{STUDENT}(x) \rightarrow \Diamond\, \text{FAIL}(x)]$

(39) $\Diamond\, \forall x[\text{STUDENT}(x) \rightarrow \text{FAIL}(x)]$

(40) *Some sanctions must be imposed.*

(41) $\exists x[\text{SANCTION}(x) \wedge \Box\, \text{BE-IMPOSED}(x)]$

(42) $\Box\, \exists x[\text{SANCTION}(x) \wedge \text{BE-IMPOSED}(x)]$

We will mention just one more possible source of scope ambiguity, namely the interaction between a quantifier and a propositional attitude verb. Consider the example in (43):

(43) *John thinks that he has visited every state.*

a. [*all* x: STATE(x)] (THINK(j, VISIT(j,x)))
b. THINK(j, [*all* x: STATE(x)] VISIT(j,x))

The (a) reading could be true and the (b) reading false if John has no idea how many states there are in the United States, but for each of the 50 states, when you ask him whether he has visited that specific state, he answers "I think so." The (b) reading could be true and the (a) reading false if John believes that there are only 48 states and knows that he has visited all of them, and he knows that he has not visited Alaska or Hawaii but doesn't believe that they are states.

[11] Abbott (2010: 48).

It is possible to analyze many cases of *de dicto-de re* ambiguity (Chapter 12) as scope ambiguities involving propositional attitude verbs, if we treat the indefinite article as an existential quantifier. An example is presented in (44). The (a) reading says that there is some specific individual who is a cowboy, and Susan wants to marry this individual. This is the *de re* reading. It could be true even if Susan does not realize that her prospective husband is a cowboy. The (b) reading says that whoever Susan marries, she wants him to be a cowboy. This is the *de dicto* reading. It could be true even if Susan does not yet have a specific individual in mind.

(44) *Susan wants to marry a cowboy.*

a. $\exists x[\text{COWBOY}(x) \wedge \text{WANT}(s, \text{MARRY}(s,x))]$

b. $\text{WANT}(s, \exists x[\text{COWBOY}(x) \wedge \text{MARRY}(s,x)])$

Based on this analysis, the *de re* reading is often referred to as the "wide scope" reading, meaning that the existential quantifier takes scope over the propositional attitude verb. The *de dicto* reading is often referred to as the "narrow scope" reading, meaning that the quantifier occurs within the scope of the propositional attitude verb.[12]

14.6 Conclusion

We have argued that the meaning contribution of a quantifier, whether expressed by a determiner, adverb, or some other category, is best understood as a relationship between two sets. We introduced a new format for logical formulae involving quantification, the restricted quantifier notation, which is flexible enough to handle all sorts of quantifiers. This notation also makes it possible to state rules of semantic interpretation which treat quantifiers in a more uniform way, although we did not spell out the technical details of how we might do this. A very important step in the interpretation of a quantifier is determining its scope, and we discussed several contexts in which scope interactions can create ambiguous sentences.

These concepts will be important in later chapters, especially in Chapter 16 where we discuss modality. As discussed in that chapter, a very influential analysis of modality is based on the claim that modal expressions like *may, must, could,* etc. are really a special type of quantifier.

[12]Some scholars argue that *de dicto-de re* ambiguity cannot always be reduced to scope relations; see for example Fodor & Sag (1982).

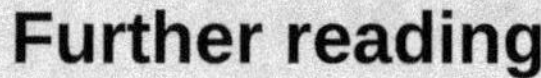

Further reading

Kearns (2000: ch. 4) provides a clear and helpful introduction to quantification. A brief overview of this very large topic is provided in Gutierrez-Rexach (2013), a longer overview in Szabolcsi (2015). D. Lewis (1975) is the classic work on quantifying adverbs. Barwise & Cooper (1981) is one of the foundational works on Generalized Quantifiers, and a detailed discussion is presented in Peters & Westerståhl (2006).

Discussion exercises

A. Restricted quantifier notation. Express the following sentences in restricted quantifier notation, and provide an interpretation in terms of set relations:

1. *Every Roman is patriotic.*

   > Model answer
   > [*every* x: ROMAN(x)] PATRIOTIC(x)
   > $[\![\text{ROMAN}]\!] \subseteq [\![\text{PATRIOTIC}]\!]$

2. Some wealthy Romans are patriotic.
3. Both Romans are patriotic.
4. Caesar loves all Romans who obey him.
5. Most loyal Romans love Caesar.

B. Scope Ambiguities. Use logical notation to express the two readings for the following sentences, and state which reading seems most likely to be intended, if you can tell.

1. Some man loves every woman.
2. Many theologians do not understand this doctrine.
3. This doctrine is not understood by many theologians.
4. Two-thirds of the members did not vote for the amendment.
5. You can fool some of the people all of the time. [Note: for now you may ignore the modal *can*.]
6. A woman gives birth in the United States every five minutes.
7. He tries to read Plato's *Republic* every year.[a]

[a] Marilyn Quayle, on the reading habits of her husband; *Wall Street Journal*, January 20, 1993.

Homework exercises

Exercise A: Translate the following sentences into predicate logic, using the STANDARD [not restricted] format for the existential and universal quantifiers, ∃ and ∀. If any sentence allows two interpretations, provide the logical formulae for both readings.

1. Solomon answered every riddle.

   Model answer

   ∀x[RIDDLE(x) → ANSWER(s,x)]

2. All ambitious politicians visit Paris.

3. Someone betrayed Caesar.
4. All critical systems are not working.
5. No German general supported Stalin.
6. Not every German general supported Hitler.
7. Some people believe every wild rumor.
8. Socrates inspires all sincere scholars who read Plato.

Exercise B: Translate the sentences below into logical formulae, using restricted quantifier notation.[a]

1. Arthur eats everything that Susan cooks.

   Model answer

   [Every x: THING(x) ∧ COOK(s,x)] EAT(a,x)

2. Boris mistrusts most reports from Brussels.
   [hint: treat *from* as a two-place predicate]
3. Few who know him like Arthur.
4. William sold Betsy every arrowhead that he found.
5. Twenty-one movies were directed and produced by Alfred Hitchcock.
6. Most travelers entering or leaving Australia visit Sydney.
7. No one_i remembers every promise he_i makes.
8. Some officials who boycotted both meetings were sacked by Reagan.
9. Jane Austen and E. M. Forster wrote six novels each.
10. Rachel met and interviewed several famous musicians.
11. Most children will not play if they are sad.

Exercise C: The bolded phrases in the sentences below can be analyzed as quantifiers. State the truth conditions for these sentences in terms of set relations.

1. More than twenty senators are guilty.

> Model answer
>
> $| [\![\text{SENATOR}]\!] \cap [\![\text{GUILTY}]\!] | > 20$

2. **Between six and twelve generals** are loyal.
3. **Both** sisters are champions.
4. **The twelve** apostles were Jewish.
5. **Just two of the seven** guides are bilingual.
6. **Neither** candidate is honest.
7. **Fewer than five** crewmen are sober.

The discontinuous determiners in the next examples express three-place quantifier meanings:

8. **More** men **than** women snore.
9. **Exactly as many** Americans are lawyers **as** are prisoners.[b]
10. **Fewer** wrestlers **than** boxers are famous.

[a]Ex. B-C are patterned after Kearns (2000: 89–90).

[b]Actually the figures are only approximately equal, but there are clearly too many of both.

15 Intensional contexts

15.1 Introduction

In Chapter 12 we discussed the apparent failure of compositionality in the complement clauses of propositional attitude verbs (*believe, expect, want,* etc.). This apparent failure is observable in several ways. First, the principle of substitutivity does not seem to hold in these complement clauses: replacing one NP with another that has the same referent can change the truth value of the proposition expressed by the sentence as a whole. For example, even if sentences (1a–b) are assumed to be true, we cannot apply the principle of substitutivity to conclude that (1c) must be true as well.

(1) a. Charles Dickens was the author of *Oliver Twist.*
b. George Cruikshank claimed to be the author of *Oliver Twist.*[1]
c. George Cruikshank claimed to be Charles Dickens.

Second, as illustrated in Chapter 12, a sentence which contains a propositional attitude verb may have a truth value even if the complement clause contains a NP which lacks a denotation. A third special property of these complement clauses is that NPs occurring within them may exhibit the *de re* vs. *de dicto* ambiguity.

These three properties are characteristic of OPAQUE contexts, i.e., contexts in which the denotation of a complex expression cannot be composed or predicted just by looking at the denotations of its constituents; we must look at senses as well. In recent work these contexts are often referred to as INTENSIONAL contexts, for reasons that will be explained in §15.2.

In this chapter we discuss several types of intensional contexts. §15.2 reviews our earlier discussion of propositional attitude verbs, and explains the term INTENSION. §15.3 discusses certain types of adjectives whose composition with the noun they modify cannot be modeled as simple set intersection. These adjectives are often referred to as INTENSIONAL ADJECTIVES. §15.4 briefly discusses some

[1]Actually, George Cruikshank only claimed that "the original ideas and characters... emanated from me." (http://www.bl.uk/collection-items/george-cruikshanks-claims-of-plagiarism-against-charles-Dickens)

other intensional contexts involving tense, modality, counterfactuals, and "intensional verbs" such as *want* and *seek.* §15.5 provides some examples of languages in which the subjunctive mood is used as a grammatical marker of intensionality. §15.6 briefly discusses the lambda operator, which is used to define functions, and how it can be used to represent intensions as functions.

15.2 When substitutivity fails

In Chapter 12 we used the following examples to illustrate the apparent failure of the law of substitutivity in the complement clauses of propositional attitude verbs:

(2) a. Mary believes [that *The Prince and the Pauper* was written by Mark Twain].
    b. Mary does not believe [that *The Prince and the Pauper* was written by Samuel Clemens].

Normally we can replace one word or phrase in a sentence by another word or phrase that has the same denotation, without affecting the truth value of the sentence as a whole. So, since the names *Mark Twain* and *Samuel Clemens* refer to the same individual, we would expect the two sentences in (2) to be contradictory. But this is not the case; it would be possible for both sentences to be true at the same time and for the same person named *Mary*, without any logical inconsistency. Since the denotation of the sentence is its truth value, such examples seem to challenge the Principle of Compositionality, at least as it applies to denotations.

As you will recall, Frege's solution to this apparent failure of compositionality was to suggest that the denotation of the complement clauses of these verbs is not their truth value when evaluated as independent clauses, but rather the propositions which they express. Essentially, Frege was pointing out that the speaker in (2) is not making a claim about the authorship of the book, but about Mary's current beliefs. The truth value of the sentence as a whole depends not on who the actual author was, but only on what propositions Mary believes.

The denotation of a sentence is its truth value, while the proposition which it expresses is its sense. A technical synonym for *sense* is the term INTENSION. Frege showed that sentences which contain propositional attitude verbs are in fact compositional, but we can only calculate their denotation based on the intension (sense) of the complement clause. Thus these sentences are an example of an INTENSIONAL CONTEXT, that is, a context where the denotation of a complex expression depends on the sense (intension) of one or more of its constituents.

Another special property of propositional attitude verbs discussed in Chapter 12 is the potential for *de dicto* vs. *de re* ambiguity, illustrated in (3). The speaker in (3a), for example, may be expressing either a desire to meet the individual who is the Prime Minister at the moment of speaking (*de re*), or a desire to meet the individual who will be serving in that role at the specified time (*de dicto*).

(3) a. I hope to meet with *the Prime Minister* next year.

b. I think that *your husband* is a lucky man.
(*de re*: because I saw him winning at the casino last night.)
(*de dicto*: any man who is married to you would be considered fortunate.)

Under the *de re* reading, the noun phrase gets its normal denotation in the relevant context, referring to the specific individual who is the Prime Minister at the moment of speaking (3a), or who is married to the addressee at the moment of speaking (3b). Under the *de dicto* reading, the denotation of the noun phrase is the property which corresponds to its sense: the property of being Prime Minister in (3a), the property of being married to the addressee in (3b). So under the *de dicto* reading, the truth value of the whole proposition depends on the sense, rather than the denotation, of a particular constituent.

In the next section we look at certain kinds of adjectives which pose a similar challenge to compositionality.

15.3 Non-intersective adjectives

Our paradigm example of an adjective modifier has been the word *yellow*. As we have discussed a number of times, the phrase *yellow submarine* is compositional in a very straightforward way: its denotation set will be the intersection of the denotation sets ⟦*yellow*⟧ and ⟦*submarine*⟧ . This intersection corresponds to the set of all things in our universe of discourse which are both yellow and submarines.

Adjectives that behave like *yellow* are referred to as INTERSECTIVE adjectives, because they obey the rule of interpretation formulated in Chapter 13: ⟦Adj N⟧ = ⟦Adj⟧ ∩ ⟦N⟧. Some examples of noun phrases involving other intersective adjectives are presented in (4).

(4) a. Otacilio is a *Brazilian* poet.
 b. Marilyn was a *blonde* actress.
 c. Arnold is a *carnivorous* biped.

Now the definition of intersection guarantees that if one of the sentences in (4) is true, then the individual named by the subject NP must be a member of both the denotation set of the head noun and the denotation set of the adjective modifier. This means that the inference in (5) will be valid.

(5) *Arnold is a carnivorous biped.*
Arnold is a mammal.
___
Therefore, Arnold is a carnivorous mammal.

However, there are other adjectives for which this pattern of inference will not be valid. Consider for example the syllogism in (6). It would be possible for a rational speaker of English to believe the two premises but not believe the conclusion, without being logically inconsistent. A similar example from *The Wizard of Oz* is presented in (7). Such examples force us to conclude that adjectives like *typical* are not intersective.[2]

(6) *Bill Clinton is a typical politician.*
Bill Clinton is a Baptist.
___
??Therefore, Bill Clinton is a typical Baptist. [NOT VALID]

(7) a. Dorothy: *Oh – you're a very bad man!*
Wizard: *Oh, no, my dear. I – I'm a very good man. I'm just a very bad Wizard.*
 b. *Oz is a bad Wizard.*
Oz is a man.
___
??Therefore, Oz is a bad man. [NOT VALID]

Barbara Partee (1995) suggested the following illustration: imagine a situation in which all surgeons are also violinists. For example, suppose that a certain hospital wanted to put on a benefit concert, and all the staff members were assigned to play instruments according to their specialties: all the surgeons would play the

[2]This is also true for *bad* in the sense Oz intended in the phrase *bad Wizard*; but *bad* is a tricky word, and the various senses probably do not all belong to the same semantic type. Of course the polysemy is also part of the problem with the invalid inference in (7).

violin, anesthesiologists the cello, nurses would play woodwinds, administrative staff the brass instruments, etc. Within this universe of discourse, the words *surgeon* and *violinist* have the same denotation sets; in other words, $[\![surgeon]\!]$ = $[\![violinist]\!]$. However, the phrases *skillful surgeon* and *skillful violinist* do not necessarily have the same denotation sets, as seen by the failure of the following inference:

(8) *Francis is a skillful surgeon.*
Francis is a violinist.

??*Therefore, Francis is a skillful violinist.* [NOT VALID]

This example provides another instance in which two expressions having the same denotation (*surgeon* and *violinist*) are not mutually substitutable, keeping the truth conditions constant. Yet the meanings of phrases like *typical politician* and *skillful surgeon* are still compositional, because if we know what each word means we will be able to predict the meanings of the phrases. The trick is that with adjectives like these, as with propositional attitude verbs, we need to combine senses rather than denotations.

We have seen that the meanings of adjectives like *typical* and *skillful* do not combine with meanings of the nouns they modify as the simple intersection of the two denotation sets. In other words, the rule of interpretation $[\![\text{Adj N}]\!] = [\![\text{Adj}]\!] \cap [\![\text{N}]\!]$ does not hold for these adjectives. However, the following constraint on the denotation of the phrases does hold: $[\![\text{Adj N}]\!] \subseteq [\![\text{N}]\!]$. In other words, the denotation set of the phrase will be a subset of the denotation set of the head noun. This means that anyone who is a typical politician must be a politician; and anyone who is a skillful surgeon must be a surgeon. Adjectives that satisfy this constraint are referred to as SUBSECTIVE adjectives.[3]

Subsective adjectives are intensional in the sense defined in §15.2: they combine with the senses, rather than the denotations, of the nouns they modify. One way of representing this is suggested in the following informal definition of *skillful*:

(9) *skillful* combines with a common noun (N) to form a phrase which denotes a set of individuals. Any given individual within the universe of discourse will belong to the set of all "skillful Ns" just in case that

[3] Of course, all intersective adjectives are subsective as well; but since the term "intersective" makes a stronger claim, saying that a certain adjective is subsective will trigger an implicature that it is not intersective, by the maxim of Quantity.

individual belongs to the set of all Ns and is extremely good at the activity named by N.
[SELECTIONAL RESTRICTION: *skillful* combines with nouns that denote the actor of a volitional activity.]

Certain types of adjectives turn out to be neither intersective nor subsective. Some examples are presented in (10).

(10) a. *former* Member of Parliament
b. *alleged* terrorist

The adjective *former* is not subsective because a former Member of Parliament is no longer a Member of Parliament; so any person who can be referred to as a "former Member of Parliament" will not belong to the denotation set of *Member of Parliament.* This also proves that *former* is not intersective. Moreover, it is not clear that the adjective *former* even has a denotation set; how could we identify the set of all "former" things? Similarly, an alleged terrorist may or may not actually be a terrorist; we can't be sure whether or not such a person will belong to the denotation set of *terrorist.* This means that *alleged* is not subsective. And once again, the adjective by itself doesn't seem to have a denotation set; it would have to be the set of all "alleged" things, whatever that might mean. So *alleged* cannot be intersective either.

How do we calculate the denotation of phrases like those in (10)? Although they cannot be defined as a simple intersection, the phrases are still compositional; knowing what each word means allows us to predict the meanings of the phrases. The trick is that with adjectives like these, as with propositional attitude verbs, we need to combine senses rather than denotations. In other words, these adjectives are intensional: they combine with the senses of the nouns they modify. Informal definitions of *former* and *alleged* are suggested in (11):

(11) a. *former* combines with a common noun (N) to form a phrase which denotes a set of individuals. Any given individual within the universe of discourse will belong to the set of all "former Ns" just in case that individual has belonged to the set of all Ns at some time in the past, but no longer does.
b. *alleged* combines with a common noun (N) to form a phrase which denotes a set of individuals. Any given individual (x) within the universe of discourse will belong to the set of all "alleged Ns" just in case there is some other individual who claims that x belongs to the set of all Ns.

The adjective *former* has the interesting property that a "former N" cannot be a member of the denotation set ⟦N⟧. In other words, denotation sets of phrases containing the word *former* are subject to the following constraint: ⟦Adj N⟧ ∩ ⟦N⟧ = ∅. Adjectives that satisfy this constraint are referred to as PRIVATIVE adjectives. Other privative adjectives include: *counterfeit, spurious, imaginary, fictitious, fake, would-be, wannabe, past, fabricated* (in one sense). Some prefixes have similar semantics, e.g. *ex-, pseudo-, non-*.

As we have seen, the adjective *alleged* is not subsective; but it is not privative either, because an alleged terrorist may or may not belong to the denotation set of *terrorist*. We can refer to this type of adjectives as NON-SUBSECTIVE. Other non-subsective adjectives include: *potential, possible, arguable, likely, predicted, putative, questionable.*

At first glance, many common adjectives like *big, old,* etc. seem to be intensional as well. Partee (1995) discusses the invalid inference in (12), which seems to indicate that adjectives like *tall* are non-intersective. The crucial point is that a height which is considered tall for a 14-year-old boy would probably not be considered tall for an adult who plays on a basketball team. This variability in the standard of tallness could lead us to conclude that *tall* does not define a denotation set on its own but combines with the sense of the head noun that it modifies, in much the same way as *typical* and *skillful.*

(12) *Win is a tall 14-year-old.*
Win is a basketball player.

??Therefore, Win is a tall basketball player. [NOT VALID]

However, Siegel (1976) argues that words like *tall, old,* etc. are in fact intersective; but they are also context-dependent and vague. The boundaries of their denotation sets are determined by context, including (but not limited to) the specific head noun which they modify. Once the boundary is determined, then the denotation set of the adjective can be identified, and the denotation set of the NP can be defined by simple intersection.

One piece of evidence supporting this analysis is the fact that a variety of contextual factors may contribute to determining the boundaries, and not just the meaning of the head noun. Partee notes that the standard of tallness which would apply in (13a) is probably much shorter than the standard which would apply in (13b), even though the same head noun is being modified in both examples.

(13) a. My two-year-old son built a really tall snowman yesterday.
b. The fraternity brothers built a really tall snowman last weekend.

She adds (1995: 331):

> Further evidence that there is a difference between truly non-intersective subsective adjectives like *skillful* and intersective but vague and context-dependent adjectives like *tall* was noted by Siegel (1976): the former occur with *as*-phrases, as in *skillful as a surgeon*, whereas the latter take *for*-phrases to indicate comparison class: *tall for an East coast mountain.*

Bolinger (1967) noted that some adjectives are ambiguous between an intersective and a (non-intersective) subsective sense; examples are presented in (14–16).[4] The fact that the (b) sentences can have a non-contradictory interpretation shows that this is a true lexical ambiguity; contrast #*Arnold is a carnivorous biped, but he is not carnivorous.*

(14) a. *Marya is a beautiful dancer.* (Siegel 1976)
intersective: Marya is beautiful and a dancer.
subsective: Marya dances beautifully.
b. *Marya is not beautiful, but she is a beautiful dancer.*

(15) a. *Floyd is an old friend.*
intersective: Floyd is old and a friend.
subsective: Floyd has been a friend for a long time.
b. *Floyd is an old friend, but he is not old.*

(16) a. *He is a poor liar.* (cf. Bolinger 1967)
intersective: Floyd is poor and a liar.
subsective: Floyd is not skillful in telling lies.
b. *He is a poor liar, but he is not poor.*

Thus far we have only considered adjectives which occur as modifiers within a noun phrase; but many adjectives can also function as clausal predicates, as illustrated in (17). In order to be used as a predicate in this way, the adjective must have a denotation set. Since all intersective adjectives must have a denotation set, they can generally (with a few idiosyncratic exceptions) be used as predicates, as seen in (18).

(17) John is happy/sick/rich/Australian.

[4] Examples adapted from Morzycki (2015: ch. 2). The adjective *bad* mentioned above is probably also ambiguous in this way.

(18) a. Otacilio is a Brazilian poet; therefore he is Brazilian.
b. Marilyn was a blonde actress; therefore she was blonde.
c. Arnold is a carnivorous biped; therefore he is carnivorous.

When an adjective which is ambiguous between an intersective and a subsective sense is used as a predicate, generally speaking only the intersective sense is available (19). So, for example, (19c) is most naturally interpreted as a pun which makes a somewhat cynical commentary on the way of the world.

(19) a. # Marya is a beautiful dancer; therefore she is beautiful.
b. # Floyd is an old friend; therefore he is old.
c. He is a poor liar; therefore he is poor.

We have already noted that the adjectives *former* and *alleged* don't seem to have a denotation set. As predicted, these adjectives cannot be used as predicates, and the same is true for many other non-subsective adjectives as well (20a). However, given the right context, some non-subsective adjectives can be used as predicates (20b, c). In such cases it appears that information from the context must be used in order to construct the relevant denotation set. In addition, cases like (20c) may require a kind of coercion to create a new sense of the word *money*, one which refers to things that look like money. As Partee points out, similar issues arise with phrases like *stone lion* and *chocolate bunny*.

(20) a. * That terrorist is former/alleged/potential/...
b. His illness is imaginary.
c. This money is counterfeit.

The main conclusion to be drawn from this brief introduction to the semantics of adjectives is that compositionality cannot always be demonstrated by looking only at denotations. All of the adjectives that we have discussed turned out to be compositional in their semantic contributions; but we have seen several classes of adjectives whose semantic contributions cannot be defined in terms of simple set intersection. These adjectives are said to be INTENSIONAL, because their meanings must combine with the sense (intension) of the head nouns being modified.

15.4 Other intensional contexts

As discussed above, intensional contexts are contexts where the denotation of an expression (e.g., the truth value of a sentence) cannot be determined from the denotations of its constituent parts. In addition to those we have already mentioned, namely propositional attitude verbs and non-intersective adjectives, a number of other linguistic features are known to create such contexts as well. These include tense, modality, and counterfactuals. We will discuss these topics in more detail in later chapters; here we focus only on issues of compositionality.

To begin with, let us contrast the intensional behavior of modality (markers of possibility and necessity) with the behavior of a non-intensional operator, negation. Modals are similar to negation in certain ways: both combine with a single proposition to create a new proposition. The crucial difference is this: in order to determine the truth value of a negated proposition, we only need to know the truth value of the original proposition. For example, both of the sentences in (21), if spoken in 2006, would have been false. For that reason, we can be sure that both of the negated sentences in (22), if spoken in 2006, would have been true.

(21) (spoken in 2006)

a. Barack Obama is the first black President of the United States. [F]
b. Nelson Mandela is the first black President of the United States. [F]

(22) (spoken in 2006)

a. Barack Obama is not the first black President of the United States. [T]
b. Nelson Mandela is not the first black President of the United States. [T]

But with modal operators like *might, could, must,* etc., it is not enough to know the truth value of the original proposition; we need to evaluate its meaning, in combination with that of the modal operator. Even though both of the sentences in (21) had the same truth value in 2006, the addition of the modal in (23) creates sentences which would have had different truth values at that time.

(23) (spoken in 2006)

a. Barack Obama could be the first black President of the United States. [T]
b. Nelson Mandela could be the first black President of the United States. [F]

Tense is another operator which combines with a single proposition to create a new proposition. As with modality, knowing the truth value of the original proposition does not allow us to determine the truth value of the tensed proposition. Both of the present tense sentences in (24a–b), spoken in 2014, are false; but the corresponding past tense sentences in (24c–d) have different truth values.

(24) (spoken in 2014)

a. Hillary Clinton is the Secretary of State. [F]
b. Lady Gaga is the Secretary of State. [F]
c. Hillary Clinton was/has been the Secretary of State. [T]
d. Lady Gaga was/has been the Secretary of State. [F]

Similarly, knowing that the present tense sentence in (25a) is true does not allow us to determine the truth value of the corresponding future tense sentence (25b).

(25) a. Henry is Anne's husband. [assume T]
b. In five years, Henry will (still) be Anne's husband. [?]

As we have seen, one of the standard diagnostics for intensional contexts is the failure of substitutivity: in intensional contexts, substituting one expression with another that has the same denotation may affect the truth value of the sentence as a whole. The examples in (26) illustrate again the failure of substitutivity in the complement clause of a propositional attitude verb. They refer to an Englishman named James Brooke who, through a combination of military success and diplomacy, made himself the king (or *Rajah*) of Sarawak, comprising most of northwestern Borneo. During the years 1842 to 1868, the phrases *James Brooke* and *the White Rajah of Borneo* referred to the same individual. Suppose that sentence (26a) was spoken in 1850, perhaps by one of Brooke's old mates from the Bengal Army. Even if (26a) was true at the time of speaking, sentence (26b) spoken at that same time by the same speaker would certainly have been false.

(26) (spoken in 1850)

a. I do not believe that James Brooke is the White Rajah of Borneo.
b. I do not believe that James Brooke is James Brooke.

The examples in (27) illustrate the failure of substitutivity in a counterfactual statement. Sentence (27a) is something that a rational person might believe; at least it is a claim which could be debated. Sentence (27b) is derived from (27a) by substituting one NP (*the first black President of the United States*) with another (*Barack Obama*) that has the same denotation. Clearly sentence (27b) is not something that a rational person could believe.

(27) a. Martin Luther King might have become the first black President of the United States.
b. Martin Luther King might have become Barack Obama.

The examples in (28) also illustrate the failure of substitutivity in a counterfactual; but instead of replacing one NP with another, this time we replace one clause with another. The two consequent clauses are based on propositions which have the same truth value in our world: both would be false if expressed as independent assertions. But replacing one clause with the other changes the truth value of the sentence as a whole: (28a) is clearly true, while (28b) is almost certainly false.

(28) a. If Beethoven had died in childhood, we would never have heard his magnificent symphonies.
b. If Beethoven had died in childhood, Columbus would never have discovered America.

Another class of verbs which create intensional contexts are the so-called INTENSIONAL VERBS. Prototypical examples of this type are the verbs of searching and desiring. These verbs license *de dicto* vs. *de re* ambiguities in their direct objects, as illustrated in (29). Sentence (29a) could mean that the speaker is looking for a specific dog (*de re*), perhaps because it got lost or ran away; or it could mean that the speaker wants to acquire a dog that fits that description but does not have a specific dog in mind (*de dicto*). Sentence (29b) could mean that John happens to be interested in the same type of work as the addressee (*de re*); or that John wants to be doing whatever the addressee is doing (*de dicto*).

(29) a. I'm looking for *a black cocker spaniel.*
b. John wants *the same job as you.*

The direct objects of such verbs are referentially opaque, meaning that substitution of a coreferential NP can affect the truth value of a sentence. Suppose that Lois Lane is looking for Superman, and that she does not know that Clark Kent is really Superman. Under these circumstances, sentence (30a) would be true, but (30b) would (arguably) be false.[5]

(30) a. Lois Lane is looking for *Superman.*
b. Lois Lane is looking for *Clark Kent.*

[5] This example comes from Forbes (2013). Forbes points out that not all semanticists share this judgement about (30b).

Furthermore, if the direct objects of intensional verbs fail to refer in a particular situation, it may still be possible to assign a truth value to the sentence. Both sentences in (31) could be true even though in each case the denotation set of the direct object is empty. All of these properties are characteristic of intensional contexts.

(31) a. Arthur is looking for *the fountain of youth.*

b. John wants *a unicorn* for Christmas.

15.5 Subjunctive mood as a marker of intensionality

In some languages, intensional contexts may require special grammatical marking. A number of European languages (among others) use subjunctive mood for this purpose. Let us note from the very beginning that the distribution of the subjunctive is a very complex topic, and that there can be significant differences in this regard even between closely related dialects.[6] It is very unlikely that all uses of subjunctive mood in any particular language can be explained on the basis of intensionality alone. But it is clear that intensionality is one of the factors which determine the use of the subjunctive.

Consider the Spanish sentences in (32), which are discussed by Partee (2008).[7] Partee states that neither sentence is ambiguous in the way that the English translations are. The relative clause in indicative mood (32a) can only refer to a specific individual, whereas the relative clause in subjunctive mood (32b) can only have a non-specific interpretation.

(32) a. María busca a un profesor que enseñ-a griego.
Maria looks.for to a professor who teaches-IND Greek.
'Maria is looking for a professor who teaches Greek.' [*de re*]

b. María busca (a) un profesor que enseñ-e griego.
Maria looks.for to a professor who teaches-SBJV Greek.
'Maria is looking for a professor who teaches Greek.' [*de dicto*]

A similar pattern is found in relative clauses in modern Greek. The marker for subjunctive mood in modern Greek is the particle *na.* Giannakidou (2011) says that the indicative relative clause in (33a) can only refer to a specific individual,

[6] See for example Marques (2004).

[7] This contrast is also discussed by Quine (1956) and a number of subsequent authors.

whereas the subjunctive relative clause in (33b) can only have a non-specific interpretation.

(33) a. Theloume na proslavoume mia gramatea [pu gnorizi kala
want.1PL SBJV hire.1PL a secretary REL know.3SG good
japonezika.]
Japanese
'We want to hire a secretary that has good knowledge of Japanese.'
(Her name is Jane Smith.) [*de re*]

b. Theloume na proslavoume mia gramatea [pu na gnorizi kala
want.1PL SBJV hire.1PL a secretary REL SBJV know.3SG good
japonezika.]
Japanese
'We want to hire a secretary that has good knowledge of Japanese.'
(But it is hard to find one, and we are not sure if we will be successful.) [*de dicto*]

Giannakidou states that because of this restriction, a definite NP cannot contain a subjunctive relative clause (34). Also, the object of a verb of creation with future time reference cannot contain an indicative relative clause, because it refers to something that does not exist at the time of speaking (34).

(34) I Roxani theli na pandrefti {enan/*ton} andra [pu na exi
the R. want.3SG SBJV marry.3SG {a/*the} man REL SBJV have
pola lefta].
much money
'Roxanne wants to marry a/*the man who has a lot of money.'

(35) Prepi na grapso mia ergasia [pu *(na)[8] ine pano apo 15 selidhes.]
must.3SG SBJV write.1SG an essay REL SBJV is more than 15 pages
'I have to write an essay longer than 15 pages.'

The pattern that emerges from these and other examples is that subjunctive mood is used when the noun phrase containing the relative clause refers to a property rather than to a specific individual.

[8]This notation indicates that the subjunctive marker is obligatory; that is, the sentence is ungrammatical without the subjunctive marker.

15.6 Defining functions via lambda abstraction

In our brief discussion of compositionality in Chapters 13–14 we focused primarily on denotations, and expressed the truth conditions of sentences in terms of set membership. So, for example, the denotation of a predicate like *yellow* or *snore*, in a particular context or universe of discourse, is the set of individuals within that context which are yellow, or which snore. The sentence *Henry snores* will be true in any model in which the individual named Henry belongs to the denotation set of *snore*.

We noted in Chapter 13 that the membership of a set can always be expressed as a function, namely its characteristic function. So it is possible to restate the truth conditions of sentences, and to show how these truth conditions are derived compositionally, in terms of functions rather than set membership. The two approaches (sets vs. functions) are essentially equivalent, but for a number of constructions the functional representation provides a simpler, more general, and more convenient way of stating the rules of interpretation.

We will not explore this approach in any detail in the present book, but it will be useful for the reader to be aware of a notation for defining functions that is very widely used in formal semantics. In the standard function-argument format that we learn in secondary school, functions generally have names. For example, the two functions defined in (36) are named "f_1" and "f_2". In this kind of definition, the function takes a bound variable (x) as argument and expresses the value as a formula which contains the bound variable. When the function is applied to a real argument, we calculate the value by substituting that argument for the bound variable in the formula. So for example, $f_1(13) = 13-4 = 9$.

(36) Named functions:
$f_1(x) = x - 4 \quad f_1(13) = 9$
$f_2(x) = 3x^2 + 1 \quad f_2(3) = 28$

Another way of defining functions, using the Greek letter lambda (λ), is illustrated in (37). These two functions are identical to f_1 and f_2, but written in a different format. Once again, when the function is applied to an argument, we calculate the value by substituting that argument for the bound variable which is introduced by the λ. However, in this format the functions have no names. Functions defined using λ are sometimes described as "anonymous functions".

(37) Anonymous functions:
$[\lambda x.\ x - 4] \quad [\lambda x.\ x - 4](13) = 9$
$[\lambda x.\ 3x^2 + 1] \quad [\lambda x.\ 3x^2 + 1](3) = 28$

We can also think of lambda (λ) as an operator which changes propositions into predicates by replacing some element of the proposition with an appropriate bound variable. For example, from the proposition *Caesar loves Brutus* we can derive "[λy. Caesar loves y]" by replacing the object NP with the variable y. This formula represents a predicate which corresponds to the property of being loved by Caesar. Alternatively, we can derive "[λx. x loves Brutus]" by replacing the subject NP with the variable x. This formula represents a predicate which corresponds to the property of being someone who loves Brutus.

This process is referred to as LAMBDA ABSTRACTION. Once again, when we apply these derived predicates to an argument, as illustrated in (38), the result is calculated by replacing the bound variable with the argument. (The argument in the first example is *b*, representing Brutus; in the second example the argument is *c*, representing Caesar; and in the third example the argument is *a*, representing Marc Antony.)

(38) [λy. LOVE(c,y)](b) = LOVE(c,b) 'Caesar loves Brutus'
[λx. LOVE(x,b)](c) = LOVE(c,b) 'Caesar loves Brutus'
[λx. LOVE(x,c) ∧ HATE(x,b)](a) = LOVE(a,c) ∧ HATE(a,b)
'Antony loves Caesar and hates Brutus'

Predicates derived by lambda abstraction can be interpreted as characteristic functions of the corresponding denotation set, as described in Chapter 13:

(39) [λy. LOVE(c,y)](n) = 1 iff Caesar loves n
0 otherwise
[λx. LOVE(x,b)](n) = 1 iff n loves Brutus
0 otherwise
[λx. LOVE(x,c)∧ HATE(x,b)](n) = 1 iff n loves Caesar and hates Brutus
0 otherwise

This means that the semantic value of an intransitive predicate like *snore* can be represented as a function which takes a single argument: [λx. SNORE(x)]. The semantic value of the sentence *Henry snores* can be derived by applying this function to the semantic value of the subject NP, as shown in (40):

(40) [λx. SNORE(x)](h) = SNORE(h)
= 1 iff Henry snores
0 otherwise

The semantic value of a transitive predicate like *love* can be represented as a function which takes two arguments: [λy. [λx. LOVE(x,y)]]. In calculating the truth conditions for a sentence like *Caesar loves Brutus*, the function named by the verb is applied first to the semantic value of the object NP, as shown in (41a), to derive the semantic value of the VP. The function named by the VP is then applied to the semantic value of the subject NP, as shown in (41b), to derive the semantic value of the sentence as a whole.

(41) a. [λy. [λx. LOVE(x,y)]](b) = [λx. LOVE(x,b)] 'is someone who loves Brutus'
b. [λx. LOVE(x,b)](c) = LOVE(c,b) 'Caesar loves Brutus'

In formal semantics, intensions (senses) are often defined as functions from possible worlds to denotations. (Roughly speaking, a "possible world" is any way the universe might conceivably be without changing the structure of the language being investigated.) The intuition behind this analysis is that, as discussed in Chapter 2, it is knowing the meaning (sense) of a word like *yellow* or *speak* that allows us to identify the set of all yellow things or speaking things in any particular context. So we can think of the senses of these words as a mapping, or function, from each possible world to the expression's denotation in that world.

Using the lambda abstraction operator, we might represent the intension of *speak* as: "[λw. [λx. SPEAK(x) in w]]". In the same way, the intension of *yellow* could be represented as: "[λw. [λx. YELLOW(x) in w]]". The *w* in these formulae is a variable over the domain of possible worlds. These functions take a possible world as their argument, and return as a value the set of all yellow things (or speaking things) in that world.

15.7 Conclusion

In chapters 13 and 14 we worked through some simple examples showing how the truth value of a sentence uttered at a particular time and situation can be calculated based on the denotations of the constituent parts of the sentence at that same time and situation. In this chapter we discussed a variety of linguistic features which make this calculation more complex. For many of these opaque (or intensional) contexts, we can only calculate the truth value of a sentence in a given situation if we know what the denotation of a constituent would be in some other situation.[9] For example, statements in the past or future tense, like examples (24–25), require knowledge about denotations at some time other than the time of speaking. Statements of possibility (23) and counterfactuals (27–28) require judgments about ways that the world might have been, i.e., other possible situations or "possible worlds". Some of the non-intersective adjectives, such as *former* and *potential*, have similar effects.

As we stated in Chapter 2, it is knowing the sense of an expression that allows speakers to identify the denotation of that expression in various situations. What all the phenomena discussed in this chapter have in common is that the denotation of some complex expression (e.g., the truth value of a sentence) cannot be compositionally determined from the denotations of its parts alone; we have to refer to senses as well.

Further reading

Kearns (2011: ch. 7) presents a good overview of referential opacity, and Zimmermann & Sternefeld (2013: ch. 8) provide a good introduction to the analysis of intensions as functions on possible worlds. Van Benthem (1988) and Gamut (1991b) provide more detailed discussions of intensional logic and its applications. Partee (1995) discusses non-intersective adjectives (among other issues) in relation to compositionality. For an introduction to lambda abstraction, see Coppock (2016: 93ff.); Kearns (2011: 62–75); Heim & Kratzer (1998: 34ff.).

[9] Cf. Cherchia & McConnell-Ginet (1990: 204–208).

Unit V

Modals, conditionals, and causation

16 Modality

16.1 Possibility and necessity

Kai von Fintel (2006: 20) defines MODALITY as "a category of linguistic meaning having to do with the expression of possibility and necessity." Most if not all languages have lexical means for expressing these concepts, e.g. *It is possible that...* or *It is necessary that...*, but in this chapter we will focus our attention on the kinds of modality which can be expressed grammatically, e.g. by verbal affixation, particles, or auxiliary verbs. In English, modality is expressed primarily by MODAL AUXILIARIES: *may, might, must, should, could, ought to,* etc. (The phrase *have to* is often included in discussions of the English modals because it is a close synonym of *must*; but it does not have the unique syntactic distribution of a true auxiliary verb in English, and the syntactic differences sometimes have semantic consequences.)

In §16.2 we outline the range of modal meanings along two basic dimensions. The first of these is strength, or degree of certainty (e.g., *must* is said to be "stronger" than *might*). The second dimension is the type of certainty or lack of certainty which is being expressed, e.g. certainty of knowledge, requirement by an authority, etc. We will see that in many languages the same modal forms can be used for two or more different types of modality. We will see some evidence suggesting that such forms are polysemous, but also some reasons for challenging this assumption.

In §16.3 we outline a very influential analysis of modal operators as quantifiers, and show how this accounts for some of the puzzling observations discussed in §16.2. In §16.4 we discuss some of the variation across languages in terms of how modal meanings are packaged, and show how the quantifier analysis can account for these differences. In §16.5 we focus on one important type of modality, referred to as EPISTEMIC modality, which expresses degree of certainty in light of what the speaker knows. Some authors have claimed that epistemic modality is not part of the propositional content of the utterance; we review several kinds of evidence that support the opposite conclusion.

16.2 The range of modal meanings: strength vs. type of modality

As we noted in Chapter 14, modality can be thought of as an operator that combines with a basic proposition (*p*) to form a new proposition (*It is possible that p* or *It is necessarily the case that p*). The range of meanings expressible by grammatical markers of modality varies along two basic semantic dimensions.[1] First, some markers are "stronger" than others. For example, the statement in (1a) expresses a stronger commitment on the part of the speaker to the truth of the base proposition (*Arthur is home by now*) than (1b), and (1b) expresses a stronger commitment than (1c).

(1) a. Arthur *must/has to* be home by now.
    b. Arthur *should* be home by now.
    c. Arthur *might* be home by now.

Second, it turns out that the concepts of "possibility" and "necessity", which are used to define modality, each include a variety of sub-types. In other words, there are several different ways in which a proposition may be possibly true or necessarily true. The two which have been discussed most extensively, EPISTEMIC vs. DEONTIC modality, are illustrated in (2–3).

(2) a. John didn't show up for work. He *must* be sick.
    [spoken by co-worker; Epistemic]
    b. John didn't show up for work. He *must* be fired.
    [spoken by boss; Deontic]

(3) a. The older students *may* leave school early (unless the teachers watch them carefully).
    b. The older students *may* leave school early (if they inform the headmaster first).

Epistemic modality indicates possibility and necessity relative to the speaker's knowledge of the situation, i.e., whether the proposition is possibly or necessarily true in light of available evidence. Deontic modality indicates possibility and necessity relative to some authoritative person or code of conduct which is relevant to the current situation, i.e., whether the truth of the proposition is required

[1]Hacquard (2011).

or permitted by the relevant authority. Examples (2a) and (3a) illustrate the epistemic sub-type, under which *He must be sick* means 'Based on the available evidence, I am forced to conclude that he is sick;' and *The older students may leave school early* means 'Based on my knowledge of the current situation, I do not know of anything which would prevent the older students from leaving school early.' Examples (2b) and (3b) illustrate the deontic sub-type, under which *He must be fired* means 'Someone in authority requires that he be fired;' and *The older students may leave school early* means 'The older students have permission from an appropriate authority to leave school early.'

The strength of modality (possibility vs. necessity) is often referred to as the modal "force", and the type of modality (e.g. epistemic vs. deontic) is often referred to as the modal "flavor".

16.2.1 Are modals polysemous?

Examples (2–3) also illustrate another important fact about modals: in English, as in many other languages, a single form may be used to express more than one type of modality. As these examples show, both *must* and *may* have two distinct uses, which are often referred to as distinct senses: epistemic vs. deontic. In fact, speakers can create puns which play on these distinct senses. One such example is found in the following passage from "The Schartz-Metterklume Method" (1911), a short story by the British author H. H. Munro (writing under the pen-name "Saki"). In this story, a young Englishwoman, Lady Carlotta, is accidentally left behind on a country railway platform when she gets out to stretch her legs. She is mistaken for a new governess who is due to arrive that day to teach the children of a local family:

> Before she [Lady Carlotta] had time to think what her next move might be she was confronted by an imposingly attired lady, who seemed to be taking a prolonged mental inventory of her clothes and looks. "*You must be Miss Hope*, the governess I've come to meet," said the apparition, in a tone that admitted of very little argument. "Very well, *if I must I must*," said Lady Carlotta to herself with dangerous meekness.

"Dangerous meekness" sounds like a contradiction in terms, but in this case it is the literal truth; Lady Carlotta's novel teaching methods turn the whole household upside down.

As discussed in Chapter 5, this kind of antagonism between the epistemic vs. deontic senses of *must* strongly suggests that the word is polysemous. Similar arguments could be made for *may*, *should*, etc. This apparent polysemy of the grammatical markers of modality is one of the central issues that a semantic analysis needs to address. But in spite of the strong evidence for distinct senses (lexical ambiguity), there is other evidence which might lead us to question whether these variant readings really involve polysemy or not.

First, as we noted in Chapter 5, distinct senses of a given word-form are unlikely to have the same translation equivalent in another language. However, this is just what we find with the English modals: the various uses of words like *must* and *may* do have the same translation equivalent in a number of other languages. This fact is especially striking because these words are not restricted to just two readings, epistemic vs. deontic; several other types of modality are commonly identified, which can be expressed using the same modal auxiliaries. Example (4) illustrates some of the uses of the modal *have to*; a similar range of uses can be demonstrated for *must*, *may*, etc. (We return to the differences among these specific types in §16.3 below. As discussed below, the term ROOT modality is often used as a cover term for the non-epistemic types.)

(4) [adapted from von Fintel 2006]

a. It *has to* be raining. [after observing people coming inside with wet umbrellas; EPISTEMIC modality]
b. Visitors *have to* leave by six pm. [hospital regulations; DEONTIC]
c. John *has to* work hard if he wants to retire at age 50. [to attain desires; BOULETIC][2]
d. I *have to* sneeze. [given the current state of one's nose; DYNAMIC][3]
e. To get home in time, you *have to* take a taxi. [in order to achieve the stated purpose; TELEOLOGICAL]

Hacquard (2007) points out that the same range of uses occurs with modal auxiliaries in French as well:

> It is a robust cross-linguistic generalization that the same modal words are used to express various types of modality. The following French examples

[2]Example (4c) is adapted from Hacquard (2011). Von Fintel (2006) offers the following definition: "BOULETIC modality, sometimes BOULOMAIC modality, concerns what is possible or necessary, given a person's desires."

[3]Von Fintel uses the term CIRCUMSTANTIAL modality for what I have called DYNAMIC modality. Huddleston & Pullum (2002: 178) define dynamic modality as being "concerned with properties and dispositions of persons, etc., referred to in the clause, especially by the subject NP." The most common examples of dynamic modality are expressions of ability with the modal *can*. The term CIRCUMSTANTIAL modality has a more general usage, as discussed below.

illustrate. The modal in (5a) receives an epistemic interpretation (having to do with what is known, what the available evidence is), while those in (5b–d) receive a 'root' or 'circumstantial' interpretation (having to do with particular circumstances of the base world): (5b) is a case of deontic modality (having to do with permissions/obligations), (5c) an ability and (5d) a goal-oriented modality (having to do with possibilities/necessities given a particular goal of the subject).

(5) a. Il est 18 heures. Anne n'est pas au bureau. Elle *peut/doit* être chez elle.
'It's 6:00pm. Anne is not in the office. She *may/must* be at home.'

b. Le père de Anne lui impose un régime très strict. Elle *peut/doit* manger du brocoli.
'Anne's father imposes on her a strict diet. She *can/must* eat broccoli.'

c. Anne est très forte. Elle *peut* soulever cette table.
'Anne is very strong. She *can* lift this table.'

d. Anne doit être à Paris à 17 heures. Elle *peut/doit* prendre le train pour aller à P.
'Anne must be in Paris at 5pm. She *can/must* take the train to go to P.'

It is somewhat unusual for the same pattern of polysemy to exist for a particular word in two languages. What we see in the case of modals is something far more surprising: multiple word forms from the same semantic domain, each of which having multiple readings translatable by a single form in not just one but many other languages. Normal polysemy does not work this way.

A second striking fact about the modal auxiliaries in English is that the ranking discussed above in terms of "strength" seems to hold across the various readings or uses of these modals. Linguistic evidence for this ranking comes from examples like those in (6–7).[4] These examples involve the deontic readings; similar evidence can be given for the epistemic readings, as illustrated in (8–9).

(6) a. You *should/ought to* call your mother, but of course you don't *have to.*

b. #You *have to* call your mother, but of course you *shouldn't.*

[4]Examples from von Fintel (2006).

(7) a. I *should* go to confession, but I'm not going to.
 b. #I *must* go to confession, but I'm not going to.

(8) a. Arthur *should* be home by now, but he doesn't *have to* be.
 b. #Arthur *must/has to* be home by now, but he *shouldn't* be. (bad on epistemic reading)
 c. Arthur *might* be home by now, but he doesn't *have to* be.
 d. #Arthur *must/has to* be home by now, but he *might* not be. (bad on epistemic reading)

(9) a. #Arthur *must/has to* be home by now, but I consider it unlikely. (bad on epistemic reading)
 b. #Arthur *should* be home by now, but I consider it unlikely. (bad on epistemic reading)
 c. Arthur *might* be home by now, but I consider it unlikely.

Evidence of this kind would lead us to define the following hierarchies for epistemic and deontic modality. What is striking, of course, is that the two hierarchies are identical. Again, this is not the type of pattern we expect to find with "normal" polysemy.

(10) a. Epistemic modal strength hierarchy:
 [NECESSITY] [POSSIBILITY]
 must/have to > *should/ought to* > *may/might/could*
 b. Deontic modal strength hierarchy:
 [OBLIGATION] [PERMISSION]
 must/have to > *should/ought to* > *may/might/could*

The challenge for a semantic analysis is to define the meanings of the modal auxiliaries in a way that can explain these unique and surprising properties. In the next section we will describe a very influential analysis which goes a long way toward achieving this goal.

16.3 Modality as quantification over possible worlds

Angelika Kratzer (1981; 1991) proposed that the English modals are not in fact polysemous. On the contrary, she suggested that English (like a number of other languages) has only one set of modal operators, which are underspecified (indeterminate) regarding the type of modality (epistemic, deontic, etc.). The strength of the modal is lexically determined, with the individual modals functioning semantically as a kind of quantifier that quantifies over situations. The specific type of modality depends on the range of situations which is permitted by the context. This section offers a brief and informal introduction to her approach.

16.3.1 A simple quantificational analysis

Kratzer's analysis builds on a long tradition of earlier work that treats a modal auxiliary as a kind of quantifier which quantifies over possible worlds. (We can think of possible worlds as possible situations or states of affairs; in other words, "ways that things might be".) A marker of necessity functions as a universal quantifier: it indicates that the basic proposition is true in all possible states of affairs. A marker of possibility functions as an existential quantifier: it indicates that there is at least one state of affairs in which the basic proposition is true.

In Chapter 14 we introduced two symbols from modal logic: ◊ = 'it is possible that'; and □ = 'it is necessarily the case that'. The use of these symbols is illustrated in the logical forms for two simple modal statements in (11).

(11) a. *Arthur must be at home.* logical form: □ AT_HOME(a)
b. *Arthur may be at home.* logical form: ◊ AT_HOME(a)

The possible worlds analysis claims that the logical forms in (11), which make use of the modal operators, express the same meaning as those in (12), which are stated in terms of the standard logical quantifiers. The *w* in (12) is a variable which stands for a possible world or state of affairs. So under this analysis, *Arthur must be home* means that the proposition *Arthur is home* is true in all possible worlds, while *Arthur might be home* means that the proposition *Arthur is home* is true in at least one possible world.

(12) a. *Arthur must be at home.* meaning: ∀w[AT_HOME(a) in w]
b. *Arthur may be at home.* meaning: ∃w[AT_HOME(a) in w]

As we noted in §16.2, words like *must* and *may* allow both epistemic and deontic readings (among others). These different types (or "flavors") of modality can be represented by different restrictions on the quantification, i.e., different limits on the kinds of possible worlds that the quantified variable (*w*) can refer to. Epistemic readings arise when *w* can range over all "epistemically accessible" worlds, i.e., situations which are consistent with what the speaker knows about the actual situation. Deontic readings arise when *w* can range over all "perfect obedience" worlds, i.e., situations in which the requirements of the relevant authority are obeyed. This analysis is illustrated in (13–14), using the restricted quantifier notation.

(13) *Arthur must be at home.*

a. **Epistemic**: [all w: w is consistent with what I know about the actual world] AT_HOME(a) in w

b. **Deontic**: [all w: w is consistent with what the relevant authority requires] AT_HOME(a) in w

(14) *Arthur may be at home.*

a. **Epistemic**: [some w: w is consistent with what I know about the actual world] AT_HOME(a) in w

b. **Deontic**: [some w: w is consistent with what the relevant authority requires] AT_HOME(a) in w

The unrestricted quantifications in (12) express logical possibility or necessity: a claim that proposition p is true in at least one imaginable situation, or in every imaginable situation. Such statements are said to involve ALETHIC modality. As von Fintel (2006) points out, "It is in fact hard to find convincing examples of alethic modality in natural language." An example of logical (or alethic) possibility might be the statement, "I might never have been born." It is possible for me to imagine states of affairs in which I would not exist (my father might have been killed in the war, my mother might have chosen to attend a different school, etc.); but none of these states of affairs are epistemically possible, because they are inconsistent with what I know about the real world. Examples of logical (alethic) necessity are probably limited to tautologies, analytically true statements, etc.; it is hard to find any other type of statement which must be true in every imaginable situation.

Analyzing modals as quantifiers accounts for a number of interesting facts. For example, the simple tautologies of modal logic stated in (15) show how either of the two modal operators can be defined in terms of the other. (15a) states that saying *p is possibly true* is equivalent to saying *it is not necessarily the case that p is false.* (15b) states that saying *p is necessarily true* is equivalent to saying *it is not possible that p is false.* It turns out that the two basic quantifiers of standard logic can be defined in terms of each other in exactly the same way, as shown by the tautologies in (16). This remarkable parallelism is predicted immediately if we analyze necessity in terms of universal quantification and possibility in terms of existential quantification.

(15) a. $(\Diamond\ p) \leftrightarrow \neg(\Box\ \neg p)$
b. $(\Box\ p) \leftrightarrow \neg(\Diamond\ \neg p)$

(16) a. $\exists x[P(x)] \leftrightarrow \neg(\forall x[\neg P(x)])$
b. $\forall x[P(x)] \leftrightarrow \neg(\exists x[\neg P(x)])$

We noted in Chapter 14 that combining quantifiers and modals in the same sentence often leads to scope ambiguities. The examples in (17–18) are repeated from Chapter 14. The quantificational analysis again predicts this fact: if modals are really quantifiers, then the ambiguities in (17–18) arise as expected from the interaction of two quantifiers.

(17) *Every student might fail the course.*[5]
a. $\forall x[\text{STUDENT}(x) \longrightarrow \Diamond\ \text{FAIL}(x)]$
b. $\Diamond\ \forall x[\text{STUDENT}(x) \longrightarrow \text{FAIL}(x)]$

(18) *Some sanctions must be imposed.*
a. $\exists x[\text{SANCTION}(x) \wedge \Box\ \text{BE-IMPOSED}(x)]$
b. $\Box\ \exists x[\text{SANCTION}(x) \wedge \text{BE-IMPOSED}(x)]$

While this analysis works well in many respects, Kratzer points out that it makes the wrong predictions in certain cases. For example, suppose that Arthur has robbed a bank, and that robbing banks is against the law. Intuitively, we would say that sentence (19a) is true in this situation. However, the analysis shown in (19b) actually predicts the opposite, because in all possible worlds consistent with what the law requires, no one robs banks. In particular, Arthur does not rob a bank (or commit any other crime) in those worlds, and so would not go to prison. Similarly, the analysis predicts that both (20a) and (20b) should be true, because the antecedent will be false in all possible worlds consistent with what the law requires. (Recall from Chapter 4 that $p \longrightarrow q$ is always considered to be true when p is false.)

(19) a. *Arthur must go to prison.* [Deontic]
b. [all w: w is consistent with what the law requires] GO_TO_PRISON(a) in w

(20) a. *If Arthur has robbed a bank, he must go to prison.*
b. *If Arthur has robbed a bank, he must not go to prison.*

[5] Abbott (2010: 48).

To take another example, suppose that when a serious crime is committed, the law allows the government to confiscate the house, car, and other assets of the guilty party to compensate the victim; but that the government is not allowed to confiscate the assets of anyone who does not commit a crime. If Arthur is convicted of a serious crime, the judge may truthfully say the sentence in (21a). But once again, the analysis in (21b) predicts that this statement should be false, since there is no possible world consistent with what the law requires in which Arthur commits a crime, so no such world in which his assets may be confiscated.

(21) a. *The state may confiscate Arthur's assets.* [Deontic]
b. [some w: w is consistent with what the law requires]
the state confiscates Arthur's assets in w

The problem with examples of this type is that we begin with an actual situation that is not consistent with what the law requires. The correct interpretation of the modal reflects the assumption that what happens next, in response to this non-ideal situation, should be as close to the ideal required by law as possible.

16.3.2 Kratzer's analysis

Kratzer addresses this problem by arguing that restrictions on the sets of possible worlds available for modal quantifiers must be stated in two components. The first, which she calls the MODAL BASE, specifies the class of worlds which are eligible for consideration, i.e., worlds that are ACCESSIBLE. The second component, which she calls the ORDERING SOURCE, specifies a ranking among the accessible worlds. It identifies the "best", or highest-ranking, world or worlds among those that are accessible. The modal's domain of quantification contains just these optimal (highest-ranking) accessible worlds.

Let us see how this approach would apply to example (19a). Deontic modality involves a CIRCUMSTANTIAL modal base, i.e., one that picks out worlds in which certain relevant circumstances of the actual world hold true. In this case, one of the relevant circumstances of the actual world is the fact that Arthur has robbed a bank. The relevant ordering source in this example is what the law requires: the optimal worlds will be those in which the law is obeyed as completely as possible, given the circumstances. An informal rendering of the interpretation of this sentence is presented in (22b). The first clause in the restriction represents the modal base, and the second clause in the restriction represents the ordering source.

(22) a. *Arthur must go to prison.* [Deontic]
b. [all w: (the relevant circumstances of the actual world are also true in w) and (the law is obeyed as completely as possible in w)]
GO_TO_PRISON(a) in w

Epistemic modals require a different kind of modal base and ordering source. The fundamental difference between the two types of modality is summarized by Hacquard (2011: 1494) as follows:

> Circumstantial [= root; PRK] modality looks at the material conditions which cause or allow an event to happen; epistemic modality looks at the knowledge state of the speaker to see if an event is compatible with various sources of information available.

The EPISTEMIC modal base, which would be relevant for epistemic modals like that in (23a), picks out worlds consistent with what is known about the actual world, i.e., consistent with the available evidence. Epistemic modals frequently invoke a STEREOTYPICAL ordering source: the optimal worlds are those in which the normal, expected course of events is followed as closely as possible, given the known facts. An informal rendering of the interpretation of (23a) is presented in (23b).

(23) a. *Arthur must be at home.* (=13a) [Epistemic]
b. [all w: (w is consistent with the available evidence) and (the normal course of events is followed as closely as possible in w)]
AT_HOME(a) in w

This rendering of the meaning of epistemic *must* is more accurate than the analysis suggested in (13a) for the same example. That earlier analysis would lead us to predict that *Arthur must be at home* entails *Arthur is at home*, since the actual world is one of the worlds that are consistent with what the speaker knows about the actual world. But this prediction is clearly wrong; saying *Arthur is at home* makes a more definite claim than *Arthur must be at home.* By using *must* in this context, the speaker is implying: "I do not have direct knowledge, but based on the evidence I can't imagine a realistic situation in which Arthur is not at home." The use of the stereotypical ordering source in (23b) helps to account for this inferential character of epistemic *must.* It helps us understand why statements of epistemic necessity are usually better paraphrased with the adverb *evidently* than with *necessarily*.[6]

Another important part of Kratzer's proposal is the claim that the modal auxiliaries in languages like English and French are not in fact polysemous. Kratzer suggests that the lexical entry for words like *must* and *may* specifies only the strength of modality (i.e., the choice of quantifier operator), and that they are indeterminate as to the type or "flavor" of modality (epistemic vs. deontic, etc.). The type of modality depends on the choice of modal base and ordering source, which are determined by context (linguistic or general).

Part of the evidence for this claim is the observation that type of modality can be overtly specified by adverbial phrases or other elements in the sentence, as seen in (24).[7] Notice that these adverbial phrases do not feel redundant, as they probably would if the modal auxiliary specified a particular type of modality as a lexical entailment. For sentences where there is no explicit indication of type of modality, the intended type will be inferred based on the context of the utterance.

(24) a. EPISTEMIC:
(In view of the available evidence,) John *must/may* be the murderer.

b. DEONTIC:
(In view of his parents' orders,) John *may* watch TV, but he *must* go to bed at 8pm.

c. ABILITY:
(In view of his physical abilities,) John *can* lift 200 lbs.

d. TELEOLOGICAL:
(In view of his goal to get a PhD,) John *must* write a dissertation.

e. BOULETIC:
(In view of his desire to retire at age 50,) John *should* work hard now.

While Kratzer's analysis provides an elegant explanation for the unusual pattern of polysemy which we discussed in §16.2, this explanation cannot be applied to all grammatical markers of modality. In the next section we discuss examples of modals for which type of modality seems to be lexically specified.

---

[6] Kratzer states that another advantage of her theory is that it provides a better way to deal with "graded modality" i.e. intermediate-strength modals of "weak necessity" like *ought* or *should*, as well as phrases such as *very likely* or *barely possible*. We will not discuss graded modality in this chapter.

[7] From Hacquard (2011).

16.4 Cross-linguistic variation

In §16.2 we noted that it is common for a single modal form to be used for several different types of modality; but there are also many languages where this does not occur. Even in English, not all modals allow both epistemic and deontic uses. *Might* is used almost exclusively for epistemic possibility, at least in main clauses.[8] *Can* is used almost exclusively for root modalities, although the negated forms *cannot* and *can't* do allow epistemic uses. What these examples show is that it is possible, even in English, for both strength and type of modality to be lexically specified.

Matthewson (2010) shows that in St'át'imcets (Lillooet Salish), clitic modality markers are lexically specified for the type of modality, with strength of modality determined by context; see examples in (25). In this regard, St'át'imcets is the mirror image of English.

(25) a. wá7=**k'a** s-t'al l=ti=tsítcw-s=a s=Philomena
be=**EPIS** STAT-stop in=DET=house-3sg.POSS=EXIS NOM=Philomena
'Philomena must/might be in her house.' [only epistemic]

b. lán=lhkacw=**ka** áts'x-en ti=kwtámts-sw=a
already=2sg.SUBJ=**DEON** see-DIR DET=husband-2sg.POSS=EXIS
'You must/can/may see your husband now.' [only deontic]

The St'át'imcets data might be analyzed roughly along the lines suggested in (26): the modal markers *=k'a* and *=ka* are both defined in terms of a quantifier which is underspecified for strength, but they lexically specify different types (or flavors) of modality:

(26) a. **Epistemic =*k'a*:**
'Philomena must/might be in her house.' (25a)
[ALL/SOME w: (w is consistent with the available evidence) and (the normal course of events is followed as closely as possible)]
AT_HOME(p) in w

b. **Deontic =*ka*:**
'You must/can/may see your husband now.' (25b)

[8] In indirect speech-type complements, *might* can function as the past tense form of *may*, e.g. *Mary said that I might visit her.* In such contexts the deontic reading is possible. (See Chapter 20 for a discussion of the "sequence of tenses" in indirect speech complements.)

> [ALL/SOME w: (the relevant circumstances of the actual world are also true in w) and (the requirements of the relevant authority are satisfied as completely as possible in w)] hearer sees husband in w

This contrast between St'át'imcets and English provides additional support for the conclusion that either strength or type of modality, or both, may be lexically specified. It is possible for both patterns to be found within a single language. The Malay modal *mesti* 'must' has both epistemic and deontic uses, like its English equivalent. The Malay modal *mungkin* 'probably, possibly' has only epistemic uses, but the strength of commitment is context-dependent, much like the clitic modality markers in St'át'imcets.

Van der Auwera & Ammann 2013 report on a study of modal marking in 207 languages, focusing on the question of whether a single modal form can be used to express both epistemic and deontic modality. They report that this is possible in just under half (102) of the languages in their sample: in 105 of the languages, all of the modal markers are lexically specified as either epistemic or deontic/root, with no ambiguity possible. Only 36 of the languages in the sample are like English and French, with markers of both possibility (*may*) and necessity (*must*) which are ambiguous between epistemic and deontic readings. In the remaining 66 languages there is a modal marker for one degree of strength, either possibility 'may' or necessity 'must', which is ambiguous between epistemic and deontic readings; but not for the other degree of strength.

The 36 languages which have ambiguous markers for both possibility and necessity are mostly spoken in Europe, and most of them express modality using auxiliary verbs; but neither of these tendencies is absolute. West Greenlandic (Eskimo) is a non-European member of this group which expresses modality with verbal suffixes. The suffix *-ssa* 'must' has a deontic/root necessity reading in (27a) and an epistemic necessity reading in (27b). The suffix *-sinnaa* 'can' has a root possibility reading in (28a) and an epistemic possibility reading in (28b).

(27) West Greenlandic[9]

a. Inna-jaa-*ssa*-atit.
go.to.bed-early-NEC-IND.2sg
'You must go to bed early.' [DEONTIC]

b. Københavni-mii-*ssa*-aq.
Copenhagen-be.in-NEC-IND.3sg
'She must be in Copenhagen.' [EPISTEMIC]

[9] Examples from Fortescue (1984: 292–294, p.c.); cited in van der Auwera & Ammann 2013

(28) Timmi-*sinnaa*-vuq.
fly-can-IND.3sg
'It can fly.' [ROOT]

(29) Nuum-mut aalla-reer-*sinnaa*-galuar-poq ...
Nuuk-ALLATIVE leave-already-can-however-3sg.IND
'He may well have left for Nuuk already, but...' [EPISTEMIC]

Most of the research on modality to this point has focused on languages of the European type. There is no obvious reason why modal markers in other types of language should not also be analyzed as quantifiers over possible worlds, since (as we have seen) lexical entries for modal markers can specify strength, type of modality, or both. However, this is a hypothesis which should probably be held lightly, pending more detailed investigation of the less-studied languages.

16.5 On the nature of epistemic modality

As mentioned in our discussion of types of modality in §16.1, the most basic distinction is between epistemic modality and all the other types. Hacquard (2011: 1486) observes that "epistemics deal with possibilities that follow from the speaker's knowledge, whereas roots deal with possibilities that follow from the circumstances surrounding the main event and its participants."

Epistemic modality is often said to be "speaker-oriented",[10] because it encodes possibility or necessity in light of the speaker's knowledge. Non-epistemic modal marking reflects some facet of the circumstances surrounding the described situation or event, such as the requirements of an authoritative person or code (DEONTIC), or the agent's abilities (DYNAMIC), goals (TELEOLOGICAL), or desires (BOULETIC).[11] Van der Auwera & Ammann (2013) use the term SITUATIONAL as a cover term for the non-epistemic types, which seems like a very appropriate choice; but the term ROOT is firmly established in linguistic usage.

Epistemic modality also differs from root modality in its interaction with time reference. Epistemic modality in the present time tends to be restricted (at least in English) to states (30a) and imperfective events, either progressive (30c) or habitual (31a). Deontic modality occurs freely with both states and events, but tends to be future oriented; deontic readings are often impossible with past events

[10] Bybee et al. (1994).

[11] These examples illustrate the most commonly recognized types of modality; but as von Fintel (2006) observes, "In the descriptive literature on modality, there is taxonomic exuberance far beyond these basic distinctions."

(31c, 32c). Epistemic necessity (*must*) is typically impossible with future events (31b), which is not surprising because speakers generally do not have certain knowledge of the future. Epistemic possibility (*may*), however, is fine with future events (32b).

(30) a. Henry must be in Brussels this week. [epistemic or deontic]
b. Henry must write a book this year. [future; only deontic]
c. Henry must be writing a book this year. [present; only epistemic]

(31) a. Mary must attend Prof. Lewis's lecture every week. [epistemic or deontic]
b. Mary must attend Prof. Lewis's lecture tomorrow. [only deontic]
c. Mary must have attended Prof. Lewis's lecture yesterday. [only epistemic]

(32) a. Mary may attend Prof. Lewis's lecture every week. [epistemic or deontic]
b. Mary may attend Prof. Lewis's lecture tomorrow. [epistemic or deontic]
c. Mary may have attended Prof. Lewis's lecture yesterday. [only epistemic]

When the modal itself is inflected for past tense, e.g. *had to* in (33), either reading is possible; but the scope of the tense feature is different in the two readings.[12]

(33) Jones had to be in the office when his manager arrived. [epistemic or deontic]

Under the deontic reading, tense takes scope over the modality: the obligation for the agent to behave in a certain way is part of the situation being described as holding true at some time in the past, prior to the time of speaking. Under the epistemic reading, the modality is outside the scope of the past tense: the speaker's knowledge now (at the time of speaking) leads him to conclude that a certain situation held true at some time in the past. As von Fintel (2006) points out, the interactions between modality and tense-aspect are complex and poorly understood, and we will not pursue these issues further here.

[12] *Have to* is used here because true modal auxiliaries in English cannot be inflected for tense.

Papafragou (2006: 1688) describes another kind of difference which has been claimed to exist between epistemic vs. "root" modality:

> It is often claimed in the linguistics literature that epistemic modality, unlike other kinds of modality, does not contribute to the truth conditions of the utterance. Relatedly, several commentators argue that epistemic modality expresses a comment on the proposition expressed by the rest of the utterance… The intuition underlying this view is that epistemic modality in natural language marks the degree and/or source of the speaker's commitment to the embedded proposition.

However, some of the standard tests for propositional content indicate that this is not the case: both types of modality can be part of the proposition and contribute to its truth conditions. We will mention three tests which provide evidence that epistemic modality does not just express a comment on or attitude toward the proposition, but is actually a part of the proposition itself. First, epistemic modality is part of what can be felicitously challenged, as illustrated in (34).[13]

(34) A: Jones is the only person who stood to gain from the old man's death; he must be the murderer.
B: That's not true; he could be the murderer, but he doesn't have to be.

In this mini-conversation, speaker B explicitly denies the truth of A's statement, but only challenges its modality. In other words, B denies $\Box p$ without denying p. In this respect epistemic modals are quite different from the speaker-oriented adverbs which we discussed in Chapter 11. Those adverbs cannot felicitously be challenged in the same way, because (as we argued) they are not a part of the proposition being asserted.

Second, epistemic modality can be the focus of a yes-no question, as illustrated in (35–36). In these questions the information requested concerns the addressee's degree of certainty, not just the identity of the murderer. The wrong choice of modal can trigger the answer "No", as in (35), showing that modality contributes to the truth conditions of the sentence. In contrast, when an inappropriate speaker-oriented adverb is added to a yes-no question, it will not cause the answer to change from "Yes" to "No" (37).

(35) A: Must Jones be the murderer?
B: Yes, he must/#is. or: No, but I think it is very likely.

[13] Cf. Papafragou (2006: 1698).

(36) A: Might Jones be the murderer?
B: Yes, he might/#is. or: No, that is impossible.

(37) A: Was Jones unfortunately arrested for embezzling?
B: Yes/#No; he was arrested for embezzling, but that is not unfortunate.

Third, epistemic modality can be negated by normal clausal negation, although this point is frequently denied. It is true that some English modals exhibit differences in this regard between their epistemic vs. deontic uses. With *may*, for example, negation takes scope over the modal in the deontic reading, but not in the epistemic reading (38). The modal *must*, on the other hand, takes scope over negation in both of these readings (39).

(38) Smith may not be the candidate. [epistemic: possible that not p]
[deontic: not permitted that p]

(39) Smith must not be the candidate. [epistemic: evident that not p]
[deontic: required that not p]

However, while most English modals (including *must* and *may*, as we have just seen) take scope over negation in the epistemic reading, there are a few counter-examples, as illustrated in (40–41).[14]

(40) Smith cannot be the candidate. [epistemic: not possible that p]

(41) Jones doesn't have to be the murderer. [epistemic: not necessary that p]

Examples like these show that even in English, epistemic modality can sometimes be negated by normal clausal negation. Moreover, German *müssen* 'must' takes opposite scope from English *must* in both epistemic and deontic readings (42).

(42) a. Er *muss nicht* zu hause bleiben.
he must not at home remain
'He doesn't have to stay home.'
[deontic: not required that p; von Fintel (2006)]

[14]The same scope holds for the "root" readings of these examples as well.

b. Er *muss nicht* zu Hause geblieben sein. Er kann auch weggegangen
he must not at home remained be he can also away.gone
sein.
be
'It doesn't have to be the case that he stayed home (or: He didn't necessarily stay home). He may also have gone away.'
[epistemic: not necessary that p; Susi Wurmbrand, p.c.]

Idris (1980) states that the Malay modal *mesti* 'must' interacts with negation much like its English equivalent, in particular, that negation cannot take scope over the epistemic use of the modal. Now auxiliary scope in Malay correlates closely with word order. When the modal precedes and takes scope over the clausal negator *tidak* 'not', as in (43a), both the epistemic and the deontic readings are possible. When the order is reversed, as in (43b), Idris states that only the deontic reading is possible.

(43) a. Dia *mesti tidak* belajar.
3SG must NEG study
'He must not study.' [epistemic: evident that not p]
(i.e., 'I am certain that he does not study.')
'He is obliged not to study.' [deontic: required that not p]

b. Dia *tidak mesti* belajar.
3SG NEG must study
'He is not obliged to study.' [deontic: not required that p]

A number of authors have cited these examples in support of the claim that epistemic modality always takes scope over clausal negation.[15] However, corpus examples like those in (44) show that the epistemic use of *mesti* is in fact possible within the scope of clausal negation.

(44) a. Inflasi *tidak mesti* ber-punca dari pemerintah...
inflation NEG must MID-source from government
'Inflation does not have to have the government as its source...'
(... it can arise due to other reasons as well)
[epistemic: not necessary that p][16]

[15] See for example de Haan (1997); Drubig (2001).
[16] http://wargamarhaen.blogspot.com/2011/09/jangan-dok-rasa-pilihanraya-lambat-lagi.html

b. Hiburan itu *tidak mesti* mem-bahagia-kan, tapi kebahagiaan
entertainment that NEG must bless/make.happy but happiness
itu sudah pasti meng-hibur-kan.
that already certain comfort/entertain

'Entertainment does not necessarily bring happiness, but happiness will definitely bring comfort.' [epistemic: not necessary that p][17]

So we have seen evidence that epistemic modality can be negated by normal clausal negation in Malay, in German, and even in English. Once again, this is not true of evaluative or speech act adverbials: they are never interpreted within the scope of clausal negation, as we demonstrated in Chapter 11. Taken together, the three types of evidence we have reviewed here provide strong support for the conclusion that epistemic modality is a part of the propositional content of the utterance and contributes to the truth conditions.

16.6 Conclusion

In this chapter we have sketched out an analysis which treats modals as quantifiers over possible worlds. This analysis helps to explain why modals are similar to quantifiers in certain ways, for example, in the scope ambiguities that arise when they are combined with other quantifiers.

The analysis also helps to explain the unusually systematic pattern of "polysemy" observed in the English modals, as well as the fact that this same pattern shows up in many other languages as well. This is not how polysemy usually works. Under Kratzer's analysis, the English modals are not in fact polysemous, but rather indeterminate for type of modality. The strength of the modal (necessary vs. possible) is lexically entailed, but the type of modality (epistemic vs. deontic etc.) is determined by context.

Modals in French and many other languages work in much the same way as the English modals; but this is certainly not the case for all languages, perhaps not even for a majority of them. However, the quantificational analysis can account for these other languages as well. Strength of modality is represented in the quantifier operator, while type of modality is represented in the restriction on the class of possible worlds. Either or both of these can be lexically specified in particular languages, or for specific forms in any language.

Epistemic modality is different in certain ways from all the other types (known collectively as ROOT modality). Some authors have claimed that epistemic modality is not part of the propositional content of the utterance. We argued that this

[17] http://skbbs-tfauzi.zoom-a.com/katahikmat.html

is wrong, based on the fact that epistemic modality can be questioned and challenged, and (at least in some languages) can be negated as well. We return to these issues in the next chapter, where we discuss the difference between markers of epistemic modality vs. markers of EVIDENTIALITY (source of information).

Further reading

Von Fintel 2006 and Hacquard (2011) provide very useful overviews of the semantic analysis of modality, as well as references to much recent work on this subject. Hacquard in particular provides a good introduction to Kratzer's treatment of modals. Matthewson (2016) presents an introduction and overview with frequent references to Salish and other languages whose modals are quite different from those of English. De Haan 2006 presents a helpful typological study of modality. A brief introduction to modal logic can be found in Garson (2016); recent textbooks on the subject include Blackburn et al. (2008) and van Benthem (2010).

Discussion exercises

A: Deontic vs. epistemic modality. Identify the type of modality in the following statements:

1. You must leave tomorrow.
2. You must have offended the Prime Minister very seriously.
3. You must be very patient.
4. You must use a Mac.
5. You must be using a Mac.

B: Ambiguous type of modality. Use the restricted quantifier notation to express two possible types of modality (deontic vs. epistemic) for the following sentences:

1. Arnold must trust you. (assume "h" = hearer)

> Model answer
>
> **Epistemic**: [all w: (w is consistent with the available evidence) ∧ (the normal course of events is followed as closely as possible in w)] TRUST(a,h) in w
>
> **Deontic**: [all w: (the relevant circumstances of the actual world are also true in w) ∧ (the relevant authority's requirements are satisfied as completely as possible in w)] TRUST(a,h) in w

2. You may annoy Mr. Roosevelt.
3. You must be very patient.

C: Scope ambiguities. Use the restricted quantifier notation to express the two possible scope relations for the indicated reading of the following sentences:

1. No terrorist must enter the White House. [deontic]

> Model answer
>
> a. [all w: (the relevant circumstances of the actual world are also true in w) ∧ (the relevant authority's requirements are satisfied as completely as possible in w)] ([no x: TERRORIST(x)] ENTER(x,wh) in w)
>
> b. [no x: TERRORIST(x)] ([all w: (the relevant circumstances of the actual world are also true in w) ∧ (the relevant authority's requirements are satisfied as completely as possible in w)] ENTER(x,wh) in w)

2. Many prisoners must be released. [deontic]
3. Every candidate could be disqualified. [epistemic]

Homework exercises

A: Epistemic vs. deontic modality. For each of the sentences below, describe two contexts: one where the modal would most likely have an epistemic reading, the other where the modal would most likely have a deontic reading:

1. Arnold must not recognize me.
2. Henry ought to be in his office by now.
3. Baxter may support Suharto.
4. George should be working late tonight.
5. You have to know how to drive.

B: Restricted quantifier representation. Use the restricted quantifier notation to express two types of modality (epistemic vs. deontic) for the following sentences. For convenience, you may use the abbreviation "sp" to refer to the speaker and "h" to refer to the hearer.

1. You must exercise regularly.
2. I should be on time this evening.
3. Rick may not remain in Casablanca.

C: Scope ambiguities.

(1) Use the restricted quantifier notation to express the deontic reading of the two indicated interpretations for the following sentence:
No professors must be fired.
   a. $\neg\exists x[\text{PROFESSOR}(x) \wedge \Box\ \text{FIRED}(x)]$
   b. $\Box\ \neg\exists x[\text{PROFESSOR}(x) \wedge \text{FIRED}(x)]$

(2) Use the restricted quantifier notation to express the two possible scope interpretations for the epistemic reading of the following sentences:

a. Every student could graduate.
b. Some of the suspects must be guilty.

17 Evidentiality

17.1 Markers that indicate the speaker's source of information

The Tagalog particle *daw* ~ *raw* is used to indicate that the speaker heard the information being communicated from someone else, as illustrated in example (1). 'Hearsay' markers like this are one of the most common types of EVIDENTIAL marker among the world's languages.

(1) Mabuti *raw* ang=ani.
good HEARSAY NOM=harvest
'*They say that* the harvest is good.' [Schachter & Otanes 1972: 423]

The term *evidential* refers to a grammatical marker which indicates the speaker's source of information. Evidentials have often been treated as a type of epistemic modality, but in this chapter we will argue that the two categories are distinct. We begin in §17.2 with a brief survey of some common types of evidential systems found across languages. In §17.3 we present a more careful definition of the term EVIDENTIAL and discuss the distinction between evidentiality and epistemic modality. In §17.4 we discuss some of the ways in which we can distinguish evidentiality from other categories, such as tense or modality, which may tend to correlate with evidentiality. §17.5 reviews a proposed distinction between two types of evidential marking. In some languages evidential markers seem to function as illocutionary (speech act) modifiers, while in other languages evidential markers seem to contribute to the propositional content of the utterance. In terms of the distinction we made in Chapter 11, the former type can be identified as contributing use-conditional meaning, while the latter can be identified as contributing truth-conditional meaning.

17.2 Some common types of evidential systems

As mentioned in the previous section, hearsay markers are one of the most common types of evidential marker cross-linguistically. Another common type of evidential marking is seen in languages like Cherokee, which distinguish DIRECT from INDIRECT knowledge. Evidentiality in Cherokee is signaled by a contrast between two different past tense forms.[1] Cherokee speakers use the direct form *-ʌʔi* to express what they have experienced personally, e.g. something they have seen, heard, smelled, felt, etc. They use the indirect form *-eʔi* to express what they have heard from someone else; or what they have inferred based on observable evidence (e.g., seeing puddles one might say 'It rained-INDIRECT'); or what they have assumed based on prior knowledge.

Many languages which have evidential systems make only a two-way distinction, e.g. between direct vs. indirect knowledge, or between hearsay/reported information vs. other sources. However, more complex systems are not uncommon. Huallaga Quechua has three contrastive evidential categories, marked by clitic particles which (in the default pattern) attach to the verb:[2] *=mi* marks "direct" knowledge (e.g. eye-witness or personal experience); *=shi* marks hearsay; and *=chi* marks conjecture and/or inference.[3] The following sentences provide a minimal contrast illustrating the use of these particles. Each of the sentences contains the same basic propositional content (*You also hit me*); the choice of particle indicates how the speaker came to believe this proposition.

(2) Huallaga Quechua evidentials (Weber 1989: 421)

a. Qam-pis maqa-ma-shka-nki *=mi.*
   you-also hit-1.OBJ-PRF-2.SUBJ =DIRECT
   'You also hit me (I saw and/or felt it).'

b. Qam-pis maqa-ma-shka-nki *=shi.*
   you-also hit-1.OBJ-PRF-2.SUBJ =HEARSAY
   '(Someone told me that) you also hit me (I was drunk and can't remember).'

c. Qam-pis maqa-ma-shka-nki *=chi.*
   you-also hit-1.OBJ-PRF-2.SUBJ =CONJECT
   '(I infer that) you also hit me.'
   (I was attacked by a group of people, and I believe you were one of them).

[1] Pulte (1985); Pulte uses the terms "experienced past" vs. "nonexperienced past".

[2] If any single constituent in the sentence gets narrow focus, the evidential clitic follows the focused constituent. If not, the clitic occupies its default position after the verb.

[3] Weber (1989).

A few languages are reported to have five or even six grammatically distinguished evidential categories. A widely cited example of a five-category system is Tuyuca, a Tucanoan language of Colombia. Evidentiality in Tuyuca is marked by portmanteau suffixes which indicate tense and subject agreement, as well as evidential category, and these suffixes are obligatory in every finite clause in the language.[4] The use of these five evidential categories is illustrated by the minimal contrasts in (3).

(3) Tuyuca evidential system (Barnes 1984)

a. díiga apé -wi
soccer play -VISUAL
'He played soccer.' (I saw him play.)

b. díiga apé -ti
soccer play -NONVISUAL
'He played soccer.' (I heard the game and him, but I didn't see it or him.)

c. díiga apé -yi
soccer play -INFERENCE
'He played soccer.' (I have seen evidence that he played: his distinctive shoe print on the playing field. But I did not see him play.)

d. díiga apé -yigi
soccer play -HEARSAY
'He played soccer.' (I obtained the information from someone else.)

e. díiga apé -hĩyi
soccer play -ASSUMED
'He played soccer.' (It is reasonable to assume that he did.)

The VISUAL category (3a) is used for states or events which the speaker actually sees, for actions performed by the speaker, and for "timeless" knowledge which is shared by the community. The NONVISUAL category (3b) is used for information which the speaker perceived directly by some sense other than seeing; that is, by hearing, smell, touch, or taste. The INFERENCE category (3c), which Barnes labels "apparent", is used for conclusions which the speaker draws based on direct evidence. The HEARSAY category (3d), which Barnes labels "secondhand", is used for information which the speaker has heard from someone else. The ASSUMED category (3e) is used for information which the speaker assumes based on background knowledge about the situation.

[4]Barnes (1984).

17.3 Evidentiality and epistemic modality

Having examined some examples of the kinds of distinctions that are typically found in evidential systems, let us think about what kind of meaning these grammatical markers express. Aikhenvald (2004: 3), in her very important book on this topic, defines evidentiality as follows:

> Evidentiality is a linguistic category whose primary meaning is source of information... [T]his covers the way in which information was acquired, without necessarily relating to the degree of speaker's certainty concerning the statement or whether it is true or not... To be considered as an evidential, a morpheme has to have 'source of information' as its core meaning; that is, the unmarked, or default interpretation.

There are several important points to be noted in this definition. First, evidentiality is a grammatical category.[5] All languages have lexical means for expressing source of information (*I was told that p*; *I infer that p*; *apparently*; *it is said*; etc.), but the term EVIDENTIAL is normally restricted to grammatical morphemes (affixes, particles, etc.). Second, an evidential marker must have source of information as its core meaning. This is significant because evidentiality often correlates with other semantic features, such as degree of certainty. Such a correlation is not surprising, since a speaker will naturally feel more certain of things he has seen with his own eyes than things he learned by hearsay. (We return below to the question of how we can know which factor represents the marker's "core meaning".)

It is not unusual for evidential meanings to arise as secondary functions of markers of modality, tense, etc. For example, the German modal verb *sollen* 'should' has a secondary usage as a hearsay marker, as illustrated in (4). This form is often cited in discussions of evidentiality; but under Aikhenvald's strict definition of the term, it would not be classified as an evidential, because its primary function is to mark modality.[6]

(4) Kim *soll* einen neuen Job angeboten bekommen haben.
Kim should a new job offered get have
'Kim has supposedly been offered a new job.' [von Fintel 2006]

[5] cf. Aikhenvald (2004: 1).

[6] Aikhenvald (2004: 1) estimates that about a quarter of the world's languages have grammatical markers of evidentiality. In contrast, de Haan (2013) indicates that evidentiality markers are present in 57% of the WALS sample (237 out of 418 languages). But this figure is based on a broader definition of the term: de Haan includes cases like German *sollen*, where a modal or some other grammatical marker has a secondary evidential function.

A third claim implicit in Aikhenvald's definition is that evidentiality is distinct from epistemic modality. She states this explicitly a bit later:

> Evidentials may acquire secondary meanings — of reliability, probability and possibility (known as epistemic extensions), but they do not have to... Evidentiality is a category in its own right, and not a subcategory of any modality... That evidentials may have semantic extensions related to probability and speaker's evaluation of trustworthiness of information does not make evidentiality a kind of modality. [Aikhenvald 2004: 7–8]

Epistemic modality of course is the linguistic category whose primary function is to indicate the speaker's degree of certainty concerning the proposition that is being expressed. As we have just noted, there is a close correlation between source of information and degree of certainty, and a number of authors have classified evidentiality as a kind of modality.[7] But Aikhenvald maintains that the two categories need to be distinguished.

Of course, the question of whether evidentiality is a type of epistemic modality depends in part on how one defines *modality*; but this is not just a terminological issue. We argued in Chapter 16 that modal markers, including epistemic modals, contribute to the propositional content of an utterance. There is good evidence that evidential markers in a number of languages do not contribute to propositional content but function as illocutionary modifiers, and so must be distinct from epistemic modality. But before we review some of this evidence, it will be helpful to think about how we go about identifying a marker's "primary function".

17.4 Distinguishing evidentiality from tense and modality

It is not always easy to distinguish empirically between evidential markers and epistemic modals. Tense and aspect markers can also be a problem, because they too can have secondary evidential functions or associations. Perfect aspect in particular often carries an indirect evidential connotation, and indirect evidence markers frequently develop out of perfect aspect markers.[8] For example, in Iranian Azerbaijani (closely related to Turkish) the suffix *-miş* is polysemous between an older perfect sense and a more recent evidential sense.[9] We can see

[7] Palmer (1986), Frawley (1992), Matthewson et al. (2007), Izvorski (1997).
[8] Izvorski (1997); Bybee et al. (1994).
[9] Lee (2008).

that the two senses are distinct in the modern language, because they can co-occur in the same word as seen in (5).

(5) zefer qazan-miş-miş-am
victory win-PRF-INDIRECT-1SG
'reportedly I have won' [Noah Lee, p.c.]

So then, when we encounter a grammatical marker which seems to indicate source of information in at least some contexts, but has other functions as well, how can we decide what to call it? In other words, how do we determine its "primary function"? The key is to search for contexts where the expected correlation does not hold, so that the two possible analyses would make different predictions.

David Weber (1989: 421ff.) compares his analysis of the Huallaga Quechua evidential clitics with an alternative analysis which treats them as VALIDATIONAL markers, that is, indicators of the speaker's degree of commitment to the truth of the proposition being expressed. The choice between these two analyses is not immediately obvious, because there is a correlation between source of information and speaker's degree of commitment. As we have noted, a speaker is likely to be more certain of knowledge gained through direct experience than of knowledge gained through hearsay or inference. In many contexts the direct evidential *=mi* (which is optional) can be used to indicate certainty; and hearers may sometimes interpret the hearsay evidential *=shi* as indicating uncertainty on the part of the speaker.

However, when there is a conflict between source of information and degree of commitment, it is source of information that determines the choice of clitic. For example, if someone were to say 'My mother's grandfather's name was John,' the direct evidential *=mi* would be extremely unnatural, no matter how firmly the speaker believes what he is saying. The hearsay evidential *=shi* must be used instead, because it is very unlikely in that culture for the speaker to have actually met his great-grandfather. Similarly, in describing cultural practices which the speaker firmly believes but has not personally experienced (e.g., 'Having chewed coca, their strength comes to them'), the hearsay evidential is strongly preferred.

The general principle is that when we are trying to identify the meaning of a certain form, and there are two or more semantic factors that seem to correlate with the presence of that form, we need to find or create situations in which only one of those factors is possible and test whether the form would appear in such situations.

17.5 Two types of evidentials

In §17.3 we mentioned that evidential markers in some languages do not contribute to propositional content but function as illocutionary modifiers. One of the best documented examples of this type is Cuzco Quechua as described by Martina Faller.[10] Faller analyzes the evidential enclitics in Cuzco Quechua as "illocutionary modifiers which add to or modify the sincerity conditions of the act they apply to." She notes that "they do not contribute to the main proposition expressed, can never occur in the scope of propositional operators such as negation, and can only occur in illocutionary force bearing environments."[11]

We present here some of her evidence for saying that the evidential enclitics do not contribute to the propositional content of the utterance, focusing on the Reportative clitic *=si*. First, the evidential is always interpreted as being outside the scope of negation. In example (6), the contribution of the Reportative evidential ('speaker was told that *p*') cannot be interpreted as part of what is being negated; so (ii) is not a possible interpretation for this sentence.

(6) Ines-qa mana=s qaynunchaw ñaña-n-ta-chu watuku-rqa-n.
Inés-TOP not=REPORT yesterday sister-3-ACC-NEG visit-PAST$_1$-3
propositional content = 'Inés didn't visit her sister yesterday.'
evidential meaning: (i) speaker was told that Inés did not visit her sister yesterday
not: (ii) # speaker was not told that Inés visited her sister yesterday
[Faller 2002, §6.3.1]

Second, the contribution of the Reportative evidential is not part of what can be challenged. If a speaker makes the statement in (7a), a hearer might challenge the truth of the statement based on the facts being reported, as in (7b); but it would be infelicitous to challenge the truth of the statement based on source of information, as in (7c). (This test is sometimes called the ASSENT/DISSENT DIAGNOSTIC.[12]) In other words, the contribution of the evidential does not seem to be part of what makes the statement true or false.

(7) a. Ines-qa qaynunchay ñaña-n-ta=s watuku-sqa.
Inés-TOP yesterday sister-ACC=REPORT visit-PAST$_2$
propositional content = 'Inés visited her sister yesterday.'

[10]Faller (2002; 2003; 2006), inter alia.
[11]Faller (2002: v).
[12]Papafragou (2006).

evidential meaning: speaker was told that Inés visited her sister yesterday

b. Mana=n chiqaq-chu. Manta-n-ta-lla=n watuku-rqa-n.
not=DIRECT true-NEG mother-3-ACC-LIMIT=DIRECT visit-$PAST_1$-3
'That's not true. She only visited her mother.'

c. Mana=n chiqaq-chu. #Mana=n chay-ta willa-rqa-sunki-chu.
not=DIRECT true-NEG not=DIRECT this-ACC tell-$PAST_1$-3S.2O-NEG
'That's not true. #You were not told this.' [Faller 2002, §5.3.3]

Third, Faller's statement that the evidential enclitics "can only occur in illocutionary force bearing environments" means that they are restricted to main clauses or clauses which express an independent speech act. This is a characteristic feature of many illocutionary modifiers. In particular, conditional clauses are typically not the kind of environment where illocutionary modifiers can occur.[13] Faller states that evidential enclitics cannot occur within conditional clauses, as illustrated in (8).

(8) Mana(*=si) para-sha-n-chu chayqa ri-sun-chis.
not=REPORT rain-PROG-3-NEG then go-1.FUT-PL
'If it is not raining we will go.' [Faller 2003, ex. 8]

The German auxiliary *sollen* 'should', when used as a reportative or hearsay marker, behaves quite differently. For example, it is possible for *sollen* to occur within a conditional clause, as illustrated in (9).

(9) F.C.B.F.A.N.: Bei uns *soll* es heute schneien!!
'It is *said* (=predicted) to snow near us today.'
FAHRBACH: Also *wenn es bei dir schneien soll*, dann schneit es bei mir auch.
'*If it said to snow near you*, then it will snow near me as well.'[14]

The assent/dissent diagnostic reveals another difference. German Reportative *sollen*, like the Quechua Reportative evidential, allows the hearer to challenge the basic propositional content of the sentence. But in addition, it is possible to

[13] Ernst (2009), Haegeman (2010).

[14] http://www.kc-forum.com/archive/index.php/t-45696, cited in Faller (2006). A reviewer points out that this is not a typical hypothetical conditional, but what we will call in Chapter 19 a REALITY conditional, which has somewhat specialized functions. It is not clear whether the reportative use of *sollen* is possible within hypothetical conditionals.

challenge the truth of a statement with *sollen* based on the source of information, as illustrated in (10).[15] This is impossible with the Quechua Reportative. Both of these differences are consistent with the hypothesis that German Reportative *sollen* is part of the propositional content of the utterance.

(10) A: Laut Polizei *soll* die Gärtnerin die Juwelen gestohlen haben.
'According to the police, the gardener *is said* to have stolen the jewels.'

B: Nein, das stimmt nicht. Das ist die Presse, die das behauptet.
'No, that's not true. It is the press who is claiming this.' (Faller 2006)

A number of languages have evidentials which behave much like those of Cuzco Quechua. However, there are other languages in which evidentials seem to contribute to the propositional content of the utterance, like German Reportative *sollen*. Murray (2010) suggests that we need to recognize two different types of evidential, which we will refer to as ILLOCUTIONARY EVIDENTIALS and PROPOSITIONAL EVIDENTIALS.[16] Illocutionary evidentials function as illocutionary operators; examples are found in Quechua, Kalaallisut, and Cheyenne. Propositional evidentials are part of the propositional content of the utterance; examples are found in German, Turkish, Bulgarian, St'át'imcets (Lillooet Salish), and Japanese.

These two types of evidentials share a number of properties in common, but Murray identifies several tests that distinguish the two classes. For example, illocutionary evidentials cannot be embedded within a conditional clause (8), while this is possible for propositional evidentials (9). Second, a speaker who makes a statement using a hearsay or reportative evidential of the illocutionary type is not committed to believing that the propositional content of the utterance is possibly true. So it is not a contradiction, nor is it infelicitous, for a speaker to assert something as hearsay and then deny that he believes it, as illustrated in (11).

(11) a. Para-sha-n=si, ichaqa mana crei-ni-chu.
rain-PROG-3=REPORT but not believe-1-NEG
'It is raining (someone says), but I don't believe it.'
[Cuzco Quechua; Faller (2002: 194)]

b. É-hoo'kȯhó-nėse naa oha ná-sáa-oné'séomátsésto-he-∅.
3-rain-REPORT.INAN.SG and CONTR 1-NEG-believe$_{\text{INAN}}$-MOD$_{\text{ANIM}}$-DIR
'It's raining, they say, but I don't believe it.'
[Cheyenne; Murray 2010: 58]

[15] Faller (2006).

[16] Murray uses the terms ILLOCUTIONARY EVIDENTIALS vs. EPISTEMIC EVIDENTIALS.

A hearsay or reportative evidential of the propositional type, however, commits the speaker to believing that it is at least possible for the expressed proposition to be true. For this reason, the St'át'imcets example in (12) is infelicitous.

(12) (Context: You had done some work for a company and they said they put your pay, $200, in your bank account; but actually, they didn't pay you at all.)
*Um'-en-tsal-itás ku7 i án'was-a xetspqíqen'kst táola,
give-DIR-1sg.OBJ-3pl.ERG REPORT DET.PL two-DET hundred dollar
t'u7 aoz kw s-7um'-en-tsál-itas ku stam'.
but NEG DET NOM-give-DIR-1sg.OBJ-3pl.ERG DET what
'They gave me $200 [I was told], but they didn't give me anything.'
[Matthewson et al. 2007]

Third, illocutionary evidentials are always speaker-oriented. This means that they indicate the source of information of the speaker, and cannot be used to indicate the source of information of some other participant. This is illustrated in the Quechua example in (13).

(13) Pilar-qa yacha-sha-n Marya-q
Pilar-TOP know-PROG-3 Marya-GEN
hamu-sqa-n-ta{-n/-s/-chá}.
come-PAST.PTCP-3-ACC{-DIR/-REPORT/-CONJECT}
propositional content = 'Pilar knows that Marya came.'
evidential meaning: (i) speaker has direct/reportative/conjectural evidence that Pilar knows that Marya came.
not: (ii) #Pilar has direct/reportative/conjectural evidence that Marya came. [Faller 2002, ex. 184]

Propositional evidentials, in contrast, can be used to indicate the source of information of some participant other than the speaker. In the St'át'imcets example in (14), for example, the reportative evidential is interpreted as marking Lémya7's source of information. It indicates that Lémya7's statement was based on hearsay evidence. The speaker in (14) already had direct evidence for this information before hearing it from Lémya7.

(14) Tsut s-Lémya7 kw sqwemémn'ek ku7 s-Mary, t'u7
say NOM-name DET pregnant REPORT NOM-name but
plán-lhkan ti7 zwát-en — áts'x-en-lhkan s-Mary áta7
already-1sg.SUBJ DEM know-DIR — see-DIR-1sg.SUBJ NOM-name DEIC
tecwp-álhcw-a inátcwas.
buy-place-DET yesterday
'Lémya7 said that [she was told that] Mary is pregnant, but I already knew that — I had seen Mary at the store yesterday.'[17]

A fourth difference demonstrated by Murray is that markers of tense or modality never take semantic scope over illocutionary evidential markers, whereas this is possible with propositional evidentials.[18]

There seems to be a strong tendency for illocutionary evidential markers to be "true evidentials" in Aikhenvald's sense, i.e., grammatical morphemes whose primary function is to mark source of information; and for propositional evidentials to be evidential uses/senses of morphemes whose primary function is something else: perfect aspect in Turkish and Bulgarian; modality in German and St'át'imcets. In terms of the distinction we made in Chapter 11, illocutionary evidentials seem to contribute use-conditional meaning, while propositional evidentials seem to contribute truth-conditional meaning.

17.6 Conclusion

We have suggested that a single type of meaning (source of information) can be contributed on two different levels or dimensions: truth-conditional vs. use-conditional. In Chapter 18 we will argue that a similar pattern is observable with adverbial reason clauses. The conjunction *because* expresses a causal relationship, but this causal relationship may either be asserted as part of the truth-conditional propositional content of the sentence, or may function as a kind of illocutionary modifier.

There is much more to be said about evidentials, but we cannot pursue the topic further here. In addition to the semantic issues introduced (all too briefly) above, the use of grammatical evidential markers interacts in interesting ways with discourse genre, world-view, first and second language acquisition, language contact, and translation, to name just a few.

[17] Matthewson et al. (2007).
[18] See Murray (2010: §3.4.2) for examples.

Further reading

Aikhenvald (2004) is the primary source for typological and descriptive details about the meanings and functions of evidential markers, and for discussion of the other issues mentioned in the last sentence of this chapter. De Haan (2012) provides a useful overview of the subject, while de Haan (1999; 2005) discusses the relationship between evidentiality and epistemic modality.

18 *Because*

18.1 Introduction

In this chapter we explore the meaning of the conjunction *because* by asking what contribution it makes to the meaning of a sentence. *Because* is used to connect two propositions, so its contribution to the meaning of the sentence will be found in the semantic relationship between those two propositions.

We begin in §18.2 by comparing reason clauses introduced by *because* with time clauses introduced by *when*. Time clauses function as adverbial modifiers, but we will argue that *because* has a different function: it combines two propositions into a new proposition which asserts that a causal relationship exists. An important piece of evidence for this analysis comes from certain scope ambiguities which arise in *because* clauses but not in time clauses.

Conjunctions are often polysemous,[1] and various authors have noted that *because* can be used in more than one way. We examine the various uses of *because* in §18.3, but we will argue that *because* is not polysemous. Rather, it has just one sense which can be used in different domains, or dimensions, of meaning: truth-conditional vs. use-conditional. The term PRAGMATIC AMBIGUITY has been proposed to describe such cases, and this term seems appropriate based on the evidence presented below.

In §18.4 we will see that the various uses of *because* correlate with different syntactic structures. We will propose diagnostic tests for distinguishing co-ordinate from subordinate *because* clauses. We argue that all of the semantic functions of *because* are possible in the co-ordinate structure, but only one function is possible in the subordinate structure. In §18.5 we show that a similar situation holds in German, where the difference between co-ordinate and subordinate structures is clearly marked.

[1]Aikhenvald (2009).

18.2 *Because* as a two-place operator

Adverbial clauses occur in complex sentences, in which two (or more) propositions are combined to produce a single complex proposition. However, not all adverbial clauses have the same semantic properties. The examples in (1–2) illustrate some of the differences between time clauses and reason clauses:

(1) a. Prince Harry wore his medals when he visited the Pope.
  b. Prince Harry didn't wear his medals when he visited the Pope.
  c. Did Prince Harry wear his medals when he visited the Pope?

(2) a. Arthur married Susan because she is rich.
  b. Arthur didn't marry Susan because she is rich.
  c. Did Arthur marry Susan because she is rich?

All three sentences in (1) imply that Harry visited the Pope. As we noted in Chapter 3, time clauses trigger a presupposition that the proposition they contain is true. Reason clauses do not trigger this kind of presupposition. While sentence (2a) implies that Susan is rich, sentences (2b–c) do not carry this inference. Sentence (2b) could be spoken appropriately by a person who does not believe that Susan is rich, and sentence (2c) could be spoken appropriately by a person who does not know whether Susan is rich.

So *q because p* does not presuppose that *p* is true; but it entails that both *p* and *q* are true. This entailment is demonstrated in (3).

(3) a. George VI became King of England because Edward VIII abdicated; #but George did not become king.
  b. George VI became King of England because Edward VIII abdicated; #but Edward did not abdicate.

A second difference between time clauses and reason clauses involves the effect of negation. The negative statement in (2b) is ambiguous. It can either mean 'Arthur didn't marry Susan, and his reason for not marrying her was because she is rich;' or 'Arthur did marry Susan, but his reason for marrying her was not because she is rich.' No such ambiguity arises in sentence (1b).

The time clause in (1a) functions as a modifier; it makes the proposition expressed in the main clause more specific or precise, by restricting its time reference. *Because* clauses seem to have a different kind of semantic function. Johnston (1994) argues that *because* is best analyzed as an operator CAUSE, which combines two propositions into a single proposition by asserting a causal relationship between the two.[2] We might define this operator as shown in (4):

(4) *CAUSE(p,q)* is true iff *p* is true, *q* is true, and *p* being true causes *q* to be true.

For example, if *p* and *q* are descriptions of events in the past, *CAUSE(p,q)* would mean that *p* happening caused *q* to happen. A truth table for *CAUSE* would look very much like the truth table for *and*; but there is a crucial additional element of meaning that would not show up in the truth table, namely the causal relationship between the two propositions.[3]

This analysis provides an immediate explanation for the ambiguity of sentence (2b) in terms of the scope of negation:

(5) *Arthur didn't marry Susan because she is rich.*

a. ¬CAUSE(RICH(s), MARRY(a,s))
b. CAUSE(RICH(s), ¬MARRY(a,s))

If this approach is on the right track, we would expect to find other kinds of scope ambiguities involving *because* clauses as well. This prediction turns out to be correct: in sentences of the form *p because q*, if the first clause contains a scope-bearing expression such as a quantifier, modal, or propositional attitude verb, that expression may be interpreted as taking scope either over the entire sentence or just over its immediate clause. Some examples are provided in (6–7).

(6) *Few people admired Churchill because he joined the Amalgamated Union of Building Trade Workers.*

a. CAUSE(JOIN(c,aubtw), [few x: person(x)] ADMIRE(x,c))
b. [few x: person(x)] CAUSE(JOIN(c,aubtw), ADMIRE(x,c))

(7) *I believed that you love me because I am gullible.*

a. BELIEVE(s, CAUSE(GULLIBLE(s), LOVE(h,s))
b. CAUSE(GULLIBLE(s), BELIEVE(s, LOVE(h,s)))
[s = speaker; h = hearer]

---

[2] This operator is probably different from the causal operator involved in morphological causatives, which is often thought of as a relation between an individual and an event/situation.

[3] The definition of causality is a long-standing problem in philosophy, which we will not address here. One way to think about it makes use of a counter-factual (see Chapter 19): *CAUSE(p,q)* means that if *p* had not happened, *q* would not have happened either.

One reading for sentence (6), which is clearly false in our world, is that only a few people admired Churchill, and the reason for this was that he joined the AUBTW. The other reading for sentence (6), very likely true in our world, is that only a few people's admiration of Churchill was motivated by his joining of the AUBTW; but many others may have admired him for other reasons. (The reader should work out the two readings for sentence (7).)

18.3 Use-conditional *because*

Now let us consider the apparent polysemy of *because.* Sweetser (1990: 76–78) suggests that *because* (and a number of other conjunctions) can be used in three different ways:

> Conjunction may be interpreted as applying in one of (at least) three domains [where] the choice of a "correct" interpretation depends not on form, but on a pragmatically motivated choice between viewing the conjoined clauses as representing content units, logical entities, or speech acts. [p. 78]

(8) a. John came back because he loved her. [CONTENT domain]
    b. John loved her, because he came back. [EPISTEMIC domain]
    c. What are you doing tonight, because there's a good movie on. [SPEECH ACT domain]

The content domain has to do with "real-world causality"; in (8a), John's love causes him to return. The epistemic domain (8b) has to do with the speaker's grounds for making the assertion expressed in the main clause: the content of the *because* clause (*he came back*) provides evidence for believing the assertion (*John loved her*) to be true. Sweetser explains the speech act domain (8c) as follows:

> [T]he *because* clause gives the cause of the *speech act* embodied by the main clause. The reading is something like 'I *ask* what you are doing tonight because I want to suggest that we go see this good movie.' [1990: 77]

Sweetser denies that the three uses above involve different senses of *because.* Rather, she argues that *because* has a single sense which can operate on three different levels, or domains, of meaning. She describes this situation, taking a term from Horn (1985), as a case of PRAGMATIC AMBIGUITY; in other words, an ambiguity of usage rather than an ambiguity of sense.

This seems like a very plausible suggestion; but any such proposal needs to account for the fact that the various uses of *because* are distinguished by a number of real differences, both semantic and structural. The most obvious of these is the presence of pause, or "comma intonation", between the two clauses. The pause is optional with content domain uses of *because*, as in (9a), but obligatory with other uses. If the pause is omitted in (9b–c), the sentences can only be interpreted as expressing real-world causality, even though this interpretation is somewhat bizarre. (With the pause, (9b) illustrates an epistemic use while (9c) illustrates a speech act use.)

(9) a. Mary scolded her husband (,) because he forgot their anniversary.
b. Arnold must have sold his Jaguar #(,) because I saw him driving a 1995 minivan.
c. Are you hungry #(,) because there is some pizza in the fridge?

Several of the tests that we used in previous chapters to distinguish truth-conditional propositional content from use-conditional meaning also distinguish the content domain use from the other uses of *because*: questionability, capacity for being negated, and capacity for being embedded within conditional clauses. Let us look first at the interpretation of yes-no questions. When content domain uses of *because* occur as part of a yes-no question, the causal relationship itself is part of what is being questioned, as in (10a). With other uses, however, the causal relationship is not questioned; the scope of the interrogative force is restricted to the main clause, as in (10b, epistemic) and (10c, speech act). If we try to interpret (10b–c) as questioning the causal relationship (the reading which is required if we omit the pause), we get rather bizarre content domain interpretations.

(10) a. Did Mary scold her husband because he forgot their anniversary?
b. Did Arnold sell his Jaguar, because I just saw him driving a 1995 minivan?
c. Are you going out tonight, because I would like to come and visit you?

We find a similar difference regarding the scope of negation. As noted in §18.2, when a sentence containing a *because* clause is negated, the negation can be interpreted as taking scope over the whole sentence including the causal relationship. But this is only possible with content domain uses of *because*, like (11a). With epistemic (11b) or speech act (11c) uses, negation only takes scope over the main clause. Once again, attempting to interpret negation with widest scope in (11b–c) results in bizarre readings involving real-world causality.

(11) a. Arthur didn't marry Susan because she is rich.
b. You couldn't have failed phonetics, because you graduated.
c. Mary is not home, because I assume that you really came to see her.

Similarly, content domain uses of *because* can be embedded within conditional clauses, as seen in (12a); but this is impossible with epistemic (12b) or speech act (12c) uses:

(12) a. If Mary scolded her husband because he forgot their anniversary, they will be back on speaking terms in a few days.
b. ?? If Arnold sold his Jaguar because I just saw him driving a 1995 minivan, he is likely to regret it.
c. ?? If you are hungry because there is some pizza in the fridge, please help yourself.

Looking back at the differences we have listed so far, we see that in each case the content domain use of *because* behaves differently from the other two uses, while the epistemic and speech act uses always seem to behave in the same way. In other words, the evidence we have considered up to this point provides solid grounds for distinguishing two uses of *because*, but not for distinguishing the epistemic and speech act uses.

The evidence we have considered thus far suggests that content domain uses of *because* contribute to truth-conditional propositional content, while epistemic and speech act uses of *because* contribute use-conditional meaning. In light of this evidence, we will adopt Sweetser's suggestion that *because* has a single sense, treating the different uses as a case of pragmatic ambiguity. However, we will posit just two (rather than three) relevant domains (or dimensions) of meaning: truth-conditional vs. use-conditional.[4]

In use-conditional functions of *because*, the conjunction expresses a causal relationship between the proposition expressed by the *because* clause and the speech act expressed in the main clause, as illustrated in (13b–c).

(13) a. *John came back because he loved her.* [TRUTH-CONDITIONAL]
CAUSE(LOVE(j,m), COME_BACK(j))
b. *John loved her, because he came back.* [USE-CONDITIONAL]
CAUSE(COME_BACK(j), I assert that LOVE(j,m))

[4] A number of other authors have made a similar two-way distinction for *because* clauses, with use-conditional *because* clauses treated as a type of speech act adverbial; see for example Scheffler (2008; 2013) and Thompson et al. (2007).

c. *What are you doing tonight, because there's a good movie on.* [USE-CONDITIONAL]
CAUSE(there's a good movie on, I ask you what you are doing tonight)

The nature of the causal relationship in use-conditional functions is often closely related to the felicity conditions for the particular speech act involved. One of the felicity conditions for making an assertion is that the speaker should have adequate grounds for believing that the assertion is true. Sweetser's epistemic *because* clauses, like the one in (13b), provide evidence which forms all or part of the grounds for the assertion expressed in the main clause.

Sweetser's speech act *because* clauses often explain the speaker's reason for performing the speech act or why it is felicitous in that specific context. The *because* clause in (13c) explains why the speaker is asking the question, and so provides guidance for the hearer as to what kind of answer will be relevant to the speaker's purpose.

Two clauses which are joined by use-conditional *because* behave in some ways like separate speech acts. As illustrated in examples (8c), (9c), and (10b–c) above, a main clause that is followed by a use-conditional *because* clause can contain a question, even when the *because* clause itself is an assertion. It is also possible for the main clause to contain a command in this context, as illustrated in (14).[5]

(14) a. Give me the tickets, because I know that you will forget them somewhere.
b. Take my sandwich, because I know that you have not eaten anything today.

Such examples show that a use-conditional *because* clause and its main clause can have separate illocutionary forces, and so can constitute distinct speech acts.

18.4 Structural issues: co-ordination vs. subordination

An additional difference between truth-conditional vs. use-conditional *because* clauses is that only the truth-conditional type can be fronted, as illustrated in (15). Sentences (15b–c) would most naturally be interpreted as use-conditional examples if the *because* clause followed the main clause. But when the *because*

[5] The fact that the *because* clauses in these examples start with *I know that* … blocks any potential interpretion as "content domain" *because* clauses.

clause is fronted they can only be interpreted as expressing real-world causality, even though this interpretation is somewhat bizarre.

(15) a. Because it's raining, we can't go to the beach. [TRUTH-CONDITIONAL]

b. ?? Because I saw Arnold driving a 1995 minivan, he sold his Jaguar. [*USE-CONDITIONAL]

c. ?? Because I assume that you came to see her, Mary hasn't come home yet. [*USE-CONDITIONAL]

Haspelmath (1995) points out that subordinate clauses can often be fronted, but this is typically impossible for co-ordinate clauses. The examples in (16–18) show that a variety of subordinate clauses in English can be fronted. The examples in (19–20) show that this same pattern of fronting is not possible with co-ordinate clauses (though of course it would be possible to reverse the order of the clauses leaving the conjunction in place between them). In light of this observation, the fact that use-conditional *because* clauses cannot be fronted suggests that they may actually be co-ordinate clauses rather than subordinate clauses.

(16) a. George will give you a ride when you are ready.

b. When you are ready, George will give you a ride.

(17) a. Paul will sing you a song if you ask him nicely.

b. If you ask him nicely, Paul will sing you a song.

(18) a. Ringo draped towels over his snare drum in order to deaden the sound.

b. In order to deaden the sound, Ringo draped towels over his snare drum.

(19) a. George played the sitar and John sang a solo.

b. * And John sang a solo, George played the sitar.

(20) a. Paul asked for tea but the waiter brought coffee.

b. * But the waiter brought coffee, Paul asked for tea.

As we noted above, a pause (comma intonation) is optional before truth-conditional *because* clauses but obligatory before use-conditional *because* clauses. (We focus here on the situation where the *because* clause follows the main clause, since pause is always obligatory when the *because* clause is fronted.) We can explain this observation if we assume that a pause in this context is an indicator of co-ordinate structure, and that use-conditional functions of *because* are only possible in co-ordinate structures. Truth-conditional interpretations of *because* are possible in either co-ordinate or subordinate structures, i.e., with or without a pause. Only the truth-conditional interpretation is possible in subordinate structures (where there is no pause), even when this interpretation is pragmatically unlikely or bizarre (see 9b-c).

Additional support for the hypothesis that a pause is a marker of co-ordination comes from the fact that the scope ambiguities discussed in §18.2 disappear when a pause is inserted between the two clauses. The examples in (21) are not ambiguous, whereas the corresponding examples with no pause are (see 2b, 6, and 7). It is not surprising that an operator in a matrix clause can take scope over a subordinate clause; it would be much less common for an operator in one half of a co-ordinate structure to take scope over the other half.

(21) a. Arthur didn't marry Susan, because she is rich.
b. Few people admired Churchill, because he joined the trade union.
c. I believed that you love me, because I am gullible.

Interrogative force exhibits similar scope effects: example (22) shows that when a pause is present, the causal relationship cannot be part of what is being questioned. And example (23) shows that a co-ordinate *because* clause cannot be embedded within a conditional clause.[6]

(22) Did Mary scold her husband, because he forgot their anniversary? (can only be understood as reason for asking, not as reason for scolding)

(23) #If Mary scolded her husband, because he forgot their anniversary, they will be back on speaking terms in a few days.

In the previous section we used negation, questioning, and embedding within *if* clauses to argue that Sweetser's "epistemic" and "speech act" *because* clauses contribute use-conditional rather than truth-conditional meaning. But if those uses of *because* are only possible in co-ordinate structures, one might wonder whether perhaps the different behavior of negation, questioning and embedding is due to purely structural factors, and is therefore not semantically relevant?

[6]The *because* clause set off by pauses in (23) cannot be interpreted as part of the conditional clause. It could only be interpreted as a parenthetical comment, which in this context produces a very incoherent sentence meaning.

However, there is at least one test that can be applied to co-ordinate structures, and this test confirms the semantic distinction we argued for in the previous section. This is the challengeability test: the truth of a statement can typically only be challenged on the basis of truth-conditional propositional content. As the following examples show, the truth of a statement which contains a content *because* clause can be appropriately challenged based on the causal relationship itself, even when the co-ordinate structure is used as in (24). With epistemic and speech act *because* clauses, however, the truth of the statement can be challenged based on the content of the main clause, but not based on the causal relationship or the content of the *because* clause (25–26).

(24) A: Mary is leaving her husband, because he refuses to look for a job.
B: That is not true; Mary is leaving her husband because he drinks too much.

(25) A: Mary is at home, because her car is in the driveway.
B1: That is not true. She is not home; she went out on her bicycle.
B2: #That is not true; you know that Mary is home because you just talked with her.

(26) A: There is some pizza in the fridge, because you must be starving.
B1: That is not true; we ate the pizza last night.
B2: #That is not true; you told me about the pizza because want to get rid of it.

To summarize, we have proposed that adverbial clauses introduced by *because* can occur in two different structural configurations, co-ordinate or subordinate. Co-ordinate *because* clauses must be separated from the main clause by a pause (comma intonation), but this pause is not allowed before subordinate *because* clauses (when they follow the main clause). The co-ordinate structure allows either truth-conditional or use-conditional interpretations of *because*, but only the truth-conditional use is possible in the subordinate structure. Subordinate *because* clauses can occur within the scope of clausal negation and interrogative force, and can be embedded within conditional clauses; but none of these things is possible with co-ordinate *because* clauses.

18.5 Two words for 'because' in German

The situation in German is very similar, but the distinction between co-ordinate and subordinate structures is much easier to recognize in German than in English.[7] German has two different words which are translated as 'because'. Both of these words can be used to describe real-world causality, as illustrated in (27–28). In each case, the a and b sentences have the same English translation.

(27) a. Ich habe den Bus verpasst, *weil* ich spät dran war.
1SG AUX the.ACC bus missed because 1SG late there was
'I missed the bus because I got there late.'

b. Ich habe den Bus verpasst, *denn* ich war spät dran. (same meaning)[8]

(28) a. Die Straße ist ganz naß, *weil* es geregnet hat.
the.NOM street is all wet because it rained AUX
'The street is wet because it rained.'

b. Die Straße ist ganz naß, *denn* es hat geregnet. (same meaning)[9]

However, in other contexts the two words are not interchangeable. Only *denn* can be used to translate use-conditional functions of *because*. This includes both Sweetser's "epistemic" use, as in (29), and her "speech act" use, as in (30). *Weil* cannot be used in such sentences.

(29) a. Es hat geregnet, *denn* die Straße ist ganz naß.
it has rained because the.NOM street is all wet
'It was raining, because the street is wet.'

b. *Es hat geregnet, *weil* die Straße ganz naß ist.

(30) a. Ist vom Mittag noch etwas übrig? *Denn* ich habe schon wieder Hunger.
is from midday still anything left.over because 1SG have already again hunger
'Is there anything left over from lunch? Because I'm already hungry again.'

b. ?? Ist vom Mittag noch etwas übrig? *Weil* ich schon wieder Hunger habe.

There are structural differences between the two conjunctions as well: *weil* is a subordinating conjunction, whereas *denn* is a co-ordinating conjunction. The difference between subordination and co-ordination in German is clearly visible

[7] The material in this section is based almost entirely on the work of Tatjana Scheffler (2005; 2008), and all examples that are not otherwise attributed come from these works.

[8] http://answers.yahoo.com

[9] Scheffler (2008: §3.1)

due to differences in word order. In German main clauses, the auxiliary verb (or tensed main verb if there is no auxiliary) occupies the second position in the clause, as illustrated in (31a). In subordinate clauses, however, the auxiliary or tensed main verb occupies the final position in the clause, as illustrated in (31b).[10]

(31) a. Ich *habe* zwei Hunde gekauft.
1sg.nom have two dogs bought.ptcp
'I have bought two dogs.'

b. Sie sagt, daß er dieses Buch gelesen *hätte.*
3sg.f.nom says that 3sg.m.nom this.acc book read have.sbjv
'She says that he has read this book.'

Looking back at examples (27–28), we can see that the tensed verbs *war* 'was' and *hat* 'has' occur in second position following *denn* but in final position following *weil.* This contrast provides a clear indication that *weil* clauses are subordinate while *denn* clauses are co-ordinate. Further evidence that *weil* clauses are subordinate while *denn* clauses are co-ordinate comes from their syntactic behavior. First, *weil* clauses can be fronted but *denn* clauses cannot, as shown in (32). Second, *weil* clauses can stand alone as the answer to a *why*-question like that in (33), whereas *denn* clauses cannot. This is one of the classic tests for syntactic constituency. The contrast in (33) suggests that *weil* combines with the clause that it introduces to form a complete syntactic constituent, whereas *denn* does not. This is what we would expect if *weil* is a subordinating conjunction and *denn* is a co-ordinating conjunction.[11]

(32) a. *Weil* es geregnet hat, ist die Straße naß.
'Because it rained, the street is wet.'

b. **Denn* es hat geregnet, ist die Straße naß.

(33) a. Warum ist die Katze gesprungen?
why aux the.nom cat jumped
— *Weil* sie eine Maus sah.
— because she a mouse saw
'Why did the cat jump? — Because it saw a mouse.'

b. —**Denn* sie sah eine Maus.

[10] This is true for subordinate clauses which are introduced by a conjunction or complementizer. Where there is no conjunction or complementizer at the beginning of the subordinate clause, the auxiliary or tensed main verb occupies the second position.

[11] Notice that the tensed verb *sah* 'saw' occupies the final position in (33a).

In our earlier discussion we demonstrated that subordinate *because* clauses in English can be negated, questioned, or embedded within conditional clauses; whereas none of these things is possible with co-ordinate *because* clauses. Interestingly, a very similar pattern emerges in German. As illustrated in (34), *weil* clauses can be interpreted within the scope of main clause negation, whereas *denn* clauses cannot.

(34) a. Paul ist nicht zu spät gekommen, *weil* er den Bus verpaßt
Paul AUX NEG too late come because he the.ACC bus missed
hat. [Sondern er hatte noch zu tun.]
AUX rather he had still to do
'Paul wasn't late because he missed the bus. [But rather, because he still had work to do.]'

b. #Paul ist nicht zu spät gekommen, *denn* er hat den Bus verpaßt. [Sondern er hatte noch zu tun.]

Similarly, *weil* clauses in questions can be interpreted as part of what is being questioned, that is, within the scope of the interrogative force (35a). *Denn* clauses cannot be interpreted in this way, as shown in (35b).

(35) a. Wer kam zu spät, *weil* er den Bus verpaßt hat?
who came too late because he the bus missed has
'Who was late because he missed the bus?'

b. ?? Wer kam zu spät, *denn* er hat den Bus verpaßt?

Denn clauses cannot be embedded within a subordinate clause, whereas this is possible with *weil* clauses. Example (36) illustrates this contrast in a complement clause, and (37) in a conditional clause.

(36) a. Ich glaube nicht, daß Peter nach Hause geht, *weil* er
1SG believe NEG COMP Peter to home goes because he
Kopfschmerzen hat.
headache has
'I don't believe that Peter is going home because he has a headache.'

b. #Ich glaube nicht, daß Peter nach Hause geht, *denn* er hat Kopfschmerzen.

(37) a. Wenn Peter zu spät kam, *weil* er den Bus verpaßt hat, war es seine eigene Schuld.
'If Peter was late because he missed the bus, it was his own fault.'

b. #Wenn Peter zu spät kam, *denn* er hat den Bus verpaßt, war es seine eigene Schuld.

Scheffler (2008) points out that *denn* clauses are normally unacceptable if the content of the *because*-clause is evident or has been previously mentioned. This explains why only *weil* is possible in the mini-conversation in (38). This interesting observation suggests that *denn* clauses, because of their coordinate structure, count as independent assertions. As we noted in Chapter 3, in our discussion of entailments, asserting a fact which is already part of the common ground typically creates an unnatural redundancy.

(38) a. Es hat heute sehr geregnet.
it has today very rained
Ja, die ganze Straße steht unter Wasser, *weil* es geregnet hat.
yes the whole street stands under water because it rained has
'It rained a lot today.'
'Yes, the whole street is submerged under water because it rained.'

b. Es hat heute sehr geregnet.
#Ja, die ganze Straße steht unter Wasser, *denn* es hat geregnet.

A number of other languages also have two words for 'because', including Modern Greek, Dutch, and French.[12]

18.6 Conclusion

We have identified two basic uses of *because* in English: truth-conditional vs. use-conditional. These two uses can be distinguished using familiar tests for truth-conditional propositional content. First, truth-conditional *because* clauses can be part of what is negated or questioned when the sentence as a whole is negated or questioned, but this is not the case with use-conditional *because.* Second, truth-conditional *because* clauses can be embedded within *if* clauses, but use-conditional *because* clauses cannot. Third, the truth of a statement can be appropriately challenged based on the causal relationship expressed in a truth-conditional *because* clause, but not on that expressed in a use-conditional *because* clause.

We have also identified two different structural configurations in which *because* may occur: co-ordinate vs. subordinate. Diagnostics for distinguishing

[12] Pit (2003); Kitis (2006).

these two structures include the following: (i) Subordinate *because* clauses can be fronted, but co-ordinate *because* clauses cannot. (ii) Co-ordinate *because* clauses must be separated from the main clause by a pause (comma intonation), but this pause is not allowed before subordinate *because* clauses. (iii) Scope ambiguities involving negation, quantifiers, modals, or propositional attitude verbs are possible with subordinate *because* clauses, but not with co-ordinate *because* clauses.

We proposed the following structural constraint on the interpretation of *because*: the truth-conditional use of *because* may occur in either a subordinate or a co-ordinate clause, but the use-conditional interpretation is possible only in the co-ordinate structure. This same constraint holds in German as well, but in German the two structures are introduced by different conjunctions: *weil* for subordinate reason clauses, and *denn* for co-ordinate reason clauses.

Further reading

Sæbø (1991) and (2011: §3.3) provide a good overview of the semantics of causal connectives like *because*, and a comparison with other types of adverbial connectives. D. Lewis (1973a) and (2000) lay out two different versions of his counterfactual analysis of causation. Scheffler (2013: ch. 4) provides a detailed discussion of the syntax and semantics of the two German conjunctions meaning 'because'.

Discussion exercises

A: Explain the scopal ambiguity of the following sentences, and state the two readings in logical notation:

1. Arthur didn't marry Susan because she is rich.

Model answer

a. ¬CAUSE(RICH(s), MARRY(a,s))

b. CAUSE(RICH(s), ¬MARRY(a,s))

2. Mrs. Thatcher will not win because she is a woman. (spoken in 1979)

3. Tourists rarely visit Delhi because the food is so spicy.

4. I doubt that Peter is happy because he was fired.

B: Show how you could use some of the tests discussed in this chapter to determine whether the *because* clauses in the following examples contribute truth-conditional or use-conditional meaning:

1. Arthur works for the State Department, because he has a STATE.GOV e-mail address.

2. Oil prices are rising, because OPEC has agreed to cut production.

Homework exercises

In §18.2 we proposed the following analysis for the scopal ambiguity of sentence (2b): *Arthur didn't marry Susan because she is rich.*

i. ¬CAUSE(RICH(s), MARRY(a,s))

ii. CAUSE(RICH(s), ¬MARRY(a,s))

Provide a similar analysis showing the two possible readings for each of the following sentences. If you wish, you may write out the clauses in prose rather than using formal logic notation, e.g.: ¬CAUSE(*Susan is rich, Arthur marry Susan*).

1. Steve Jobs didn't start Apple because he loved technology.[a]
2. Arnold must have sold his Jaguar because I saw him driving a minivan.
3. Few Texans voted for Romney because he is a Mormon.
4. Susan believes that A.G. Bell was rich because he invented the telephone.

[a] https://www.fastcompany.com/3001441/do-steve-jobs-did-dont-follow-your-passion

19 Conditionals

Exactly what conditionals mean and how they come to mean what they mean is one of the oldest problems in natural language semantics. According to Sextus Empiricus, the Alexandrian poet Callimachus reported that the Greek philosophers' debate about the semantics of the little word if had gotten out of hand: 'Even the crows on the roof-tops are cawing about which conditionals are true'. (von Fintel 2011).

19.1 Conditionals and modals

A CONDITIONAL sentence is a bi-clausal structure of the form *if p (then) q*. The conjunction *if* seems to indicate that a certain kind of relationship holds between the meanings of the two clauses. However, as the passage quoted above demonstrates, the exact nature of this relationship has been a topic of controversy for thousands of years.

An intuitive description of the construction, suggested by the term CONDITIONAL, is that the *if* clause describes some condition under which the *then* clause is claimed to be true. For example, the conditional sentence in (1) claims that the proposition *you are my second cousin* is true under a certain condition, namely that Atatürk was your great-grandfather.

(1) If Atatürk was your great-grandfather, then you are my second cousin.

Much recent work on the meaning of conditional constructions builds on the similarities between conditionals and modals. The analysis of modality that we sketched in Chapter 16 treats modal operators as quantifiers over possible worlds: modals of necessity are universal quantifiers, while modals of possibility are existential quantifiers. The difference between epistemic vs. deontic or other types of modality is the result of restricting this quantification to specific kinds of worlds. For example, we analyzed epistemic *must* as meaning something like, "In all worlds which are consistent with what I know about the actual world, and in which the normal course of events is followed..."

Conditionals can also be analyzed in terms of possible worlds. One way of evaluating the truth of a conditional statement like (1) is to adopt the following procedure:[1] Add the content of the *if* clause to what is currently known about the actual world. Under those circumstances, would the *then* clause be true? We might suggest the following paraphrase for sentence (1): "In all possible worlds which are consistent with what I know about the actual world, and in which the normal course of events is followed, and in which Atatürk was your great-grandfather, you are my second cousin."

An adequate analysis needs to provide not only a reasonable paraphrase but also an explanation for how this meaning is derived compositionally, addressing questions like the following: What do the individual meanings of the two clauses contribute to the meaning of the sentence as a whole? What does *if* mean? These questions lead to some very complex issues, to which this chapter can provide only a brief introduction.

It will be easier to talk about conditional sentences if we introduce some standard terminology for referring to the parts of such sentences. We refer to the *if* clause as the ANTECEDENT (also known as the PROTASIS); and to the *then* clause as the CONSEQUENT (or APODOSIS). The names *antecedent* and *consequent* reflect the most basic ordering of these clauses (*if p, q*), not only in English but (apparently) in all languages.[2] But in many languages the opposite order (*q if p*) is possible as well. Regardless of which comes first in any particular sentence, the antecedent names the condition under which the consequent is claimed to be true.

One factor that makes the analysis of conditional sentences so challenging is that the conditional structure can be used for a variety of different functions, not only in English but in many other languages as well. We introduce the most common of these in §19.2. In §19.3 we focus on "standard" conditionals, i.e. those in which neither the antecedent nor the consequent is asserted or presupposed to be true. In many languages these conditionals may be marked by tense, mood, or other grammatical indicators to show the speaker's degree of confidence as to how likely the antecedent is to be true.

In §19.4 we will return to the question raised in Chapter 9 as to whether the meaning of English *if* can be adequately represented or defined in terms of the material implication operator (⟶) of propositional logic. We will see that, for a number of reasons, this does not seem to be possible. (Of course, that does not mean that the material implication operator is useless for doing natural language semantics; it is an indispensible part of the logical metalanguage. It just means that material implication does not provide a simple translation equivalent for English *if*.)

[1]This is a version of the "Ramsey Test" from Stalnaker (1968).
[2]Greenberg (1963: 84–85); Comrie (1986: 83).

We go on in §19.5 to discuss one very influential approach to defining the meaning of *if*, which takes it to be a marker of restriction for modals or other types of quantifiers. §19.6 discusses some of the special challenges posed by COUNTERFACTUAL conditionals, in which the antecedent is presupposed to be false. Finally, in §19.7 we argue for a distinction between truth-conditional vs. speech act conditionals, and provide some evidence for the claim that speech act conditionals are not part of the propositional content that is being asserted, questioned, etc.

19.2 Four uses of *if*

In this section we introduce the most commonly discussed functions of the conditional construction. As noted above, the STANDARD conditional, illustrated in (2), does not commit the speaker to believing either the antecedent or the consequent to be true, but does seem to commit the speaker to believing that some type of relation exists (often a causal relationship) between the two propositions. Most authors take this to be the most basic usage of *if*.

(2) STANDARD CONDITIONALS

a. If it does not rain, we will eat outside.
b. If the TV Guide is correct, there is a good documentary on PBS tonight.
c. There are biscuits on the sideboard if Bill has not moved them.
d. If you take another step, I'll knock you down.
e. If Mary's husband forgets their anniversary (again!), she will never forgive him.
f. If you see George, you should invite him to the party.

The sentences in (3) are examples of RELEVANCE CONDITIONALS, also known as "biscuit conditionals" because of the famous example listed here as (3a). When the consequent is a statement, as in (3a–d), the relevance conditional seems to commit the speaker to believing the consequent to be true, regardless of whether the antecedent is true or not.[3]

(3) RELEVANCE CONDITIONALS (a.k.a. "biscuit conditionals"):

a. There are biscuits on the sideboard if you want them. (Austin 1956)

[3] This claim has been challenged by some authors.

b. PBS will broadcast *Die Walküre* tonight, if you like Wagner.[4]

c. If I may say so, you do not look well.

d. He's not the sharpest knife in the drawer, if you know what I mean.

e. If you went to the office party, how did Susan look?

The replies in (4–5) illustrate FACTUAL CONDITIONALS.[5] Factual conditionals carry the presupposition that someone other than the speaker (often the addressee) believes or has said that the proposition expressed by the antecedent is true.

(4) A. This book that I was assigned to read is really stupid.
B. I haven't read it, but if it is that stupid you shouldn't bother with it.

(5) A. My boyfriend Joe is really smart.
B. Oh yeah? If he's so smart why isn't he rich?

The final type that we will mention is the CONCESSIVE CONDITIONAL, illustrated in (6). (Small caps are used here to indicate intonation peak.) A speaker who uses a concessive conditional asserts that the consequent is true no matter what, regardless of whether the antecedent is true or false. This is made explicit when, as is often the case, the antecedent is preceded by *even if*. Notice that the most basic order for concessive conditionals seems to be the opposite of that for standard conditionals, i.e., the consequent comes first. In order for the antecedent to be stated first, it must be marked by *even*, focal stress, or some other special marker.

(6) CONCESSIVE CONDITIONALS

a. I wouldn't marry you if you were the last man on EARTH.

b. (Even) if the bridge were STANDING I wouldn't cross. (Bennett 1982)

c. I'm going to finish this project (even) if it KILLS me.

We need to distinguish concessive conditional clauses from concessive adverbial clauses,[6] which can be marked with various conjunctions including *if*. Some examples of concessive adverbial clauses are presented in (7), and examples of concessive adverbial clauses with *if* in (8).[7] This kind of concessive construction

---

[4]Bennett (2003).

[5]These examples are adapted from Bhatt & Pancheva (2006: 671).

[6]Thompson et al. (2007).

[7]The examples in (8) come from LanguageLog: http://itre.cis.upenn.edu/~myl/languagelog/archives/000408.html

commits the speaker to believing that both the antecedent and the consequent are true.

(7) a. Even though the bridge is still standing, I won't cross it.
b. Although she loves him, she does not plan to marry him.
c. While no one has seen Bigfoot, few people here doubt its existence.

(8) a. It's all perfectly normal – if troublesome to varying degrees.
b. Virtual colon dissection is promising, if flawed.
c. It was fair and balanced if perhaps a little old.
d. Today hashing is a global, if little known, pursuit.
e. If Eskimos have dozens of words for snow, Germans have as many for bureaucracy. [*The Economist*, October 11th, 2003, p. 56, col. 2]
f. If Mozart was a life-long admirer of J. C. Bach, his views on Clementi were disparaging, to put it mildly.
[OED, citing 1969 *Listener* 24 Apr. 585/1]

The contrast in truth commitments mentioned above is illustrated in (9). The standard conditional in (9a) does not imply that the speaker believes either the antecedent or the consequent to be true, so denying the consequent does not lead to contradiction or anomaly. The concessive conditional in (9b) and the relevance conditional in (9c) both imply that the speaker believes the consequent to be true, regardless of the truth of the antecedent; so denying the consequent is a contradiction, as indicated by the #.

(9) a. I wouldn't marry Bill if he were a starving linguist; but as things stand I might end up marrying him (since he is a dentist). [STANDARD CONDITIONAL]
b. I wouldn't marry Bill if he were the last man on EARTH; #but I suppose I might end up marrying him. [CONCESSIVE CONDITIONAL]
c. If you really want to know, I would never marry Bill; #but I suppose I might end up marrying him. [RELEVANCE CONDITIONAL]

In the long history of the study of conditionals and their meanings, a variety of additional functions and gradations have been identified and named (often with multiple competing names for the same function, as we have already seen in the case of "relevance" or "biscuit" conditionals). §19.7 below provides some evidence for making a distinction between truth-conditional vs. speech act uses of the conditional form. This is of course the same distinction that we were led to in the previous chapter in our discussion of causation. We will argue that the standard conditionals in (2) involve a truth-conditional usage, whereas the relevance conditionals in (3) involve a speech act usage. The factual and concessive conditionals in (4–6) are harder to classify.

19.3 Degrees of hypotheticality

One widely discussed property of standard conditionals is that they can be used to express varying degrees of hypotheticality,[8] reflecting the speaker's judgment as to how likely it is that the antecedent is actually true. In languages where verbs are inflected for tense and/or mood, verbal morphology is often used to signal these distinctions. However, other kinds of marking are also found, as illustrated below; and in some languages this distinction is not grammatically marked at all, but is determined entirely by contextual clues.

As a number of authors have noted, there is a cross-linguistic tendency for the antecedent to be interpreted as more hypothetical (less certain) when it is stated in the past tense than in present tense. However, tense marking also serves to indicate the actual time frame of the described event. (See Chapter 21 for a detailed discussion of tense marking.) For this reason, there is generally no one-to-one correlation between tense and degree of hypotheticality. Some English examples are presented in (10–12).

(10)
a. If Bill *is* your uncle, then you must know his daughter Margaret.
b. If David *was* your thesis advisor, then he knows your work pretty well.
c. If Susan *wins* the election, she will become the mayor of Des Moines.
d. Results have not yet been announced, but if Susan *won* the election, the current mayor will have to find a new job.
e. "It would make it more important if that *be* the case," he [Ralph Nader] said yesterday.[9]

In the indicative mood, either present or past tense can be used when the speaker has reason to believe that the antecedent is true, as illustrated in (10a–b). Such examples are sometimes referred to as REALITY conditionals.[10] These

[8] See for example Comrie (1986); Thompson et al. (2007).
[9] New York Daily News, 5 February 2007; cited in Gomes (2008).
[10] Thompson et al. (2007).

same two verb forms can also be used in HYPOTHETICAL conditionals, those in which the speaker simply doesn't know whether the antecedent is true or not, as illustrated in (10c–d). In these examples, the tense marking of the verb in the antecedent functions in the normal way, to indicate the location in time of the situation described by that clause. The subjunctive mood can be used for hypothetical conditionals as well, as illustrated in (10e). However, it is not always easy to recognize the subjunctive in English. The past indicative and past subjunctive are distinguished in Modern English only for the verb *to be*, as illustrated in (11a).[11]

COUNTERFACTUAL conditionals, which normally presuppose that the speaker believes the antecedent to be false, tend to be expressed in the subjunctive as seen in (11–12). Example (11a) demonstrates the preference for the subjunctive over the past indicative in counterfactual conditionals, although many speakers will use or at least accept the past indicative in casual speech.

(11) a. If I *were/?was* you, I would apply for a different job.
b. If I *had been* your thesis advisor, you would have been lucky to finish at all.

(12) "Sir, if you *were* my husband, I would poison your drink."
"Madam, if you *were* my wife, I would drink it."
(Exchange between Lady Astor and Winston Churchill)

Comrie (1986) argues that the degrees of hypotheticality associated with conditionals are not limited to three discrete categories, but rather form a continuum from most certain (reality conditionals) to most doubtful (counterfactuals). The examples in (13) lend some support to this claim, at least for English. All three of these examples can be interpreted as hypothetical conditionals referring to a present situation, i.e., the state of the world at the time of speaking; none of them requires that the speaker know whether the antecedent is true or not. However, the past indicative in (13b) seems more doubtful than the present indicative in (13a), and the subjunctive mood in (13c) seems more doubtful than the indicative mood in (13b).[12] In the same way, both (14a) and (14b) can be interpreted as hypothetical conditionals, but (14b) expresses more doubt than (14a). Notice

[11] The present subjunctive is identical to the bare infinitive form. It is archaic in conditionals, though still used occasionally in formal registers as in (10e), but preserved in other uses, including optatives (*God bless you; long live the King*).

[12] Without any additional context, the subjunctive conditional in (13c) would most likely be interpreted as a counterfactual; but given the right context, the hypothetical reading is certainly possible as well.

that in (14b), the tense marking of the antecedent does not reflect the time of the described situation, but is used to mark a high degree of hypotheticality.

(13) a. If Alice *is* a spy, she probably carries a gun.
b. If Alice *was* a spy, she would probably carry a gun.
c. If Alice *were* a spy, she would probably carry a gun.

(14) a. If Arthur still *loves* her, he will catch the first train home.
b. If Arthur still *loved* her, he would catch the first train home.

These examples show that, in English conditional clauses, tense and mood morphology have partly overlapping functions. Both past tense and subjunctive mood can serve to make the antecedent seem less likely. Similar patterns are found in other languages as well.

The use of tense and mood in Portuguese conditionals is illustrated in (15).[13] Example (15a) is what we have called a reality conditional, (15b) is a hypothetical conditional, and (15c) is a counterfactual conditional. Notice that the difference between the hypothetical and counterfactual conditionals is formally a difference in tense inflection, rather than mood, on the antecedent verb. Notice too the "conditional mood" form of the verb in the consequent of (15c). A number of Romance languages have such forms, which occur in the consequent of counterfactual conditionals and typically have several other uses as well (e.g. "future in the past" tense; see Chapter 21).

(15) a. Se ela é italiana, ela é européia.
if she is Italian she is European
'If/since she is Italian she is European.' (I know that she is Italian.)
b. Se ela for italiana, ela é européia.
if she be.3sg.FUT.SBJV Italian she is European
'If she be Italian she is European.' (I do not know whether she is Italian or not.)
c. Se ela fosse italiana, ela seria européia.
if she be.3sg.IPFV.SBJV Italian she would.be.COND European
'If she were Italian she would be European.' (I know that she is not Italian.)

[13] Examples from Gomes (2008).

In Russian counterfactual conditionals, both the antecedent and consequent appear in the subjunctive-conditional mood (16b), in contrast to the indicative mood used in hypothetical conditionals (16a):[14]

(16) a. Esli ja pribudu na vokzal, menja posadjat v tjur'mu.
if I arrive.IND at station me put.IND in prison
'If I arrive at the station, they will throw me in prison.'

b. Esli by ja pribyl na vokzal, menja by posadili v tjur'mu.
if COND I arrive.COND at station me COND put.COND in prison
'If I had shown up at the station, they would have thrown me in prison.'

The contrast between hypothetical vs. counterfactual conditionals can also be marked in other ways. Irish has two distinct words for 'if': *dá* is used in counterfactual conditionals (17a), while *má* is used in hypothetical conditionals (17b).[15] A similar situation is reported in Welsh and some varieties of Arabic.

(17) a. Dá leanfadh sé dá chúrsa, bheadh deireadh leis.
if follow.COND he of.his course be.COND end with.him
'If he had persisted in his course, he'd have been finished.'

b. Má leanann tú de do chúrsa, beidh aithreachas ort.
if follow.PRES you of your course be.FUT regret on.you
'If you persist in your (present) course, you'll be sorry.'

In Tolkapaya (also known as Western Yavapai), a Yuman language of North America, counterfactuals are distinguished from other kinds of conditionals by the suffix *–th* attaching to the auxiliary of the consequent clause (Hardy & Gordon 1980). In other (non-conditional) contexts, this suffix is used to mark "non-factual" propositions, including "failed attempts, unfulfilled desires, descriptions of a state that formerly obtained but which no longer does, and situations where the realization of one event precludes that of another" (Hardy & Gordon 1980: 191).

A very similar case is found in Kimaragang Dusun, spoken in northeastern Borneo (Kroeger 2017). The frustrative particle *dara* appears in main clauses which express failed attempts, unfulfilled desires or intentions, former states

[14] These examples are from Chung & Timberlake (1985: 251), who use the term IRREALIS mood for what I have called the subjunctive-conditional mood.

[15] McCloskey (2001).

that no longer obtain, and things done in vain. This same particle appears in the consequent clause of counterfactual conditionals, as seen in (18), distinguishing counterfactuals from other types of conditionals like those in (19). Notice that non-past tense is used in the consequent of a counterfactual even if the situation which failed to materialize would have been prior to the time of speaking, as in (18b).

(18) a. Ong noguring no koniab ino, atanaman
if plowed.POTENT.PST already yesterday that planted.POTENT.NPST
no do paray benoy *dara.*
already ACC rice today FRUS
'If that (field) had been plowed yesterday, it could have been planted with rice today.'

b. Amu *dara* agamit i kambing ong konoko
NEG FRUS caught.POTENT.NPST NOM goat if not
ginipit sid susut.
trapped.PST LOC below
'The goat could not have been caught if we hadn't trapped it under the house.'

(19) a. Ong amu nu ibaray ino siin dino, mangan tekaw posutay.
if NEG you pay that money that AUX I.you cane
'If you don't pay that money I'll cane you.'

b. Kaanak=i' dati yalo dilo' ong sumambat do=duktur.
able.to.bear.child=EMPH PROB 3SG that if meet ACC=doctor
'She could probably have children if she goes to the doctor.'

Some languages do not mark the degree of hypotheticality at all, at least not in their most common conditional sentence patterns. In these languages, a single sentence can be ambiguous between the reality, hypothetical, and counterfactual conditional readings; the intended meaning must be determined from context. For example, the Japanese sentence in (20) could be interpreted either as a hypothetical conditional (expressing the hope of a father whose son is missing in action), or as a counterfactual conditional (expressing the sorrow of a father whose son has been killed). Comrie (1986) mentions Mandarin and Indonesian as examples of other languages where a similar ambiguity is normal.

(20) Musuko=ga ikite i-tara, ii noni naa!
son=NOM alive be-if good though EXCLAM
'If my son is alive, I'll be so happy.'
or: 'If my son were alive, I would be so happy.'[16]

To sum up, counterfactual conditionals get distinctive marking in many languages, but not in all languages. Now let us return to the fundamental question raised in §19.1: what does *if* mean?

19.4 English *if* vs. material implication

In Chapter 9 we presented evidence in support of Grice's analysis of the English words *and* and *or.* Grice suggested that the lexical semantic content of these words is actually equivalent to their logical counterparts (∧ and ∨), and that apparent differences in meaning are best understood as conversational implicatures. This approach seems to work fairly well for those two words; could a similar approach work for English *if*? Grice argued that it could, specifically proposing that the lexical semantic content of English *if* is equivalent to the material implication operator (⟶). However, there are a number of reasons to believe that this approach will not work for *if.*

First, if *if* really means material implication, then the truth table for material implication predicts that the sentences in (21) should all be true. (Recall that $p \longrightarrow q$ is only false when p is true and q is false.) However, this does not match our intuitions about these sentences; most English speakers are very reluctant to call any of them true.

(21) a. If Socrates was a woman then $1 + 1 = 3$.[17]
b. If the Amazon flows through Paris then triangles have three sides.
c. If the Chinese invented gunpowder then Martin Luther was German.

What makes these sentences seem so odd is that there is no relationship between the antecedent and consequent. Whatever *if* means, it seems to require that some such relationship be present. Grice argued that this inference of relationship between antecedent and consequent is only a conversational implicature. Several other authors have also proposed that the semantic content of *if* is simply material implication, and that the apparent differences between the

[16] Akatsuka (1985: 627).
[17] http://en.wikipedia.org/wiki/Material_conditional

two are pragmatic rather than semantic in nature. Other authors have tried to account for the requirement of relationship between antecedent and consequent by suggesting that *if p then q* expresses the claim that $p \longrightarrow q$ is true in all possible worlds, i.e., under any imaginable circumstances.[18] But any attempt to derive the meaning of *if* from material implication must deal with a number of problems.

As discussed in Chapter 4, the meaning of the material implication operator is entirely defined by its truth table. We need to know the truth values for both p and q (but nothing else) before we can determine the truth value for $p \longrightarrow q$. But this does not match our judgments about the truth of English conditionals. It would be entirely possible for a competent native speaker to believe that sentence (22) is true without knowing whether either of the two clauses alone expresses a true proposition. What is being asserted in (22) is not a specific combination of truth values, but a relationship between the meanings of the clauses.[19]

(22) If this test result is accurate, your son has TB.

This point is further demonstrated by the fact that, in addition to statements, questions and commands may also appear as the consequent clause of a conditional, as illustrated in (23). This is significant because questions and commands cannot be assigned a truth value.

(23) a. If you are offered a fellowship, will you accept it?
b. If you want to pass phonetics, memorize the IPA chart!

Finally, as we will argue in more detail below, the antecedent in a speech act conditional like (24) does not specify conditions under which the consequent is true, but rather conditions under which the speech act performed by the consequent may be felicitous.[20]

(24) a. If you have a pen, may I please borrow it?
b. If you want my advice, don't invite George to the party!
c. If I may say so, you do not look well.

[18] C. I. Lewis (1918), cited in von Fintel (2011).

[19] The material in this paragraph and the next are based on observations made by Podlesskaya (2001).

[20] In order to account for such examples under the assumption that *if* is equivalent to the material implication operator, we could interpret them as conditional speech acts; so (24c) would have an interpretation something like: "If I am permitted to say so, then I hereby assert that you do not look well." But in fact someone who says (24c) seems to be asserting the consequent unconditionally; it is only the felicity of the assertion that is conditional.

Even if we focus only on truth values, the logical properties of $\longrightarrow$ make predictions which do not seem to hold true for English *if*. For example, it is easy to show (from the truth table for $\longrightarrow$) that $\neg(p\rightarrow q)$ logically entails p. So if the semantic value of *if* is material implication, anyone who believes that (25a) is false is committed to believing that (25b) is true. However, it does not seem to be logically inconsistent for a speaker to believe both statements to be false.

(25) a. If I win the National Lottery, I will be happy for the rest of my life.
b. I will win the National Lottery.

Counterfactuals raise a number of special problems for the material implication analysis. We will mention here just one famous example, shown in (26).[21] It is easy to show that $p\rightarrow q$ logically implies $(p\wedge r) \longrightarrow q$. So if the semantic value of *if* is material implication, anyone who believes that (26a) is true should be committed to believing that (26b) is true. However, it does not seem to be logically inconsistent for a speaker to believe the first statement to be true while believing the second to be false.

(26) a. If kangaroos had no tails, they would topple over.
b. If kangaroos had no tails and they used crutches, they would topple over.

Many other similar examples have been pointed out, and various solutions have been proposed.[22] As we noted in §19.1 above, even if material implication is not logically equivalent to English *if*, that does not mean that it is irrelevant to natural language semantics. It will always be an important part of the logical metalanguage that semanticists use. But in view of the many significant differences between material implication and English *if*, it seems reasonable to look for some other way of capturing the meaning of *if*.

19.5 *If* as a restrictor

A radically different approach to defining the meaning of *if* was proposed by Kratzer (1986), based on a suggestion by D. Lewis (1975). As we mentioned in Chapter 14, Lewis analyzes adverbs like *always, sometimes, usually, never*, etc. as "unselective quantifiers", because they can quantify over various kinds of things.

[21] This example comes from D. Lewis (1973b).
[22] See Von Fintel (2011) for a good summary; see also Gazdar (1979: 83–87); Bennett (2003: ch2–3).

He points out that conditional clauses can be used to specify the situations, entities, or units of time which are being quantified over, as illustrated in (27). However, it is difficult to say exactly what the *if* means in such examples.

(27) a. If it is sunny, we *always/usually/rarely/sometimes/never* play soccer.[23]
always: $\forall_d$ [SUNNY(d) $\longrightarrow$ (we play soccer on d)]
sometimes: $\exists_d$ [SUNNY(d) $\wedge$ (we play soccer on d)]
usually: ???

b. If a man wins the lottery, he *always/usually/rarely/sometimes/never* dies happy.
always: $\forall_x$ [(MAN(x) $\wedge$ WIN(x,lottery)) $\longrightarrow$ DIE_HAPPY(x)]
sometimes: $\exists_x$ [MAN(x) $\wedge$ WIN(x,lottery) $\wedge$ DIE_HAPPY(x)]
usually: ???

Example (27a) is a standard conditional whose antecedent expresses the proposition SUNNY(d), using *d* as a variable for days. The adverbs *always, sometimes,* etc, specify the quantifier part of the meaning. The word *if* seems to name the relation between the antecedent and the consequent; but with *always* this relation is expressed by $\longrightarrow$, with *sometimes* the relation is expressed by $\wedge$, and with adverbs like *usually* and *rarely* there is no way to express the relation in standard logical form. A similar problem arises in (27b). What these examples show is that we cannot identify any consistent contribution of the word *if* to the meaning of the sentence in this construction.

Using the restricted quantifier notation allows us to give a uniform analysis for such sentences, regardless of which adverb is used. As shown in (28), the antecedent of the conditional clause contributes material to the restriction on the quantifier, and the consequent specifies the material in the scope of the quantifier. But notice that there is no element of meaning in these expressions corresponding to the word *if.* Lewis concludes that in this construction, *if* "has no meaning apart from the adverb it restricts."

(28) If a man wins the lottery, he *always/usually/rarely/sometimes/never* dies happy.
always: [*all* x: MAN(x) $\wedge$ WIN(x,lottery)] DIE_HAPPY(x)
sometimes: [*some* x: MAN(x) $\wedge$ WIN(x,lottery)] DIE_HAPPY(x)
usually: [*most* x: MAN(x) $\wedge$ WIN(x,lottery)] DIE_HAPPY(x)
rarely: [*few* x: MAN(x) $\wedge$ WIN(x,lottery)] DIE_HAPPY(x)
never: [*no* x: MAN(x) $\wedge$ WIN(x,lottery)] DIE_HAPPY(x)

[23] D. Lewis (1975).

Kratzer (1986) proposed that Lewis's analysis could be extended to all indicative (i.e., non-counterfactual) standard conditionals. If the conditional sentence contains a quantifier-like element in the consequent, the word *if* serves only as a grammatical marker introducing material that contributes to the restriction on the quantifier. This is illustrated in (29) for normal quantifier phrases, and in (30) for epistemic and deontic modality.

(29) a. *Every student will succeed if he works hard.*
[*all* x: STUDENT(x) ∧ WORK_HARD(x)] SUCCEED(x)
b. *No student will succeed if he goofs off.*
[*no* x: STUDENT(x) ∧ GOOF_OFF(x)] SUCCEED(x)

(30) a. *If John did not come to work, he must be sick.* [epistemic necessity]
[*all* w: (w is consistent with what I know about the actual world) ∧ (the normal course of events is followed as closely as possible in w) ∧ (John did not come to work in w)] SICK(j) in w
b. *If John did not come to work, he must be fired.* [deontic necessity]
[*all* w: (the relevant circumstances of the actual world are also true in w) ∧ (the relevant authority's requirements are satisfied as completely as possible in w) ∧ (John did not come to work in w)] FIRED(j) in w

Kratzer suggests that when a conditional sentence does not contain an overt quantifier-like element, the presence of *if* leads the hearer to assume a default quantifier. In some contexts, this default element would be epistemic necessity, as in (31a). In other contexts, the default element could be generic frequency, as in (31b).[24]

(31) a. *If John left at noon, he's home by now.* [implied: epistemic necessity]
[*all* w: (w is consistent with what I know about the actual world) ∧ (the normal course of events is followed as closely as possible in w) ∧ (John left at noon in w)] HOME(j) in w (by time of speaking)
b. *If John leaves work on time, he has dinner with his family.* [implied: generic frequency]
[*all* d: (d is a day) ∧ (John leaves work on time in d)] John has dinner with his family in d

[24] Examples from Von Fintel (2011). As we will see in Chapter 21, the English simple present tense has special properties which explain the generic frequency interpretation of examples like (31b).

Kratzer (1986: 11) summarizes her proposal as follows:

> The history of the conditional is the story of a syntactic mistake. There is no two-place *if* ... *then* connective in the logical forms for natural languages. *If*-clauses are devices for restricting the domains of various operators. Whenever there is no explicit operator, we have to posit one.

Her point is that the conditional meaning, the sense of relationship between antecedent and consequent, is not encoded by the word *if*. Rather, it comes from the structure of the quantification itself. The function of *if* is to mark certain material (the antecedent) as belonging to the restriction rather than the scope of the quantifier.

The proposal that *if* "does not carry any distinctive conditional meaning"[25] may get some support from the observation that conditional readings can arise in sentences where two clauses are simply juxtaposed without any marker at all, as seen in (32–33).

(32) Examples of juxtaposed conditionals from LanguageLog:[26]

a. "Listen," Renda said, "*we get to a phone we're out of the country before morning.*"

b. "He could have been a little rusty early on, and then the inning he gave up four runs I think he kind of lost his composure a little bit," Orioles manager Sam Perlozzo said. "*He just did a little damage control in that situation, we're OK.*"[27]

(33) INIGO: We're really in a terrible rush.
MIRACLE MAX: Don't rush me, sonny.
You rush a miracle man, you get rotten miracles.[28]

19.6 Counterfactual conditionals

The Lewis-Kratzer proposal provides a great deal of help in understanding how the meaning of a conditional sentence is compositionally derived. However, determining the right meanings for certain types of conditionals is still a significant challenge.[29] Counterfactuals are an especially challenging case. Consider

[25] Von Fintel (2011).

[26] http://itre.cis.upenn.edu/~myl/languagelog/archives/004521.html

[27] AP Recap of Toronto-Baltimore game of May 22, 2007; David Ginsburg, AP Sports Writer.

[28] From the 1987 movie *The Princess Bride*.

[29] This section draws heavily on von Fintel (2012).

the contrast between the hypothetical conditional in (34a) and the counterfactual conditional in (34b).[30]

(34) a. If Shakespeare did not write *Hamlet*, someone else did.
b. If Shakespeare had not written *Hamlet*, someone else would have.[31]

Most English speakers would probably agree that the hypothetical conditional in (34a) is true, but would probably judge the counterfactual conditional in (34b) to be false. This contrast suggests that some different rule of interpretation must apply to counterfactual conditionals. We have said that a counterfactual conditional presupposes that the antecedent is false; but this by itself is not sufficient to cause sentence (34b) as a whole to be regarded as false. Notice that even a speaker who believes the antecedent in (34a) to be false, i.e., who believes that Shakespeare did write *Hamlet*, would probably judge the sentence as a whole to be true.

Ideally we would like to apply the same analysis of *if* to both types of conditionals, but this would make it hard to explain why the two sentences in (34), which are structurally very similar have different truth conditions. What makes the counterfactual conditional in (34b) so odd is that it seems to imply that there is (or was) something about our world which made the writing of *Hamlet* inevitable. The hypothetical conditional in (34a) carries no such inference. How can we account for this difference?

In the preceding section we sketched out a procedure for interpreting conditionals that do not contain an overt quantifier. In many contexts, an epistemic necessity modal has to be assumed in order to arrive at the intended interpretation. The truth conditions of the sentence are calculated by adding the content of the antecedent to what is known about the actual world in order to derive the appropriate restriction on the set of possible worlds. This procedure yields an interpretation something like (35) for the hypothetical conditional in (34a). Intuitively, this feels like a reasonable interpretation. Part of what we know about the world is that plays do not grow on trees, so if a play such as *Hamlet* exists (another part of what we know about the actual world), then someone must have written it.

[30] Counterfactual and hypothetical conditionals are often referred to as "subjunctive" and "indicative" conditionals, respectively; but as we noted in §19.3, there is not always a perfect correlation between verb morphology and the degree of hypotheticality.

[31] These examples come from Morton (2004).

(35) [*all* w: (w is consistent with the available evidence) ∧ (the normal course of events is followed as closely as possible in w) ∧ (Shakespeare did not write *Hamlet* in w)] someone else wrote *Hamlet* in w

With the counterfactual conditional in (34b), the process is more complex. We cannot simply add the content of the antecedent to what is known about the actual world, because the antecedent is assumed to be false in the actual world. One approach is to quantify over those possible worlds in which the antecedent is true, but which are otherwise as similar as possible to the actual world. Roughly speaking, (34b) could be paraphrased as follows: "For all worlds w in which Shakespeare did not write *Hamlet*, but which are otherwise as similar as possible to the actual world *in the relevant ways*: someone else wrote *Hamlet* in w." Of course, the success of such an analysis depends on how one determines the relevant points of similarity that need to be considered.

This general approach can help explain why the counterfactual conditionals in (26a–b), repeated here as (36a–b), have different truth conditions. Sentence (36a) restricts the domain of quantification to worlds which are as similar as possible to the actual world, aside from the stipulation that kangaroos have no tails. In these worlds presumably kangaroos do not use crutches, since that would constitute an extra unforced difference as compared to the actual world. Sentence (36b) however adds the additional stipulation that kangaroos do use crutches in all the relevant worlds. For this reason, kangaroos would be more likely to topple over in the worlds relevant to evaluating (36a) than in those relevant to evaluating (36b).

(36) a. If kangaroos had no tails, they would topple over.
b. If kangaroos had no tails and they used crutches, they would topple over.

Now the phrase "as similar as possible" is admittedly vague, and it is reasonable to wonder whether using this criterion to restrict the domain of quantification will be very helpful in determining the meaning of a sentence. However, some authors have argued that the vagueness and context-dependence of the term are in fact good things, because counterfactuals themselves are somewhat vague, and the correct interpretation depends heavily on context.[32] Consider the following examples from Quine (1960: 221):

(37) a. If Caesar were in command, he would use the atom bomb.

[32] D. Lewis (1973b: 91ff); von Fintel (2012).

b. If Caesar were in command, he would use catapults.

A given feature of the real world may be given more or less priority in determining relative closeness between two worlds depending on various contextual factors, including the purposes of the speaker. In (37a), for example, Caesar's ruthless nature may outrank his historical setting, but in (37b) the technological resources of his era are given higher priority. The speaker's purpose plays an important role in determining which ordering source should be applied in each case. Quine (1960: 221) expresses this principle in the following words:

> The subjunctive [= counterfactual; PK] conditional depends, like indirect quotation and more so, on a dramatic projection: we feign belief in the antecedent and see how convincing we then find the consequent. What traits of the real world to suppose preserved in the feigned world of the contrary-to-fact antecedent can only be guessed from a sympathetic sense of the fabulist's likely purpose in spinning his fable.

The pair of sentences in (34) above is quite similar to the famous pair in (38). Once again, the hypothetical conditional in (38a) seems to be true, while most people would probably judge the counterfactual conditional in (38b) to be false. However, the historical facts in this case are still somewhat controversial and poorly understood, which makes it difficult to decide which points of comparison would be relevant for determining the "most similar" possible worlds.

(38) a. If Oswald didn't kill Kennedy, someone else did.
b. If Oswald hadn't killed Kennedy, someone else would have.[33]

Consider instead the counterfactual conditional in (39). While not everyone would consider this sentence to be true, it at least makes a claim that a historian could consider as a serious hypothesis:

(39) If John Wilkes Booth hadn't killed Abraham Lincoln, someone else would have.

What claim does (39) make? Based on our discussion above, this sentence could be paraphrased roughly as follows: "For all worlds w in which Booth did not kill Lincoln, but which are otherwise as similar as possible to the actual world in the relevant ways: someone else killed Lincoln in w." In this context, relevant points of similarity to the real world on April 14, 1865 (the night when Lincoln was shot) might include the following:

[33] These examples come from Adams (1970).

- The on-going civil war: Gen. Lee's army had surrendered in Virginia on April 9, 1865 but fighting continued for a few more months to the south and west;
- The location of the capital city, Washington DC, on the border between a Confederate state (Virginia) and a nominally Union state (Maryland) where many residents (including Booth) were pro-slavery and sympathetic to the Confederacy;
- The lax provisions in place for protecting the President during that era;
- The anger aroused among supporters of slavery by Abraham Lincoln's speech of April 11, 1865, in which he announced his intention to extend voting rights to at least some African-Americans, including those who had fought for the Union.

By asserting that Lincoln's assassination would take place in *any* world which shares these properties (and perhaps others) with the real world, sentence (39) seems to imply that the assassination was inevitable.

There is much more to be said about counterfactuals, but further discussion would be beyond the scope of the present book. We turn now to another use of the conditional sentence pattern, which we will argue contributes use-conditional rather than truth-conditional meaning.

19.7 Speech Act conditionals

Relevance conditionals are often referred to as SPEECH ACT CONDITIONALS, and in this section we try to understand why this label is appropriate. Let us begin by considering how a relevance conditional is used. As we noted in §19.2, relevance conditionals like those in (40) commit the speaker to believing that the consequent is true; and this raises the question of why a speaker who believes *q* would choose to say *if p then q* rather than just *q*?

(40) a. If you are hungry, there's some pizza in the fridge.
 b. If you need anything, my name is Arnold.
 c. I am planning to watch Brazil vs. Argentina tonight, if you are interested.
 d. You look like you need to sit down, if you don't mind my saying so.

One important function of the *if* clause in such cases is to prevent unintended implicatures from arising and/or guide the hearer toward the intended implicature.[34] If the speaker in (40a) simply announces *There's some pizza in the fridge*, in a context where the topic of conversation is something other than left-over food, the comment will seem irrelevant. This could lead the hearer, who assumes that the speaker is observing the Maxim of Relevance (see Chapter 8), to seek an implicature which renders the statement relevant. But the context may not be adequate for the hearer to succeed in this attempt. (Was I supposed to clean the fridge? Is this fridge only supposed to be used for bio-medical supplies?) The conditional clause functions first as a relevance hedge, warning the hearer that the statement which follows may not be relevant if certain conditions do not hold. The conditional clause also serves to guide the hearer toward the intended implicature: in this example, the statement *There's some pizza in the fridge* is intended as an indirect speech act, specifically an offer or invitation to have something to eat.

Similarly, the *if* clause in (40b) helps the hearer to correctly interpret the assertion in the consequent as an offer to be of service, rather than (for example) an initiation of mutual introductions. The *if* clause in (40c) helps the hearer to correctly interpret the consequent as an invitation to watch a soccer match.

The term RELEVANCE CONDITIONAL reflects what is perhaps the most common function of the *if* clause in this construction, namely to specify the conditions under which the assertion in the consequent will be relevant. Now relevance is one of the felicity conditions for making an assertion; so the conditional clause is used by the speaker to avoid making an infelicitous assertion. The *if* clause in (49d) (*if you don't mind my saying so*) functions as a politeness hedge, rather than a relevance hedge; but the basic function is again to avoid making an infelicitous assertion.

An important feature of relevance conditionals is that the consequent need not be an assertion at all; other speech acts are possible as well. The examples below show that the consequent of a relevance conditional may be a command (41a) or a question (41b–c).

(41) a. If you want my advice, ask her to marry you right away.
b. If you have heard from Michael recently, how is he doing?
c. What did you do with that left-over pizza, if you don't mind my asking?

[34] DeRose & Grandy (1999); Franke (2007).

Once again, the *if* clause in such examples refers to the felicity conditions for performing the speech act expressed by the consequent. One of the felicity conditions for asking a question is that the speaker believes that the hearer has access to the information being requested. The *if* clause in (41b) specifies a condition under which it is reasonable to expect that the addressee will know something about Michael's current situation. The *if* clauses in (41a, c) seem to address the preparatory conditions for commands and questions, respectively, which include the relationship between speaker and hearer, and the degree to which the speaker feels free to advise or ask the hearer on a particular topic.

In view of the fact that this construction can be used to hedge a variety of felicity conditions, and not just relevance, the more general term SPEECH ACT CONDITIONALS seems quite appropriate. This label also suggests that these conditional clauses may function as speech act modifiers, similar to the speech act adverbials we discussed in Chapter 11. This hypothesis is supported by the fact that the conditional relation between the two clauses can be questioned with standard conditionals, but not with speech act conditionals.

There is an important difference between relevance conditionals that contain questions, like that in (42b), vs. "questions about conditionals", illustrated in (42a).[35]

(42) a. Q: If you inherit, will you invest?
A: Yes, if I inherit, I will invest.

b. Q: If you saw John, did you talk to him?
A: Yes, I talked to him.
A: #Yes, if I saw John, I talked to him.

In questions about conditionals (i.e., a standard conditional within an interrogative sentence), the conditional meaning is part of what is being questioned. Therefore it is natural and appropriate to include the conditional clause in the answer, as seen in (42a). In a speech act conditional that contains a question, however, the conditional meaning is not part of what is being questioned. Rather, the *if* clause specifies a condition under which it would be appropriate or felicitous to ask the question. Therefore it is not appropriate to include the conditional clause in the answer, as in (42b), except perhaps as a somewhat annoying joke. This contrast suggests that speech act conditionals function as illocutionary modifiers, rather than as part of the at-issue propositional content of the sentence.

Several syntactic differences have been noted between speech act conditionals

[35]This point is made by van der Auwera (1986), which is also the source of the examples in (42).

and standard conditionals.[36] First, speech act conditionals can only be embedded in the complements of indirect speech verbs, and not under propositional attitude verbs (43). Both kinds of embedding are possible for standard conditionals (44).

(43) a. John said that if you are thirsty there is beer in the fridge.
b. * John believes that if you are thirsty there is beer in the fridge.

(44) a. John said that if he drinks too much wine he gets dizzy.
b. John believes that if he drinks too much wine he gets dizzy.

Second, standard conditionals allow the consequent to be introduced with the pro-form *then* (45), but speech act conditionals do not (46).

(45) a. If it does not rain, then we will eat outside.
b. If I see him again, then I will invite him.

(46) a. #If I may be honest, then you are not looking good.
b. #If you want to know, then 4 isn't a prime number.
c. #If you are thirsty, then there is beer in the fridge.

Third, the word order in Dutch and German seems to indicate that standard conditionals occupy a different structural position from speech act conditionals. As we mentioned in Chapter 18, Dutch and German are "verb-second" (V2) languages. This means that in main clauses (or, more generally, clauses not introduced by a complementizer), the inflected verb or auxiliary must immediately follow the first constituent of the clause. As the Dutch examples in (47–48) show,[37] standard conditionals occupy the clause-initial position, causing the inflected verb to immediately follow the conditional clause. However, this is not the case with speech act conditionals. The fact that the main clause subject in (48) must precede the verb indicates that the conditional clause is not a constituent of the main clause at all; it attaches to some higher node in the sentence.

(47) a. [Als Jan weg-gaat] ga ik ook weg.
if John away-goes go I also away
'If John goes away, I will go away too.' [STANDARD CONDITIONAL]
b. *[Als Jan weggaat] ik ga ook weg.

[36] Bhatt & Pancheva (2006).
[37] Examples (47–48) are originally from Iatridou (1991: ch. 2).

(48) a. [Als je het wil weten] 4 is geen priem getal.
if you it want know 4 is no prime number
'If you want to know, 4 is not a prime number.'
[SPEECH ACT CONDITIONAL]

b. *[Als je het wil weten] is 4 geen priem getal.

The minimal pair in (49) shows how word order can disambiguate standard conditionals vs. speech act conditionals in German.[38] The main clause verb in (49a) immediately follows the conditional clause, forcing it to be interpreted as a standard conditional: *I will stay home only if you need me.* In contrast, the main clause verb in (49b) follows its subject NP, forcing it to be interpreted as a speech act conditional: *I'll be at home all day and you can reach me there if you need me.* Again, the word order facts indicate that the standard conditional is embedded within the main clause, whereas the speech act conditional is not.

(49) a. [Wenn Du mich brauchst], bleibe ich den ganzen Tag zu Hause.
if you me need stay I the whole day at house
'[If you need me], (only then) I will stay at home all day.'
[STANDARD CONDITIONAL]

b. [Wenn Du mich brauchst], ich bleibe den ganzen Tag zu Hause.
if you me need I stay the whole day at house
'[If you need me], I'll be at home all day (anyway).'
[SPEECH ACT CONDITIONAL]

A final difference that we will mention here concerns the potential for pronouns to function as bound variables. A pronoun which occurs in the antecedent clause of a standard conditional can be interpreted as being bound by a quantifier phrase that occurs in the consequent clause. This was seen in example (29) above, repeated here as (50). However, this interpretation is not available in speech act conditionals, as illustrated in (51). This contrast provides additional evidence that the antecedent clause of a standard conditional is more tightly integrated into the syntax of the main clause than the antecedent clause of a speech act conditional.[39]

(50) a. [Every student]$_i$ will succeed if he$_i$ works hard.

b. [No student]$_i$ will succeed if he$_i$ goofs off.

[38] The examples in (49) are from Scheffler (2013: 102).

[39] See Ebert et al. (2008) for similar examples in German.

(51) a. #[Every student]$_i$ should study trigonometry, if he$_i$ wants my opinion.
b. #[No student]$_i$ gave a very impressive speech, if he$_i$ doesn't mind my saying so.

Concessive conditionals share some of these properties with relevance conditionals. For example, the concessive meaning is lost when the consequent contains *then* (52a), or when the conditional is embedded in the complement of a propositional attitude verb (52b). But the semantic function of concessive conditionals seems quite different from that of relevance conditionals.

(52) a. #If you were the last man on earth, then I would not marry you.
b. #Mary believes that if John were the last man on earth, she would not marry him.

Some of the similarities between concessive conditionals and relevance conditionals seem to be related to the fact that in both types, the speaker asserts that the consequent is true, without condition. This limits the kinds of inferences that can be triggered. For example, standard conditionals of the form *if p then q* typically create a generalized conversational implicature: *p if and only if q*. This implicature can be explained in terms of the maxim of Quantity. If the speaker was in a position to assert that *q* was true, whether or not *p* was true, then the most informative way to communicate this fact would be to simply say *q*. Saying *if p then q* is less informative, and so gives the hearer reason to infer that the speaker is not in a position to assert that *q* is true (53a). However, this implicature is not triggered by relevance or concessive conditionals (53b–c).

(53) a. If you take another step, I'll knock you down.
(implicature: If you do not take another step, I will not knock you down.)
b. If you are hungry, there is some pizza in the fridge.
(does not implicate: If you are not hungry, there is no pizza in the fridge.)
c. I wouldn't marry you if you were the last man on EARTH.
(does not implicate: I would marry you if you were not the last man on earth.)

We mentioned a related fact in Chapter 9, namely that the rule of *modus tollens* (denying the consequent) does not hold for all uses of the English word *if*. We can now see that the rule works for standard conditionals (54a), but not for relevance or concessive conditionals (54b–c).

(54) a. Mother said that if her meeting was cancelled, she would come home; but she's not home, so I guess her meeting was not cancelled.
b. Mother says that if we are hungry, there's some pizza in the fridge; but there's no pizza in the fridge, #so I guess we are not hungry.
c. I wouldn't marry that man (even) if he became a millionaire; #so if I end up marrying him, you will know that he did not become a millionaire.

It seems natural to ask whether the analysis we outlined in §19.5 for standard conditionals can be extended to account for speech act conditionals as well. In Chapter 18 we analyzed the contrast between truth-conditional vs. speech act uses of *because* as a case of pragmatic ambiguity: a single sense used in two different ways. In the truth-conditional use (55a), *because* indicates a causal relation between two propositions. In the speech act use, *because* indicates a causal relation between the truth of a proposition and the performance of a speech act. We might paraphrase (55b) as meaning something like: 'Because I would like to come and visit you, I hereby ask you whether you are going out tonight.'

(55) a. Mary scolded her husband because he forgot their anniversary again.
b. Are you going out tonight, because I would like to come and visit you.

A somewhat parallel approach to speech act conditionals is possible. Our discussion at the beginning of this section suggests that the antecedent of a speech act conditional specifies a condition under which the speech act performed in the consequent will be felicitous, whereas the antecedent in standard conditionals specifies a condition under which the proposition expressed in the consequent will be true.

19.8 Conclusion

We began with the intuition that in a conditional sentence *if p (then) q*, the *if* clause describes some condition under which the *then* clause will be true. We noted that modals have a somewhat similar function, in that modal operators (in particular, modal markers of necessity) specify sets of possible worlds in which the basic proposition will be true. In Chapter 16 we analyzed modals as quantifiers over possible worlds, and it seems plausible that a similar approach might work for conditionals as well.

A quantificational analysis of conditionals is further supported by the observation that, when the consequent clause in a conditional sentence contains a quantifier-type expression (e.g. *all, usually, should,* etc.), the word *if* seems to have no independent meaning. Rather, the antecedent of the conditional is added to the restriction of the quantifier, as illustrated in (27–30) above. When there is no overt quantifier in the consequent, the meaning of the conditional sentence can generally be well paraphrased in terms of epistemic necessity or (given the appropriate tense marking on the consequent's verb) generic frequency.

This kind of quantificational analysis for conditionals seems to work well for hypothetical conditionals, but other uses of the conditional form present additional challenges. In the case of counterfactuals, some more elaborate means seems to be required to restrict the set of relevant possible worlds. In the case of speech act conditionals, the issue does not seem to be the truth of the consequent but the felicity or appropriateness of the associated speech act. Whether all the various uses of *if* can be unified under a single sense remains an open and much-discussed question.

Further reading

Von Fintel (2011) provides a good introduction to the study of conditionals, including a summary of much recent work on the topic. Comrie (1986) offers a useful typological study of the construction. Kratzer (1986) provides a very clear and readable argument for her restrictor analysis. Kearns (2000: 61–64) provides a brief and helpful introduction to the analysis of counterfactual conditionals, and von Fintel (2012) provides an excellent overview of the topic. Bhatt & Pancheva (2006) discuss the syntactic structure of conditionals and how the structure relates to the meaning. They also present a good discussion of the various uses of *if.*

Discussion exercises

A: Types of conditionals. Identify the type of conditional expressed in each of the following sentences. Use one of the following labels: STANDARD, RELEVANCE, CONCESSIVE, or FACTUAL; and for standard conditionals, add one of the following: REALITY, HYPOTHETICAL, COUNTERFACTUAL.

1. I wouldn't eat that stew if you paid me.
2. If you place your order now, I will include the batteries for free.
3. If you have no money, where did you get all this electronic equipment?
4. If wishes were horses, beggars would ride.
5. I just told you that I have a meeting with a client this evening. And if I have a meeting with a client, there is no way I can go to the game with you.
6. If you like seafood, there is a great restaurant down by the harbor.
7. If you had waited for me, I would have married you.
8. I'll show you the agenda if you promise not to tell anyone.

B: Restrictor analysis. Use the restricted quantifier notation to express the interpretation of the following sentences, omitting the words in parentheses:

1. Few boxers are famous if they lose.
2. Subtitles are often funny if they are mistranslated.
3. John must pass Greek if he drops Hebrew.
4. If the Bishop was preaching, we used to be late (for Sunday dinner).

Homework exercises

A: Types of conditionals. Show how you could use some of the tests discussed in Chapter 19 to determine whether the conditional clauses in the following examples conditional are STANDARD conditionals or SPEECH ACT conditionals.

(1) If you want my advice, I will do some research and send you an e-mail.

(2) If you want my advice, Arnold is not the right man for you.

B: Restrictor analysis.

(3) Use the restricted quantifier notation to express the interpretation of the following sentences:
  a. Most students are happy if they pass.
  b. If the light is on, Arthur must be at home.
  c. If it rains, I drive to work.

(4) Use the restricted quantifier notation to express the two possible interpretations for the following sentence:
  d. Arthur may not visit Betty if she insults him.

Unit VI

Tense & aspect

20 Aspect and *Aktionsart*

20.1 Introduction

In this final unit of the book we look at the meanings of grammatical morphemes that mark tense and aspect. Tense and aspect markers both contribute information about the time of the event or situation being described. Broadly speaking, tense markers tell us something about the situation's location in time, as illustrated in (1), while aspect markers tell us something about the situation's distribution over time, as illustrated in (2).

(1) Lithuanian tense marking (Chung & Timberlake 1985: 204)

  a. dirb-*au*
  work-1SG.PAST
  'I worked/ was working'

  b. dirb-*u*
  work-1SG.PRESENT
  'I work/ am working'

  c. dirb-*s*-iu
  work-FUTURE-1SG
  'I will work/ will be working'

(2) Aspect marking in English

  a. When I got home from the hospital, my wife *wrote* a letter to my doctor.

  b. When I got home from the hospital, my wife *was writing* a letter to my doctor.

As we will see, many of the same issues that we encountered in our study of word meanings are also relevant to the study of tense and aspect markers: distinguishing entailments from selectional restrictions and other presuppositions; implicature and coercion as sources of new meanings; potential for polysemy and idiomatic senses; etc.

This chapter focuses on aspect, while the next chapter looks at tense. We begin in §20.2 with a discussion of SITUATION TYPE, sometimes referred to as SITUATION ASPECT or *Aktionsart* (German for 'action type'). It turns out that situation type, e.g. the difference between events vs. states, can have a significant effect on the interpretation of both tense and aspect markers.

In §20.3 we introduce the notion of TOPIC TIME, the time under discussion, which will play an important role in our approach to both tense and aspect. §20.4 discusses grammatical aspect, exploring the kinds of aspectual meaning that are most commonly distinguished by grammatical markers across languages. §20.5 and §20.6 explore some of the ways that situation type (*Aktionsart*) and grammatical aspect interact with each other.

20.2 Situation type (*Aktionsart*)

Before we think about the kinds of meanings that tense and aspect markers can express, we need to think first about the kinds of situations that speakers may want to describe. We can divide all situations into two basic classes, STATES vs. EVENTS. (This is why we speak of "situation type" rather than "event type"; we need a term that includes states as well as events.[1]) Informally we might define events as situations in which something "happens", and states as situations in which nothing happens.

Roughly speaking, if you take a video of a state it will look like a snapshot, because nothing changes; but if you take a video of an event, it will not look like a snapshot, because something will change. In more precise terms we might define a state as a situation which is homogeneous over time: it is construed as being the same at every instant within the time span being described. Examples of sentences which describe stative situations include: *this tea is cold*; *my puppy is playful*; *George is my brother.* Of course, to say that a state is a situation in which nothing changes does not mean that these situations will never change. Tea can be re-heated, puppies grow up, etc. It simply means that such changes are not part of the situation currently being described.

Conversely, we can define an EVENT as a situation which is not homogeneous over time, i.e., a situation which involves some kind of change. In more technical terminology, events are said to be DYNAMIC, or internally complex. Examples of sentences which describe eventive situations include: *my tea got cold*; *my puppy is playing*; *George hit my brother; Susan will write a letter.*

[1]Some authors use the terms *eventuality* or *actionality* instead of *situation.*

In classifying situations into various types, we are interested in those distinctions which are linguistically relevant, so it is important to have linguistic evidence to support the distinctions that we make.[2] A number of tests have been identified which distinguish states from events. For example, only sentences which describe eventive situations can be used appropriately to answer the question *What happened?*[3] Applying this test leads us to conclude that sentences (3a–d) describe eventive situations while sentences (3e–h) describe stative situations.

(3) What happened was that...

a. Mary kissed the bishop.
b. the sun set.
c. Peter sang Cantonese folk songs.
d. the grapes rotted on the vine.
e. * Sally was Irish.
f. * the grapes were rotten.
g. * William had three older brothers.
h. * George loved sauerkraut.

A second test is that only eventive situations can be naturally described using the progressive (*be V-ing*) form of the verb, although with some states the progressive can be used to coerce a marked interpretation. This test indicates that sentences (4a–c) describe eventive situations while sentences (4d–g) describe stative situations. Sentences (4h-i) involve situations which, based on other evidence, we would classify as stative. Here the progressive is acceptable only with a special, coerced interpretation: (4h) is interpreted to mean that this situation is temporary and not likely to last long, while (4i) is interpreted to mean that Arthur is behaving in a certain way (an eventive interpretation). In some contexts, (4e) might be acceptable with a coerced interpretation like that of (4i).

(4) a. Mary is kissing the bishop.
b. The sun is setting.
c. Peter is singing Cantonese folk songs.
d. * This room is being too warm.
e. * Sally is being Irish.

[2]It turns out that situation type plays an important role in syntax as well as semantics.
[3]Jackendoff (1976: 100, 1983: 179).

f. * William is having a headache.
g. * George is loving sauerkraut.
h. George is loving all the attention he is getting this week.
i. Arthur is being himself.

A third test is that in English, eventive situations described in the simple present tense take on a HABITUAL interpretation, whereas no such interpretation arises with states in the simple present tense. For example, (5c) means that Peter is in the habit of singing Cantonese folk songs; he does it on a regular basis. In contrast, (5e) does not mean that William gets headaches frequently or on a regular basis; it is simply a statement about the present time (=time of speaking). This test indicates that sentences (5a–c) describe eventive situations while sentences (5d–e) describe stative situations.

(5) a. Mary kisses the bishop (every Saturday).
b. The sun sets in the west.
c. Peter sings Cantonese folk songs.
d. This room is too warm.
e. William has a headache.

Some authors have cited certain tests as evidence for distinguishing state vs. event, which in fact are tests for agentive/volitional vs. non-agentive/non-volitional situations. For example, only agentive/volitional situations can normally be expressed in the imperative; be modified by agent-oriented adverbials (e.g. *deliberately*); or appear as complements of Control predicates (*try, persuade, forbid,* etc.). It turns out that most states are non-agentive, but not all non-agentive predicates are states (e.g. *die, melt, fall, bleed,* etc.). Moreover, some stative predicates can occur in imperatives or control complements (*Be careful! He is trying to be good. I persuaded her to be less formal.*), indicating that these states are at least potentially volitional. It is important to use the right tests for the right question.

A second important distinction is between TELIC vs. ATELIC events. A telic event is one that has a natural endpoint. Examples include dying, arriving, eating a sandwich, crossing a river, and building a house. In each case, it is easy to know when the event is over: the patient is dead, the sandwich is gone, the house is built, etc.

Many telic events (e.g. *build, destroy, die,* etc.) involve some kind of change of state in a particular argument, generally the patient or theme. This argument "measures out" the event, in the sense that once the result state is achieved, the event is over.[4] Some telic events are measured out by an argument that does not undergo any change of state, e.g. *read a novel*: when the novel is half read, the event is half over, but the novel does not necessarily change in any way. Other telic events are measured out or delimited by something which is not normally expressed as an argument at all, e.g. *run five miles, fly to Paris, drive from Calgary to Vancouver*, etc. Motion events like these are measured out by the path which is traversed; the progress of the theme along the path reflects the progress of the event. As Dowty (1991) points out, with many such predicates the path can optionally be expressed as a syntactic argument: *swim the English channel, ford the river, hike the Annapurna Circuit, drive the Trans-Amazonian Highway*, etc.

Atelic events are those which do not have a natural endpoint. Examples include singing, walking, bleeding, shivering, looking at a picture, carrying a suitcase, etc. There is no natural part of these events which constitutes their end point. They can continue indefinitely, until the actor decides to stop or something else intervenes to end the event. Atelic events do not involve a specified change of state, and no argument "measures them out".

Dowty (1979) identifies several tests which distinguish telic vs. atelic events. The two most widely used are illustrated in (6–7). A description of an atelic event can naturally be modified by time phrases expressing duration, as in (6); this is unnatural with telic events. In contrast, a description of a telic event can naturally be modified by time phrases expressing a temporal boundary, as in (7); this is unnatural with atelic events.

(6) For ten minutes Peter...

  a. sang in Cantonese.
  b. chased his pet iguana.
  c. stared at the man sitting next to him.
  d. * broke three teeth.
  e. * recognized the man sitting next to him.
  f. * found his pet iguana.

(7) In ten minutes Peter...

  a. ?? sang in Cantonese. (could only mean, 'In ten minutes Peter began to sing...')

[4]The term "measures out" comes from Tenny (1987). Dowty (1991) uses the term "incremental theme" for arguments that "measure out" the event in gradual/incremental stages, so that the state of the incremental theme directly reflects the progress of the event.

b. * chased his pet iguana.
c. * stared at the man sitting next to him.
d. broke three teeth.
e. recognized the man sitting next to him.
f. found his pet iguana.

Situation Aspect is sometimes referred to as "lexical aspect", because certain verbs tend to be associated with particular situation types. For example, *die* and *break* are inherently telic, whereas *chase* and *stare* are fundamentally atelic. However, in many sentences the whole VP (and sometimes the whole clause) helps to determine the situation type which is being described. For example, with many transitive verbs the telicity of the event depends on whether or not the object NP is quantified or specified in some way: *eat ice cream* is atelic, but *eat a pint of ice cream* is telic; *sing folk songs* is atelic, but *sing "The Skye boat song"* is telic. Similarly, as noted above, the telicity of motion events may depend on whether or not the path is delimited in some way: *walk* is atelic, but *walk to the beach* is telic.

Based on the two distinctions we have discussed thus far, we can make the following classification of situation types:

(8)

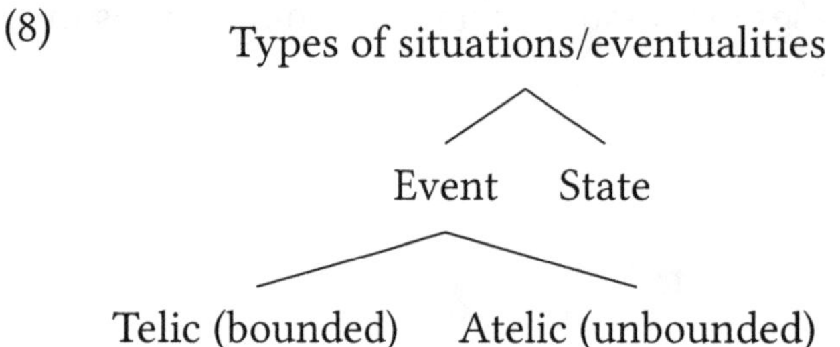

A third distinction which will be important is that between DURATIVE VS. PUNCTILIAR (=instantaneous) situations. Durative situations are those which extend over a time interval (singing, dancing, reading poetry, climbing a mountain), while punctiliar situations are those which are construed as happening in an instant (recognizing someone, reaching the finish line, snapping your fingers, a window breaking). One test that can help in making this distinction is that punctiliar situations described in the progressive (*He is tapping on the door/blinking his eyes*/etc.) normally require an iterative interpretation (something that happens repeatedly, over and over). This is not the case with durative situations (*He is reading your poem/climbing the mountain*/etc.).

Five major situation types are commonly recognized, and these can be distinguished using the three features discussed above as shown in Table 20.2.[5] Activities are atelic events such as *dance, sing, carry a sword, hold a sign*, etc. Achievements are telic events (normally involving a change of state) which are construed as being instantaneous: *break, die, recognize, arrive, find*, etc. Accomplishments are durative telic events, meaning that they require some period of time in order to reach their end-point. Accomplishments often involve a process of some kind which results in a change of state. Examples include *eat a pint of ice cream, build a house, run to the beach, clear a table*, etc. Semelfactives are instantaneous events which do not involve any change of state: *blink, wink, tap, snap, clap, click*, etc. Although they are punctiliar, they are considered to be atelic because they do not involve a change of state and nothing measures them out.

Table 20.1: Aktionsart (situation types) (C. Smith 1997: 3)

Situations	Static	Durative	Telic
State	+	+	–[a]
Activity	–	+	–
Accomplishment	–	+	+
Achievement	–	–	+
Semelfactive	–	–	–

[a]Smith leaves the telicity of states unspecified, because it is not contrastive; here I follow Van Valin & LaPolla (1997: 93) in specifying states as atelic.

For some purposes it is helpful to make a further distinction between two kinds of states: stage-level (temporary) vs. individual-level (permanent).[6] We will refer to these situation types often in our discussion of the meanings of tense and aspect markers. But first we begin that discussion by identifying three "cardinal points" for time reference: the time of speaking, the time of situation, and "topic time".

[5]The first four of these types are well known from the work of Dowty (1979) and Vendler (1957). The Semelfactive class was added by C. Smith (1997), based on Comrie (1976: 42).

[6]Carlson (1977), Kratzer (1995).

20.3 Time of speaking, time of situation, and "topic time"

Tense markers are often described as "locating" a situation in time, as seen in the following widely-cited definitions of tense (9):

(9) a. "TENSE is grammaticalised expression of location in time... [T]enses locate situations either at the same time as the present moment..., or prior to the present moment, or subsequent to the present moment." (Comrie 1985: 9, 14)

b. "TENSE refers to the grammatical expression of the time of the situation described in the proposition, relative to some other time." (Bybee 1992: 144)

These definitions state that tense markers specify the time of a situation relative to some other time, generally the "present moment" (= the time of speaking). However, as Klein (1994) points out, examples like the following seem to pose a problem for the claim that tense "locates situations in time":

(10) a. I took a cab back to the hotel. *The cab driver was Latvian.*[7]

b. They found John in the bathtub. *He was dead.*[8]

c. Tuesday morning we ate leftovers from Chili's for breakfast and checked out of the Little America Hotel... *The Grand Canyon was enormous.* We walked along the rim taking pictures amazed at how beautiful and massive the canyon is.[9]

If the past tense in the italicized portions of these examples indicates that the described situation is located prior to the time of speaking, does that mean that the cab driver was no longer Latvian at the time of speaking, or that John was no longer dead at the time of speaking, or that the Grand Canyon was no longer enormous at the time of speaking? In light of examples like these, Klein suggests that tense actually locates or restricts the speaker's ASSERTION, rather than locating the situation itself. That is, tense indicates the location of the time period about which the speaker is making a claim.

Klein uses the term TOPIC TIME to refer to the time period about which the speaker is making a claim, or in his words, "the time span to which the speaker's claim on this occasion is confined" (1994:4). This choice of terminology builds on

[7]Michaelis (2006).

[8]Klein (1994: 22).

[9]http://scottnmegan.blogspot.com/2009/04/arizona-part-2.html

the widely used definition of "Topic" as "what we are talking about." So Topic Time is the time span that we are talking about. Klein distinguishes Topic Time (TT) from the two other significant times mentioned above: TSit, the time of the event or situation which is being described; and TU, the Time of Utterance (=time of speaking).[10]

The Topic Time can be specified by time adverbs like *yesterday* or *next year*, or by temporal adverbial clauses as seen in example (2) above (*When I got home from the hospital*). It can also be determined by the context. For example, in a narrative sequence like that in (10c), the Topic Time is partly determined by the clause's position in the sequence. Event-type verbs in the simple past tense move the Topic Time forward, whereas stative predicates in the simple past tense inherit the Topic Time from the previous main-line event. The italicized portion of that example makes an assertion only about the Topic Time at that stage of the narrative; no assertion is made about the Time of Utterance.

Klein (1994: 4) describes an imaginary mini-dialogue between a judge and a witness in a courtroom. He points out that the second sentence of the witness's reply cannot be felicitously expressed in the present tense, even though the book in question is presumably still in Russian at the time of speaking. That is because the judge's question establishes a specific topic time (*when you looked into the room*) prior to the time of the current speech event, and any felicitous reply must be relevant to the same topic time.

(11) Judge: What did you notice when you looked into the room?
Witness: There was a book on the table. *It was/#is in Russian.*[11]

Klein assumes that the values of TSit and TT are time intervals, rather than simple points in time, whereas TU can be treated as a point. Using these three concepts, Klein defines tense and aspect as follows:

(12) a. Tense indicates a temporal relation between TT and TU;
b. Aspect indicates a temporal relation between TT and TSit.

We can illustrate Klein's definition of aspect using the examples in (2), repeated here as (13). As noted above, the temporal adverbial clause in these examples (*When I got home from the hospital*) specifies the location of Topic Time. The duration of Topic Time in this case seems to be somewhat vague and context-dependent, influenced partly by our knowledge of how long it takes to write a

[10]As we will discuss in Chapter 21, Klein's framework is based on a proposal by Reichenbach (1947: §51).

[11]Klein 1994: 4.

letter. The use of PERFECTIVE aspect in (13a) indicates that the writing of the letter occurred completely within Topic Time. Under the most natural interpretation, the writing began after the speaker arrived home, and was completed shortly thereafter. The use of IMPERFECTIVE aspect in (13b) indicates that the writing of the letter extended beyond the limits of Topic Time. Under the most natural interpretation, the writing began before the speaker arrived home, and may not even be completed at the time of speaking.[12]

(13) a. When I got home from the hospital, my wife *wrote* a letter to my doctor.
b. When I got home from the hospital, my wife *was writing* a letter to my doctor.

We will discuss Klein's definition of tense in Chapter 21. In the remainder of this chapter we focus on aspect.

20.4 Grammatical Aspect (= "viewpoint aspect")

Situation type (*Aktionsart*) is an inherent property of the situation itself. Grammatical aspect is a feature of the speaker's description of the situation, i.e., a part of the claim that is being made about the situation under discussion. Grammatical aspect is sometimes referred to as VIEWPOINT ASPECT, reflecting the intuition that grammatical aspect markers indicate something about the way the speaker chooses to view or describe the situation, rather than some property of the situation itself.

This intuition is reflected in some widely cited definitions of aspect. Comrie (1976: 3), for example, says: "Aspects are different ways of viewing the internal temporal constituency of a situation." C. Smith (1997: 2–3) states: "Aspectual viewpoints present situations with a particular perspective or focus, rather like the focus of a camera lens. Viewpoint gives a full or partial view of the situation talked about." Using Smith's metaphor of the camera lens, we could describe PERFECTIVE aspect as a wide angle view: the situation fits inside the time frame of the speaker's perspective. The IMPERFECTIVE is like a zoom or close-up view, focusing on just a part of the situation being described, with the situation as a whole extending beyond the boundaries of the speaker's perspective.

Both of these definitions are helpful, but they may tend to obscure a very important point about the nature of grammatical aspect, namely that grammatical

[12]The terms PERFECTIVE and IMPERFECTIVE will be defined more carefully in §20.4 below.

aspect markers contribute to the truth conditions of the sentence. For example, sentences (14a–b) differ only in their aspect. Both are marked for past tense, but (14b) is marked for IMPERFECTIVE aspect while (14a) involves PERFECTIVE aspect. If spoken in the year 2010, (14b) would (reportedly) be true while (14a) would be false, due to the intervention of a neighboring country. So different aspect markers represent different claims about the world.

(14) a. The Syrians *built* a nuclear weapon with North Korean technology.
b. The Syrians *were building* a nuclear weapon with North Korean technology.

Klein's definition of aspect, which was mentioned in the previous section, reflects this insight by relating the time structure of the situation not to the speaker's perspective, but to the time about which a claim is being asserted (Topic Time): aspect indicates a temporal relation between TT and TSit. As a first approximation, we can define PERFECTIVE aspect as indicating that the situation time fits inside Topic Time (TSit $\subseteq$ TT); and IMPERFECTIVE aspect as indicating that Topic Time fits completely inside situation time (TT $\subset$ TSit). These are objective claims about the relationship between two time intervals, which can be evaluated as being true or false in a particular situation.

To take another example, the temporal adverbial clause in (15a–b) establishes the topic time for the main clause in each sentence. The imperfective form of the main clause in (15a) indicates that the topic time is completely contained within the situation time. In other words, the boundaries (and in particular the end point) of TSit, the "digging a tunnel" event, extend beyond the boundaries of TT, the time during which the guards were at the Christmas party. For this reason, the imperfective description of the event in (15a) may be true even if the tunnel was never completed. In contrast, the perfective form of the main clause in (15b) indicates that the situation time is contained within the topic time. This means that the entire "digging a tunnel" event took place within the time span of the guards attending the party.

(15) a. While the guards were at the Christmas party, the prisoners *were digging* a tunnel under the fence (but they never finished it).
b. While the guards were at the Christmas party, the prisoners *dug* a tunnel under the fence (#but they never finished it).

Digging a tunnel is a telic situation, specifically an accomplishment; so its endpoint, or culmination, is an integral part of the event. For this reason, the perfective description of the event in (15b) would not be true if the tunnel was not completed. This example illustrates how an imperfective description of an event may be true in a situation in which a perfective description of that same event would be false. The diagrams in (16) represent the relative locations of the Time of Utterance, Topic Time (time during which the guards were at the party), and Situation Time (prisoners digging a tunnel) for examples (15a–b).

(16) a.

```
      [ TT ]          +
 ____________________________
   ...===TSit===...   TU
```
[15a; IMPERFECTIVE ASPECT]

b.

```
   [    TT    ]    +
 _______________________
      |=TSit=|    TU
```
[15b; PERFECTIVE ASPECT]

20.4.1 Typology of grammatical aspect

Comrie (1976) classifies the most commonly marked aspectual categories in the following hierarchy, which starts with the contrast between perfective vs. imperfective.

(17)

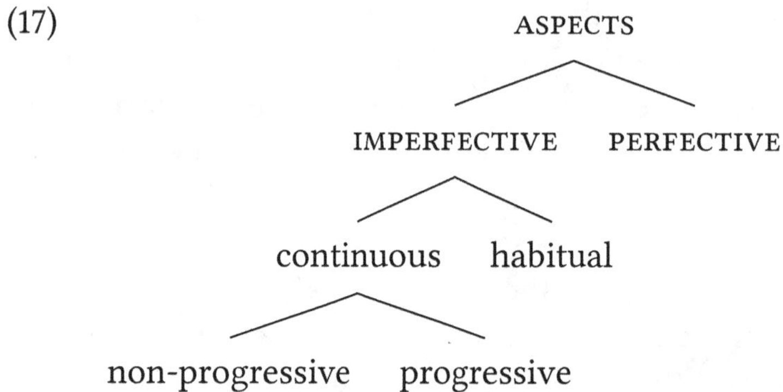

In many languages, including English, perfective is the default or unmarked way of describing an event in the past. It simply asserts that the event happened. Notice that we illustrated the perfective in examples (14–15) using the simple past tense; the lack of overt aspect marking indicates perfective aspect. However, aspect is distinct from tense. Many languages distinguish perfective vs. imperfective in the future (e.g. *will eat* vs. *will be eating*) as well as the past.

Different kinds of imperfective meaning are grammatically distinguished in some languages. HABITUAL aspect describes a recurring event or on-going state which is a characteristic property of a certain period of time.[13] Imperfective as-

[13] Comrie (1976: 27–28).

pect which is not habitual is typically called either CONTINUOUS or PROGRESSIVE. The difference between these two categories lies in their selectional restrictions, rather than in their entailments. The term PROGRESSIVE is generally applied to non-habitual imperfective markers that are used only for describing events, and not for states. Comrie uses the term CONTINUOUS for non-habitual imperfective aspect markers that are not restricted in this way, but can be used for both states and events. In some languages, however, the term CONTINUOUS is applied to aspect markers that are used primarily for states.

English does not have a general imperfective aspect marker. The *be + V-ing* form illustrated in (18a) is specifically progressive in meaning. Habitual meaning can be expressed using the simple present tense as in (18b), or (for habituals in the past) with the auxiliary *used to* as in (18c).

(18) a. Mary is playing tennis.
b. Mary plays tennis.
c. Mary used to play tennis.

Spanish does have a general imperfective form as well as a more specific progressive. The imperfective form is ambiguous between habitual vs. continuous meaning, as illustrated in (19b).[14]

(19) a. *Juan llegó.* 'Juan arrived.' [PERFECTIVE]
b. *Juan llegaba.* 'Juan was arriving/used to arrive.' [IMPERFECTIVE]
c. *Juan estaba llegando.* 'Juan was arriving.' [PROGRESSIVE]

20.4.2 Imperfective aspect in Mandarin Chinese

The Mandarin imperfective aspect markers *zài* 'progressive' and *–zhe* 'continuous' are often cited as a paradigm example of Comrie's distinction between continuous and progressive aspects. The most important difference between the two morphemes lies in the types of situations that each one can modify. *Zài* occurs only with events (20a); it cannot be used to mark states (20b). In main clauses, -*zhe* is used primarily for states (21a–b), and is generally unacceptable with events (21c), though there appears to be some dialect variation in this regard.[15]

[14]Comrie 1976: 25.

[15]See for example Klein et al. (2000: 738), ex. 10. Also, Li & Thompson (1981) state that the combination of *–zhe* plus final particle *ne* has a distinct sense and can be used with events. Unless otherwise indicated, the examples in (20)-(23) come from Li & Thompson (1981: 220–222).

(20) a. Zhāngsān zài tiào.
Zhangsan PROG jump
'Zhangsan is jumping.'

b. *Wo zài xǐhuān Měiguó.
1SG PROG like America
(intended: 'I am liking America.') [16]

(21) a. Chēzi zài wàimian tíng-zhe.
car at outside remain-CONT
'The car is parked outside.'

b. Tā zài chuáng-shàng tǎng-zhe.
3SG at bed-on lie-CONT
'He is lying on the bed.'

c. *Zhāngsān tiào-zhe.
Zhangsan jump-CONT
(intended: 'Zhangsan is jumping.')

Some verbs allow both a stative and an eventive sense. For example, *chuān* can mean either 'wear' or 'put on'; *ná* can mean either 'hold' or 'pick up'. In such cases, *zài* selects the eventive reading and *–zhe* the stative.

(22) a. Tā zài chuān pí-xié.
3SG PROG wear leather-shoe
'He is putting on leather shoes.'

b. Tā chuān-zhe pí-xié.
3SG wear-CONT leather-shoe
'He is wearing leather shoes.'

(23) a. Tā zài ná bàozhǐ.
3SG PROG hold newspaper
'He is picking up a/the newspaper.'

b. Tā ná-zhe bàozhǐ.
3SG hold-CONT newspaper
'He is holding a/the newspaper.'

[16] Sun (2008: 90).

Yeh (1993) and a number of subsequent authors have noted that only individual-level (temporary) states can be marked with *–zhe*; it is generally incompatible with stage-level (permanent) states.[17]

(24) *Tā cōnghuì-zhe.
3SG intelligent-CONT
(for: 'He is intelligent.')

Although these examples have all been translated in the present tense, present time reference is not part of the meaning of either marker, as illustrated by the past time reference in (25).

(25) Nǐ dāngshí mí-zhe Mǎkèsī, Ēngésī Lièníng.
2SG then fascinate-CONT Marx Engels Lenin
'At that time you were fascinated by Marx, Engels and Lenin.'

So far we have considered only main clause uses of these markers. In adverbial clauses like those in (26), *–zhe* occurs freely with both stative and eventive predicates.[18] As C. Smith (1997: 275) notes, *-zhe* is grammatically obligatory in this context; it cannot be replaced by *zai*. This illustrates an important general point: the function of a tense or aspect marker in subordinate clauses may be quite different from its function in main clauses. When we are trying to determine the semantic properties of a morpheme, it may be necessary to treat these two uses separately.

(26) a. Tā kū-zhe pǎo huí jiā qù le.
3SG cry-CONT run return house go COS
'He ran home crying.'

b. Xiǎo gǒu yáo-zhe wěiba pǎo le.
small dog shake-CONT tail run COS
'The little dog ran away wagging its tail.'

20.4.3 Perfect and prospective aspects

Using Klein's terminology, we can define PERFECT (or RETROSPECTIVE) aspect as indicating that the situation time is prior to Topic Time (TSit < TT); and PROSPECTIVE aspect as indicating that the situation time is later than Topic Time (TT <

[17]The examples in (24)-(25) come from C. Smith (1997: 274). In addition to non-occurrence with with stage-level states, there also seem to be a number of idiosyncratic lexical restrictions concerning which stative predicates can combine with *–zhe*.

[18]The examples in (26) come from Li & Thompson (1981: 223).

TSit). The perfect in English is marked by the auxiliary *have* + past participle, e.g. *has eaten, has arrived*, etc. Comrie (1976: 64) suggests that the *going to V* construction (e.g., *the ship is going to sail*) is a way of expressing the prospective aspect in English. Other ways to express this meaning include *the ship is about to sail* and *the ship is on the point of sailing*.

The terms PERFECT and PERFECTIVE are often confused, even by some linguists, but it is important to be clear about the distinction. We will discuss the perfect in some detail in Chapter 22.

20.4.4 Minor aspect categories

A number of languages have aspect markers which refer to the "phase" of the situation being described. For example, some languages have an INCEPTIVE aspect, which indicates that the beginning of the situation falls within the topic time. Such markers often get translated as *begin to X*. (The term INCHOATIVE is sometimes used for this meaning, but more commonly this term is restricted to changes of state or entering a state, e.g. *to become fat, get old, get rich*, etc.) Some languages have a TERMINATIVE or COMPLETIVE aspect, which indicates that the end of the situation falls within the topic time. CONTINUATIVE aspect would mean *continue to X*, or *keep on X-ing*.

ITERATIVE (or REPETITIVE) aspect is used to refer to events which occur repeatedly. Such forms are often translated into English using phrases like *over and over, more and more, here and there*, etc. DISTRIBUTIVE aspect might be considered a sub-type of iterative; it indicates that an action is done by or to members of a group, one after another.[19]

20.5 Interactions between situation type (*Aktionsart*) and grammatical aspect

The definitions we have adopted predict that certain grammatical aspects will not be available for certain situation types. For example, the definition of imperfective aspect as indicating that $TT \subset TSit$ implies that a situation expressed in the imperfective cannot be strictly punctiliar; the situation time must have some duration. A semelfactive event is construed as being instantaneous; it has no duration. For this reason, when a semelfactive event is described in the imperfective (e.g., *he was tapping on the window*), it cannot be interpreted as referring

[19] http://www-01.sil.org/linguistics/GlossaryOflinguisticTerms/WhatIsDistributiveAspect.htm

to a single instance, but must receive an iterative (= repetitive) interpretation. Similarly, an instantaneous change of state cannot be described in the imperfective (e.g. ??*He was recognizing his old classmate*) without some very unusual context. With other changes of state, the use of the imperfective (e.g., *he was dying*) may shift the reference from the change itself to the process leading up to the change. This kind of shift can be seen as a type of coercion.

The same constraint applies to semelfactives in Mandarin. In Chinese as in English, a semelfactive event described in the imperfective cannot be interpreted as referring to a single instance, but must receive an iterative interpretation (27). As we would predict, this is possible only with the progressive *zai*, and not with the continuous *–zhe*.

(27) Zhāngsān zài qiāo mén.
Zhangsan PROG knock door
'Zhangsan is knocking on the door.' (C. Smith 1997: 272)

Similarly, the definition of perfective aspect as indicating that TSit ⊆ TT makes predictions about the kinds of situations that can appropriately be expressed in the perfective. When a state is described in the perfective aspect, what is asserted is that the state was true during the topic time, as discussed above. When an event is described in perfective aspect, what is being asserted is that the whole event took place within the topic time. For activities, which do not have an inherent endpoint, perfective descriptions in the past can be interpreted as bounded events, as in (28a): 'I played tennis *for a while*.' Alternatively, as illustrated in (28b), they can get a habitual interpretation, which has properties similar to a state.

(28) a. I played tennis yesterday.
b. I played tennis when I was in high school.

For telic events, and in particular for accomplishments, the end-point or culmination is an intrinsic part of the event; so a perfective description of that event should be false if the culmination is not in fact attained. This prediction holds true for English, as illustrated in example (15b) above, and for many other languages. However, a number of languages have been identified in which this culmination is only an implicature, rather than an entailment, for accomplishments expressed in the perfective. In Tagalog, for example, it is not a contradiction to say: 'I removed the stain, but I ran out of soap, so I couldn't remove it.'[20] Other languages

[20] Dell (1983: 186).

in which such "non-culminating accomplishments" are possible include Hindi, Mandarin, Thai, several Tibeto-Burman languages, various Philippine-type languages, and at least two Salish languages.[21]

The exact conditions under which "non-culminating accomplishments" can occur vary from one language to another, but the existence of such cases might suggest that we need to modify our definition of PERFECTIVE in some way. Another alternative that we might consider starts with the recognition that accomplishments are composed of two "phases": the first phase is a process or activity which leads to the second phase, a change of state.[22] In building a house, for example, the first phase would be doing the work of building and the second phase would be the coming into existence of a completed house. We might account for the difference between languages like English vs. languages like Chinese or Tagalog by recognizing that for languages of the latter type, there are certain conditions under which a VP that normally describes an accomplishment can be used to refer to just the first phase of the event, i.e. a process or activity.

This two-phase analysis also gives us a way of thinking about a puzzling fact concerning accomplishment predicates in English, which Dowty (1979) refers to as the "imperfective paradox". Building on Vendler's (1957) discussion of these facts, Dowty points out that with state and activity predicates a statement in the imperfective (29a, 30a) entails the corresponding statement in the perfective (29b, 30b). With accomplishment predicates, however, this entailment does not hold (31–32).

(29) a. Arnold was wearing a wig.
     b. Arnold wore a wig. [a entails b]

(30) a. George was speaking Etruscan.
     b. George spoke Etruscan. [a entails b]

(31) a. Felix was writing a letter.
     b. Felix wrote a letter. [a does not entail b]

(32) a. Sarah was running to the library.
     b. Sarah ran to the library. [a does not entail b]

Dowty goes on to ask: Given the fact that accomplishments always have a natural end-point, how can the imperfective description of the event be considered

[21]References: Hindi (Singh 1991; 1998), Mandarin (Soh & Kuo 2005; Koenig & Chief 2008), Thai (Koenig & Muansuwan 2000), Salish (Bar-el et al. 2005), Tibeto-Burman (Larin Adams, p.c.).

[22]Klein et al. (2000).

true if that end-point was never achieved?[23] It seems that English, like Chinese and Tagalog, allows a shift in meaning so that a VP which normally describes an accomplishment can be used to refer to just the first phase of the event. In English, however, this shift seems to be possible only in the imperfective.

20.6 Aspectual sensitivity and coercion effects

A predicate which normally describes one type of situation can sometimes be coerced into a different situation type (Aktionsart) by contextual factors. De Swart (1998: 360) describes this process as follows:

> Typically, coercion is triggered if there is a conflict between the aspectual character [i.e., Aktionsart—PK] of the eventuality description and the aspectual constraints of some other element in the context. The felicity of an aspectual reinterpretation is strongly dependent on linguistic context and knowledge of the world.

In example (33a), for example, a basically stative predicate (*know the answer*) is coerced into a change-of-state (achievement) interpretation by the adverb *suddenly*, which emphasizes the starting point of the state.[24]

(33) a. Suddenly I knew the answer.
  b. I read *The Lord of the Rings* for a few minutes.
  c. John played the sonata for about eight hours.
  d. For months, the train arrived late.

Examples (33b–c) both involve predicates which normally describe telic events (*read The Lord of the Rings* and *play the sonata*), specifically accomplishments. In

[23]Dowty's solution was to propose that the progressive encodes not only aspect but also modality, that is, quantification over a certain class of possible worlds. He designated the relevant class of possible worlds INERTIA WORLDS, which he defined as follows: an inertia world is a possible world which is exactly like the actual world under discussion up to and including the topic time, "and in which the future course of events after this time develops in ways most compatible with the past course of events" (Dowty 1979: 148). In other words, inertia worlds are possible worlds in which the expected outcomes from a given situation are actually realized. Dowty then proposed a new definition of the progressive which says that *John was X-ing* will be true when asserted about a time interval I just in case (i) there is some longer time interval I′ which contains I and extends beyond the end-point of I; and (ii) *John X-ed* is true in all inertia worlds when asserted about time interval I′.

[24]The examples in (33) are adapted from de Swart (1998: 359).

both cases an activity reading is coerced by an adverbial PP which specifies the duration of the event. In (33b) the time span that is specified (*a few minutes*) is much too short for the entire event of reading *The Lord of the Rings* to be accomplished. As a result, we interpret the statement to mean that the speaker carried out a certain activity, namely reading portions of *The Lord of the Rings*, for a few minutes. In (33c) the time span that is specified (*for about eight hours*) is much longer than it would normally take to play a sonata. The most natural interpretation is that John played the sonata over and over again for about eight hours. This iterative interpretation describes an activity, because it has no natural endpoint.

Example (33d) involves a predicate (*arrive*) which is both telic and instantaneous, i.e., an achievement. The instantaneous nature of the basic meaning conflicts with the long duration specified by the adverbial phrase (*for months*), which results in a habitual interpretation: the train always or usually arrived late whenever it ran during those months. As mentioned above, habitual situations can be considered to be a type of state.

De Swart (1998) points out that coercion effects are often triggered by a kind of selectional restriction that is associated with some tense and aspect markers. In Sections 20.2 and 20.4.2 above we discussed examples of grammatical morphemes (the progressive aspect markers in English and Mandarin) which can normally be used only for describing events, and not for states. Similar restrictions are found in a number of other languages as well: certain tense or aspect markers may select for specific situation types (Aktionsart). De Swart (1998) refers to selectional restrictions of this kind as ASPECTUAL SENSITIVITY.

In §20.2 we illustrated the principle that stative predicates cannot normally be expressed in the progressive with examples like those in (34a–c). However, we noted there that some such examples might be acceptable with a coerced interpretation in certain contexts. The progressive in (34d), for example, suggests that the described state is temporary and likely to last only a short time. The progressive form of (34e) seems to coerce a basically stative proposition, which would be a tautology in the simple present (*he is himself*), into an eventive (activity) interpretation, roughly 'acting in a way typical of him'.

(34) a. * This room is being too warm.
b. * I am knowing the answer.
c. * George is loving sauerkraut.
d. George is loving all the attention he is getting this week.
e. Arthur is being himself.

De Swart discusses two past tense forms in French: the *passé simple* vs. the *imparfait*. She suggests that they differ primarily in terms of their aspectual sensitivity: the *passé simple* occurs only with bounded situations, while the *imparfait* occurs only with unbounded situations. The normal way of expressing a state that was true in the past is with the *imparfait*, as in (35a), because states are not naturally bounded. When the *passé simple* is used for stative predicates, as in (35b), the sentence must receive a bounded interpretation through some kind of coercion effect. Depending on context, it could be bounded either by referring to the beginning of the state (ingressive/inchoative reading), or by describing a state that held true only for a limited period of time.

(35) a. Anne *était* triste.
Anne was(IMP) sad.
'Anne was sad.'

b. Anne *fut* triste.
Anne was(PS) sad.
'Anne became sad.' or: 'Anne was sad for a while.'

The use of the *passé simple* in the second sentence of (36a) causes the normally stative predicate to be interpreted as an event (change of state) which takes place subsequent to the previous event in the narrative. The use of the *imparfait* in (36b) is interpreted as describing a state which overlaps the event described in the preceding sentence.

(36) a. Georges annonça sa résignation. Anne *fut* triste.
George announced his resignation. Anne was(PS) sad.
'George announced his resignation. Anne became sad (as a result).'

b. Georges annonça sa résignation. Anne *était* triste
George announced his resignation. Anne was(IMP) sad.
'George announced his resignation. Anne was sad (during that time).'

A similar contrast is illustrated in (37). The use of the *passé simple* in the second clause of (37a) causes 'cross the street' to be interpreted as a bounded event (an accomplishment) which takes place subsequent to the event in the previous clause. The use of the *imparfait* in (37b) is interpreted as describing an unbounded event (an activity) which overlaps with the event described in the previous clause.

(37) a. Quand elle vit Georges, Anne *traversa* la rue.
when she saw George Anne crossed(PS) the street
'When/after she saw George, Anne crossed the street.'

b. Quand elle vit Georges, Anne *traversait* la rue.
when she saw George Anne crossed(IMP) the street
'When she saw George, Anne was crossing the street.'

The adverbial phrase 'for two hours' in (38) imposes bounds on an activity (playing the piano) which would otherwise be unbounded. In this context, the most natural description of a past event would use the *passé simple*, as in (38a). De Swart states that the use of the *imparfait* in (38b) cannot describe a single event of Anne playing the piano for two hours, but could receive a habitual interpretation: whenever she played the piano, she used to play for two hours.

(38) a. Anne *joua* du piano pendant deux heures.
Anne played(PS) the piano for two hours
'Anne played the piano for two hours.'
b. Anne *jouait* du piano pendant deux heures.
Anne played(IMP) the piano for two hours
'Anne used to play the piano for two hours.'

We will see more examples of coercion effects arising from aspectual sensitivity in the next two chapters.

20.7 Conclusion

Aktionsart (situation aspect) is a way of classifying situations (events and states) on the basis of their temporal contour, that is, the shape of their "run time". A state is a situation which is homogeneous over time (nothing changes within the time span being described), while an event involves some kind of change. The primary features which are used to distinguish different classes of events are duration and telicity (boundedness).

Grammatical aspect (or "viewpoint aspect") is a choice that the speaker makes in describing a situation, part of the claim that is being made about the situation. It is expressed by grammatical morphemes which indicate the relation between the run time of the situation and the "Topic Time", or time about which a claim is being made. The most basic distinction is between perfective aspect, which indicates that the situation time is contained within Topic Time, vs. imperfective aspect, which indicates that the situation time extends beyond the boundaries of Topic Time.

Some tense and aspect markers impose selectional restrictions on the types of situations which they can be used to describe. De Swart (1998) refers to selectional restrictions of this kind as ASPECTUAL SENSITIVITY. When the expected temporal contour of the described situation clashes with the aspectual sensitivity of the tense or aspect marker that is used in the description, or with some other element of the clause (e.g. an adverbial phrase), a new interpretation may be coerced that involves a different *aktionsart*. This type of coercion is an important factor in explaining how the basic meanings (established sense(s)) of tense and aspect markers can account for their observed range of uses.

Further reading

Comrie (1976) is still an excellent resource on the typology of grammatical aspect. C. Smith (1997) is another foundational work on grammatical (or "viewpoint") aspect and *aktionsart* (situation aspect). Binnick (2006) provides a helpful overview of these topics, and Klein (2009) provides a helpful introduction to his theory of tense and aspect. Dowty (1979) provides an very good description of the *aktionsart* categories and summarizes a number of useful tests for identifying and distinguishing them.

Discussion exercises

A: Identify the most likely situation type (*aktionsart*) for the following predicates (options: STATE, ACTIVITY, ACHIEVEMENT, ACCOMPLISHMENT, SEMELFACTIVE):[a]

1. *swim*
2. *be happy*
3. *wake up*

4. *snap your fingers*
5. *compose a sonnet*
6. *swim the English channel*
7. *drink coffee*
8. *drink two cups of coffee*
9. *expire* (e.g., visa, passport, etc.)
10. *own* (e.g., *John owns a parrot*)

[a]Patterned after Kearns (2000: 225).

Homework exercises

A: Some English verbs are polysemous between a stative sense and a dynamic (eventive) sense. Show how the progressive aspect can be used to distinguish these two senses for each of the following five verbs: *weigh, extend, surround, smell, apply* (e.g. *that law doesn't apply* vs. *apply for a job*).[a]

Model answer: *have*

1. Stative: She has/#is having four grown children.
2. Dynamic: She is having a baby.

B: Show how you would use time adverbials (e.g. *for an hour* vs. *in an hour*) to determine whether each of the following situations is telic or atelic:

1. Walter laughed.
2. Susan realized her mistake.
3. Horace played piano sonatas.
4. Horace played Beethoven's Pathétique sonata.
5. Martha resented George's comment.

C: Describe the coercion effects in the following examples:

1. As I walked through his door, *I was instantly aware* of the quiet strength of mind Buzz possesses.[b]
2. William recited the *Iliad* for a few minutes.
3. John knocked on the door for ten minutes.
4. The children of Atuler village in Sichuan have for many years been climbing up a sheer 800 meter cliff on rattan ladders in order to attend school.

---

[a] Adapted from Saeed (2009: 147).

[b] http://www.vvoice.org/?module=displaystory&story_id=3725&format=html

21 Tense

21.1 Introduction

As we discussed in Chapter 20, tense markers are frequently described as locating a situation in time relative to the time of speaking (or some other reference time). However, we argued (following Klein and others) that tense actually indicates the location of the TOPIC TIME (the time span which is currently under discussion), rather than the time of the situation itself. In this chapter we explore the kinds of meanings that can be expressed by tense markers.

In §21.2 we will compare Klein's theory of tense with some other well-known approaches. In §21.3 we discuss in some detail the simple present tense in English. This turns out to be a useful case study, because it illustrates how a wide range of uses can be explained in terms of a single basic sense plus coercion effects triggered by selectional restrictions, etc.

§21.4 discusses the difference between ABSOLUTE TENSE, which defines past, present, or future relative to the time of speaking, from RELATIVE TENSE, in which the reference point for tense marking is some time other than the time of speaking. Some languages also have COMPLEX TENSE forms, which combine absolute with relative time reference. In sentence (1), for example, the first clause specifies a topic time (3:15 pm) that is in the past relative to the time of speaking. That time becomes the reference point for the tense marking in the second clause, which specifies a new topic time (3:00 pm) that is in the past relative to this reference point. The form *had left* is an example of a complex tense, namely "past-in-the-past".

(1) I managed to get to the station at 3:15 pm, but the train *had left* promptly at 3:00.

Most languages that have grammatical tense markers distinguish only relative order: past is before the time of speaking, future is after the time of speaking. Some, however, make finer distinctions. §21.5 briefly illustrates some of these METRICAL TENSE systems, in which various degrees of past or future time are grammatically distinguished.

21.2 Tense relates Topic Time to the Time of Utterance

In Chapter 20 we quoted the following standard definitions of tense:

(2) a. "**Tense** is grammaticalised expression of location in time... [T]enses locate situations either at the same time as the present moment..., or prior to the present moment, or subsequent to the present moment." (Comrie 1985: 9, 14)

b. "**Tense** refers to the grammatical expression of the time of the situation described in the proposition, relative to some other time." (Bybee 1992: 144)

An important feature of these definitions is that they are restricted to "grammatical(ized) expressions" of location in time. Every language has a variety of content words which can be used to specify the time of an event. These may include NPs (*last year, that week, the next day*), PPs (*in the morning, after the election*), temporal adverbs (*soon, later, then*), adverbial clauses (*While Hitler was in Vienna, ...*), etc. But not all languages have tense markers. The traditional use of the term TENSE in linguistics has been restricted to grammatical morphemes: inflectional affixes, auxiliary verbs, particles, etc.

One way to represent the "location" of a situation in time is to define logical operators (e.g. PAST and FUTURE) which will add tense information to a basic proposition. These tense operators can be defined as existential quantifiers over times, as suggested in (3).[1] This definition says that PAST(p) will be true at the time of speaking just in case there was some time prior to the time of speaking when p was true; and similarly for FUTURE(p). (The letter *t* stands for 'time', and "<" in this context means 'prior to'. TU represents the time of speaking; this is typically the time for which the truth value of a statement is evaluated.)

(3) PAST(p) is true at TU iff $\exists_t$[t < TU ∧ (p is true at time t)]
FUTURE(p) is true at TU iff $\exists_t$[TU < t ∧ (p is true at time t)]

This system works fairly well in many cases, but Partee (1973) points out that it leads to problems with examples like (4):

(4) Wife to husband, as they drive away from their house: "*I didn't turn off the stove.*"

[1] A. N. Prior (1957); Arthur N. Prior (1967).

If the positive statement *I turned off the stove* is interpreted as shown in (5a), there are two possible ways of interpreting the corresponding negative statement, depending on the scope of negation, as shown in (5b). The first reading means that the speaker has never in her life turned off the stove, while the second reading means that there was at least one moment in her life when the speaker was not turning off the stove. Clearly neither of these captures the intended meaning.

(5) a. *I turned off the stove.*
$\exists_t$ [t < TU ∧ (TURN_OFF(speaker, stove) is true at t)]

b. *I didn't turn off the stove.*
$\neg\exists_t$ [t < TU ∧ (TURN_OFF(speaker, stove) is true at t)]
or: $\exists_t$ [t < TU ∧ (¬TURN_OFF(speaker, stove) is true at t)]

In Chapter 20 we introduced Klein's analysis of tense, which crucially defines tense as indicating the location of Topic Time rather than the location in time of the situation itself. Under Klein's analysis, the past tense in (4) *I didn't turn off the stove* indicates that Topic Time is prior to the Time of Utterance. The Topic Time is determined by the context; in this situation, it would be the time immediately before leaving the house. The speaker is asserting that at that particular time, she didn't turn off the stove. No assertion is made about other times. This analysis provides the correct interpretation.

To review, Klein defines tense and aspect as shown in (6), where TT = Topic Time (the time period about which the speaker is making a claim); TU = Time of Utterance (i.e., time of speaking); and TSit = the time of the event or situation which is being described.

(6) a. Tense indicates a temporal relation between TT and TU;

b. Aspect indicates a temporal relation between TT and TSit.

So, for example, past tense can be defined as a grammatical marker which indicates that TT is prior to TU. Future tense can be defined as indicating that TU is prior to TT. Present tense might be defined as indicating that TU is contained within TT.

Klein's framework is based on the very influential work of Reichenbach (1947). Reichenbach defined tense categories in terms of three cardinal points in time: speech time (S), the time of the utterance; event time (E), the time of the event or situation which is being described; and reference time (R). S and E correspond to Klein's TU and TSit, respectively. Reichenbach's "reference time" can be seen as analogous to Klein's TT, although there is some disagreement as to what Reichenbach actually meant by this term. In the discussion that follows we will use Klein's terminology, but Reichenbach's terms (E, S, and R) are also widely used, and it will be helpful to be aware of these as well.

Because tense is (normally) marked relative to the time of the speech event, tense markers are considered to be deictic elements. It is helpful to remember that tense markers normally do not fully specify the location of the topic time; rather, they impose constraints on that location, such as TT < TU (for past tense). More specific time reference can be achieved by using temporal adverbs, adverbial clauses, etc.

Klein's definition of tense as marking a temporal relation between TT and TU provides us with a foundation for analyzing the semantic content of specific tense markers. However, as Comrie (1985: 26–29, 54–55) points out, tense markers can be associated with other kinds of meaning as well, including presuppositions, implicatures, idiomatic uses, and polysemous senses. These factors often combine to create a complex range of possible uses even for tense markers whose basic semantic content is relatively simple. We can illustrate some of the challenges involved in analyzing tense systems by looking at the simple present tense in English.

21.3 Case study: English simple present tense

The simple present tense in English is notoriously puzzling, as Langacker (2001) observes:

> [T]he English present is notorious for the descriptive problems it poses. Some would even refer to it as "the so-called present tense in English", so called because a characterization in terms of present time seems hopelessly unworkable. On the one hand, it typically cannot be used for events occurring at the time of speaking. To describe what I am doing right now, I cannot felicitously use sentence [7a], with the simple present, but have to resort to the progressive, as in [7b]. On the other hand, many uses of the so-called present do not refer to present time at all, but to the future [8a], to the past [8b], or to transcendent situations where time seems irrelevant [8c]. It appears, in fact, that the present tense can be used for *anything but* the present time.

(7) a. * I *write* this paper right now.
  b. I am writing this paper right now.

(8) a. My brother *leaves* for China next month.
b. I'm eating dinner last night when the phone *rings*. I *answer* it but there's no response. Then I *hear* this buzzing sound.
c. The area of a circle *equals* pi times the square of its radius.

The concept of ASPECTUAL SENSITIVITY (the potential for tense forms to select specific situation types or Aktionsart), which we introduced in Chapter 20, can help us to explain at least some of these puzzles.[2] Suppose that the basic meaning of the English simple present tense is, in fact, present tense: it indicates that TU is contained within TT. In addition, suppose that the simple present imposes a selectional restriction on the described situation: only states may be described using this form of the verb. This would immediately explain why eventive (non-stative) situations that are happening at the time of speaking cannot normally be expressed in the simple present but require the progressive, as illustrated in (7).

What happens when an event-type predicate is expressed in the simple present? Eventive predicates in the progressive can be interpreted as referring to specific events occurring at the time of speaking, as seen in (9a) and (10a), but this interpretation is not available for the simple present because of the aspectual sensitivity described in the preceding paragraph. For this reason, an event-type predicate in the simple present frequently gets a habitual interpretation, as seen in examples (9b) and (10b).[3]

(9) a. Mary is playing tennis.
b. Mary *plays* tennis.

(10) a. Sam is feeding the cat.
b. Sam *feeds* the cat.

As discussed in Chapter 20, habitual aspect describes a recurring event or ongoing state which is a characteristic property of a certain period of time.[4] Examples (9b) and (10b) describe not what Mary and Sam are doing at the time of speaking, but characteristic properties of Mary and Sam; thus these sentences actually refer to states, not events. This is an example of coercion: since the aspectual sensitivity of the simple present blocks the normal eventive sense of these predicates, they take on a stative meaning in this context. The fact that the habitual readings encode states rather than events can be seen in the fact

[2]Much of the discussion in this section is based on Michaelis (2006).
[3]Examples (9b) and (10b) are taken from C. Smith (1997: 185).
[4]Comrie (1976: 27–28).

that (9b) and (10b) cannot be appropriately used to answer the question, "What is happening?"

A very similar use of the simple present is for GNOMIC (or universal) statements, like those in (11); see also (8c). Again, even though the verbs used in (11) are eventive, these sentences do not refer to specific events but to general properties.

(11) a. Pandas *eat* bamboo shoots.
  b. Water *boils* at 100℃.
  c. Work *expands* to fill the time available.
  d. Absolute power *corrupts* absolutely.

As Langacker illustrated in (8a), the simple present can also be used to refer to events in the future. Additional examples are provided in (12). This "futurate present" usage presents two puzzles. First, we need to explain the shift in time reference. Second, we would like to account for the apparent violation of the aspectual restriction noted above: the simple present can be used to refer to specific events in the future, whereas this is normally impossible for events in the present.

(12) a. The Foreign Minister *flies* to Paris on Tuesday (but you could see him on Monday).
  b. Brazil *hosts* the World Cup next year.
  c. This offer *ends* at midnight tonight, and will not be repeated.

Comrie (1976: 47) notes that "there is a heavy constraint on the use of the present tense with future reference, namely that the situation referred to must be one that is scheduled." He illustrates this constraint with the examples in (13). Comrie notes that (13b) would only be acceptable if God is talking, or if humans develop new technology that allows them to schedule rain.

(13) a. The train *departs* at five o'clock tomorrow morning.
  b. ?#It *rains* tomorrow.

Note also that the future interpretation of the simple present is not available within the scope of a conditional or temporal adverbial clause, as seen in (14b), since these seem to block the inference that the event is independently scheduled.

(14) a. If/When you touch me, I *will scream*.
  (main clause refers to specific event)

b. If/When you touch me, I *scream*.
(only gnomic/universal interpretation is possible)

We might explain these facts by suggesting that the futurate present is not a description of a future event, but rather an assertion that a particular event is "on the schedule" at the moment of speaking. It describes a state, specifically a property of events: the property of being scheduled. This represents another pattern of coercion. The habitual reading discussed above is unavailable because of the adverbial expressions which specify a definite future time. The scheduled future reading allows these sentences to be interpreted in a way which does not violate the aspectual sensitivity of the simple present.

There are other eventive uses of the simple present, however, which are not so easy to explain. The "historical present" illustrated in (8b) seems to be allowed primarily in a specific genre of discourse, namely informal narrative. This usage seems to involve a shift in the deictic reference point, from the current time of speaking to the time line of the narrative. We need to recognize that such shifts are possible in order to deal with examples like (15), which should be a contradiction but is often heard on telephone answering machines.

(15) I'm not here right now.

In this example the identity of the speaker and location of the speech event are interpreted in the normal way, but the hearer is expected to interpret the deictic *right now* as referring to the time when the recording is played, the time of hearing, rather than the original time of speaking. More study is needed to understand why this shift should license an apparent violation of the aspectual restrictions discussed above.

Other eventive uses of the simple present include explicit performatives, play-by-play reports by sportscasters, stage directions in the scripts of plays, etc.[5] For now, we will simply consider these to be idiosyncratic exceptions to the general rule; that is, idiomatic uses of the simple present form.

21.4 Relative tense

As noted in the definitions we cited from Comrie and Bybee, tense systems typically specify location in time relative to the time of the current utterance (TU). This type of tense marking is called ABSOLUTE TENSE. For certain tense markers,

[5]See Klein (2009) for a discussion of other special uses of the present.

however, some other reference point is used, which must be determined by the context. This type of tense marking is called RELATIVE TENSE. Because absolute tense marking is anchored to the time of the current utterance, absolute tenses are deictic elements; relative tenses might be considered anaphoric rather than deictic. A Brazilian Portuguese example is presented in (16a).[6]

(16) a. Quando você chegar, eu já saí.
when 2SG arrive.FUT.SBJV 1SG already leave.PAST
'When you arrive, I will already have left.' [Brazilian Portuguese]

b. *When you arrive, I already left.

The simple past tense form *saí* 'left' would normally have past reference, but in this context it gets a relative tense interpretation, indicating that the event described in the main clause is located in the past relative to the time of the event described in the adverbial clause. So in this context a verb marked for past tense can refer to an event which is actually in the future relative to the time of the speech event (TU). As demonstrated in (16b), the literal English translation of this sentence is ungrammatical, because the simple past tense in English normally does not allow this kind of relative tense interpretation.

We will refer to the contextually determined reference point of a relative tense marker as the PERSPECTIVE TIME (PT).[7] Absolute tense constrains the relationship between TT and TU, while relative tense constrains the relationship between TT and PT. In example (16a), the adverbial clause ('When you arrive') establishes the perspective time, which is understood to be in the future relative to the time of speaking. The past tense on the main verb *saí* 'left' gets a relative tense interpretation in this context, indicating that the topic time (i.e., the time about which an assertion is being made) is in the past relative to the perspective time.

The most likely interpretation for ex. (16a) is diagrammed in (17). Relative past tense imposes the constraint that TT < PT, but does not specify whether TT is before or after TU. The fact that TT is later than TU is a pragmatic inference; if the speaker had already left before the time of speaking, it would be more natural and informative to simply say 'I have already left.' (The relationship between

[6] Comrie (1985: 31). A reviewer notes that the Persian translation for this example would use exactly the same tenses as the Portuguese. Note that the Portuguese future subjunctive is homophonous with the infinitive paradigm for most verbs, including *chegar*; but the paradigms are distinct for certain irregular verbs, including *ter* 'have', *haver* 'have', *ser* 'be', *estar* 'be', *querer* 'want', *trazer* 'bring', *ver* 'see', *vir* 'come' (Jeff Shrum, p.c.).

[7] This terminology follows Kiparsky (2002) and Bohnemeyer (2014).

TT and TSit is determined by the perfective aspect of the simple past form, as discussed in Chapter 20.)

(17)

TU	[TT]	PT
	| TSit: my departure |	[your arrival]

In Imbabura Quechua, main clause verbs have absolute tense reference.[8] Most subordinate verbs use a distinct set of tense affixes which get a relative tense interpretation.[9] In the following examples, the subordinate verb 'live' is marked for relative past, present or future tense according to whether it refers to a situation which existed before, during or after the situation named by the main verb, which determines the perspective time. Since the main verb is marked for past tense, the actual time referred to by the subordinate verb may have been before the time of the utterance even when it is marked for 'future' tense, as in (18c):

(18) **Imbabura Quechua** (Peru; Cole 1982: 143)

a. [Marya Agatu-pi kawsa-j]-ta kri-rka-ni.
Mary Agato-in live-PRES-ACC believe-PAST-1SUBJ
'I believed that Mary was living (at that time) in Agato.'

b. [Marya Agatu-pi kawsa-shka]-ta kri-rka-ni.
Mary Agato-in live-PAST-ACC believe-PAST-1SUBJ
'I believed that Mary had lived (at some previous time) in Agato.'

c. [Marya Agatu-pi kawsa-na]-ta kri-rka-ni.
Mary Agato-in live-FUT-ACC believe-PAST-1SUBJ
'I believed that Mary would (some day) live in Agato.'

Relative past tense is sometimes referred to as ANTERIOR tense, relative future as POSTERIOR tense, and relative present as SIMULTANEOUS tense. Relative tense is most common in subordinate clauses, but is also found in main clauses in some languages (e.g., classical Arabic). Comrie (1985) points out that participles in many languages, including English and Latin, get a relative tense interpretation. Example (19) illustrates the simultaneous meaning of the English present participle (*flying*). Example (10) illustrates the posterior meaning of the Latin future participle: the event of crossing the river is described for a topic time which is in the future relative to the perspective time defined by the main clause (the time

[8]Cole (1982), Comrie (1985: 61).

[9]Verbs in relative clauses use the main-clause tense markers with absolute tense reference.

when he failed to send over the provisions). Example (21) illustrates the anterior meaning of the Latin past participle: the event of delaying is described for a topic time which is in the past relative to the perspective time defined by the main clause (the time when he orders them to give the signal).[10]

(19) a. Last week passengers *flying* with Qantas were given free tickets.
b. Next week passengers *flying* with Qantas will be given free tickets.

(20) Trāiectūrus Rhēnum commeātum nōn trānsmīsit.
cross-FUT.PTCP Rhine provisions NEG send.over-PAST.PFV.3sg
'Being about to cross the Rhine, he did not send over the provisions.'[11]

(21) Paululum *commorātus,* sīgna canere iubet.
little.bit delay-PST.PTCP signal.PL to.sound order-PRES.3sg
'Having delayed a little while, he orders them to give the signal.'

The English *be going to* construction is sometimes identified as marking posterior tense. It can express future time relative to a perspective time in the past, as in (22a), creating a "future in the past" meaning. It can express future time relative to some generic or habitual perspective time, which may be past or present relative to the time of speaking, as illustrated in (22b–c).

(22) a. I was just *going to tell* you when you first came in, only you began about Castle Richmond.[12]
b. John keeps saying that he is *going to visit* Paris some day.
c. Dibber always did tell me Pat was *going to study* to be a doctor.[13]
d. John *is going to visit* you very soon.

Comrie (1985) points out that if a relative tense is used in contexts where the perspective time is equivalent to the time of speaking, then its meaning is equivalent to the corresponding absolute tense. For example, the interpretation of the

[10]Example (21) comes from Sallust, Catilina 59; cited in Allen & Greenough (1903: §496). The past participle in Latin, as in English, normally has a passive meaning; but the verb meaning 'delay' in Latin is a DEPONENT verb, meaning that passive morphology does not create a passive meaning.

[11]Suetonius; cited in Comrie (1985: 61).

[12]Anthony Trollope (1860), *Castle Richmond*; cited at: http://grammar.about.com/od/fh/g/Future-In-The-Past.htm

[13]John Fante, "Horselaugh on Dibber Lannon"; cited at: http://grammar.about.com/od/fh/g/Future-In-The-Past.htm

posterior tense in (22d) is equivalent to a simple future tense. English does not have a fully natural way of indicating "future in the future". Comrie states that the closest equivalent would make use of the *about to* construction, which marks immediate future: *he will be about to X.*

21.4.1 Complex ("absolute-relative") tense marking

The perspective time (PT) for relative tense markers like those discussed above is not grammatically specified but is determined by contextual features. However, Comrie points out that some languages do have tense forms which grammatically specify both the location of PT (relative to TU) and the location of TT (relative to PT). Comrie refers to such cases as "absolute-relative" tense marking; we will use the term COMPLEX TENSE.

The English Pluperfect construction (*I had eaten*) can be used to express "past in the past", as illustrated in (23). In example (23a), the event of Sam reaching the base camp is asserted to be true at a topic time which is in the past relative to a perspective time in the past, which is defined by the preceding clause (the time when the speaker arrived there). In example (23b), the event of Einstein publishing a paper (in 1905) is asserted to be true at a topic time which is in the past relative to a perspective time in the past, i.e. the time at which he won the Nobel prize (1922).

(23) a. I reached the base camp Tuesday afternoon; Sam *had arrived* the previous evening.
b. Einstein was awarded the Nobel prize in 1922, for a paper that he *had published* in 1905.

Similarly, the Future Perfect construction (*I will have eaten*) can be used to express "past in the future". In example (24a), the event of Sam reaching the base camp is asserted to be true at a topic time which is in the past relative to a perspective time in the future (the time when the speaker arrives there). Another complex tense, "future in the past", is illustrated in (24b). This sentence asserts that the event of Einstein winning the Nobel prize (1922) was in the future relative to a perspective time in the past, i.e. the year in which he published four ground-breaking papers (1905).

(24) a. I expect to reach the base camp on Tuesday afternoon; Sam *will have arrived* the previous evening.
b. Einstein published four ground-breaking papers in 1905, including the one for which he *would win* the Nobel prize in 1922.

The relative positions of TT, PT and TU for the italicized verbs in examples (23b), (24a), and (24b) are shown in the diagrams in (25).

(25) a. [TT: 1905] PT TU — | TSit | (1922) (now) — "past in the past" (23b)

b. TU [TT: Mon. eve.] PT — (now) | TSit | (Tues. pm) — "past in the future" (23a)

c. PT [TT: 1922] TU — (1905) | TSit | (now) — "future in the past" (23b)

As we will see in Chapter 22, the Pluperfect and Future Perfect forms are ambiguous. In addition to the complex tense readings illustrated in (23–24), they can also be used to indicate perfect aspect. In this chapter we consider only their tense functions.[14]

Comrie (1985) points out that cross-linguistically, most forms which express complex tense meanings are morphologically complex; that is, they involve combinations of two or more morphemes, like the English Pluperfect and Future Perfect constructions. However, occasional exceptions to this generalization do exist, e.g. the mono-morphemic pluperfect *–ara* in literary Portuguese.

21.4.2 Sequence of tenses in indirect speech

The difference between direct vs. indirect speech is that direct speech purports to be an exact quotation of the speaker's words, as in (26a), whereas indirect speech does not (26b).[15]

(26) a. Yesterday Arthur told me, "I will meet you here again tomorrow." [DIRECT]

b. Yesterday Arthur told me that he would meet me there again today. [INDIRECT]

One of the most important differences between the two forms is seen in the use of the deictic elements. Deictics within the direct quote (26a) are anchored

[14] As discussed in Chapter 22, the temporal adverbs used here ensure that only the complex tense readings are available.

[15] Most languages probably make a distinction between direct vs. indirect speech, but in some languages the difference is quite subtle. A number of languages are reported to have an intermediate form, "semi-direct speech", in which some but not all of the deictic elements (especially pronouns and/or agreement markers) shift their reference point.

to the perspective of the original speaker (Arthur) and the time and place of the original speech event: *I* = Arthur; *you* = the addressee in the original speech event, who is also the speaker in the current, reporting event; *here* = place of the original speech event; *tomorrow* = the day following the original speech event; etc. Deictics within the indirect quote (26b) are anchored to the perspective of the speaker in the current, reporting event (= the addressee in the original speech event), and the time and place of the current speech event. So *I* shifts to *he*; *you* shifts to *me*; *here* shifts to *there*; *tomorrow* shifts to *today*, etc.

Notice that the tense of the verb also shifts: *will meet* in the direct quote (26a) becomes *would meet* in the indirect quote (26b). Since (absolute) tense is a deictic category, anchored to the time of speaking, this is hardly surprising. It would be natural to assume that this shift in tenses follows automatically from the shift in deictic reference point. This may in fact be the case in some languages, but in English and a number of other languages, the behavior of tense in indirect speech is more complex. (The same issues often arise in other types of finite complements, e.g. complements of verbs of thinking and knowing, in addition to verbs of saying.)

Comrie (1985) presents an interesting contrast between the use of tense in indirect speech in English vs. Russian. In Russian, the tense of the verb in indirect speech is identical to the tense in direct speech, i.e., the tense that was used by the original speaker in the original speech act. However, all of the other deictic elements shift to the perspective of the current speaker, just as they do in English. An example is presented in (27), reporting a speech act by John at some unspecified time in the past:[16]

(27) a. Džon skazal: "Ja ujdu zavtra."
John said 1SG will.leave tomorrow
John said, "I will leave tomorrow." [DIRECT]

b. Džon skazal, čto on ujdet na sledujuščij den.
John said COMP 3SG will.leave on next day
John said that he would leave (lit: will leave) on the following day. [INDIRECT]

In other words, verbs in Russian indirect speech complements (and other finite complements) get relative tense marking: the reference point is not the current time of speaking, but the time of the reported speech event (or, more generally, the topic time of the main clause). English verbs behave differently in this regard.

[16]Data from Comrie (1985: 109). The non-past tense used in these examples would be interpreted with future reference in this context.

For example, in (26b) and the English translation of (27b), where the original speaker used a simple future tense (*will leave*), the form used in indirect speech is the complex "future in the past" tense (*would leave*). As noted above, this is what we would expect to happen due to the shift in the deictic reference point, from the time of the original speech event to the time of the current, reporting speech event. However, there are other contexts where this shift by itself cannot account for the English tense forms.

The examples in (28) suggest that the form of the complement verb depends on the tense of the matrix (main clause) verb. Assume that John's actual words in both (28a) and (28b) use the present progressive form (*I am studying*). When the matrix verb occurs in the future tense, as in (28b), English seems to follow the same pattern as Russian: the tense of the complement verb in indirect speech is identical to the tense that would have been used by the original speaker. However, when the matrix verb occurs in the past tense, this is not always true: in (28a), for example, we see the past progressive form (*was studying*) instead of the present progressive (*is studying*).

(28) a. Yesterday I asked John what he was doing, and he said that he *was/*is studying.*
b. If I ask him the same thing tomorrow, he will say that he *is/*will be studying.*

Some additional examples illustrating this contrast are presented below. One general pattern that emerges is that, when the complement clause contains an auxiliary verb, that auxiliary retains its original tense form if the matrix verb occurs in the future (b, b, b). However, if the matrix verb occurs in the past, the auxiliary is normally "back-shifted", i.e., replaced by the corresponding past tense form, as seen in (a, a, b).[17]

(29) a. Yesterday I invited John to go out for pizza, but he said that he *had/ *has* just *eaten.*
b. If you invite him for pizza tomorrow, he will say that he *has/ will have* just *eaten.*

(30) (spoken in 1998):
a. In 2008 Ebenezer will say, "I *will* get tenure in 2011."
b. In 2008 Ebenezer will say that he *will* get tenure in 2011.

[17] Many of the examples in the remainder of this section are adapted from Declerck (1991).

(31) (spoken in 1998):

a. In 1987 Ebenezer said, "I *will* get tenure in 1992."

b. In 1987 Ebenezer said that he *would/*will* get tenure in 1992.

When the original, reported utterance contains a verb in the simple past tense, the original tense form is again retained if the matrix verb occurs in the future (32). This can result in a past tense form being used to describe an event which is in the future relative to the current time of speaking, as in (32b). Back-shifting of a simple past form is often optional when the matrix verb occurs in the past, as in (33).

(32) (spoken in 1998):

a. In 2008 Ebenezer will say, "I *got* tenure in 2004."

b. In 2008 Ebenezer will say that he *got/*will get* tenure in 2004.

(33) (spoken in 1998):

a. In 1987 Ebenezer said, "I *got* tenure in 1982."

b. In 1987 Ebenezer said that he *got/had gotten* tenure in 1982.

There are certain other contexts where back-shifting appears to be optional as well. For example, if the matrix verb occurs in the past and the complement clause describes a situation which is still true at the current time of speaking, either past or present can often be used for the complement verb in place of the present tense used by the original speaker (34). However, even in this context back-shifting is sometimes obligatory, as illustrated in (35).

(34) a. Yesterday the mayor revealed that he *is/was* terminally ill.

b. Last week John told me that he *likes/liked* you.

c. The ancient Babylonians did not know that the earth *circles/circled* the sun.

(35) a. I KNEW you *liked/*like* her.

b. This is John's wife.
— Yes, I THOUGHT he *was/*is* married.

The set of rules which determine the tense forms in indirect speech complements is traditionally referred to as the "sequence of tenses." A full discussion of the sequence of tenses in English is beyond the scope of this chapter. Scholars disagree as to whether the sequence of tenses in English can be explained on semantic grounds. Some (e.g. Comrie 1985) argue that the rules are purely grammatical, and cannot be predicted from the semantic content of the tense forms. Others (e.g. Declerck 1991) argue that a semantic analysis is possible, though the rules would need to be fairly complex.

Our purpose in this section has been to show that verb forms in indirect speech complements may require special treatment: these verbs may not exhibit the same kind of relative tense marking found in other kinds of subordinate clauses within the same language, and the normal shift in deictic reference point may not explain the usage of the tenses. Finally, this is an area where even closely related languages can exhibit significant differences from each other.

21.5 Temporal Remoteness markers ("metrical tense")

Among languages in which tense is marked morphologically, the most common tense systems involve a two-way distinction: either past vs. non-past or future vs. non-future.[18] A three-way morphological distinction, like the Lithuanian past vs. present vs. future paradigm mentioned in Chapter 20 (and repeated here as 36) is actually somewhat unusual.

(36) Lithuanian tense marking (Chung & Timberlake 1985: 204)

a. dirb-*au*
   work-1SG.PAST
   'I worked/ was working'

b. dirb-*u*
   work-1SG.PRESENT
   'I work/ am working'

c. dirb-*s*-iu
   work-FUTURE-1SG
   'I will work/ will be working'

However, a number of languages have verbal affixes which distinguish more than one degree of past and/or future time reference, e.g. 'immediate past' vs. 'near past' vs. 'distant past'. Such systems are especially well-known among the Bantu languages. Example (37) presents a paradigm from the Bantu language

[18] Chung & Timberlake (1985).

ChiBemba, which has (in addition to the present tense, not shown here) a symmetric set of four past and four future time markers.

(37) ChiBemba (Bantu)[19]

a. remote past
ba-*àlí*-bomb-*ele*
'they worked (before yesterday)'

b. removed past
ba-*àlíí*-bomba
'they worked (yesterday)'

c. near past
ba-*àcí*-bomba
'they worked (today)'

d. immediate past
ba-*á*-bomba
'they worked (within the last 3 hours)'

e. immediate future
ba-*áláá*-bomba
'they'll work (within the next 3 hours)'

f. near future ba-*léé* -bomba
'they'll work (later today)'

g. removed future ba-*kà*-bomba
'they'll work (tomorrow)'

h. remote future
ba-*ká* -bomba
'they'll work (after tomorrow)'

A slightly less complex system is found in Grebo (Niger-Kordofanian), as illustrated in (38):

(38) Grebo (Niger-Kordofanian)[20]

a. remote past
ne du-*da* bla
'I pounded rice (before yesterday)'

[19] Chung & Timberlake (1985: 208), based on Givón (1972).
[20] Frawley (1992: 365–367); based on Innes (1966).

b. yesterday past
ne du-*də* bla
'I pounded rice (yesterday)'

c. today (past or future)
ne du-*e* bla
'I pounded/will pound rice (today)'

d. tomorrow future
ne du-*a* bla
'I will pound rice (tomorrow)'

e. remote future
ne du-*də*$_2$ bla
'I will pound rice (after tomorrow)'

These systems are sometimes referred to as "metrical tense" or "graded tense" systems. However, some recent research has argued that at least in some languages, these markers indicate the location of the situation time (TSit), rather than the topic time (TT), relative to the time of speaking.[21] If this is true, then these markers would not fit Klein's definition of tense. The widely-used label TEMPORAL REMOTENESS is general enough to include this type as well.

As examples (37–38) illustrate, Temporal Remoteness systems frequently make distinctions such as 'today' vs. 'yesterday', 'yesterday' vs. 'before yesterday', etc. In such systems, the "today" category is sometimes referred to as HODIERNAL, and the "yesterday past" category is sometimes referred to as HESTERNAL, based on the Latin words for 'today' and 'yesterday'. In some languages, temporal remoteness is measured in other units of time, e.g. months or years; and in some, there can be a shift in the choice of unit depending on which unit would be contextually most relevant. Some languages make other kinds of distinctions, e.g. between remembered past vs. non-remembered past.[22]

The ChiBemba and Grebo systems illustrated above are both symmetrical, with equal numbers of past and future categories. It is also fairly common for a language with Temporal Remoteness markers to make more distinctions in the past than in the future. Nurse (2008) reports that in his sample of 210 Bantu languages, about half have only a single future category, whereas 80% have more than one degree of past time marking.

When languages do have multiple contrastive future markers, it is not uncommon for one or more to take on secondary meanings relating to degree of

[21]Cable (2013); LaCross (2016).
[22]Botne (2012).

certainty (remote future marking less certainty). Such secondary meanings are also associated with past time markers in some languages, with remoteness indicating reduced certainty.[23]

21.6 Conclusion

We have adopted Klein's definition of (absolute) tense as indicating a temporal relation between TT and TU, and aspect as indicating a temporal relation between TT and TSit. We assume further that relative tense indicates a temporal relation between TT and some perspective time (PT), which is determined by context. It is important to remember that the observed uses of tense-aspect markers do not depend only on the semantic content of these morphemes. When we seek to analyze the meanings of these markers, we need to consider the following additional factors as well:

- *aspectual sensitivity* (restriction to specific aktionsart/situation types);
- potential for different semantic functions in different situation types;
- coercion effects;
- potential for different uses in main vs. subordinate clauses;
- presuppositions triggered by the marker;
- implicatures which may add extra meaning;
- potential polysemy and/or idiomatic senses.

Several of these points were illustrated in our discussion of the simple present tense in English.

Further reading

Comrie (1985: ch. 1) provides a good introduction to the study of tense, and (in §1.8) a good discussion of the importance of distinguishing mean-

[23]Botne (2012); Nurse (2008).

ing from usage, for tense markers in particular. Michaelis (2006) is another helpful introduction, focusing primarily on English. Botne (2012) summarizes what we know about "metrical tense" systems.

Discussion exercises

A: Draw time-line diagrams and provide an appropriate label for the italicized verb in the following sentences:

Model answer

I managed to get to the station at 3:15 pm, but the train *had left* promptly at 3:00.

[TT: 3:00] PT TU "past in the past"

| TSit | (3:15)

1. When I got home from the hospital, my wife *wrote* a letter to my doctor.
2. When I got home from the hospital, my wife *was writing* a letter to my doctor.
3. I fled from the Khmer Rouge in 1976; my brother *would escape* two years later.
4. I can get to the station by 5:00 pm, but the train *will have departed* at 3:00 pm.
5. This morning the President rescinded an executive order that he *had issued* just 12 hours earlier.

Homework exercises

A: Draw time-line diagrams for the clauses which contain the italicized verb forms, and name the tense/aspect expressed by those forms:

Model answer

Einstein published four ground-breaking papers in 1905, including the one for which he *would win* the Nobel prize in 1922.

PT	[TT: 1922]	TU	"future in the past"
(1905)	| TSit |	(2016)	

1. When I got back from my trip, a family of stray cats *were living* in my garage.
2. The new President will move into the White House on Jan. 20th; the previous President and his family *will have vacated* the premises on Jan. 19th.
3. Kipling was sent back to England at the age of five; he *would return* to India eleven years later to work as a journalist.
4. The road to Fort Driant began for the United States Third Army when it landed on Utah Beach at 3 pm on August 5, 1944. The Third Army *had been activated* four days earlier in England under the command of Lt. Gen. George S. Patton Jr.[a]

[a] http://warfarehistorynetwork.com/daily/wwii/general-george-s-pattons-lost-battle/

22 Varieties of the Perfect

22.1 Introduction: PERFECT VS. PERFECTIVE

The terms PERFECT and PERFECTIVE are often confused, or used interchangeably, but there is an important difference between them. The contrast between the perfect (e.g. *have eaten*) and perfective (*ate*) in English is illustrated in the examples in (1). In some contexts there seems to be very little difference in meaning between the two, as illustrated in (1a–b). In other contexts, however, the two are not interchangeable (1c–e). For example, the perfect cannot be used with certain kinds of time adverbials which are fine with the perfective (1c–d). We will discuss this very interesting restriction in §22.3.

(1) a. I just *ate* a whole pizza.
b. I *have* just *eaten* a whole pizza.
c. Last night I *ate/#have eaten* a whole pizza.
d. When I was a small boy, I *broke/#have broken* my leg.
e. Gutenberg *discovered/#has discovered* the art of printing.[1]

Notice that the English perfect can be combined with imperfective (specifically progressive) aspect, as in (2). This shows clearly that perfect and perfective are distinct categories, because perfective and imperfective are incompatible and could not co-occur in the same clause.

(2) a. I *have been standing* in this line for the past four hours.
b. Smith *has been paying* a lot of visits to New York lately. (Grice 1975)
c. Nixon *has been writing* an autobiography.

There is a large measure of agreement about the basic meaning of the perfective. As stated in Chapter 20, it is an aspectual category which refers to an entire event as a whole, or as completely contained within Topic Time. In contrast, the meaning of the perfect has been and remains a highly contentious issue.

---

[1]McCoard (1978).

We will begin our discussion in §22.2 by illustrating four or five well-known uses or readings of the perfect. Whether or not all of these uses can be explained in terms of a single core meaning remains one of the issues in the controversy. In §22.3 we examine a much-discussed puzzle concerning the co-occurrence of time adverbials with the English present perfect. In §22.4 we will review some of the properties of the various readings which have been cited as evidence supporting the claim that the English present perfect form is in fact polysemous. In §22.5–§22.6 we examine the properties of perfect markers in two non-Indo-European languages.

22.2 Uses of the perfect

McCawley (1971), Comrie (1976), and others identify four major uses, or semantic functions, of the present perfect in English: (i) EXPERIENTIAL (or EXISTENTIAL) perfect, illustrated in (3); (ii) perfect of persistent situation (also known as the UNIVERSAL reading), illustrated in (4); (iii) perfect of CONTINUING RESULT, illustrated in (5); (iv) perfect of RECENT PAST (the "hot news" reading), illustrated in (6). Similar uses are found in a number of other languages.

(3) Experiential (or Existential) reading

a. Have you ever tasted fresh durian?
b. I have climbed Mt. Fuji twice in the past six months.

(4) Perfect of persistent situation (Universal perfect)

a. He has lived in Canberra since 1975.
b. I have been waiting for three days.

(5) Perfect of continuing result

a. I have lost my glasses, so I can't read this telegram.
b. The governor has fainted; don't let the press know until he regains consciousness.

(6) Recent past (or "hot news") reading

a. A group of former city employees has just abducted the Mayor.
b. The American president has announced new trade sanctions against the Vatican.

Kiparsky (2002) mentions a fifth use of the perfect, attested in languages such as Swahili, Sanskrit, and ancient Greek, which he calls the Stative Present. In these languages, the perfect form can be used to refer to events, as in English; but it can also be used to refer to the state that results from an event. Some Swahili examples are provided in (7).[2]

(7) Swahili (Ashton 1944)

Root		Perfect form	
-fika	'arrive'	*a-me-fika*	'he has arrived'
-iva	'ripen'	*ki-me-iva*	'it is ripe'
-choka	'get tired'	*a-me-choka*	'he is tired'
-simama	'stand up'	*a-me-simama*	'he is standing'
-sikia	'hear, feel'	*a-me-sikia*	'he understands'

We will focus our discussion on the four uses illustrated in (3–6). Comrie (1976) and others have attempted to unify these four readings under a single definition in terms of "current relevance". Comrie says that the perfect is used to express a past event which is relevant to the present situation. That is, it signals that some event in the past has produced a state of affairs which continues to be true and significant at the present moment.

Other authors have suggested that what the various uses of the perfect share is reference to an indefinite past time. Klein (1992; 1994) for example, building on the analysis of Reichenbach (1947), suggests that the perfect indicates that Time of Situation precedes Topic Time. A number of other authors have adopted some version of Reichenbach's analysis as well, often arguing that the different readings arise through various pragmatic inferences.

A very influential proposal by McCoard (1978) argues that the meaning of the perfect locates the described event within the "Extended Now", an interval of time which begins in the past and includes the utterance time.

> The intuitive idea of the Extended Now is that we typically count a longer stretch of time than the momentary "now" as the present for conversational purposes. Its exact duration is contextually determined, since what we count as "the present" in this sense may vary depending on the conversational topic. (Portner 2003)

[2] Kiparsky notes that this reading is available in English only with a single verb: *I've got (=I have) five dollars in my pocket* (cf. Jespersen 1931: 47). Comrie treats the Stative Present as a sub-type of his "perfect of result".

Some authors, however, including McCawley (1971; 1981b), Michaelis (1994; 1998), and Kiparsky (2002), have argued that the English perfect is polysemous, and that at least some of the readings listed above must be recognized as fully distinct senses. We will discuss some of the evidence which supports this claim in §22.4.

22.3 Tense vs. aspect uses of English *have* + participle

22.3.1 The present perfect puzzle

As illustrated in (1c–d), the English present perfect cannot normally co-occur with adverbial phrases which name the time in the past when the event occurred; further evidence is provided in (8b).

(8) a. George left for Paris *yesterday*/*last week*.
b. George has left for Paris (**yesterday*/**last week*).

This constraint may seem puzzling, since the use of the present perfect clearly indicates that the described event took place in the past. Klein's definition of perfect aspect as indicating that Time of Situation precedes Topic Time may offer at least a partial explanation.[3]

In English, the perfect can be combined with the various tenses to create the present perfect, past perfect, and future perfect forms: the present perfect combines present tense with perfect aspect, and so forth. Recall that tense indicates the position of Topic Time relative to the Time of Utterance; so in the present perfect, the Topic Time equals or includes the Time of Utterance. This helps to explain the "current relevance" constraint on the use of the present perfect: if the Topic Time is now, then in using the perfect to describe an event or situation in the past, we are actually "talking about" or making an assertion about the present moment.

Time adverbials like those in (1) and (8) generally modify the Topic Time. In the present perfect, the Topic Time is "now"; so time adverbials which locate the Topic Time in the past will be incompatible with the present perfect. The present perfect is, however, compatible with time adverbials which include the present moment, as illustrated in (9).

(9) a. I have *now* built hospitals on five continents.
b. I have interviewed ten students *today*/**yesterday*.
c. I have built five hospitals *this year*/**last year*.

[3]See Klein (1992) for a detailed discussion of this topic.

The use of the perfect aspect constrains the Time of Situation by indicating that it precedes Topic Time, but it does not provide a precise location in time for the Time of Situation. The result is an "indefinite past" interpretation, which stands in contrast to the simple past form of the verb. The simple past tense indicates that Topic Time precedes the Time of Utterance (past tense) and contains the Time of Situation (perfective aspect). Topic Time must be identifiable by the hearer, and so will generally be specified, with whatever degree of precision is required, by some combination of adverbial phrases, contextual clues, etc.

Comrie (1976: 55) points out that past time adverbials actually can be used with the present perfect form of the verb in certain contexts, such as in non-finite clauses (10a–c), or in the presence of a modal auxiliary (10d–f).

(10) a. Having eaten a whole pizza **last night**, I skipped breakfast this morning.
  b. Einstein's *having visited* Princeton **in 1921** eventually led to his permanent appointment there.
  c. Charlie Chaplin was believed *to have been born* **on April 16, 1889**.
  d. I should not *have eaten* a whole pizza **last night**.
  e. Einstein must *have visited* Princeton **in 1921**.
  f. Charlie Chaplin may *have been born* **on April 16, 1889**.

McCawley (1971: 101) observes that these environments have something in common: in these contexts past tense cannot be morphologically expressed by the normal past tense suffix *-ed*. This suggests that the perfect form (*have* + V-*en*) may have a different function in such contexts, namely as a marker of past time, i.e., an "allomorph" of past tense.

The acceptability of the time adverbials in (10) shows that the italicized verbs in these sentences do not have the interpretation normally associated with the present perfect form. But of course, it is also possible for a true perfect to occur with modals or in non-finite clauses, as illustrated in (11). So in these contexts the perfect form is ambiguous: it may either mark past tense, as in (10), or perfect aspect, as in (11). The two uses are distinguished by the interpretation of the time adverbials: if the time adverbs specify the time of the situation itself, as in (10), we are dealing with past tense.

(11) a. *Having lived* in Tokyo since 1965, I know the city fairly well.
b. Arthur was believed *to have climbed* Mt. Fuji four times.
c. Einstein must *have visited* Princeton several times before he emigrated to America.

The same ambiguity can be observed in the past perfect and future perfect as well. The examples in (12) involve true perfect aspect. The time adverbials shown in boldface in these examples refer to Topic Time, which precedes the time of speaking in the past perfect (12a) and follows the time of speaking in the future perfect (12b). In both cases, perfect aspect indicates that the Situation Time (the time when Mt. Fuji is climbed) occurs before Topic Time.

(12) a. **In 1987**, when I first met Arthur, he *had* (already) *climbed* Mt. Fuji four times.
b. **Next Christmas**, when you come to see me, I *will have climbed* Mt. Fuji four times.

The examples in (13) illustrate the use of the perfect form as a tense marker. In these examples the time adverbials shown in boldface refer to the time when the event actually took place. The perfect form is used to locate the situation prior to some perspective time which is different from the time of speaking. The result is a compound tense, as discussed in Chapter 21: "past in the past" in (13a), "past in the future" in (13b).

(13) a. Einstein was awarded the Nobel prize in 1922, for a paper that he *had published* **in 1905**.
b. I will reach Tokyo at 6:00 pm, but George *will have arrived* **at noon**.

22.3.2 Distinguishing perfect aspect vs. relative tense

There is a long tradition of regarding the aspectual vs. complex tense uses of the past perfect and future perfect forms as instances of polysemy.[4] However, some authors disagree with this view. Klein (1994) for example argues that both the "perfect in the past" (12a) and the "past in the past" (13a) interpretations of the pluperfect (= past perfect) form can be assigned to a single basic sense: TSit<TT<TU. He states, "The notion of relative tense is not necessary to account for the Pluperfect nor for the Future Perfect" (1994: 131).

[4] Jespersen (1924); Comrie (1976).

Bohnemeyer (2014) argues that perfect aspect does need to be distinguished from anterior (relative past) tense. The empirical basis for this claim is that some languages (e.g. Kalaallisut (=West Greenlandic) and Yucatec Maya) have a perfect aspect that cannot be used to express anterior tense, while other languages (e.g. Japanese, Kituba, and Korean) have anterior tenses that cannot be used to express perfect aspect. The critical diagnostic that Bohnemeyer uses is the interpretation of time adverbials. Time adverbials can be used with the perfect aspect in Kalaallisut and Yucatec Maya to specify a topic time before which the event had occurred, as illustrated in (14), but not to specify the time of the event itself, as in (15). The opposite pattern holds for the anterior tense forms in Japanese, Kituba, and Korean: these are compatible with time adverbials that specify the time of the event itself, as in (15), but not with time adverbials that specify a topic time before which the event had occurred, as in (14).

(14) PERFECT ASPECT:

a. In 1912, when Theodore Roosevelt challenged William Howard Taft for the Republican nomination, both men *had been elected* President of the United States. Taft was now an unpopular incumbent, Roosevelt his beloved predecessor.

b. When you see me again next Christmas, I *will have graduated* from law school.

(15) ANTERIOR TENSE:

a. Arthur's theft of government documents was discovered on May 21st, but he *had left* the country on April 16th.

b. I expect to reach the base camp on Tuesday afternoon; Sam *will have arrived* the previous evening.

The crucial difference between perfect aspect vs. anterior (= relative past) tense is this: With relative past tense the time of the described situation can be specified precisely, as seen in (15), because TSit must overlap with Topic Time. With perfect aspect, however, the time of the described situation is generally not specified precisely; all we know is that TSit must be sometime prior to Topic Time, as illustrated in (14).

22.4 Arguments for polysemous aspectual senses of the English Perfect

As noted above, McCawley (1971; 1981b), Michaelis (1994; 1998), and Kiparsky (2002) have argued that the various aspectual uses of the English perfect are in fact distinct polysemous senses. In this section we discuss some of the evidence that has been proposed in support of this hypothesis.

McCawley observed that the existential reading presupposes that a similar event could happen again, i.e., is currently possible. "In particular, the referents of the NP arguments must exist at [the time of speaking], and the event must be of a repeatable type" (Kiparsky 2002). The examples in (16b–c) are odd because the subject NPs are no longer alive at the time of speaking. Example (17) is odd because the described event clearly cannot happen again.

(16) a. I have never tasted fresh durian.
  b. #Julius Caesar has never tasted fresh durian.
  c. #Einstein has visited Princeton. (spoken after he died)[5]

(17) #Fred has been born in Paris.[6]

Leech (1971: 33) notes that the perfect form in (18a) would be appropriate if the Gauguin exhibition is still running, so the addressee could still attend. Once the exhibit has closed for good, however, only (18b) would be felicitous. McCawley (1971: 107) points out that other circumstances could also make (18a) infelicitous, for example if the addressee has "recently suffered an injury which will keep him in the hospital until long after the exhibition closes."

(18) a. Have you visited the Gauguin exhibition?
  b. Did you visit the Gauguin exhibition?

The examples in (16a–b) and (18a) show that the "current possibility" requirement is a presupposition, because it applies even to negative statements and questions. They also give us reason to believe that this presupposition is better stated in terms of current possibility than repeatability, since neither sentence assumes that the event has happened in the past.

Jespersen (1931: 66–67) notes that the choice between perfect and perfective can be significant because of this presupposition: "The difference between the

[5]Example (16c) is from Chomsky (1970).
[6]Kiparsky (2002).

reference to a dead man and to one still living is seen in the following quotation [19] which must have been written between 1859, when Macaulay died, and 1881, when Carlyle died (note also Mr. before the latter name)."[7]

(19) Macaulay *did not impress* the very soul of English feeling as Mr. Carlyle, for example, *has done.* [attributed to McCarthy]

Kiparsky points out that the presupposition of current possibility does not attach to the recent past (or "hot news") reading, as illustrated in (20). He cites this contrast as evidence that the existential and "hot news" readings are in fact distinct senses.

(20) a. Fred has just eaten the last doughnut.[8]
b. Einstein has just died.

A second argument is based on the observation that the various readings listed above do not all have the same truth conditions. Kiparsky notes that sentence (21) is ambiguous between the existential vs. universal (or persistent situation) readings, and that these two readings have different truth conditions. The universal reading asserts that at all times from 1977 to the present, the speaker was in Hyderabad; it is false if there were any times within that period at which he was elsewhere. The existential reading asserts only that there was at least one time between 1977 and the present moment at which the speaker was in Hyderabad. We could easily construct a context in which the existential reading is true and the universal reading false. This suggests that we are dealing with true semantic ambiguity, rather than mere vagueness or generality.

(21) I have been in Hyderabad since 1977.

Third, the various readings have different translation equivalents in other languages. Kiparsky notes that some languages which have a perfect, e.g. German

[7]Jespersen also points out that topicality can affect the use of the perfect: "Thus we may say: *Newton has explained the movements of the moon* (i.e. in a way that is still known or thought to be correct, while *Newton explained the movements of the moon from the attraction of the earth* would imply that the explanation has since been given up). On the other hand, we must use the preterit in *Newton believed in an omnipotent God*, because we are not thinking of any effect his belief may have on the present age" (Jespersen 1931: 66). The "effect on the present age" is relevant because the Topic Time of the present perfect is the time of speaking. Topicality also seems to be responsible for the contrast which Chomsky (1970) noted between *Einstein has visited Princeton*, which seems to imply that Einstein is still alive, vs. *Princeton has been visited by Einstein*, which can still be felicitous after Einstein's death.

[8]Kiparsky (2002).

and modern Greek, would use the simple present tense rather than the perfect to express the universal reading.[9] In addition, some languages (e.g. Hungarian and Najdi Arabic) have a distinct form which expresses only the existential/experiential perfect. Mandarin seems to be another such language; see §22.6 below.

A fourth type of evidence is seen in the following play on words (often attributed to Groucho Marx, but probably first spoken by someone else) which seems to demonstrate an antagonism between the (expected) "hot news" sense and the (unexpected) existential sense of the perfect:

(22) I've had a perfectly wonderful evening, but this wasn't it.

Authors supporting the polysemy of the perfect have also pointed out that the various readings have different aspectual requirements. The universal reading, in contrast to all other uses of the perfect, is possible only with atelic situations. This would include states or activities (23a–b), coerced states such as habituals (23c), and accomplishments expressed in the imperfective (thus involving an atelic assertion, 23d). Telic situations like those in (24) cannot normally be expressed in the universal perfect. In contrast, the perfect of continuing result illustrated in (5) is possible only with telic events (achievements or accomplishments).

(23) a. I have loved Charlie Chaplin ever since I saw *Modern Times.*
b. Fred has carried the food pack for the past 3 hours, and needs a rest.
c. I have attended All Saints Cathedral since 1983.
d. I've been writing a history of Nepal for the past six years, and haven't had time to work on anything else.

(24) a. #Fred has arrived at the summit for the past 3 hours.
b. #I have written a history of Nepal for the past six years.

This correlation between situation type and "sense" of the perfect is clearly an important fact which any analysis needs to account for; but by itself it does not necessarily prove that the perfect is polysemous. We have already seen several cases where a single sense of a tense or aspect marker gives rise to different interpretations with different situation types (*Aktionsart*), so this is a possibility that we should consider with the perfect as well. Here we leave our discussion of the English perfect, in order to examine the uses of the perfect in two other languages.

[9]See also Comrie (1976), Klein (2009).

22.5 Case study: Perfect aspect in Bạraïn (Chadic)

Baraïn is an East Chadic (Afroasiatic) language spoken by about 6,000 people in the Republic of Chad. Lovestrand (2012) discusses the contrast between perfect vs. perfective in Baraïn. He shows that the perfect form of the verb can be used for four of the five common uses of the perfect discussed above, specifically all but the experiential perfect. Examples of the four possible uses are presented in (25).

(25) a. **Resultative**:

kà gūsē ándì
kà gūs- -ē ándì
SBJ:3.M go.out PRF Andi
'He has left Andi (and has not returned).'

b. **Universal**:

kà súlē máŋgò wàlèɟì kúr
kà súl- -ē móŋgò wālō -ɟì kúr
SBJ:3.M sit PRF Mongo year POSS:3.M ten
'He has lived in Mongo for ten years (and lives there now).'

c. **Recent past**:

kà kólē sòndé kāj
kà kól- -ē sòndé kājē
SBJ:3.M go PRF now here
'He has just left this moment.'

d. **Present state**:

rámà āt:ē màlpì
rámà ăt:- -ē màlpì
Rama remain PRF Melfi
'Rama has stayed in Melfi (and is there now).'
French: *Il est resté à Melfi.*

Lovestrand states that "what is labeled the 'existential' or 'experiential' perfect is not expressed with the Perfect, but instead with the Perfective marker." An example is presented in (26).

(26) kì kólá āt:á ān:áŋ ɲɟàménà
kiˋ kól- -à āt:á ān:áŋ ɲɟamena
Sbj:2.s go PFV time how.many N'Djamena
'How many times have you been to N'Djamena?'

The perfect in Baraïn, in all four of its uses, entails that the situation is still true or the result state still holds at the time of speaking. Semelfactives, which do not have a result state, cannot be expressed in the perfect:

(27) a. kà ás:á tā āt:á pańiŋ́
kà ás:- -à tā āt:á pańiŋ́
Sbj:3.m cough pfv prtcl time one
'He coughed once.'

b. #kà as:e āt:á pańiŋ́
kà ás:- -ē āt:á pańiŋ́
Sbj:3.m cough prf time one

The requirement that the result state still hold true at the time of speaking is illustrated in (28a). If the same event is described in the perfective, as in (28b), it implies that the result state is no longer true.

(28) a. kà kólá wò kà láawē
kà kól- -à wò kà láaw- -ē
Sbj:3.m go pfv and S:3.m return prf
'He left but he has returned (and is still here).'

b. kà kólá wò kà láawá tā
kà kól- -à wò kà láaw- -à tā
Sbj:3.m go pfv and S:3.m return pfv prtcl
'He left and he returned (but he is not here now).'

Events which result in a permanent change of state, like those in (29a) and (30a), must normally be expressed in the perfect. If these events are described in the perfective, as in (29b) and (30b), it implies that some extraordinary event has taken place to undo the result state of the described event.

(29) a. át:ù tōklē
át:á -ɟù tǒkl- -ē
arm poss:1sg remove prf
'My arm was removed.'

b. át:ù tòklá tā
át:á -ɟù tǒkl- -à tā
arm poss:1sg remove pfv prtcl
'My arm was removed once (but somebody reattached it).'

(30) a. kà móté̄
kà mót- -ē
SBJ:3.M die PRF
'He died.'

b. ?kà mótá
kà mót- -à
SBJ:3.M die PFV
'He *was* dead (but is miraculously no longer dead).'

The inference illustrated in (29–30), by which the perfective signals that the result state is no longer true, seems to be an implicature triggered by the speaker's choice not to use the perfect, where that would be possible. This inference does not arise in all contexts. For example, verbs describing main-line events in a narrative sequence can occur in the perfective without any implication that the result state is no longer true. In contrast, the requirement that the result state of an event in the perfect hold true at the time of speaking is an entailment which cannot be cancelled, as demonstrated in (31b).

(31) a. kà mótá tā wò kà ɲīrē
kà mót- -à tā wò kà ɲīr -ē
SBJ:3.M die PFV PRTCL and SBJ:3.M resurrect PRF
'He died, but he has been resurrected.'

b. #kà mótē wò kà ɲīrē
kà mót- -ē wò kà ɲīr -ē
SBJ:3.M die PRF and SBJ:3.M resurrect PRF
(intended: 'He has died, but he has been resurrected.')

22.6 Case study: Experiential *-guo* in Mandarin

In our discussion of the English perfect we noted that some languages have a perfect marker which expresses only the existential/experiential sense. Mandarin is one such language. The meaning of the verbal suffix *-guo* is in some ways the polar opposite of the meaning of the perfect marker in Baraïn. While the perfect in Baraïn can express all of the standard perfect readings except the experiential, *-guo* expresses only the experiential perfect. While the perfect in Baraïn requires that the result state of the event still holds true at the time of speaking, *-guo* requires that the result state no longer holds true at the time of speaking.

The meaning of Mandarin *-guo* is similar in many ways to the existential/experiential perfect in English; but there are important differences as well. Chao (1968) refers to the suffix *-guo* as a marker of "indefinite past aspect". Li & Thompson (1981: 226) identify *-guo* as a marker of "experiential aspect", stating that it indicates that the situation has been experienced at least once, at some indefinite time in the past.[10] They provide the following minimal pair illustrating the contrast between the perfective (32a), in which the described event occurs within Topic Time, vs. the experiential (32b), in which the described event occurs at some arbitrary time prior to Topic Time.[11]

(32) a. Nǐ kànjian-le wǒ=de yǎnjìng ma?
2SG see-PFV 1SG=POSS glasses Q
'Did you see my glasses?' (recently; I'm looking for them)

b. Nǐ kànjian-guo wǒ=de yǎnjìng ma?
2SG see-EXPER 1SG=POSS glasses Q
'Have you ever seen my glasses?'

Wu (2009) states: "an eventuality presented by *-guo* is temporally independent of others in the same discourse." This constraint follows from the fact that normally *-guo* has indefinite time reference, and so does not establish a new Topic Time to which other clauses or sentences can refer. As a result, clauses marked with *-guo* are not interpreted as a narrative sequence of events. Iljic (1990: 308) provides the following contrast between the two verbal suffixes *–le* and *-guo*, showing that a series of clauses marked with *–le* is interpreted as a chronological sequence, while the same series of clauses marked with *-guo* is interpreted as a mere inventory of activities.

(33) a. Qùnián wǒ zuò-le mǎimài, xué-le jìsuànjī, shàng-le yèdàxué.
last.year 1SG do-PFV business study-PFV computer go-PFV evening.university
'Last year I *did* some business, (then) *studied* computers, (then) *attended* evening university.' (chronological perspective)

[10] Some authors take the term "experiential aspect" quite literally, assuming that an animate experiencer must be involved. For example, Xiao & McEnery (2004: 144) write: "The distinguishing feature of *-guo* is that it conveys a mentally experienced situation." C. Smith (1997: 267) states that "sentences with-*guo* ascribe to an experiencer the property of having participated in the situation." However, *-guo* can also be used in clauses which contain no animate arguments.

[11] Examples from Ma (1977: 19); Li & Thompson (1981: 227).

b. Qùnián wǒ *zuò-guo* mǎimài, *xué-guo* jìsuànjī, *shàng-guo* yèdàxué.
last.year 1SG do-EXPER business study-EXPER computer go-EXPER evening.university
'Last year I *did* some business, (and) *studied* computers, (and) *attended* evening university.' (inventory perspective)

Examples like (34) are sometimes cited as counter-examples to the generalization that *-guo* marks indefinite time in the past. The speaker in this sentence is clearly not just claiming to have eaten food at some time in the past, but rather is stating that he has finished eating the most recently scheduled meal.

(34) Wǒ chī-guò fàn le.
1SG eat-finish rice COS[12]
'I have already eaten.' (Ma 1977)

Chao (1968: 251), Comrie (1976: 59) and Xiao & McEnery (2004: 139ff.) state that the *-guò* in such examples is not the aspectual suffix but a verb root occurring as the second member of a compound verb. Both of these forms are derived from the verb *guò* 'to pass by', and both are written with the same Chinese character. However, the aspectual suffix can be distinguished from the compound verb by phonological and morphological evidence. Phonologically, the aspectual suffix is always toneless (i.e., takes neutral tone) whereas the compound verb takes an optional 4th tone, as marked in (34).[13] Morphologically, the compound verb *-guò* can be followed by the perfective suffix *-le*, whereas the aspectual suffix *-guo* cannot. Chu (1998: 39–40) shows that temporal adverbial clauses like the first clause of (35) are another context where the compound verb *-guò* rather than the aspectual suffix *-guo* is used. Some authors introduce unnecessary complexity into the discussion of aspectual *-guo* by failing to make this distinction.

(35) Nǐ míngtian kàn-guò jiù zhīdao le.
2SG tomorrow see-finish then know COS
'After you see it tomorrow, you will know.' (G.-t. Chen 1979)

Many authors have noted an interesting semantic restriction on the use of the aspectual suffix *-guo*: as first observed by Chao (1968:439; cf. Yeh 1996), there

[12]The abbreviation COS stands for 'change-of-state', the label used by Soh (2009) for the sentence-final particle which indicates that a situation is currently true but was not true in the past. Li & Thompson (1981: 238ff.) use the label "Currently Relevant State" for this particle.

[13]Comrie states that this 4th tone is optional but is usually pronounced.

must be a "discontinuity" between Situation Time and Topic Time. If the described event produces a result state, the result state must be over before Topic Time, as seen in (36a). We might represent this discontinuity as follows: TSit ∩ TT = ∅ (here we assume that the result state is included in TSit). Some authors (e.g. Iljic 1990, Yeh 1996) have suggested that this discontinuity effect is merely an "inference"; but examples (37a) and (38a) seem to indicate that the requirement is an entailment and not just an implicature.[14]

(36) a. Wǒ shuāi-duàn-guo tuǐ.
1SG fall-break-EXPER leg
'I have broken my leg (before).' (It has healed since.)

b. Wǒ shuāi-duàn-le tuǐ.
1SG fall-break-PFV leg
'I broke my leg.' (It may be still in a cast.)

(37) a. Tā qùnián dào Zhōngguó qù-guo, (#xiànzai hái zài nàr ne).
3SG last.year to China go-EXPER now still at there PRTCL
'He has been to China sometime last year (#and is still there now).'

b. Tā qùnián dào Zhōngguó qù-le, (xiànzai hái zài nàr ne).
3SG last.year to China go-PFV now still at there PRTCL
'He went to China last year (and is still there now).'

(38) a. Tā ài-guo Huáng Xiǎojie, (#xiànzai hái ài-zhe tā ne).
3SG love-EXPER Huang Miss now still love-CONT there PRTCL
'He once loved Miss Huang (#and he still loves her now).'

b. Tā ài Huáng Xiǎojie le, (xiànzai hái ài-zhe tā ne).
3SG love Huang Miss COS now still love-CONT there PRTCL
'He has fallen in love with Miss Huang (and he still loves her now).'

Interestingly, this discontinuity requirement is (partially?) dependent on the definiteness of the affected argument.[15] When the patient is definite, as in (39a), the use of *-guo* indicates that the result state no longer obtains; but when the patient is indefinite, as in (39b), there is no such implication/entailment.[16]

[14]Examples (36)–(38) come from Ma (1977: 18, 25) and Chao (1968).
[15]Lin (2007); Wu (2008); C.-c. Chen (2009).
[16]Examples from C.-c. Chen (2009); cf. Lin (2007).

(39) a. Lǐsì nòng-huài-guo zhè bù bǐjìxíng-diànnǎo.
Lisi make-broken-EXPER this CL laptop
'Lisi has broken this laptop before.'
(strongly implies that the laptop has been fixed at the time of speech)

b. Lǐsì nòng-huài-guo yī bù bǐjìxíng-diànnǎo.
Lisi make-broken-EXPER one CL laptop
'Lisi has broken a laptop before.'
(no commitment as to whether the laptop has been fixed or not)

A number of authors[17] have claimed that the situation marked by *-guo* must be repeatable. If it is an event, there must be a possibility for the same kind of event to happen again. This is a well-known property of the experiential (or existential) perfect in English, and its applicability to *-guo* is supported by examples like (40), from Ma (1977: 15). However, this claim has been challenged by number of other authors.[18] Consider the contrast in (41). Neither being old nor young are states that are repeatable for a single individual. The contrast between the two sentences seems best explained in terms of the discontinuity requirement: a person who is no longer young can still be alive, but not a person who is no longer old.

(40) * Tā sǐ-guo.
3SG die-EXPER
(intended: 'He has died before.')

(41) a. Nǐ yě niánqīng-guo.
you also young-EXPER
'You also have been young before.'

b. *Nǐ yě lǎo-guo.
you also old-EXPER
'You have also been old before.'

It appears that all of the data which has been proposed in support of the repeatability hypothesis can equally well be explained in terms of the discontinuity requirement. Support for the idea that discontinuity, rather than repeatability, is the operative factor comes from the observation that "repeatability" effects are sensitive to definiteness in exactly the same way as demonstrated above for the

[17] Ma (1977); Li & Thompson (1981: 230); Yeh (1996); C. Smith (1997: 268).

[18] G.-t. Chen (1979), Iljic (1990), Xiao & McEnery (2004: 147–148), Pan & Lee (2004), Lin (2007).

discontinuity requirement; this is illustrated in (42).[19] The fact that it is possible to use *-guo* when talking about the actions of dead people, as in (42b), gives further support to the claim that there is no repeatability requirement in Mandarin. Such examples are normally quite unnatural in the English experiential/existential perfect.

(42) a. * Columbus fāxiàn-guo měizhōu.
Columbus discover-EXPER America
(intended: 'Columbus has discovered America before.')

b. Columbus fāxiàn-guo yī gè xiǎo dǎo.
Columbus discover-EXPER one CL small island
'Columbus has discovered a small island before.'

It is useful to compare the semantic effect of the aspectual suffix *-guo* in various situation types (*Aktionsart*). With stative predicates, *-guo* indicates that the state no longer exists (43).[20] Therefore, permanent states cannot normally be marked with *-guo* (44).[21]

(43) a. Zhāng Xiǎojie guòqù pàng-guo.
Zhang Miss in.past fat-EXPER
'Miss Zhang has been fat.' (implying she is not fat now)

b. Měiguo níuròu yě guì-guo.
America beef also expensive-EXPER
'Beef America has also been expensive (in the past but not now).'

c. Tā zài Zhōngguó zhù-guo sān nián.
3SG at China live-EXPER three year
'He has lived in China for three years before (but does not live there now).'

(44) * Dāngdì nóngmín zhīdào-guo nà gèzhā yǒudú.
local farmer know-EXPER that chrome.dreg poisonous
(intended: 'Local farmers knew that those chrome dregs were poisonous.')

[19] Examples from Yeh (1996: 153, 163)
[20] Examples from Ma (1977: 20, 23)
[21] Example (44) comes from Xiao & McEnery (2004: 149).

With atelic events such as activities (45) and non-culminating accomplishments (46), the suffix *-guo* has the same interpretation as the perfective suffix *–le*, indicating that the event has terminated.[22]

(45) Lǐsì dǎ-guo wǎngqiú.
Lisi play-EXPER tennis
'Lisi has played tennis before.'

(46) a. # Wǒ xiě-guo gěi Wáng de xìn, hái zài xiě.
1SG write-GUO to wang LNK letter, still PROG write
'I wrote Wang's letter and am still writing it.'

b. Wǒ xiě-guo gěi Wáng de xìn, kěshì méi xiě-wán.
1SG write-GUO to wang LNK letter, but not write-finish
'I wrote Wang's letter but didn't finish it.'

In light of what we have said above, we would predict that the aspectual suffix *-guo* cannot occur with telic predicates whose result state is permanent, because this would mean that discontinuity with Topic time is impossible. This prediction turns out to be true when the patient (or affected argument) is definite. However, as noted above, the discontinuity requirement does not apply when the patient is indefinite; so the aspectual suffix *-guo* is possible in such contexts.

The examples in (47a–b) contain a Result Compound Verb (RCV), which means that the culmination of the event is entailed. As predicted, *-guo* is not allowed when the object NP is definite (47a), but is possible when the object NP is indefinite (47b). However, (47c) contains the simple root 'kill' with no RCV, and so the culmination of the event would normally be implicated but not entailed. In this example, *-guo* functions as an explicit indicator that the result state was not achieved.[23]

(47) a. * Tā shā-sǐ-guo nèi-ge rén.
3SG kill-die-EXPER that-CLASS person
(intended: 'He has killed that person.')

b. Tā shā-sǐ-guo sān-ge rén.
3SG kill-die-EXPER three-CLASS person
'He has killed three people.'

[22] Examples from C. Smith (1997: 267).
[23] The examples in (47) come from Ma (1977: 23).

c. Tā shā-guo nèi-ge rén.
3SG kill-EXPER that-CLASS person
'He tried (at least once) to kill that person (without success).'

A similar pattern is seen in (48). The aspectual suffix *-guo* can occur with the predicate 'die' only when the patient is indefinite (48c). In (48d), which Chu (1998) and Xiao & McEnery (2004) describe as a figurative use of the word 'die', *-guo* functions as an indicator that the result state was not achieved.

(48) a. * Tā sǐ-guo.
3SG die-EXPER
(intended: 'He has died before.') (Ma 1977: 15)

b. Tā sǐ-le.
3SG die-PFV
'He died.' (Ma 1977: 15)

c. Yǒu rén zài zhè tiáo hé lǐ yān-sǐ-guo.
have person at this CL river in drown-die-EXPER
'Someone has drowned in this river (before).' (Yeh 1996: 163)

d. Wǒ sǐ-guo hǎojǐ cì.
1SG die-EXPER quite.a.few time
'I almost died quite a few times.' (Chu 1998: 41)

Huang & Davis (1989: 151) point out that *-guo* can also be used to indicate partial affectedness of a definite object, another way in which the culmination of the event might not be achieved:

(49) a. Gǒu gāngcái chī-le nǐ de píngguǒ.
dog just.now eat-PFV you POSS apple
'The dog just ate your apple.'

b. Gǒu gāngcái chī-guo nǐ de píngguǒ.
dog just.now eat-EXPER you POSS apple
'The dog just took a bite of your apple.'

22.7 Conclusion

We have discussed a number of different uses of the perfect in various languages. What all of these various uses have in common is the fact that (all or part of) the Situation Time precedes Topic Time. As mentioned at the beginning of this chapter, this is the component of meaning which Klein (1992) identifies as the defining feature of perfect aspect.

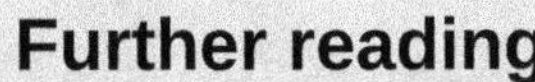

Further reading

Comrie (1976: ch. 3) is a foundational work, and still a good place to start. Portner (2011) and Ritz (2012) provide good overviews of the empirical challenges and competing analyses for the perfect.

Discussion exercises

A. Identify the sub-type (i.e., the semantic function: Experiential, Universal, Result, or "hot news") of the present perfect forms in the following examples:

1. Russia *has* just *accused* the American curling team of doping.
2. Rupert *has visited* Brazil three times.
3. Horace *has been playing* that same sonata since four o'clock.
4. The Prime Minister *has resigned*; it happened several weeks ago, but we still don't know who the next Prime Minister will be.
5. Martha *has known* about George's false teeth for several years.

Homework exercises

Based on the examples provided below, describe the Tok Pisin Tense-Aspect system and suggest an appropriate label for each of the five italicized grammatical markers (e.g. *subjunctive mood*, *iterative aspect*, etc.). These markers are glossed simply as 'AUX'. Some of these forms can also be used as independent verbs, but you should consider those meanings (shown in the section headings) to be distinct senses. Base your description on the 'AUX' functions only. You can ignore the somewhat mysterious "predicate marker" *i*.[a]

A. *bin*

1. Bung i *bin* stat long Mande na *bai* pinis long Fraide.
   meeting PRED AUX start at Monday and AUX end at Friday

   'The meeting began on Monday and will finish on Friday, April 22.'

2. Asde/#Tumora mi *bin* lukim tumbuna bilong mi.
   yesterday/#tomorrow 1SG AUX see grandparent POSS 1sg

   'Yesterday/#tomorrow I saw my grandparent.'

3. Wanem taim sik i *bin* kamap nupela?
   what time illness PRED AUX appear new

   'When did the illness first appear?'

4. Ol tumbuna i no *bin* wari long dispela.
   PL ancestor PRED not AUX worry about this

   'The ancestors did not worry about this.'

5. Ol i *bin* slip long haus bilong mi.
   3pl PRED AUX sleep at house POSS 1sg

   'They were sleeping in(side) my house.'

B. *bai*

6. Long wanem taim *bai* yu go?
   at what time AUX 2SG go

   'At what time will you go?'

7. Tumora/#Asde *bai* mi askim em.
   tomorrow/#yesterday AUX 1SG ask 3sg

   'Tomorrow/#yesterday I will ask him/her.'

8. Ating apinun *bai* mi traim pilai ping-pong namba.wan taim.
   maybe afternoon AUX 1SG try play ping-pong first time.'

   'Maybe this afternoon I will try to play ping-pong for the first time.'

9. Sapos yu kaikai planti pinat *bai* yu kamap strong olsem phantom.
   if 2SG eat much peanut AUX 2SG become strong like phantom

   'If you eat many peanuts, you will become strong like the Phantom.'

C. *save* (short form: *sa*) [main verb sense: 'know']

10. Mipela i no *save* kaikai bulmakau.
    1pl.EXCL PRED NEG AUX eat cow

    'We don't (customarily) eat beef.'

11. Mi *save* wokabaut go wok.
    1SG AUX walk go work

    'I always walk to work.'

12. Long nait mi slip na ol natnat i *save* kam long
at night 1SG sleep, and PL mosquitoes PRED AUX come to
haus bilong mi.
house POSS 1sg

'At night I sleep, and then the mosquitoes come into my house.'

13. Mipla stap lo(ng) skul, ol ami ol *sa* pait wantem ol
1pl.EXCL be in school, PL soldier 3PL AUX fight with PL
man ia.
man here

'When we were in school, the soldiers used to fight with the men (rebels).' [East New Britain dialect]

D. *stap* [main verb sense: 'be, stay, remain']

14. Ol i kaikai i *stap.*
3pl PRED eat PRED AUX

'They are/were eating.'

15. Ol lapun meri i subim ka i go i *stap.*
pl old woman PRED push car PRED go PRED AUX

'The old women are/were pushing a car.'

16. Dua i op nating i *stap.*
door PRED open just PRED AUX

'The door was just open like that...'

17. Em i tisa i *stap* yet.
3SG PRED teacher PRED AUX still

'He is still a teacher.'

18. Hamas de pikinini i sik i *stap*?
how.many day child PRED sick PRED AUX

'How many days has the child been sick?'

19. Taim em i kam i lukim Dogare i sindaun tanim
    time 3SG PRED come PRED see (name) PRED sit roll
    smok i *stap*.
    smoke PRED AUX

    'When he came he saw Dogare sitting down rolling a cigarette.'

20. Bai sampela ol i toktok i *stap* na ol i no harim
    AUX some 3pl PRED talk PRED AUX and 3pl PRED not listen
    gut tok bilong yu.
    well talk POSS 2sg

    'Some of them will be talking and not listen well to your speech.'

E. *pinis* [main verb sense: 'finish, stop, complete']

21. Mipela i wokim sampela haus *pinis*.
    1pl.EXCL PRED build some house AUX

    'We [excl.] have built some houses.'

22. Gavman i putim *pinis* planti didiman.
    government PRED place AUX many agricultural.officer

    'The government has appointed many agricultural officers.'

23. Dok i dai *pinis*.
    dog PRED die AUX

    'The dog has died/is dead.'

24. Mi lapun *pinis*.
    1SG old.person AUX

    'I am already old.' Or: 'I have grown old.'

25. a. Ol i bikpela *pinis*.
       3pl PRED big AUX

       'They have become big/are grown-ups (now).'

b. *Ol i liklik *pinis.*
3pl PRED small AUX

(intended: 'They are already small' or 'they were small once.')

26. Pen i stap longpela taim *pinis*, o, nau tasol em i kamap?
pain PRED exist long time AUX or now only 3SG PRED become

'Has the pain been there for a long time, or has it just started?

27. Em i kamap meija *pinis* taim mipela i harim dispela
3SG PRED become major AUX time 1pl.EXCL PRED hear this
stori hia.
story here

'He had become a major by the time we [excl.] heard this story.'

28. a. Esra i sanap long dispela ples.
Esra PRED stand at this place

'Ezra stood on this platform (while reading the Law).'
[Neh. 8:4]

b. Man i sanap *pinis.*
man PRED stand AUX

'The man has stood up (and is standing now).'

29. a. Wanpela diwai i sanap namel tru.
one tree PRED stand middle very

'One tree stood right in the middle (of the Garden).' [Gen. 3:3]

b. #Diwai i sanap *pinis.*
tree PRED stand AUX

'The tree has stood up (and is standing now).'

---

[a]Most of the examples in this exercise come from Verhaar (1985). Other data sources include: Dutton (1973); Wohlgemuth (1999); Holm (2000); Sebba (1997); G. Smith (2002); Joyce Wood and Liisa Berghäll (p.c.).

References

Abbott, Barbara. 2010. *Reference* (Oxford Surveys in Semantics and Pragmatics 2). Oxford University Press.

Adams, Ernest W. 1970. Subjunctive and indicative conditionals. *Foundations of Language* 6. 89–94.

Aikhenvald, Alexandra Y. 2004. *Evidentiality*. Oxford: Oxford University Press.

Aikhenvald, Alexandra Y. 2009. Semantics and grammar in clause linking. In R. M. W. Dixon & Alexandra Aikhenvald (eds.), *The semantics of clause linking: A cross-linguistic typology*, 380–402. Oxford, UK: Oxford University Press.

Akatsuka, Noriko. 1985. Conditionals and the epistemic scale. *Language* 61(3). 625–639.

Allen, J. H. & J. B. Greenough. 1903. *Allen and Greenough's new Latin grammar for schools and colleges*. Boston: Ginn & Company. Edited by J. B. Greenough, G. L. Kitteredge, A. A. Howard, and Benjamin L. D'Ooge.

Allwood, Jens, Lars-Gunnar Andersson & Östen Dahl. 1977. *Logic in linguistics*. Cambridge & New York: Cambridge University Press.

Apresjan, Jurij. 1974. Regular polysemy. *Linguistics* 142. 5–32.

Arka, I. Wayan. 2005. Speech levels, social predicates and pragmatic structure in Balinese: A lexical approach. *Pragmatics* 2/3. 169–203. elanguage.net/journals/pragmatics/article/download/490/418.

Aronoff, Mark & Kirsten Fudeman. 2011. *What is morphology?* 2nd edn. Malden, MA: Wiley-Blackwell.

Ashton, E. O. 1944. *Swahili grammar (including intonation)*. London: Longman.

Austin, J. L. 1956. Ifs and cans. *Proceedings of the British Academy* 42. 107–132.

Austin, J. L. 1961. *Performative utterances*. J. O. Urmson & G. J. Warnock (eds.). Oxford: Oxford University Press. 2nd edition, 1970.

Austin, J. L. 1962. *How to do things with words*. Oxford: Clarendon Press. Edited by James O. Urmson and Marina Sbisá.

Bach, Emmon. 1989. *Informal lectures on formal semantics*. Albany, NY: State University of New York Press.

Bach, Kent. 1994. Conversational impliciture. *Mind and Language* 9. 124–162.

Bach, Kent. 2010. Impliciture vs explicature: What's the difference? In Belén Soria & Esther Romero (eds.), *Explicit communication: Robyn Carston's pragmatics*, 126–137. London: Palgrave Macmillan.

Baker, Mark C. 1995. On the absence of certain quantifiers in Mohawk. In E. Bach, E. Jelinek, A. Kratzer & B. H. Partee (eds.), *Quantification in natural languages*, 21–58. Dordrecht & Boston: Kluwer Academic Publishers.

Bar-el, Leora, Henry Davis & Lisa Matthewson. 2005. *On non-culminating accomplishments* (Proceedings of the North Eastern Linguistics Society 35). Amherst, MA: GLSA. http://faculty.arts.ubc.ca/lmatthewson/pdf/accomplishments.pdf.

Bariki, Ozidi. 2008. On the relationship between translation and pragmatics. *International Journal of Translation* 20(1–2). 67–75.

Barker, Chris. 2002. Lexical semantics. In *Encyclopedia of cognitive science.* Macmillan Reference Ltd.

Barnes, Janet. 1984. Evidentials in the Tuyuca verb. *International Journal of American Linguistics* 50. 255–271.

Barwise, Jon & Robin Cooper. 1981. Generalized quantifiers in natural language. *Linguistics and Philosophy* 4. 159–219.

Beekman, John & John Callow. 1974. *Translating the word of God.* Grand Rapids, MI: Zondervan.

Bennett, Jonathan. 1982. Even if. *Linguistics and Philosophy* 5. 403–18.

Bennett, Jonathan. 2003. *A philosophical guide to conditionals.* Oxford: Oxford University Press.

Bhatt, Rajesh & Roumyana Pancheva. 2006. Conditionals. In Martin Everaert & Henk van Riemsdijk (eds.), *The Blackwell companion to syntax*, vol. 1, 638–687. London: Blackwell.

Binnick, Robert I. 2006. Aspect and aspectuality. In Bas Aarts & April McMahon (eds.), *The handbook of English linguistics*, 244–268. Malden, MA: Blackwell Publishing.

Birner, Betty J. 2012/2013. *Introduction to pragmatics.* Malden, MA & Chichester, UK: Wiley-Blackwell.

Bittner, Maria. 1995. Quantification in Eskimo: a challenge for compositional semantics. In E. Bach, E. Jelinek, A. Kratzer & B. H. Partee (eds.), *Quantification in natural languages*, 59–80. Dordrecht & Boston: Kluwer Academic Publishers.

Blackburn, P., M. de Rijke & Y. Venema. 2008. *Modal logic.* Cambridge: Cambridge University Press.

Blum-Kulka, S., J. House & G. Kasper (eds.). 1989. *Cross-cultural pragmatics: Requests and apologies* (Advances in Discourse Processes XXXI). New Jersey: Ablex Publishing Corporation.

Bohnemeyer, Jürgen. 2014. Aspect vs. relative tense: The case reopened. *Natural Language and Linguistic Theory* 32. 917–954.

Bolinger, Dwight. 1967. Adjectives in English: Attribution and predication. *Lingua* 18. 1–34.

Botne, Robert. 2012. Remoteness distinctions. In R. Binnick (ed.), *The handbook of tense and aspect*, 536–562. Oxford: Oxford University Press.

Bross, Fabian. 2012. German modal particles and the common ground. *Helikon: A Multidisciplinary Online Journal* 2. 182–209. http://helikon-online.de/2012/Bross_Particles.pdf.

Brown, Penelope & Stephen C. Levinson. 1978. Universals in language usage: Politeness phenomena. In E. N. Goody (ed.), *Questions and politeness: Strategies of social interaction*, 56–311. Cambridge: Cambridge University Press.

Bybee, Joan. 1992. Tense, aspect, and mood. In William Bright (ed.), *International encyclopedia of linguistics*, vol. 4, 144–145. New York & Oxford: Oxford University Press.

Bybee, Joan, Revere Perkins & William Pagliuca. 1994. *The evolution of grammar: Tense, aspect and modality in the languages of the world.* Chicago: University of Chicago Press.

Cable, Seth. 2013. Beyond the past, present and future: Towards the semantics of 'graded tense' in Gĩkũyũ. *Natural Language Semantics* 21(3). 219–276.

Cann, Ronnie. 2011. Sense relations. In Claudia Maienborn, Klaus von Heusinger & Paul Portner (eds.), *Semantics*, vol. 1, 456–478. Berlin: Walter de Gruyter.

Carlson, Greg. 1977. *Reference to kinds in English.* MIT dissertation.

Carston, Robyn. 1988. Implicature, explicature and truth-theoretic semantics. In R. Kempson (ed.), *Mental representations: The interface between language and reality*, 155–181. Cambridge: Cambridge University Press. Reprinted in Davis, S. (ed.) (1991).

Carston, Robyn. 1998. Informativeness, relevance and scalar implicature. In R. Carston & S. Uchida (eds.), *Relevance theory: Applications and implications*, 179–236. Amsterdam: John Benjamins.

Carston, Robyn. 2002. *Thoughts and utterances: The pragmatics of explicit communication.* Oxford: Blackwell.

Carston, Robyn. 2004. Relevance theory and the saying/implicating distinction. In Laurence Horn & Gregory Ward (eds.), *The handbook of pragmatics*, 633–656. Oxford: Blackwell.

Carston, Robyn & Alison Hall. 2012. Implicature and explicature. In Hans-Jörg Schmid (ed.), *Cognitive pragmatics* (Handbooks in Pragmatics 4), 47–84. Berlin: Mouton de Gruyter.

Chang, Chen Chung & H. Jerome Keisler. 1990. *Model theory*. 3rd edn. (Studies in Logic and the Foundations of Mathematics 73). Amsterdam: Elsevier.

Chao, Yuen-Ren. 1968. *A grammar of spoken Chinese*. Berkeley: University of California Press.

Chen, Chien-chou. 2009. Experientiality and reversibility of the aspectual morpheme *guo* in Mandarin Chinese: Temporal and atemporal perspectives. *Dong Hwa Journal of Humanities* (東華人文學報) 1. 247–94. ir . ndhu . edu . tw / bitstream/987654321/4910/1/14-247-294.pdf.

Chen, Gwang-tsai. 1979. The aspect markers *le*, *guo* and *zhe* in Mandarin Chinese. *Journal of the Chinese Language Teachers Association* 14(2). 27–46.

Cherchia, Gennaro & Sally McConnell-Ginet. 1990. *Meaning and grammar: An introduction to semantics*. Cambridge MA: MIT Press.

Chomsky, Noam. 1965. *Aspects of the theory of syntax*. Cambridge: MIT. Press.

Chomsky, Noam. 1970. Deep structure, surface structure and semantic interpretation. In R. Jakobson & S. Kawamoto (eds.), *Studies in general and Oriental linguistics*, 62–119. Tokyo: TEC Corporation.

Chu, Chauncey. 1998. *A discourse grammar of Mandarin Chinese*. New York: Peter Lang Publishing.

Chung, Sandra & Alan Timberlake. 1985. Tense, aspect, and mood. In Timothy Shopen (ed.), *Language typology and syntactic description: Grammatical categories and the lexicon*, vol. 3, 202–258. Cambridge: Cambridge University Press.

Cohen, L. Jonathan. 1971. The logical particles of natural language. In Y. Bar-Hillel (ed.), *Pragmatics of natural language*, 50–68. Dordrecht: Reidel.

Cole, Peter. 1982. *Imbabura Quechua* (Lingua Descriptive Studies 5). Amsterdam: North-Holland.

Comrie, Bernard. 1976. *Aspect*. Cambridge: Cambridge University Press.

Comrie, Bernard. 1985. *Tense*. Cambridge: Cambridge University Press.

Comrie, Bernard. 1986. Conditionals: A typology. In Elizatbeth C. Traugott, Alice ter Meulen, Judy Snitzer Reilly & Charles Ferguson (eds.), *On conditionals*, 77–99. Cambridge: Cambridge University Press.

Coppock, Elizabeth. 2016. *Semantics boot camp*. http://eecoppock.info/semantics-boot-camp.pdf. Unpublished ms.

Cotterell, Peter & Max Turner. 1989. *Linguistics and biblical interpretation*. Illinois: InterVarsity Press.

Croft, William & D. Alan Cruse. 2004. *Cognitive linguistics*. Cambridge: Cambridge University Press.

Cruse, D. Alan. 1986. *Lexical semantics*. Cambridge: Cambridge University Press.

Cruse, D. Alan. 2000. *Meaning in language: An introduction to semantics and pragmatics*. New York & Oxford: Oxford University Press.

Cruse, D. Alan. 2004. Lexical facets and metonymy. *Revista Ilha do Desterro: A Journal of English Language, Literatures in English and Cultural Studies* 47. 73–96. http://www.periodicos.ufsc.br/index.php/desterro/article/view/7348/6770.

de Haan, Ferdinand. 1997. *The interaction of modality and negation*. New York: Garland.

de Haan, Ferdinand. 1999. Evidentiality and epistemic modality: Setting boundaries. *Southwest Journal of Linguistics* 18. 83–101.

de Haan, Ferdinand. 2005. Encoding speaker perspective: Evidentials. In Zygmunt Frajzyngier & David Rood (eds.), *Linguistic diversity and language theories*, 379–397. Amsterdam: Benjamins.

de Haan, Ferdinand. 2006. Typological approaches to modality. In William Frawley (ed.), *Modality*, 27–69. Berlin: Mouton de Gruyter.

de Haan, Ferdinand. 2012. Evidentiality and mirativity. In Robert I. Binnick (ed.), *The Oxford handbook of tense and aspect*, 1020–1046. Oxford: Oxford University Press.

de Haan, Ferdinand. 2013. Semantic distinctions of evidentiality. In Matthew S. Dryer & Martin Haspelmath (eds.), *The world atlas of language structures online*. Leipzig: Max Planck Institute for Evolutionary Anthropology. http://wals.info/chapter/77.

de Swart, Henriette. 1998. Aspect shift and coercion. *Natural Language and Linguistic Theory* 16. 347–385.

Declerck, Renaat. 1991. *Tense in English*. London: Routledge.

DeLancey, Scott. 1995. *Verbal Case Frames in English and Tibetan*. Unpublished ms., Department of Linguistics, University of Oregon, Eugene, OR.

DeLancey, Scott. 2000. The universal basis of case. *Logos and Language* 1(2). 1–15.

Dell, François. 1983. An aspectual distinction in Tagalog. *Oceanic Linguistics* 22-23. 175–206.

DeRose, Keith & Richard E. Grandy. 1999. Conditional assertions and "biscuit" conditionals. *Noûs* 33(3). 405–420.

Dowty, David. 1979. *Word meaning and Montague grammar: The semantics of verbs and times in generative semantics and in Montague's PTQ*. Dordrecht & Boston: Reidel.

Dowty, David. 1991. Thematic proto-roles and argument selection. *Language* 67. 547–619.

Dowty, David, Robert Wall & Stanley Peters. 1981. *Introduction to Montague semantics.* Dordrecht: Reidel.

Drubig, Hans B. 2001. *On the syntactic form of epistemic modality.* Unpublished ms. Tübingen, University of Tübingen.

Dutton, Thomas E. 1973. *Conversational New Guinea Pidgin* (Pacific Linguistics D-12). Canberra: The Australian National University.

Ebert, Christian, Cornelia Endriss & Stefan Hinterwimmer. 2008. A unified analysis of indicative and biscuit conditionals as topics. In Tova Friedman & Satoshi Ito (eds.), *Proceedings of Semantics and Linguistic Theory 18*, 266–283. Ithaca: Cornell University.

Egner, Inge. 2002. *The speech act of promising in an intercultural perspective* (SIL Electronic Working Papers). SIL. http://www.sil.org/silewp/2002/001/SILEWP2002-001.pdf.

Enderton, Herbert B. 1977. *Elements of set theory.* New York: Academic Press.

Engelberg, Stefan. 2011. Lexical decomposition: Foundational issues. In Claudia Maienborn, Klaus von Heusinger & Paul Portner (eds.), *Semantics: An international handbook of natural language meaning*, vol. 1, 122–142. Berlin, New York: de Gruyter.

Ernst, Thomas. 2009. Speaker-oriented adverbs. *Natural Language and Linguistic Theory* 27. 497–544. DOI:10.1007/s11049-009-9069-1

Faller, Martina. 2002. *Semantics and pragmatics of evidentials in Cuzco Quechua.* Department of Linguistics, Stanford University dissertation. http://personalpages.manchester.ac.uk/staff/martina.t.faller/documents/thesis-a4.pdf.

Faller, Martina. 2003. Propositional- and illocutionary-level evidentiality in Cuzco Quechua. In Jan Anderssen, Paula Menendez-Benito & Adam Werle (eds.), *The Proceedings of SULA 2 (The Second Conference on the Semantics of Under-Represented Languages in the Americas),Vancouver, BC*, 19–33. Amherst: GLSA. http://www.umass.edu/linguist/events/SULA/SULA_2003_cd/files/faller.pdf.

Faller, Martina. 2006. *Evidentiality above and below speech acts.* http://semanticsarchive.net/Archive/GZiZjBhO/.

Fillmore, Charles. 1970. The grammar of *hitting* and *breaking*. In Roderick Jacobs & Peter Rosenbaum (eds.), *Readings in English transformational grammar*, 120–33. Washington, DC: Georgetown University Press.

Fillmore, Charles. 1977. The case for case reopened. In Peter Cole & Jerrold Sadock (eds.), *Grammatical relations* (Syntax and Semantics 8), 59–81. New York: Academic Press.

Fillmore, Charles & Beryl T. Atkins. 2000. Describing polysemy: The case of 'crawl'. In Yael Ravin & Claudia Leacock (eds.), *Polysemy: Theoretical and computational approaches*, 1–29. Oxford: Oxford University Press.

Finegan, Edward. 1999. *Language: Its structure and use.* Vol. 3. Fort Worth: Harcourt Brace College Publishers.

Fodor, Janet & Ivan Sag. 1982. Referential and quantificational indefinites. *Linguistics and Philosophy* 5. 355–398.

Fodor, Jerry A. 1975. *The language of thought.* New York: Crowell.

Fortescue, Michael. 1984. *West Greenlandic* (Croom Helm Descriptive Grammars). London: Croom Helm.

Fortin, Antonio. 2011. *The morphology and semantics of expressive affixes.* University of Oxford dissertation.

Franke, Michael. 2007. The pragmatics of biscuit conditionals. In Maria Aloni, Paul Dekker & Floris Roelofsen (eds.), *Proceedings of the 16th Amsterdam colloquium*, 91–96. http://www.sfs.uni-tuebingen.de/~mfranke/Papers/AC07_Paper.pdf.

Frawley, William. 1992. *Linguistic semantics.* Hillsdale, NJ, Hove & London: Lawrence Erlbaum.

Frege, Gottlob. 1892. Über Sinn und Bedeutung. *Zeitschrift für Philosophie und Philosophische Kritik* 100. 25–50. Translated as 'On sense and reference', in P. Geach and M. Black (eds.), *Translations from the philosophical writings of Gottlob Frege*, 56–78. Oxford: Blackwell.

Frege, Gottlob. 1918–1919. Der Gedanke. Eine logische Untersuchung. *Beiträge zur Philosophie des deutschen Idealismus* Band I. 58–77. Translated by Peter Geach (1956) as 'The thought: A logical inquiry' in *Mind* 55: 289–311.

Gamut, L. T. F. 1991a. *Logic, language and meaning.* Vol. I. Chicago: University of Chicago Press.

Gamut, L. T. F. 1991b. *Logic, language and meaning: Intensional logic and logical grammar.* Vol. II. Chicago: University of Chicago Press.

Garson, James. 2016. Modal logic. In Edward N. Zalta (ed.), *The Stanford encyclopedia of philosophy (spring 2016 edition).* Stanford. https://plato.stanford.edu/archives/spr2016/entries/logic-modal/.

Gass, Susan & Joyce Neu (eds.). 2006. *Speech acts across cultures.* Berlin: Walter de Gruyter.

Gazdar, Gerald. 1979. *Pragmatics: Implicature, presupposition and logical form.* New York: Academic Press.

Geurts, Bart. 2011. *Quantity implicatures.* Cambridge: Cambridge University Press.

Geurts, Bart & David Beaver. 2011. Presupposition. In E. Zalta (ed.), *The Stanford encyclopedia of philosophy*. Stanford: Stanford University. http://plato.stanford.edu/entries/presupposition/. revised version: Beaver, David and Bart Geurts. 2012. Presupposition. In Claudia Maienborn, Klaus von Heusinger & Paul Portner (eds.), *Semantics: an international handbook of natural language meaning*, Vol. 3, 2432–2460. Berlin: Mouton de Gruyter.

Giannakidou, Anastasia. 2011. (Non)veridicality and mood choice: Subjunctive, polarity and time. In Renate Musan & Monika Rathert (eds.), *Tense across languages*, 59–90. Berlin, Boston: De Gruyter.

Gillon, Brendan. 1990. Ambiguity, generality and indeterminacy: Tests and definitions. *Synthese* 85. 391–416.

Givón, Talmy. 1972. Studies in ChiBemba and Bantu grammar. *Studies in African linguistics, supplement* 3. 1–247.

Goldberg, Adele E. 2015. Compositionality. In Nick Riemer (ed.), *The Routledge handbook of semantics*, 419–433. London: Routledge. http://semanticsarchive.net/Archive/jcyZDc1Y/Goldberg.Compositionality.RoutledgeHandbook.pdf.

Gomes, Gilberto. 2008. Three types of conditionals and their verb forms in English and Portuguese. *Cognitive Linguistics* 19(2). 219–40.

Green, Georgia. 1990. The universality of Gricean interpretation. In *Proceedings of the Sixteenth Annual Meeting of the Berkeley Linguistics Society*, 411–428.

Greenberg, Joseph H. 1963. Some universals of grammar with particular reference to the order of meaningful elements. In Greenberg (ed.), *Universals of language*, 73–113. Cambridge MA: MIT Press. 2nd edition 1966.

Grice, H. Paul. 1961. The causal theory of perception. *Arisotelian Society Supplement* 35. 121–152. http://www.jstor.org/stable/4106682.

Grice, H. Paul. 1975. Logic and conversation. In Peter Cole & Jerry L. Morgan (eds.), *Syntax and semantics 3: Speech acts*, 41–58. New York: Academic Press.

Grice, H. Paul. 1978. Further notes on logic and conversation. In Peter Cole & Jerry L. Morgan (eds.), *Pragmatics* (Syntax and Semantics 9), 113–127. New York: Academic Press.

Grice, H. Paul. 1981. Presupposition and conversational implicature. In Peter Cole (ed.), *Radical pragmatics*, 183–198. New York: Academic Press.

Grosz, Patrick. 2010. German *doch*: An element that triggers a contrast presupposition. In T. Grinsell, A. Baker, J. Thomas, R. Baglini & J. Keane (eds.), *Proceedings of the Chicago Linguistic Society*, vol. 46, 163–177.

Guerssel, Mohamed, Kenneth Hale, Mary Laughren, Beth Levin & Josie White Eagle. 1985. A crosslinguistic study of transitivity alternations. In William Eilfort, Paul Kroeber & Karen Peterson (eds.), *Papers from the parasession on causatives and agentivity at the 21st regional meeting*, 48–63. Chicago: Chicago Linguistic Society.

Gutierrez-Rexach, Javier. 2013. Quantification. In Philipp Strazny (ed.), *Encyclopedia of linguistics*, 885–887. London: Routledge.

Gutzmann, Daniel. 2015. *Use-conditional meaning: Studies in multidimensional semantics* (Oxford Studies in Semantics and Pragmatics 6). Oxford: Oxford University Press.

Hacquard, Valentine. 2007. Speaker-oriented vs. subject-oriented modals: A split in implicative behavior. In E. Puig-Waldmüller (ed.), *Proceedings of Sinn und Bedeutung 11*, 305–319. Barcelona: Universitat Pompeu Fabra.

Hacquard, Valentine. 2011. Modality. In Claudia Maienborn, Klaus von Heusinger & Paul Portner (eds.), *Semantics: An international handbook of natural language and meaning*, vol. 2 (HSK 33.2), 1484–1515. Berlin: Walter de Gruyter.

Haegeman, Liliane. 2010. The internal syntax of adverbial clauses. *Lingua* 120. 628–648.

Hale, Kenneth L. & Samuel J. Keyser. 1987. *A view from the middle* (Lexicon Project Working Papers 10). Cambridge, MA: Center for Cognitive Science, MIT Press.

Halmos, Paul. 1960. *Naive set theory*. Princeton, NJ: D. Van Nostrand Company. Reprinted by Springer-Verlag, New York, 1974.

Harada, Shin-Ichi. 1976. Honorifics. In Masayoshi Shibatani (ed.), *Japanese generative grammar* (Syntax and Semantics 5), 499–561. New York: Academic Press.

Hardy, Heather K. & Lynn Gordon. 1980. Types of adverbial and modal constructions in Tolkapaya. *International Journal of American Linguistics* 46(3). 183–196.

Hartmann, R. R. K. & Gregory James. 1998. *Dictionary of lexicography*. London & New York: Routledge.

Haspelmath, Martin. 1995. The converb as a cross-linguistically valid category. In M. Haspelmath & E. König (eds.), *Converbs in cross-linguistic perspective: Structure and meaning of adverbial verb forms – adverbial participles, gerunds*, 1–55. Berlin: Mouton de Gruyter.

Heim, Irene & Angelika Kratzer. 1998. *Semantics in generative grammar*. Oxford: Basil Blackwell.

Hjelmslev, Louis. 1953[1943]. *Prolegomena to a theory of language*. (Indiana University Publications in Anthropology and Linguistics, IJAL Memoir 7). Baltimore: Waverly Press. (Translated by Francis J. Whitfield; first published in Danish in 1943; 2nd English edition, slightly rev., Madison: University of Wisconsin Press, 1961.)

Hockett, Charles F. 1958. *A course in modern linguistics*. New York: Macmillan.

Hockett, Charles F. 1960. The origin of speech. *Scientific American* 203. 88–96.

Hodges, Wilfrid. 1997. *A shorter model theory*. Cambridge: Cambridge University Press.

Hodges, Wilfrid. 2013. Model theory. In Edward N. Zalta (ed.), *The Stanford encyclopedia of philosophy (Fall 2013 edition)*. Stanford. https://plato.stanford.edu/archives/fall2013/entries/model-theory/.

Holm, John. 2000. *An introduction to pidgins and creoles*. Cambridge: Cambridge University Press.

Horn, Laurence. 1972. *On the semantic properties of logical operators in English*. University of California, Los Angeles dissertation.

Horn, Laurence. 1985. Metalinguistic negation and pragmatic ambiguity. *Language* 61. 121–174.

Horn, Laurence. 1989. *A natural history of negation*. Chicago: University of Chicago Press.

Horn, Laurence. 1992. The said and the unsaid. In Chris Barker & David Dowty (eds.), *SALT II: Proceedings of the 2nd Semantics and Linguistic Theory conference* (Ohio State University Working Papers in Linguistics 40), 163–192. DOI:http://dx.doi.org/10.3765/salt.v2i0.3039

Horn, Laurence. 1997. Presupposition and implicature. In Shalom Lappin (ed.), *The handbook of contemporary semantic theory*, 209–319. London: Blackwell Publishing.

Horn, Laurence. 2004. Implicature. In Laurence Horn & Gregory Ward (eds.), *The handbook of pragmatics*, 3–28. Oxford: Blackwell Publishing.

Huang, Lillian Mei-Jin & Philip W. Davis. 1989. An aspectual system in Mandarin Chinese. *Journal of Chinese Linguistics* 17. 128–66.

Huddleston, Rodney & Geoffrey K. Pullum. 2002. *The Cambridge grammar of the English language*. Cambridge: Cambridge University Press.

Iatridou, Sabine. 1991. *Topics in conditionals*. MIT dissertation.

Idris, Abdul Aziz. 1980. Modality in Malay. *Kansas Working Papers in Linguistics* 5(1). 1–14. http://kuscholarworks.ku.edu/dspace/handle/1808/531.

Iljic, Robert. 1990. The verbal suffix *–guo* in Mandarin Chinese and the notion of recurrence. *Lingua* 81. 301–326.

Innes, Gordon. 1966. *An introduction to Grebo*. London: School of Oriental & African Studies, University of London.

Izvorski, Roumyana. 1997. The present perfect as an epistemic modal. In Aaron Lawson (ed.), *Proceedings from Semantics and Linguistic Theory VII*, 222–239. Ithaca, NY: Cornell University. http://www-bcf.usc.edu/~pancheva/evidentialperfect.pdf.

Jackendoff, Ray. 1976. Toward an explanatory semantic representation. *Linguistic Inquiry* 7(1). 89–150.
Jackendoff, Ray. 1983. *Semantics and cognition.* Cambridge, MA: MIT Press.
Jespersen, Otto. 1924. *The philosophy of grammar.* London: Allen & Unwin.
Jespersen, Otto. 1931. *A modern English grammar on historical principles. Part 4, Syntax (third volume): Time and tense.* London: G. Allen & Unwin; Copenhagen: E. Munksgaard.
Jespersen, Otto. 1933. *Essentials of English grammar.* London: G. Allen & Unwin; Reprinted by University of Alabama Press, 1964.
Johnston, Michael. 1994. *The syntax and semantics of adverbial adjuncts.* University of California Santa Cruz dissertation.
Kalisz, Roman. 1992. Different cultures, different languages and different speech acts revisited. *Poznan Studies in Contemporary Linguistics* 27. 107–118.
Karagjosova, Elena. 2000. A unified approach to the meaning and function of modal particles in dialogue. In Catherine Pilire (ed.), *Proceedings of the ESSLLI 2000 Student Session, August 6-18.* Birmingham, UK: University of Birmingham. http://events.cs.bham.ac.uk/esslli/notes/student-session/proc.pdf.
Karttunen, Lauri & Stanley Peters. 1979. Conventional implicature. In Choon-Kyu Oh & David Dinneen (eds.), *Syntax and semantics, volume 11: Presupposition,* 1–56. New York: Academic Press.
Katz, Jerrold J. 1972. *Semantic theory.* New York: Harper & Row.
Katz, Jerrold J. 1978. Effability and translation. In F. Guenthner & M. Guenthner-Reutter (eds.), *Meaning and translation,* 191–234. New York: New York University Press.
Katz, Jerrold J. & Jerry A. Fodor. 1963. The structure of a semantic theory. *Language* 39. 170–210.
Kearns, Kate. 2000. *Semantics* (Modern Linguistics series). New York: St. Martin's Press.
Kearns, Kate. 2011. *Semantics.* 2nd edn. Basingstoke: Palgrave Macmillan.
Keenan, Elinor O. 1974. The universality of conversational implicatures. In Ralph W. Fasold & Roger W. Shuy (eds.), *Studies in linguistic variation: Semantics, syntax, phonology, pragmatics, social situations, ethnographic approaches,* 255–268. Georgetown: Georgetown University Press.
Kempson, Ruth. M. 1975. *Presupposition and the delimitation of semantics.* Cambridge: Cambridge University Press.
Kempson, Ruth M. 1977. *Semantic theory* (Cambridge Textbooks in Linguistics). Cambridge: Cambridge University Press.

Kennedy, Christopher. 2011. Ambiguity and vagueness: An overview. In Claudia Maienborn, Klaus von Heusinger & Paul Portner (eds.), *Semantics: An international handbook of natural language meaning*, vol. 1, 507–535. Berlin: Mouton de Gruyter.

Kim, Jong-Bok & Peter Sells. 2007. Korean honorification: A kind of expressive meaning. *Journal of East Asian Linguistics* 16(4). 303–336. http://web.khu.ac.kr/~jongbok/research/final-papers/kor-hon-kim-sells.pdf.

Kiparsky, Paul. 2002. Event structure and the perfect. In David I. Beaver, Luis D. Casillas Martínez, Brady Z. Clark & Stefan Kaufmann (eds.), *The construction of meaning*. Stanford CA: CSLI Publications.

Kiparsky, Paul & Carol Kiparsky. 1970. Fact. In Manfred Bierwisch & Karl Heidolph (eds.), *Progress in linguistics*, 143–173. The Hague: Mouton. Reprinted in L. Jakobovits and D. Steinberg (eds.), *Semantics: An Interdisciplinary Reader*. Cambridge: Cambridge University Press, 1971.

Kitis, Eliza. 2006. Causality and subjectivity: The causal connectives of Modern Greek. In Hanna Pishwa (ed.), *Language and memory: Aspects of knowledge representation*, 223–267. Berlin & New York: Mouton de Gruyter.

Klein, Wolfgang. 1992. The present perfect puzzle. *Language* 68. 525–552.

Klein, Wolfgang. 1994. *Time in language*. London: Routledge.

Klein, Wolfgang. 2009. How time is encoded. In Wolfgang Klein & Ping Li (eds.), *The expression of time*, 5–38. Berlin: De Gruyter.

Klein, Wolfgang, Ping Li & Henriette Hendriks. 2000. Aspect and assertion in Mandarin Chinese. *Natural Language and Linguistic Theory* 18. 723–770.

Koenig, Jean-Pierre & Liancheng Chief. 2008. Scalarity and state-changes in Mandarin (and other languages). In O. Bonami & P. Cabredo Hofherr (eds.), *Empirical issues in syntax and semantics*, vol. 7, 241–262. Paris: CNRS. http://www.cssp.cnrs.fr/eiss7/koenig-chief-eiss7.pdf.

Koenig, Jean-Pierre & Karin Michelson. 2010. *How to quantify over entities in Iroquoian*. Paper presented at the Society for the Study of the Indigenous Languages of the Americas, Baltimore, MD.

Koenig, Jean-Pierre & N. Muansuwan. 2000. How to end without ever finishing: Thai semi-perfectivity. *Journal of Semantics* 17. 147–184.

König, Ekkehard. 1991. *The meaning of focus particles: A comparative perspective*. London: Routledge.

König, Ekkehard, Detlef Stark & Susanne Requardt. 1990. *Adverbien und Partikeln: Ein deutschenglisches Wörterbuch [Adverbs and particles: A German–English dictionary]*. Heidelberg: Julius Groos.

Kratzer, Angelika. 1981. The notional category of modality. In H.-J. Eikmeyer & H. Rieser (eds.), *Words, worlds, and contexts: New approaches in word semantics*, 38–74. Berlin: Mouton de Gruyter.

Kratzer, Angelika. 1986. Conditionals. *Chicago Linguistics Society* 22(2). 1–15.

Kratzer, Angelika. 1991. Modality. In Arnim von Stechow & Dieter Wunderlich (eds.), *Semantics: An international handbook of contemporary research*, 639–650. Berlin: Mouton de Gruyter.

Kratzer, Angelika. 1995. Stage-level/individual-level predicates. In G. N. Carlson & F. J. Pelletier (eds.), *The generic book*, 125–175. Chicago: University of Chicago Press.

Kratzer, Angelika. 1999. *Beyond 'Ouch' and 'Oops': How descriptive and expressive meaning interact. Comment on Kaplan's paper at the Cornell Conference on Context Dependency.* http://semanticsarchive.net/Archive/WEwNGUyO/.

Kroeger, Paul. 2005. *Analyzing grammar.* Cambridge: Cambridge University Press.

Kroeger, Paul. 2010. The grammar of *hitting*, *breaking* and *cutting* in Kimaragang Dusun. *Oceanic Linguistics* 49. 2–20.

Kroeger, Paul. 2017. Frustration, culmination and inertia in Kimaragang grammar. *Glossa: a journal of general linguistics* 56(1). 1–29.

LaCross, Lisa. 2016. *Past temporal remoteness in Kimanianga.* Paper presented at the Texas Linguistic Society conference, Feb. 2016, Austin TX.

Lakoff, George. 1970. A note on vagueness and ambiguity. *Linguistic Inquiry* 1. 357–359.

Langacker, Ronald W. 2001. The English present tense. *English Language and Linguistics* 5. 251–272.

Lee, Sooman Noah. 2008. *A grammar of Iranian Azerbaijani.* Seoul: The Altaic Society of Korea.

Leech, Geoffrey N. 1971. *Meaning and the English verb.* London: Longman.

Levin, Beth. 1993. *English verb classes and alternations: A preliminary investigation.* Chicago: University of Chicago Press.

Levin, Beth. 2015. Verb classes within and across languages. In A. Malchukov & B. Comrie (eds.), *Valency classes: A comparative handbook*, 1627–1670. Berlin: De Gruyter.

Levinson, Stephen C. 1983. *Pragmatics.* Cambridge: Cambridge University Press.

Levinson, Stephen C. 1995. Three levels of meaning. In F. R. Palmer (ed.), *Grammar and meaning: Essays in honour of Sir John Lyons*, 90–115. Cambridge: Cambridge University Press.

Levinson, Stephen C. 2000. *Presumptive meanings: The theory of generalized conversational implicature.* Cambridge, MA: MIT Press.

Levinson, Stephen C. & E. Annamalai. 1992. Why presuppositions aren't conventional. In R. N. Srivastava (ed.), *Language and text: Studies in honour of Ashok R. Kelkar*, 227–242. Delhi: Kalinga Publications.

Lewis, Clarence I. 1918. *Survey of symbolic logic.* Berkeley: University of California Press.

Lewis, David. 1973a. Causation. *Journal of Philosophy* 70. 556–567.

Lewis, David. 1973b. *Counterfactuals.* Oxford: Blackwell.

Lewis, David. 1975. Adverbs of quantification. In Edward Keenan (ed.), *Formal semantics of natural language*, 3–15. Cambridge: Cambridge University Press.

Lewis, David. 2000. Causation as influence. *Journal of Philosophy* 97. 182–197.

Li, Charles & Sandra A. Thompson. 1981. *Mandarin Chinese: A functional reference grammar.* Berkeley, CA: University of California Press.

Lin, Jo-Wang. 2007. Predicate restriction, discontinuity property and the meaning of the perfective marker *guo* in Mandarin Chinese. *Journal of East Asian Linguistics* 16. 237–257.

Lovestrand, Joseph. 2012. *The linguistic structure of Baraïn (Chadic).* Graduate Institute of Applied Linguistics MA thesis. http://www.gial.edu/images/theses/Lovestrand_Joseph-thesis.pdf.

Lyons, John. 1977. *Semantics.* Cambridge: Cambridge University Press. vol. 1-2.

Lyons, John. 1995. *Linguistic semantics.* Cambridge: Cambridge University Press.

Ma, Jing Sheng. 1977. Some aspects of the teaching of *-guo* and *-le*. *Journal of the Chinese Language Teachers Association* 12(1). 14–26.

Marques, Rui. 2004. On the system of mood in European and Brazilian Portuguese. *Journal of Portuguese Linguistics* 3(1). 89–109.

Martin, John N. 1987. *Elements of formal semantics: An introduction to logic for students of language.* Orlando: Academic Press.

Martin, Samuel E. 1992. *A reference grammar of Korean: A complete guide to the grammar and history of the Korean language.* Rutland, Vermont & Tokyo: Charles E. Tuttle Company.

Matsumoto, Yo. 1995. The conversational condition on Horn scales. *Linguistics and Philosophy* 18. 21–60.

Matthewson, Lisa. 2006. Presupposition and cross-linguistic variation. *North-Eastern Linguistic Society (NELS)* 26. 63–76.

Matthewson, Lisa. 2010. Cross-linguistic variation in modality systems: The role of mood. *Semantics and Pragmatics* 3. 1–74.

Matthewson, Lisa. 2016. Modality. In Maria Aloni & Paul Dekker (eds.), *Cambridge handbook of formal semantics*, 525–559. Cambridge: Cambridge University Press.

Matthewson, Lisa, Henry Davis & Hotze Rullmann. 2007. Evidentials as epistemic modals: Evidence from St'át'imcets. *Linguistic Variation Yearbook* 7. 201–254.

McCawley, James D. 1968. Concerning the base component of a transformational grammar. *Foundations of Language* 4. 243–269.

McCawley, James D. 1971. Tense and time reference in English. In Langendoen & Fillmore (eds.), *Studies in linguistic semantics*, 97–113. New York: Holt Rinehart.

McCawley, James D. 1981a. *Everything that linguists have always wanted to know about logic... but were ashamed to ask.* Chicago: University of Chicago Press.

McCawley, James D. 1981b. Notes on the English perfect. *Australian Journal of Linguistics* 1. 81–90.

McCloskey, James. 2001. The morphosyntax of WH-extraction in Irish. *Journal of Linguistics* 37. 67–100.

McCoard, Robert W. 1978. *The English perfect: Tense choice and pragmatic inferences.* Amsterdam: North-Holland Publishing Company.

Meibauer, Jörg. 2005. Lying and falsely implicating. *Journal of Pragmatics* 37. 1373–1399.

Michaelis, Laura A. 1994. The ambiguity of the English present perfect. *Journal of Linguistics* 30. 111–157.

Michaelis, Laura A. 1998. *Aspectual grammar and past-time reference.* London: Routledge.

Michaelis, Laura A. 2006. Time and tense. In B. Aarts & A. MacMahon (eds.), *The handbook of English linguistics*, 220–234. Oxford: Blackwell.

Milsark, Gary L. 1977. Toward an explanation of certain peculiarities of the existential construction in English. *Linguistic Analysis* 3. 1–30.

Moens, Marc & Mark Steedman. 1988. Temporal ontology and temporal reference. *Computational Linguistics* 14(2). 15–28.

Morton, Adam. 2004. Indicative versus subjunctive future conditionals. *Analysis* 64(4). 289–293.

Morzycki, Marcin. 2015. *Modification* (Key Topics in Semantics and Pragmatics). Cambridge: Cambridge University Press.

Murray, Sarah E. 2010. *Evidentiality and the structure of speech acts.* Rutgers, The State University of New Jersey dissertation. http://conf.ling.cornell.edu/sem/Murray_Thesis-Rutgers-2010.pdf.

Nida, Eugene. 1951. A system for the description of semantic elements. *Word* 7. 1–14.

Nunberg, Geoffrey. 1979. The non-uniqueness of semantic solutions: Polysemy. *Linguistics and Philosophy* 3(2). 143–184.

Nunberg, Geoffrey. 1995. Transfers of meaning. *Journal of Semantics* 12(2). 109–132. http://people.ischool.berkeley.edu/~nunberg/JOS.pdf.

Nunberg, Geoffrey & Annie Zaenen. 1992. Systematic polysemy in lexicology and lexicography. In H. Tommola, K. Varantola, T. Salmi-Tolonen & J. Schopp (eds.), *Proceedings of Euralex II*, 387–398. Tampere: University of Tampere. http://www.euralex.org/elx_proceedings/Euralex1992_2/011_Geoffrey%20Nunberg%20&%20Annieen%20-Systematic%20polysemy%20in%20lexicology%20and%20lexicography.pdf.

Nurse, Derek. 2008. *Tense and aspect in Bantu.* New York: Oxford University Press.

Olshtain, Elite & Andrew Cohen. 1989. Speech act behaviour across languages. In Hans W. Dechert & Manfred Raupach (eds.), *Transfer in language production*, 53–68. Norwood, N. J.: Ablex.

Pagin, Peter & Dag Westerståhl. 2010. Compositionality II: Arguments and problems. *Philosophy Compass* 5(3). 265–282.

Pak, Miok. 2008. Types of clauses and sentence end particles in Korean. *Korean Linguistics* 14. 113–155.

Pak, Miok, Paul Portner & Raffaella Zanuttini. 2013. *Politeness, formality and main clause phenomena.* Handout for talk at LSA annual meeting, Jan. 2013.

Palmer, F. R. 1986. *Mood and modality.* Cambridge: Cambridge University Press.

Pan, H. & P. Lee. 2004. The role of pragmatics in interpreting the Chinese perfective markers *-guo* and *-le. Journal of Pragmatics* 36. 441–466.

Papafragou, Anna. 2006. Epistemic modality and truth conditions. *Lingua* 116. 1688–1702. http://papafragou.psych.udel.edu/papers/Lingua-epmodality.pdf.

Partee, Barbara Hall. 1973. Some structural analogies between tenses and pronouns in English. *The Journal of Philosophy* 70. 601–609.

Partee, Barbara Hall. 1995. Lexical semantics and compositionality. In Lila Gleitman & Mark Liberman (eds.), *Invitation to cognitive science, volume 1*, 2nd edn., 311–360. Cambridge, MA: Language MIT Press. Prepublication version is available online at: http://semanticsarchive.net/Archive/jhjMGYwM/BHP95LexicalSemanticsAndCompositionality.pdf.

Partee, Barbara Hall. 2008. Negation, intensionality, and aspect: Interaction with NP semantics. In Susan Rothstein (ed.), *Theoretical and crosslinguistic approaches to the semantics of aspect*, 291–320. Amsterdam & Philadelphia: John Benjamins.

Pelletier, Francis. 2001. Did Frege believe Frege's principle? *Journal of Logic, Language and Information* 10. 87–114.

Peters, Stanley & Dag Westerståhl. 2006. *Quantifiers in language and logic.* Oxford: Clarendon Press.

Pinker, Steven. 1994. *The language instinct.* New York: W. Morrow & Co.

Pit, Mirna. 2003. *How to express yourself with a causal connective: Subjectivity and causal connectives in Dutch, German and French.* Amsterdam: Rodopi.

Podlesskaya, Vera. 2001. Conditional constructions. In Martin Haspelmath, Ekkehard König, Wulf Oesterreicher & Wolfgang Raible (eds.), *Language typology and language universals*, vol. 2, 998–1010. Berlin: Walter de Gruyter.

Portner, Paul. 2003. The temporal semantics and modal pragmatics of the perfect. *Linguistics and Philosophy* 26. 459–510.

Portner, Paul. 2011. Perfect and progressive. In Claudia Maienborn, Klaus von Heusinger & Paul Portner (eds.), *Semantics: An international handbook of natural language meaning*, 1217–1261. Berlin: Mouton de Gruyter.

Posner, Roland. 1980. Semantics and pragmatics of sentence connectives in natural language. In John R. Searle, Ferenc Kiefer & Manfred Bierwisch (eds.), *Speech act theory and pragmatics*, 168–203. Dordrecht: Reidel.

Potts, Christopher. 2005. *The logic of conventional implicatures* (Oxford Studies in Theoretical Linguistics). Oxford: Oxford University Press.

Potts, Christopher. 2007a. Conventional implicatures, a distinguished class of meanings. In Gillian Ramchand & Charles Reiss (eds.), *The Oxford handbook of linguistic interfaces. Studies in theoretical linguistics*, 475–501. Oxford: Oxford University Press.

Potts, Christopher. 2007b. Into the conventional-implicature dimension. *Philosophy Compass* 4(2). 665–679.

Potts, Christopher. 2007c. The expressive dimension. *Theoretical Linguistics* 33(2). 165–197.

Potts, Christopher. 2012. The pragmatics of conventional implicature and expressive content. In Claudia Maienborn, Klaus von Heusinger & Paul Portner (eds.), *Semantics: An international handbook of natural language meaning*, vol. 3, 2516–2536. Berlin: Mouton de Gruyter.

Potts, Christopher. 2015. Presupposition and implicature. In Shalom Lappin & Chris Fox (eds.), *Wiley-Blackwell handbook of contemporary semantics*, 2nd edn., 168–202. Oxford: Wiley-Blackwell. http://web.stanford.edu/~cgpotts/manuscripts/potts-blackwellsemantics.pdf.

Prince, Ellen F. 1982. *Grice and universality: A reappraisal.* ftp://babel.ling.upenn.edu/papers/faculty/ellen%5C_prince/grice.ps. ms, University of Pennsylvania.

Prior, A. N. 1957. *Time and modality*. Oxford: Oxford University Press.

Prior, Arthur N. 1967. *Past, present and future*. Oxford: Oxford University Press.

Pulte, William. 1985. The experienced and non-experienced past in Cherokee. *International Journal of American Linguistics* 4. 543–544.

Pustejovsky, James. 1995. *The generative lexicon*. Cambridge, MA: The MIT Press.

Quine, Willard van Orman. 1956. Quantifiers and propositional attitudes. *Journal of Philosophy* 53. 177–187.

Quine, Willard van Orman. 1960. *Word and object*. Cambridge, MA: MIT Press.

Rappaport Hovav, Malka & Beth Levin. 1998. Building verb meanings. In Miriam Butt & Wilhelm Geuder (eds.), *The projection of arguments: Lexical and compositional factors*, 97–134. Stanford, CA: CSLI Publications.

Ravin, Yael & Claudia Leacock. 2000. Polysemy: an overview. In Yael Ravin & Claudia Leacock (eds.), *Polysemy: theoretical and computational approaches*. 91–110. Oxford: Oxford University Press.

Recanati, François. 2004. Pragmatics and semantics. In Laurence Horn & Gregory Ward (eds.), *The handbook of pragmatics*, 442–462. Oxford: Blackwell.

Reichenbach, Hans. 1947. *Elements of symbolic logic*. London: Macmillan.

Ritz, Marie-Eve. 2012. Perfect tense and aspect. In Robert I. Binnick (ed.), *The Oxford handbook of tense and aspect*, 881–907. Oxford: Oxford University Press.

Rundell, Michael. 2006. More than one way to skin a cat: Why full-sentence definitions have not been universally adopted. In Corino E., Marello C. & Onesti C. (eds.), *Proceedings of 12th EURALEX International Congress*. Alessandria: Edizioni Dell'Orso.

Russell, Bertrand. 1905. On denoting. *Mind* 14. 479–493.

Sadock, Jerry. 1978. On testing for conversational implicature. In Peter Cole (ed.), *Pragmatics* (Syntax and Semantics 9), 281–297. New York: Academic Press.

Sæbø, Kjell Johan. 1991. Causal and purposive clauses. In Arnim von Stechow & Dieter Wunderlich (eds.), *Semantics: An international handbook of contemporary research*, 623–631. Berlin: Walter de Gruyter.

Sæbø, Kjell Johan. 2011. Adverbial clauses. In Claudia Maienborn, Klaus von Heusinger & Paul Portner (eds.), *Semantics: an international handbook of natural language meaning*, vol. 2, 1420–1441. Berlin & New York: De Gruyter Mouton.

Saeed, John. 2009. *Semantics*. 3rd edn. Chichester, UK: Wiley-Blackwell.

Schachter, Paul & Fe T. Otanes. 1972. *Tagalog reference grammar*. Berkeley CA: University of California Press.

Scheffler, Tatjana. 2005. Syntax and semantics of causal *denn* in German. In *Proceedings of the 15th Amsterdam colloquium*. Amsterdam, Netherlands.

Scheffler, Tatjana. 2008. *Semantic operators in different dimensions*. University of Pennsylvania dissertation.

Scheffler, Tatjana. 2013. *Two-dimensional semantics: Clausal adjuncts and complements*. Berlin, Boston: De Gruyter Mouton.

Searle, John. 1969. *Speech acts: An essay in the philosophy of language*. Cambridge: Cambridge University Press.

Searle, John. 1975. Indirect speech acts. In P. Cole & J. L. Morgan (eds.), *Speech acts* (Syntax and Semantics 3), 59–82. New York: Academic Press.

Sebba, Mark. 1997. *Contact languages: Pidgins and creoles*. Basingstoke: Palgrave Macmillan.

Siegel, Muffy. 1976. *Capturing the adjective*. University of Massachusetts dissertation.

Singh, Mona. 1991. The perfective paradox or how to eat your cake and have it too. In *Proceedings of the Seventeenth Annual Meeting of the Berkeley Linguistics Society: General Session and Parasession on The Grammar of Event Structure*, 469–479. http://elanguage.net/journals/bls/article/viewFile/2738/2719.

Singh, Mona. 1998. On the semantics of the perfective aspect. *Natural Language Semantics* 6. 171–199.

Smith, Carlota. 1997. *The parameter of aspect*. 2nd edn. Dordrecht: Kluwer Academic. (1st edition 1991).

Smith, Geoff. 2002. *Growing up with Tok Pisin: Contact, creolization, and change in Papua New Guinea's national language*. London: Battlebridge Publications.

Soh, Hooi Ling & Jenny Yi-Chun Kuo. 2005. Perfective aspect and accomplishment situations in Mandarin Chinese. In Angeliek van Hout, Henriette de Swart & Henk Verkuyl (eds.), *Perspectives on aspect*, 199–216. Dordrecht: Springer.

Soh, Hooi-Ling. 2009. Speaker presupposition and Mandarin Chinese sentence final *-le*: A unified analysis of the "change of state" and the "contrary to expectation" reading. *Natural Language and Linguistic Theory* 27. 623–657.

Sohn, Ho-Min. 1999. *The Korean language*. New York: Cambridge University Press.

Sperber, Dan & Deirdre Wilson. 1986. *Relevance: communication and cognition*. Oxford: Blackwell.

Stalnaker, Robert. 1968. A theory of conditionals. In Nicholas Rescher (ed.), *Studies in logical theory*, vol. 2 (American Philosophical Quarterly Monograph Series), 98–112. Oxford: Basil Blackwell.

Stalnaker, Robert. 1973. Presuppositions. *Journal of Philosophical Logic* 2. 447–457.

Stalnaker, Robert. 1974. Pragmatic presuppositions. In Milton K. Munitz & Peter K. Unger (eds.), *Semantics and philosophy*, 197–213. New York: New York University Press.

Strawson, Peter. 1950. On referring. *Mind* 59. 320–344. Reprinted in A. P. Martinich (ed.), 1990, *The Philosophy of Language*. New York: Oxford University Press, pp. 219–234.

Strawson, Peter. 1952. *Introduction to logical theory*. London: Methuen.

Sun, Chen-Chen. 2008. *Variations in the* ba *construction and its relevance to DP: A minimalist perspective*. Arizona State University dissertation.

Svensén, Bo. 2009. *A handbook of lexicography: The theory and practice of dictionary-making*. Cambridge: Cambridge University Press.

Sweetser, Eve. 1990. *From etymology to pragmatics: Metaphorical and cultural aspects of semantic structure*. Cambridge: Cambridge University Press.

Szabolcsi, Anna. 2015. Varieties of quantification. In Nick Riemer (ed.), *The Routledge handbook of semantics*, 320–337. London: Routledge.

Tannen, Deborah. 1975. Communication mix and mixup, or how linguistics can ruin a marriage. *San Jose State Occasional Papers in Linguistics*. 205–211.

Tannen, Deborah. 1981. Indirectness in discourse: Ethnicity as conversational style. *Discourse Processes* 4(3). 221–238.

Tannen, Deborah. 1986. *That's not what I meant! How conversational style makes or breaks relationships*. New York: Ballantine.

Tenny, Carol. 1987. *Grammaticalizing aspect and affectedness*. Massachusetts Institute of Technology dissertation.

Thompson, Sandra A., Robert E. Longacre & Shin Ja Hwang. 2007. Adverbial clauses. In Timothy Shopen (ed.), *Language typology and syntactic description*, 2nd edn., vol. 2, 237–300. Cambridge: Cambridge University Press.

Tonhauser, Judith, David Beaver, Craige Roberts & Mandy Simons. 2013. Towards a taxonomy of projective content. *Language* 89(1). 66–109.

Tuggy, David. 1993. Ambiguity, polysemy and vagueness. *Cognitive Linguistics* 4(3). 273–290.

van der Auwera, Johan. 1986. Conditionals and speech-acts. In Elizabeth C. Traugott, Alice ter Meulen, Judy Snitzer Reilly & Charles Ferguson (eds.), *On conditionals*, 197–214. Cambridge: Cambridge University Press.

van der Auwera, Johan & Andreas Ammann. 2013. Overlap between situational and epistemic modal marking. In Matthew S. Dryer & Martin Haspelmath (eds.), *The world atlas of language structures online*. Leipzig: Max Planck Institute for Evolutionary Anthropology. http://wals.info/chapter/76.

Van Valin, Robert D. & Randy J. LaPolla. 1997. *Syntax: Structure, meaning and function*. Cambridge: Cambridge University Press.

van Benthem, Johan. 1988. *A manual of intensional logic*. 2nd edn. Stanford, CA: CSLI.

van Benthem, Johan. 2010. *Modal logic for open minds*. Stanford, CA: CSLI.

Vendler, Zeno. 1957. Verbs and times. *Philosophical Review* 66. 143–160. Reprinted in Vendler (1967), *Linguistics in Philosophy*, 97–121. Ithaca NY: Cornell University Press.

Verhaar, John W. M. 1985. *Toward a reference grammar of Tok Pisin: An experiment in corpus linguistics* (Oceanic Linguistics Special Publication 26). Honolulu: University of Hawai'i Press.

Vogel, Alan R. 2005. *Jarawara verb classes*. University of Pittsburgh Doctoral dissertation.

von Fintel, Kai. 2004. Would you believe it? The king of France is back! Presuppositions and truth-value intuitions. In Anne Bezuidenhout & Marga Reimer (eds.), *Descriptions and beyond: An interdisciplinary collection of essays on definite and indefinite descriptions and other related phenomena*, 315–341. Oxford: Oxford University Press.

von Fintel, Kai. 2006. Modality and language. In Donald M. Borchert (ed.), *Encyclopedia of philosophy*, 2nd edn., vol. 10, 20–27. Detroit: MacMillan Reference USA.

von Fintel, Kai. 2011. Conditionals. In *Semantics: An international handbook of meaning*, vol. 2, 1515–1538. Berlin: Mouton de Gruyter.

von Fintel, Kai. 2012. Subjunctive conditionals. In Gillian Russell & Delia Graff Fara (eds.), *The Routledge companion to philosophy of language*, 466–477. New York: Routledge.

von Fintel, Kai & Lisa Matthewson. 2008. Universals in semantics. *The Linguistic Review* 25. 139–201.

von Heusinger, Klaus. 2011. Specificity. In Klaus von Heusinger, Claudia Maienborn & Paul Portner (eds.), *Semantics: An international handbook of natural language meaning*, vol. 2, 1024–1057. Berlin: de Gruyter.

Waltereit, Richard. 2001. Modal particles and their functional equivalents: A speech-act-theoretic approach. *Journal of Pragmatics* 33(9). 1391–1417.

Weber, David J. 1989. *A grammar of Huallaga (Huánuco) Quechua* (University of California Publications in Linguistics 112). Berkeley: University of California Press.

Wierzbicka, Anna. 1985. Different languages, different cultures, different speech acts: English vs. Polish. *Journal of Pragmatics* 9. 145–178.

Wohlgemuth, Jan. 1999. *Grammatische Kategorien und ihre Ausprägungen im Tok Pisin von Papua-Neuguinea [Grammatical categories and their realisations in Tok Pisin of Papua New Guinea]*. Münster: Institute for general linguistics, Westfälische Wilhelms-Universität Münster. http://www.linguist.de/TokPisin/index.htm.

Wu, Jiun-Shiung. 2008. Terminability, wholeness and the semantics of the experiential *guo*. *Journal of East Asian Linguistics* 17(1). 1–32. http://tjl.nccu.edu.tw/volume7-2/7.2-1Wu.pdf.

Wu, Jiun-Shiung. 2009. Aspectual influence on temporal relations: A case study of the experiential *guo* in Mandarin. *Taiwan Journal of Linguistics* 7(2). 1–24.

Xiao, Richard & Tony McEnery. 2004. *Aspect in Mandarin Chinese: A corpus-based study*. Amsterdam/Philadelphia: John Benjamins Publishing Company.

Yeh, Meng. 1993. Stative situations and the imperfective *-zhe* in Mandarin. *Journal of the Chinese Language Teachers Association* 28. 69–98.

Yeh, Meng. 1996. An analysis of the experiential *guo* in Mandarin: A temporal quantifier. *Journal of East Asian Linguistics* 5. 151–182.

Zalta, Edward N. 2011. Gottlob Frege. In E. Zalta (ed.), *The Stanford encyclopedia of philosophy (Spring 2017 edition)*. Stanford CA: Stanford University. https://plato.stanford.edu/archives/spr2017/entries/frege/.

Zimmermann, Malte. 2011. Discourse particles. In Paul Portner, Claudia Maienborn & Klaus von Heusinger (eds.), *Semantics* (Handbücher zur Sprach- und Kommunikationswissenschaft 33.2), 2011–2038. Berlin: Mouton de Gruyter. http://www.ling.uni-potsdam.de/~mzimmermann/papers/MZ2011-Particles-HSK.pdf.

Zimmermann, Thomas & Wolfgang Sternefeld. 2013. *Introduction to semantics: An essential guide to the composition of meaning*. Berlin: DeGryter Mouton.

Zwicky, Arnold & Jerry Sadock. 1975. Ambiguity tests and how to fail them. In J. P. Kimball (ed.), *Syntax and semantics*, vol. 4, 1–36. New York: Academic Press.

Name index

Language index